AF479002

Natacha Nisic

Echo

JEU DE PAUME

ACTES SUD

2

Contents

Natacha Nisic

Echo

JEU DE PAUME

ACTES SUD

What is the connection between a gesture and a landscape, between a landscape and a voice, or between several voices and a single body? Are there any links between Bavaria and Korea, between the Nikkei index and spirits, between a natural disaster and collateral damage?

All these seemingly unrelated issues are "echoed" in the work of Natacha Nisic by means of sinuous narratives that twist and turn, time and again, before coming together and taking shape in this exhibition.

Nisic's oeuvre reflects the growing interest shown by certain contemporary artists in examining the tensions between de facto power and diffused power, between the visible and the invisible. On the one hand, Nisic explores the contradictions of beliefs, of the fear of the unknown and of the reversibility / irreversibility of perception. On the other, in subtly critical works her focus shifts from the effects of colonialism to the vagaries of Orientalism.

Thus, from her first *Catalogue de gestes* to her latest pieces, such as *Indice Nikkei, e* and, above all, *f* and *Andrea en conversation*, produced specifically for this exhibition, Nisic's images conjure up no end of symbolic, perceptual and sensory associations that viewers must needs view in a kaleidoscopic manner in the light of past and present.

The Jeu de Paume would like to thank the artist for her enthusiasm and her dedication to the project, and the authors of the essays in the catalogue, Philippe-Alain Michaud, Beck Jee-sook and Florent Perrier, for their pertinent and enlightening contributions.

Last but not least, we should like to express our gratitude to the Ministère de la Culture et de la Communication, to Neuflize Vie, our chief partner, and to the Fondation Nationale des Arts Graphiques et Plastiques for their invaluable support, as well as the Amis du Jeu de Paume for their generous support for the catalogue.

Marta Gili
Director of the Jeu de Paume

—
Translated from Spanish by Josephine Watson

Philippe-Alain
Michaud

*World of
Dew*

p. 82

*Monde de
rosée*

This world of dew
is only the world of dew
and yet . . . oh and yet
  Kobayashi Issa[1]

I

In 1995, Natacha Nisic began working on a *Catalogue de gestes* [fig. 1 + p. 15–25], which has grown incessantly over the years. It is an open-ended catalogue, made up of a series of films shot in Super 8, each one lasting as long as a cartridge (between one and two and a half minutes). The films show, framed in close up and slightly from above, hands performing a simple task, real or imaginary (peeling, cutting, rubbing, or cleaning), or handling an object (a flower, piece of fruit, pair of scissors, knife), or simply rubbing one against the other. They form a motif within the shot that has neither beginning nor end, that loops back on itself, with no conclusion. The faces never appear in shot: although most of the hands are those of women, marked by time and revealing something of their history through wrinkles, marks or stains, a ring on a finger, they are never joined to a body, performing entirely on their own a function detached from any subject. First projected from film, the films, now digitalized and screened on flat screens, play in a loop, installed throughout the exhibition spaces in varying number, in open compositions that can be endlessly permutated.

In Natacha Nisic's work, the *Catalogue de gestes* has taken on a character that is ever more openly inaugural, evoking memories of other films devoted to the movement of hands. In 1934, Ralph Steiner and Willard Van Dyke, members of the Film and Photo League, a group of radical documentary-makers, made *Hands* [fig. 2], a silent film produced by the Works Progress Administration (WPA) showing the hands of the unemployed, of craftsmen and factory workers, idle or at work. The two documentary-makers, who also did not show faces, used experimental techniques – editing effects, framing, highly expressive lighting – to portray workers' gestures with the aim of revealing their beauty. Like Steiner and Van Dyke's *Hands*, Natacha Nisic's *Catalogue de gestes* displays an interest in social and cultural concerns, but is more than a just a simple repertoire of forms, an archive project or exercise in conservation. Not only is she conjuring up the forgotten by contrasting it with the permanence of images, and conserving by means of photographic prints the trace of ephemeral movements, henceforth without effect, irretrievably erased by history, but she is also representing the very workings of time itself: the anonymous hands tirelessly repeat the same action in a loop, drawing in space the web of duration, like the Fates unraveling and cutting the thread of destiny. Thus in *Nord* [fig. 3], a film made in 2007, presented either as a simple screening or as an installation, the artist, gives her images an apparently documentary slant, focusing first on the gestures of the organizers of cock fights meticulously knotting the spurs on the feet of their animals, and then on the gestures of former workers at a spinning mill who were made redundant, repeating before the camera their now ghostly actions, lined up side by side, mimicking the production line that they belonged to. The spinning mills, like cock fights, are just relics: the people of the north of France became extras in *Nord*, reproducing the gestures they always used to make before allowing them to be lost as they are forgotten. As performance, the film functions both as description and symptom: it protects a dying gesture at the same time as confirming its disappearance; it knots the thread at the same time as it cuts it.

But the *Catalogue de gestes* awakens another echo, both closer and more enigmatic: in 1966, following an operation that prevented her from dancing for several months, Yvonne Rainer decided to shoot a film in which, defying immobility, she continued to dance with the fingers of her right hand. In her *Hand Movie* [fig. 4], which would inspire Richard Serra, in 1968, to start making his series of *Hand Films* [fig. 5], the movement of the hand, in replacing that of the body, takes on a discreetly prophylactic or incantatory significance, assuming the magical function associated with the gesture, which anthropology has traditionally examined in ancient societies, folk traditions and non-Western cultures [fig. 6].[2] The gesture is a way of tying things together, invisibly, by bypassing the rule of real causality: let us suggest that for Natacha Nisic, with the catalogue she began in 1995, it has become a way of conceiving of film as a shamanistic operation, using the almighty power of manipulation.

II

In May 1889, Wassily Kandinsky, then a law student, travelled around the Vologda region for almost six weeks on behalf of the Russian ethnographic society to study the religious concepts and legal structures of the Zyrian peoples. Two decades later, in 1913, he recalled his journey: "The other particularly powerful impression I experienced during my student days, which again exerted a decisive effect in later years, were Rembrandt in the Hermitage in St. Petersburg and my journey to the province of Vologda, where in the capacity of ethnographer and jurist, I was sent by the Imperial Society for Science, Anthropology, and Ethnography. My task was twofold: in the case of the Russian population to study peasant criminal law (to discover the principles of primitive law) and in the case of the fishing and hunting communities of the slowly disappearing Zyrians, to salvage the remnants of their pagan religion." Studying the categories of thought of this Finno-Ugric community, the young Kandinsky would discover a distinctive form of the soul known as *ort*, which had a palpable presence in the men's daily life: given to everyone at birth, "the *ort* appears to the relatives of a person near death and always at night, assuming the guise of the very person who is close to death."[3] At this moment, he was reputed to inflict a pinching so severe that it left a blue mark on the skin, a manifest proof of his real nature. This explains the custom of the Finno-Ugric peoples of leaving a pitcher of water and a towel on the windowsill outside their houses so that the *ort* could wash his face [fig. 7]. Zyrian ideas relating to the mystery of death would shatter Kandinsky's categories of legal thought and lead him to understand the existence of shamanistic forms of thought capable of detecting, under the stable surface of the visible, the presence of contradictory forces at work — an experience that would prove crucial in spawning his experimentation with the breaking up of the plane and the divorcing of form and color.

In 2007, Natacha Nisic was given permission to film the daily life of the Carmelite nuns of Lisieux. In *Carmel* [p. 26–32 + 36], she recorded the gestures of the recluses, the preparation of the meals, the work of sewing and gardening, the pastimes, prayer, in the somber, unadorned space of their cells and communal spaces, far from the sparkling light that bathed the convent where Robert Bresson had filmed the Carmelites transfigured by grace in *Angels of Sin*. Natacha Nisic's nuns do not change the world; they reproduce it in its prosaic reality by gliding over its surface, as if grazing it with their gestures. Similarly, the Korean shaman in *Princess Snow-Flower* (2011) [p. 37 + 72–78], living in the middle of the countryside in a place propitious for revealing the good or evil forces that rule the world, in a makeshift

shack amid a mountain of consumer products, performs ritual gestures as if doing the cooking and makes contact with the dead ("Maybe the spirit of a suicide makes his presence felt in my body," she says, or again: "You are buried so deep that you have become transparent"). She is gripped by the tremors of the trance while continually moaning about her lack of money and dreaming of a new life in Seoul. As Mircea Eliade has remarked, illnesses, dreams, and ecstasies, more or less pathological, are all ways of attaining the status of shaman: "They succeed in transforming the profane man of before 'the choice' into a technician of the sacred."[4] This is how the young Bavarian who Natacha Nisic had asked to tell her story (*Andrea*, 2012) found herself reluctantly initiated, without ever having imagined it, following a series of trials that would affect her health and her sanity [p. 36–37].[5] Shamanistic power is transmitted from afar, from generation to generation, like a predestination: the shaman is the descendant of that witch described by Jules Michelet, reborn from its ashes throughout history, under different names, like the incarnation of a principle of life: "The witch is ended forever but not the fairy. She will reappear in this form, which is immortal."[6]

III

"If the atomic bombings of Hiroshima and Nagasaki on August 6 and 9, 1945, respectively, are a surpassing disaster then beyond not only the immediate death toll and the manifest destruction of buildings, including museums, libraries and temples, and of various other sorts of physical records, but also the long-term hidden material effects, in cells that have been affected with radioactivity in the 'depth' of the body, and the latent traumatic effects that may manifest themselves *après coup*, there would be an additional immaterial withdrawal of literary, philosophical and thoughtful texts as well as of certain films, videos, and musical works, notwithstanding that copies of these continue to be physically available; of paintings and buildings that were not physically destroyed; of spiritual guides; and of the holiness / specialness of certain spaces."[7]

Natacha Nisic's works systematically set out to reveal the erasure that Jalal Toufic identifies as both the effect and symptom of a disaster he calls "excessive" because it escapes quantification, and subsequently description, an excess that the artistic or literary work can only mimic.

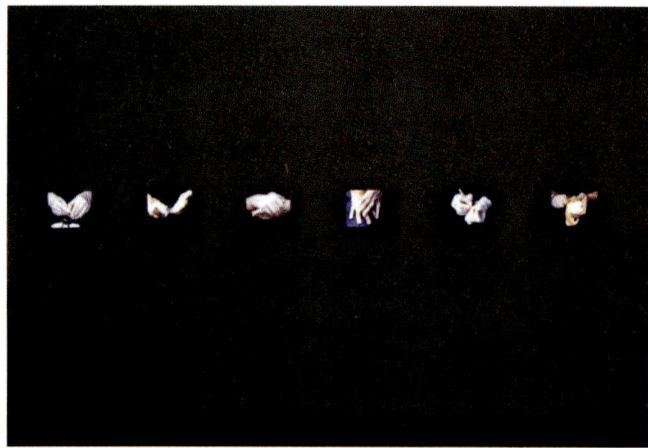

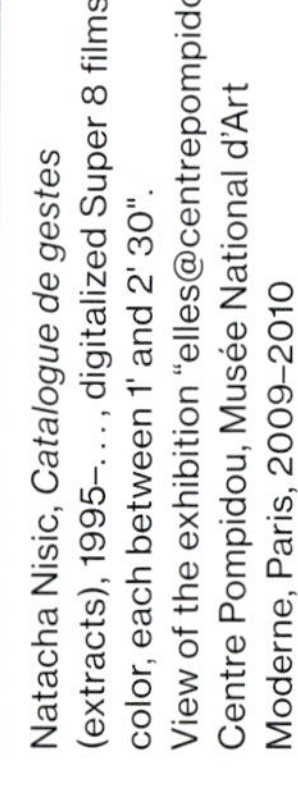

fig. 1

Natacha Nisic, *Catalogue de gestes* (extracts), 1995–…, digitalized Super 8 films, color, each between 1' and 2' 30".
View of the exhibition "elles@centrepompidou," Centre Pompidou, Musée National d'Art Moderne, Paris, 2009–2010

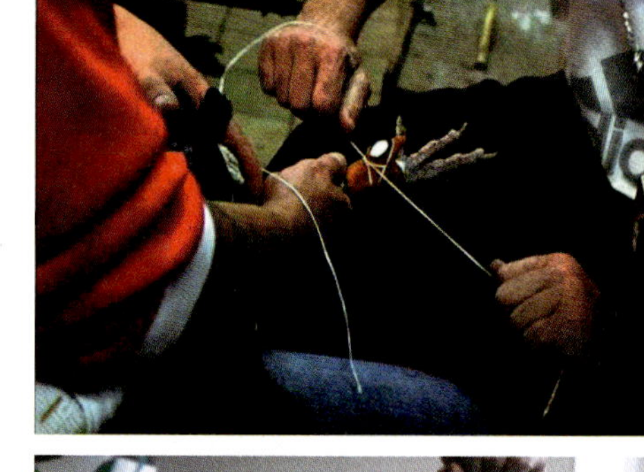

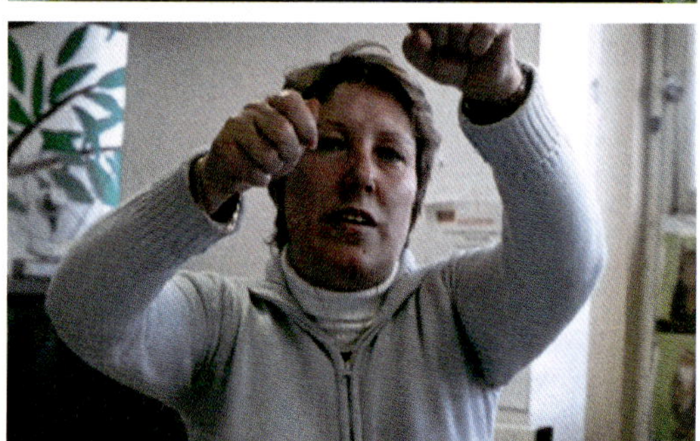

Natacha Nisic, *Nord*, 2007, installation, 5 projections of 16 mm films transferred to video, color, stereo sound, each 5' 50"

fig. 2

Ralph Steiner and Willard Van Dyke, *Hands*, 1934, 16 mm film, black and white, 4'

fig. 3

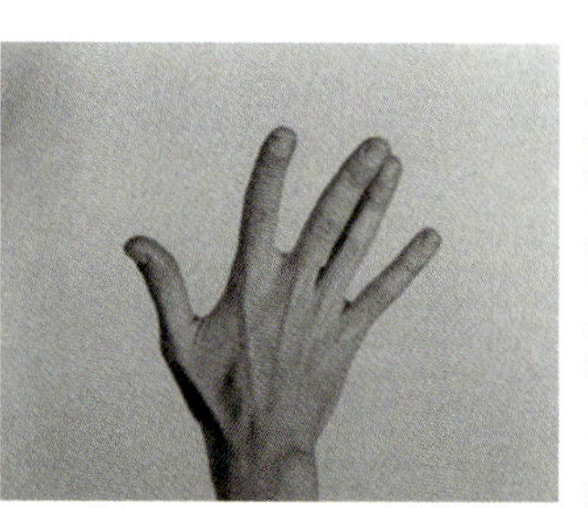

fig. 4

Yvonne Rainer, *Hand Movie*, 1966, 8 mm film, black and white, 5'

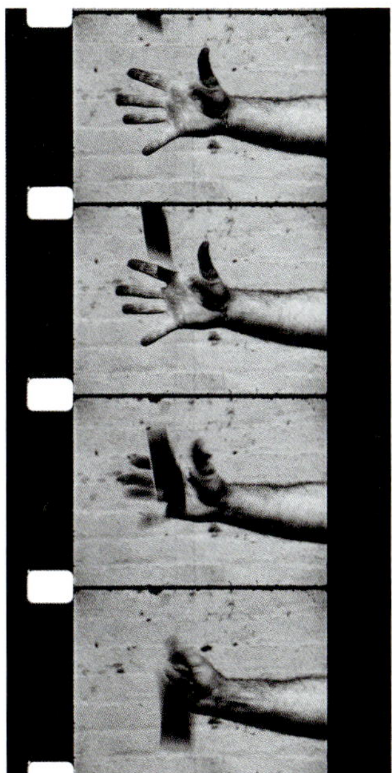

fig. 5

Richard Serra, *Hand Catching Lead*, 1968, 16 mm film, black and white, 3'.
Centre Pompidou, Musée National d'Art Moderne, Paris

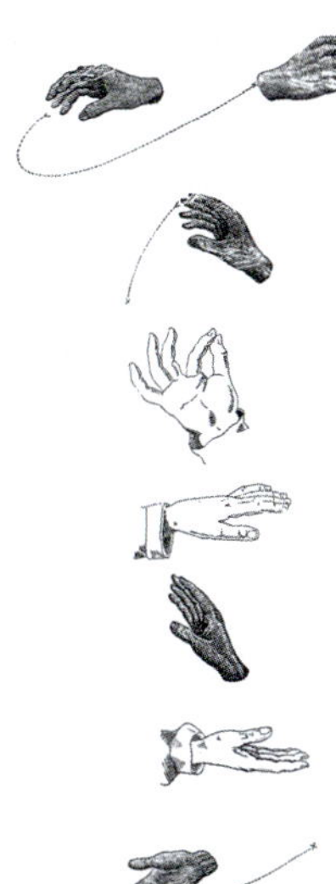

fig. 6

Sketch illustrating the study by Garrick Mallery, "Sign Language among North American Indians Compared with That among Other Peoples and Deaf-Mutes," 1881

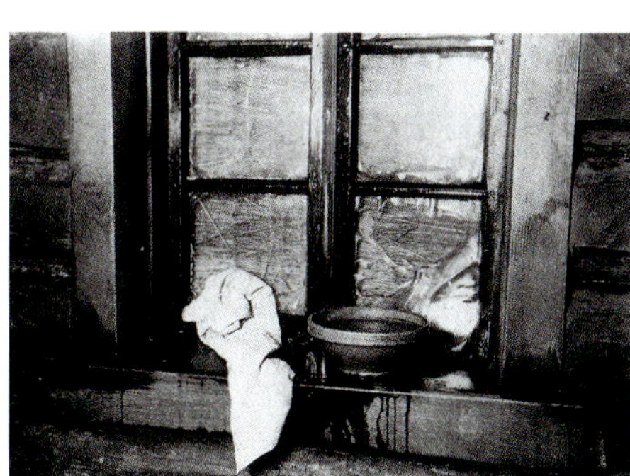

fig. 7

Towel and bowl of water at window for the soul of the dead, funerary custom among the Setukesen of Estonia; similar to the custom described by Wassily Kandinsky among the Zyrians, 1924 (?)

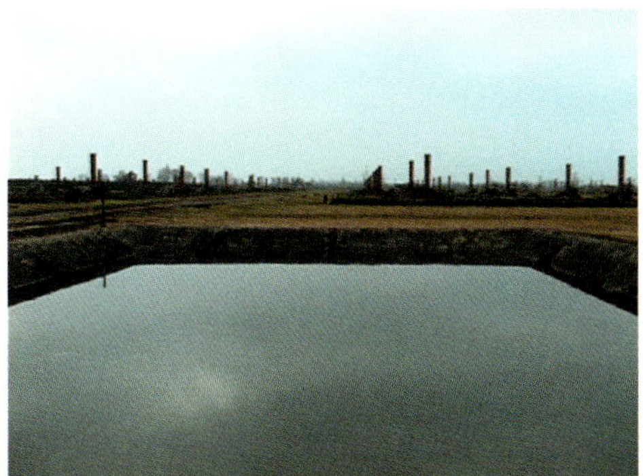

fig. 8

Natacha Nisic, *Effroi*, 2005, video, color, 7' 30"

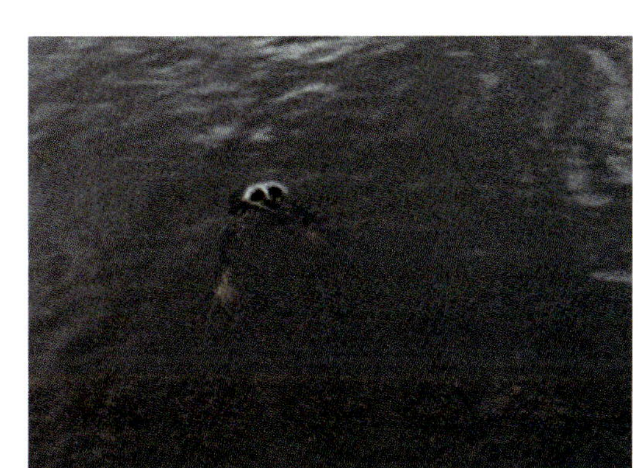

fig. 9.

Natacha Nisic, *Effroi – Réservoir* (detail), 2005, color photograph, 110 × 80 cm

e (Japanese for "image"; 2009) consists of sequences shown on three screens, exploring a region in the north of the island of Honshu ravaged by an earthquake in 2008 [p. 138 + 156–184]. One of the island's inhabitants describes having experienced, during the catastrophe, a feeling of vertigo, as if the earth, under his feet, was charged with conflicting forces: "The shelves and objects moved in opposite directions." He re-enacts his terror at the time of the quake, how he ran out of the house: in reality, he can only show the impossibility of repeating the disaster (at a certain point in his account, the image goes blank). Aerial shots, reproduced on three screens, then scan the devastated countryside, showing the land upturned by a visceral force, of which, after the event, the image can only capture surface signs. *f* [p. 143–156] was also shot in Japan, in 2013, on the contaminated site of Fukushima, a landscape of affliction across the surface of which the camera glides in a series of tracking shots that do not "fictionalize" reality, but on the contrary reveal its opacity. Mirrors positioned in the space, extending from top to bottom of the frame, render more inaccessible the background, which is a fragment of reality both visible and erased, situated beyond the mirrors, where people continue to live and work. The surface of the image is reversed and becomes reflective: by repelling examination, she introduces a moment of unreality into the imaginary space of this reversed image. The landscape elements and the doomed beings who inhabit it dissolve in the limbo of the image, creating a spatial vacuity, an echo, perhaps, of the landscape paintings of the Edo era that were split across several panels of a screen.

IV

"The image carries within it its own contradiction": this is Natacha Nisic's explanation of how she arrives at her representational devices for the objects, bodies, and landscapes she films and photographs. The image, fixed or moving, is not a description, but rather reveals a state of tension pervading things, a demonology for which the "track and zoom shot" could well be a model or the final figuration. Associating a zoom in and a track out (or, on the contrary, a zoom out and a track in), the track and zoom shot produces a contradictory movement born from the meeting of two forces, one optic (that of the lens) and the other physical (that of the camera), which act in opposition, without the possibility of continuity or resolution.

Alfred Hitchcock gave this stylistic device its pure construction in the final scene of *Vertigo* (1958), as a representation of the cause of the vertigo: a stairwell, reproduced in a model and framed in a 90° high-angle shot, is hollowed out by the effect of the zoom, forming a bottomless well that draws the gaze inexorably in, while being simultaneously brought back to the front of the image by the backwards force of the tracking out. The image becomes both elastic and static, its surface dilating without breaking, like a bridge hit by an earthquake, as a result of forces that act and form within it without cancelling each other out.

In 2005, with *La Porte de Birkenau* [p. 137], a work now installed in Paris at the Mémorial de la Shoah, Natacha Nisic reinvents this figure of immobility to produce an image of what cannot be shown: the camera, fitted to rails, physically (and imperceptibly) approaches the gates of the extermination camp, whose form stands out ever more clearly in the distance and optically resists the mechanical movement that pulls it toward the foreground. This dialectical construction is clearly a response to the famous tracking shot in Gilles Pontecorvo's *Kapo* (1959), of which Jacques Rivette commented scathingly in *Cahiers du cinéma*: "See, in *Kapo*, the shot where [Emmanuelle] Riva commits suicide by throwing herself onto the electrified barbed wire: the man who decided, at that moment, to do a tracking shot to reframe the corpse from below, while taking care to place the raised hand right in the corner of the shot at the end, this man deserves the deepest disdain." [8] Representing the ineluctability of an absolute limit, and yet at the same time the impossibility of transgressing that limit, the track and zoom shot thus becomes the very embodiment of the resistance to mise-en-scène. By preventing the lyrical resolution of the scene, that is to say its transformation into fiction, Natacha Nisic uses the image not for its power to reveal but as a symptom of the forces that, having been removed from sight, continue to act here.

The surface is not that which reveals the abyss, but that which conceals it: it is the place where it is forgotten, and this manifests itself in the form of a sudden appearance. "The first time that I took the time to wander around the camp, I found the wandering around very strange, because the weather suddenly turned fine, the birds began to sing . . . The image was very picturesque. I asked myself if I had the right to feel an emotion close to joy, to lightness. I went up to a pond situated right by the tracks that I had never heard about. It didn't correspond at all to the image I had of Auschwitz. The surface of this pond filled with water formed a perfect image, a reflection of an almost archetypical world, like a 19th-century painting … The image was very disturbing. When I got closer I heard a very strange noise, that of a toad sitting on the steps of the pond. I photographed it." [9] In *Effroi* (2005) [fig. 8], the tracking shot is thus in a way vitrified into the image: on the expanse of gray water, which is both disturbing and calm, reflective like a metal mirror, the landscape is doubled and inverted in the glare of a clear refraction, preventing the gaze from venturing into its depths, while at the bottom of the image, in the gray water, the ectoplasmic form of a toad rises to the surface [fig. 9]. Like the image floating to the surface of the world without touching it, it is the hallucinatory sign of something stubbornly, endlessly returning.

1.   *The Spring of My Life and Selected Haiku*, Boston and London: Shambala, 1997, p. 65.

2.   In historic literature, see for example Andrea de Jorio, *La Mimica degli antichi investigata nel gestire napoletano*, Naples: Dalla stamperia e cartiera del Fibreno, 1832, or Garrick Mallery, *Sign Language among North American Indians Compared with That among Other Peoples and Deaf-Mutes*, Washington: Government Printing Office, 1881.

3.   Wassily Kandinsky, "Notebook of Voyage in Vologda," 1889, quoted in Peg Weiss, *Kandinsky and Old Russia. The Artist as Ethnographer and Shaman*, New Haven and London: Yale University Press, 1985, p. 23.

4.   Mircea Eliade, *Mythes, rêves et mystères*, Paris: Gallimard, 1957, p. 106ff.

5.   For the exhibition at the Jeu de Paume in 2013, the artist produced a second version of the work entitled *Andrea en conversation* [p. 41–72], in the form of an installation consisting of nine monitors, in which the increased number and redistribution of the images perhaps reproduce the shamanistic displacement of the function of the subject.

6.   Jules Michelet (trans. A.R. Allinson), *Satanism and Witchcraft*, New York: Kensington Publishing Corporation, 1992.

7.   Jalal Toufic, *The Withdrawal of Tradition Past a Surprising Disaster*, n.p.: Forthcoming Books, 2009, p. 11 (http://www.jalaltoufic.com/downloads/Jalal_Toufic,_The_Withdrawal_of_Tradition_Past_a_Surpassing_Disaster.pdf.)

8.   Jacques Rivette, "De l'abjection," *Cahiers du cinéma*, no. 120, June 1961, p. 54–55; reprinted in Antoine de Baecque (ed.), *Théories du cinéma*, Paris: Cahiers du cinéma, 2001, p. 37–40.

9.   "The pond is situated to the left of the tracks (when looking in the direction of the ditches, back to the gate); midway between the gate to the camp and the gas chambers, which were demolished by the Nazis. There is little documentation about these ponds. They might have been used to clean the latrines or in the event of fire. One image has haunted me for a long time and almost held me back from publishing mine: that of young people – soldiers – bathing in one of these ponds. This light-hearted photograph was used by revisionists to prove that the camp at Auschwitz was a holiday camp. I haven't found other pictures of these ponds," Natacha Nisic, email, May 4, 2013.

–

Translated from French by Natasha Edwards

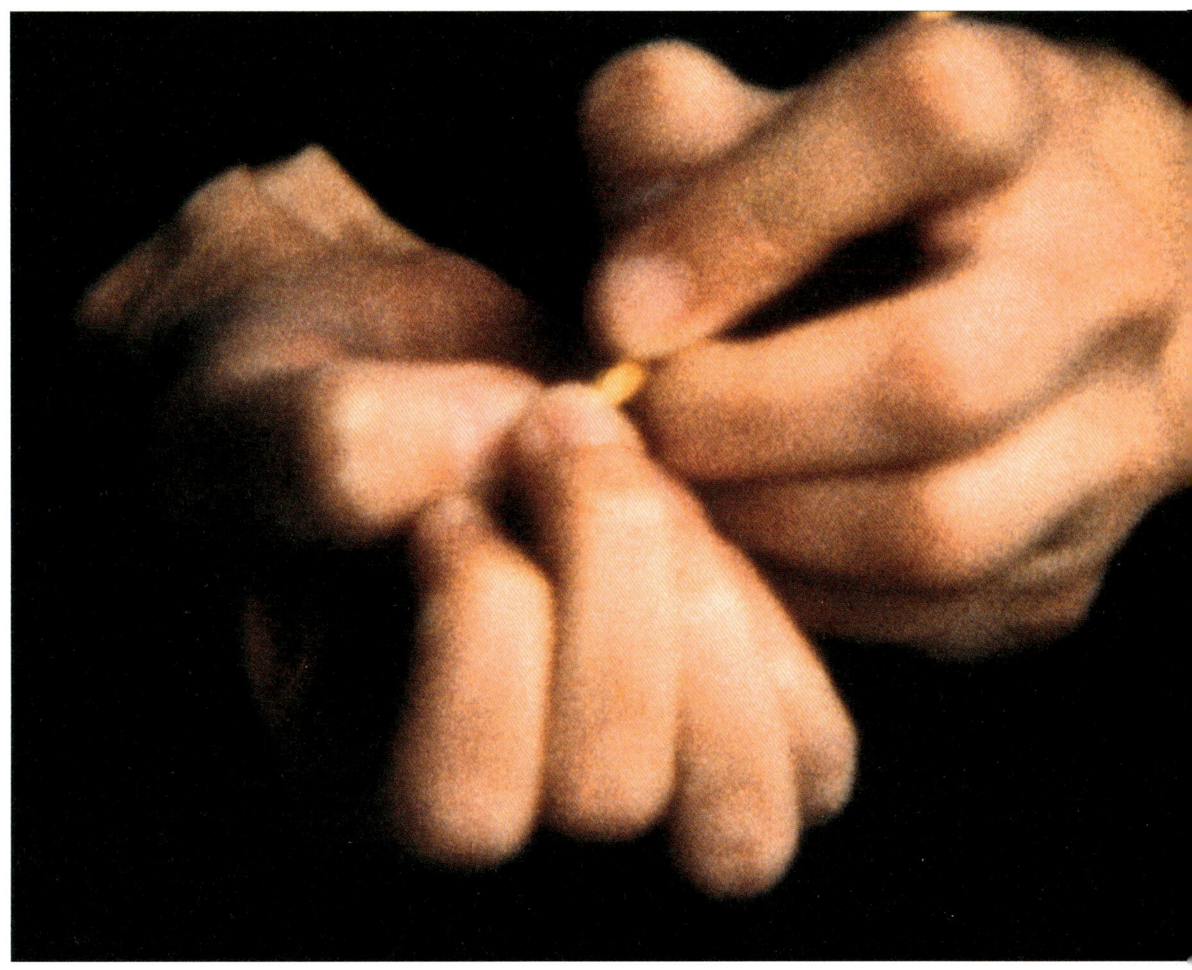

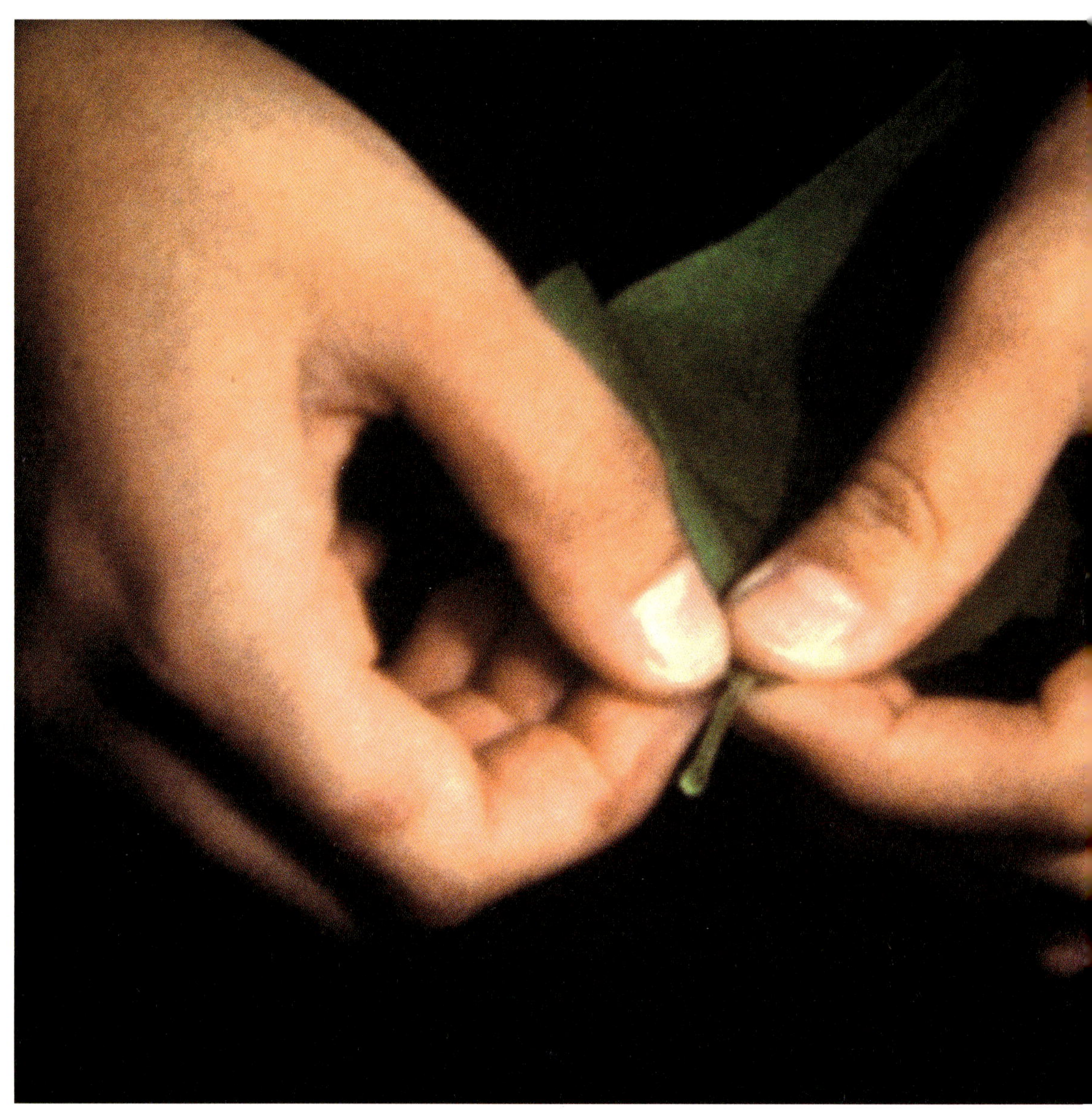

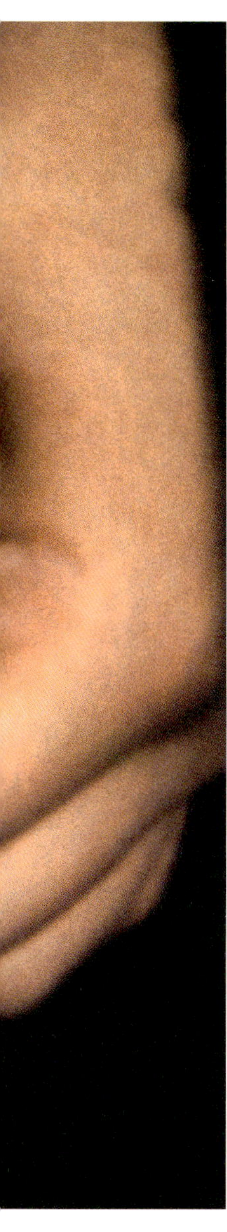
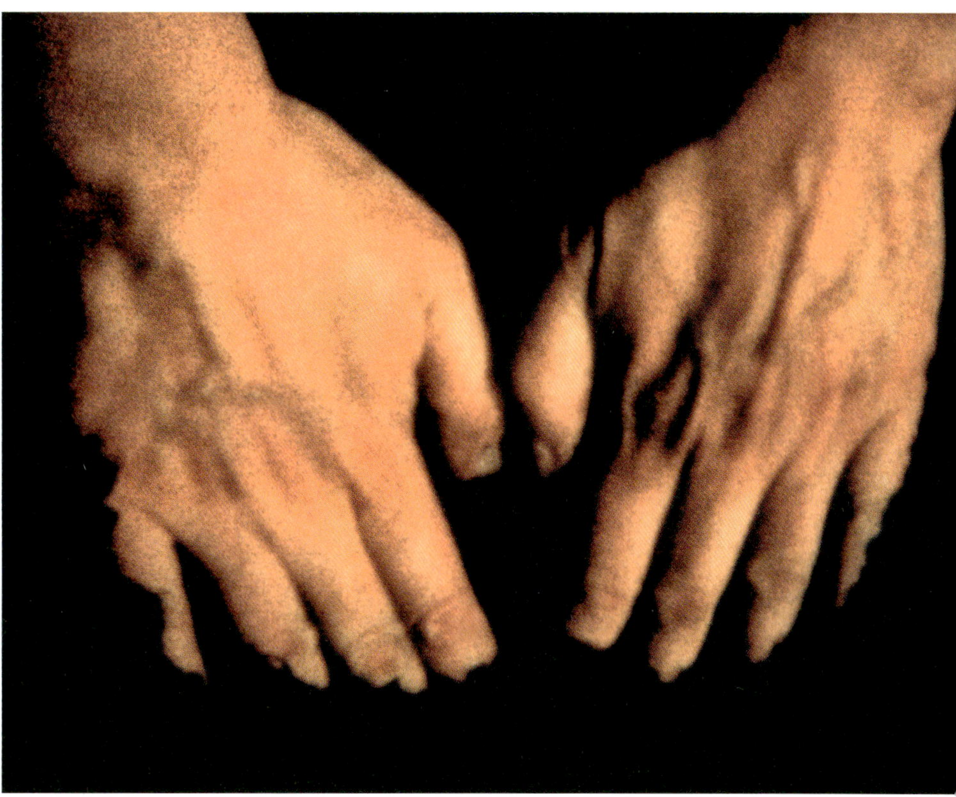

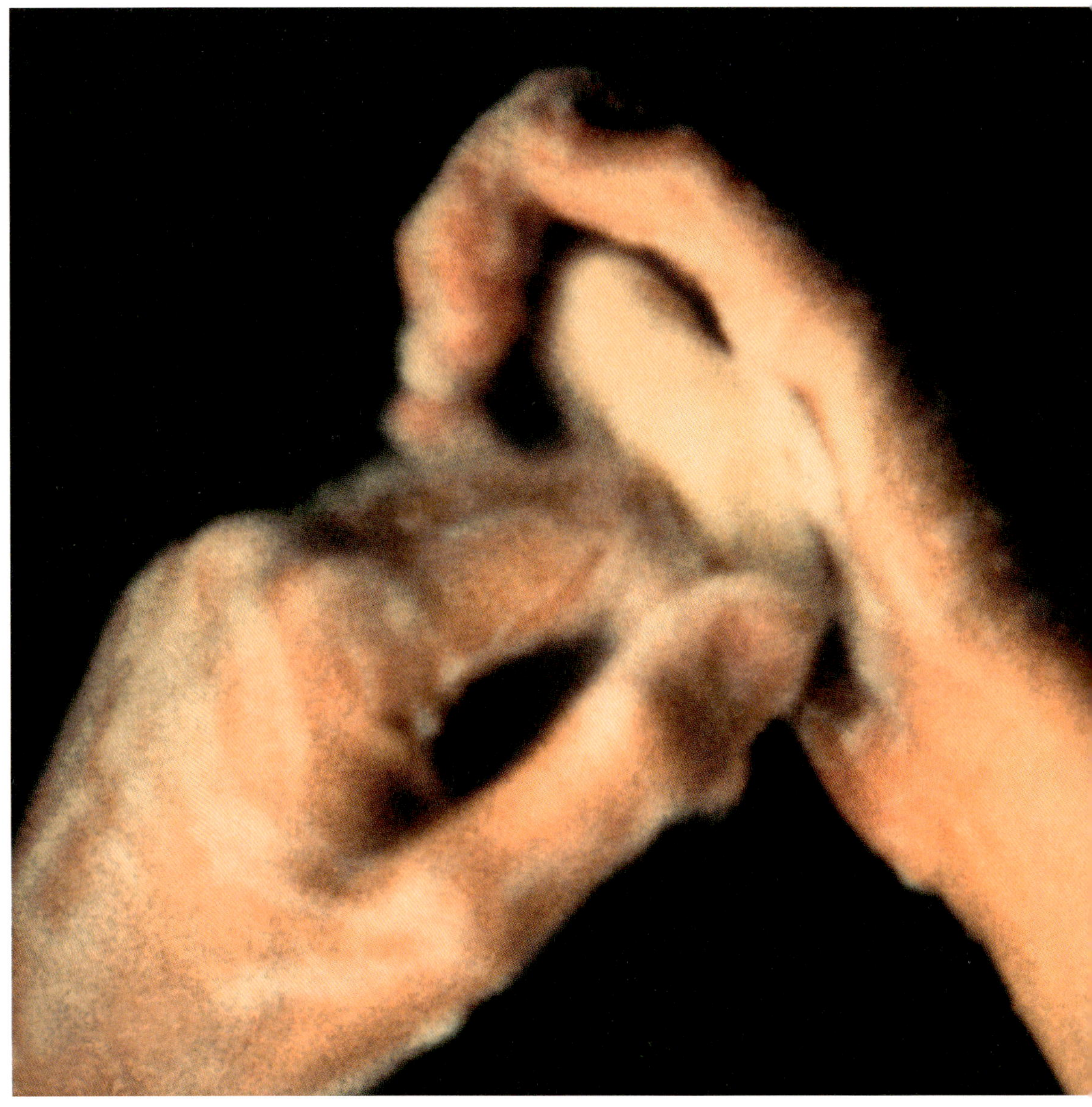

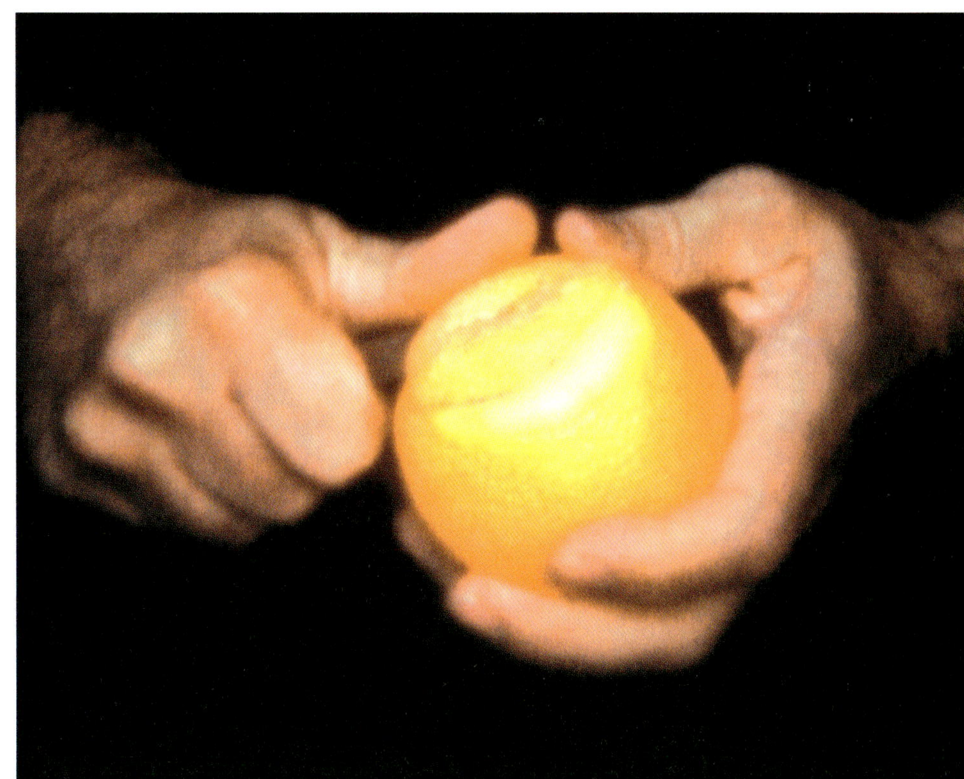

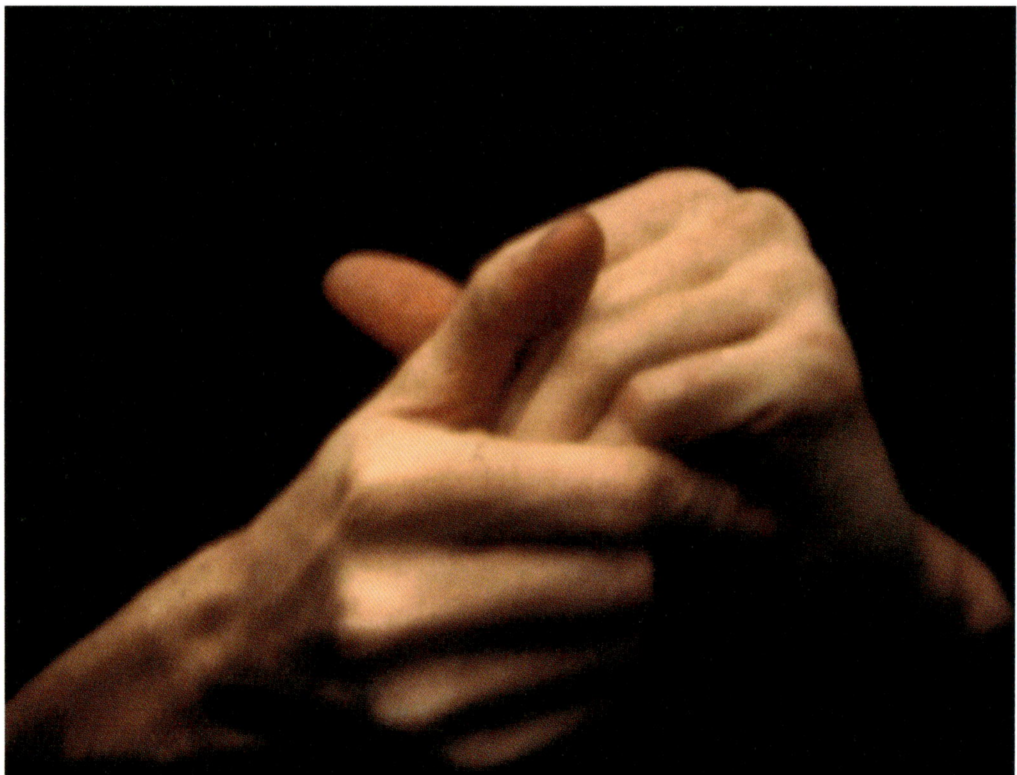

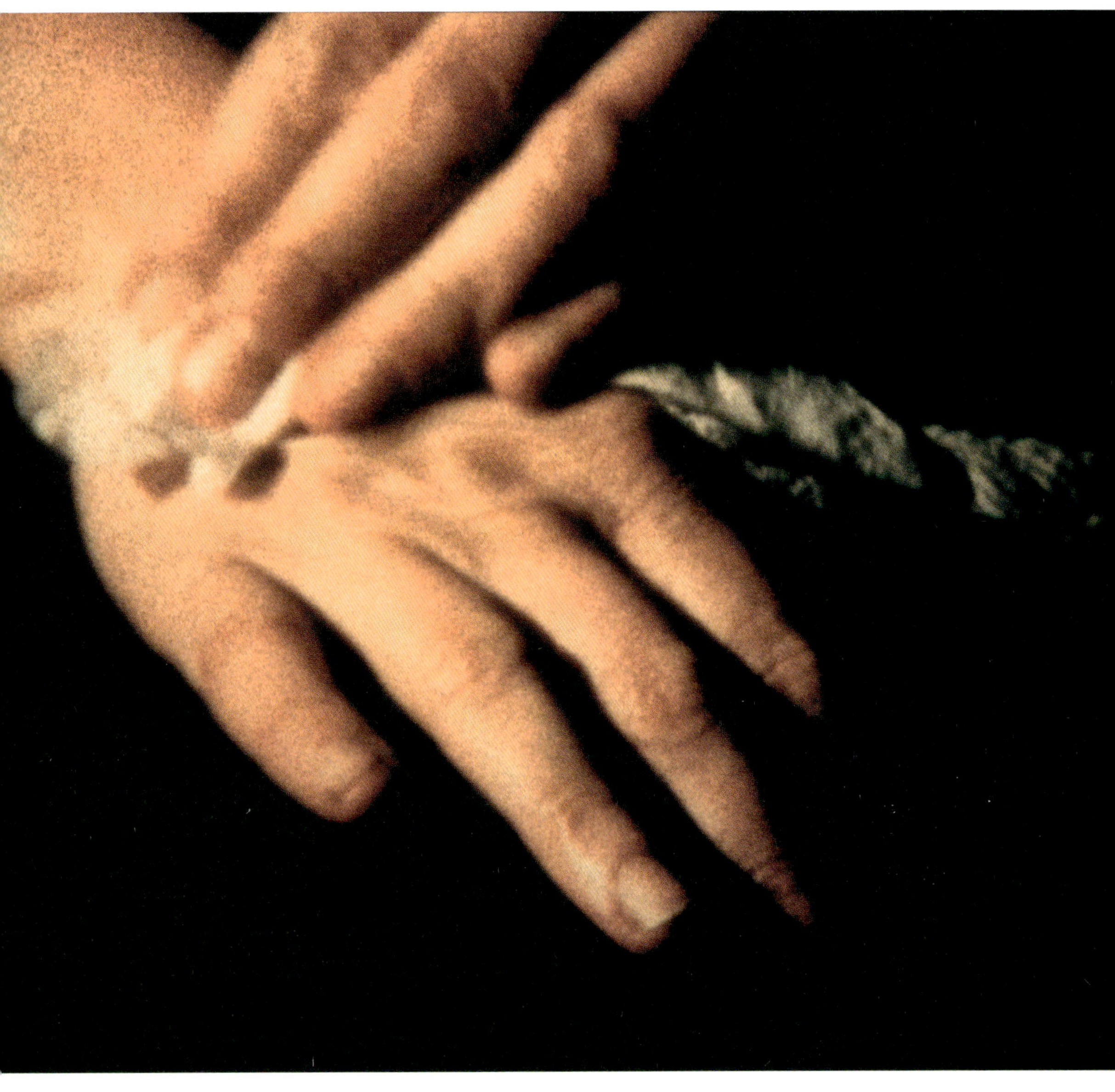

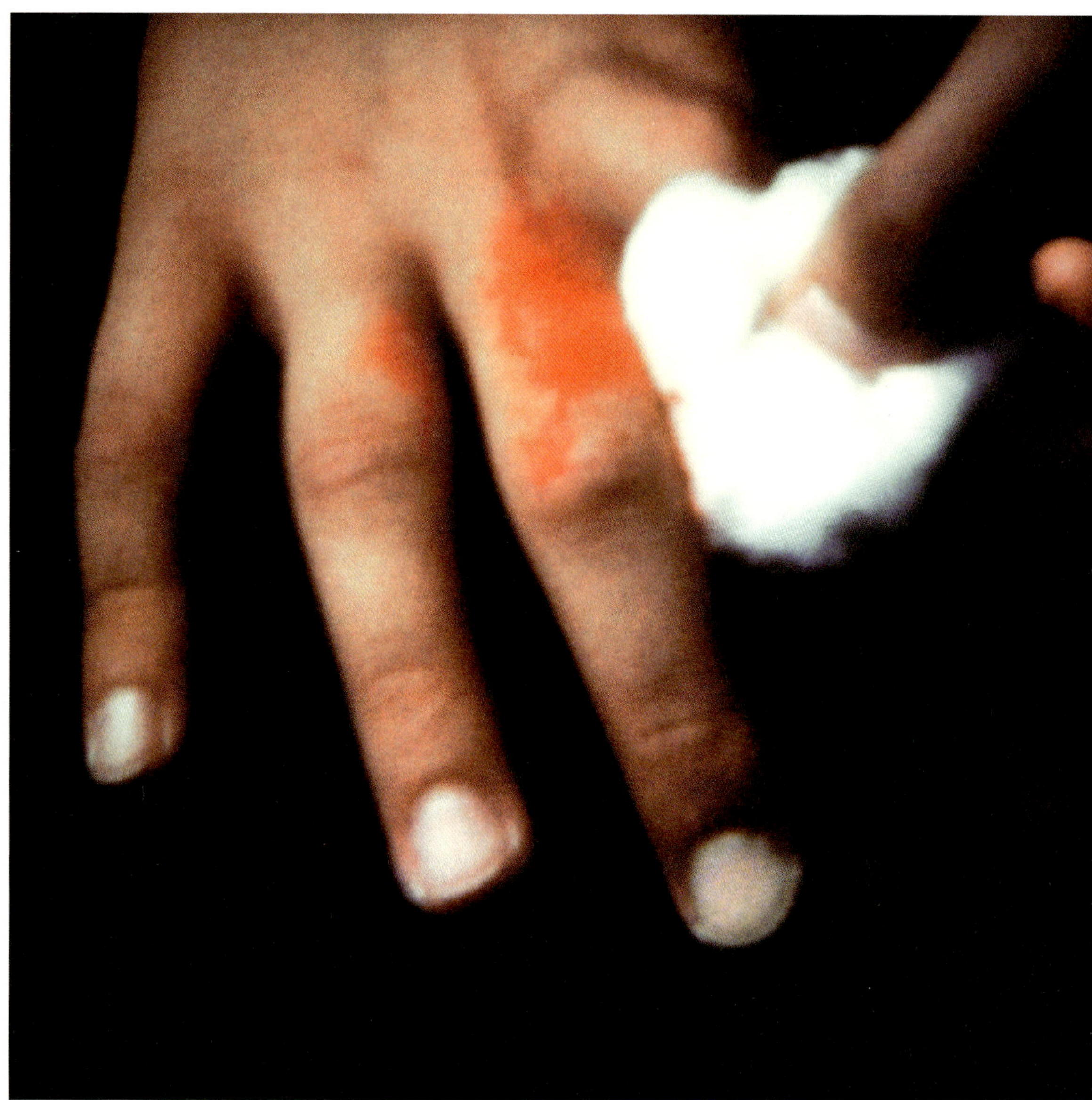

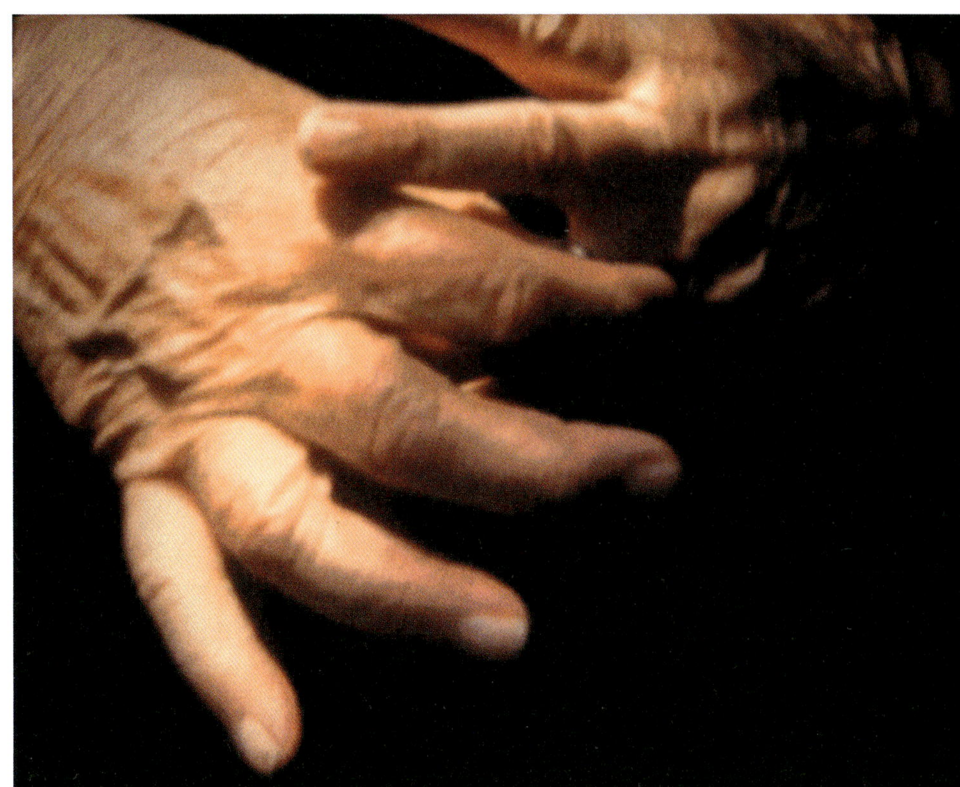

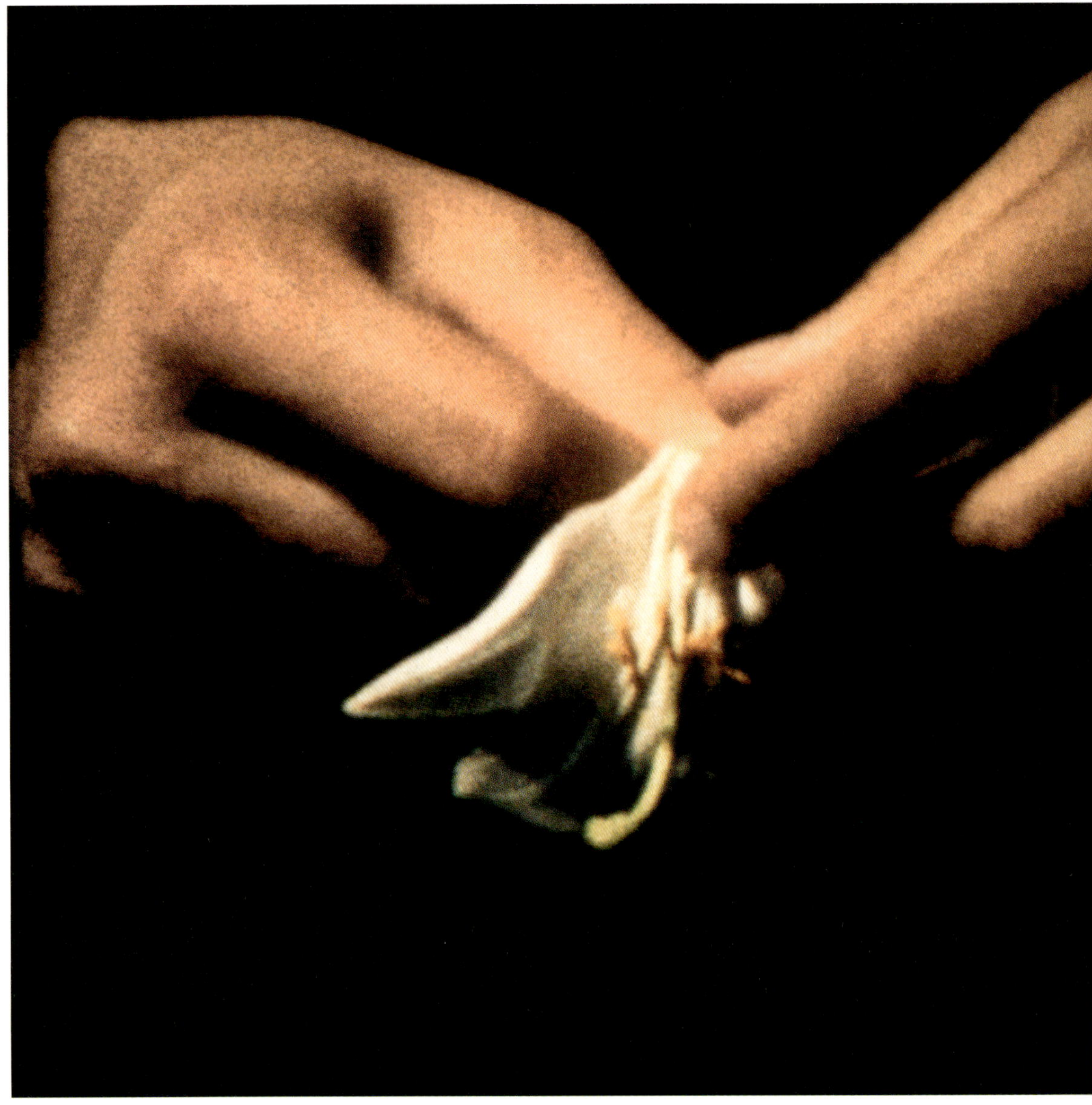

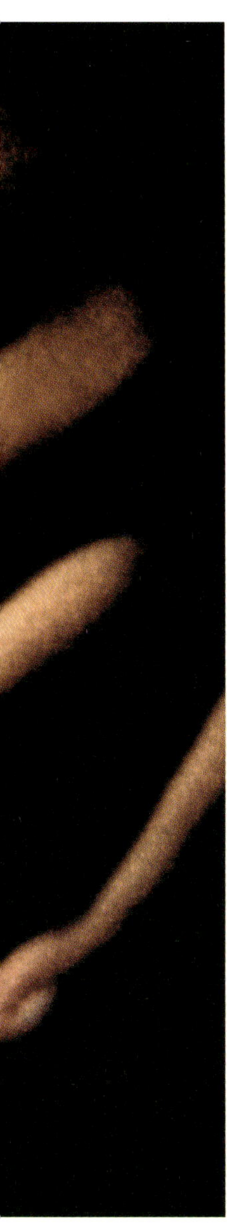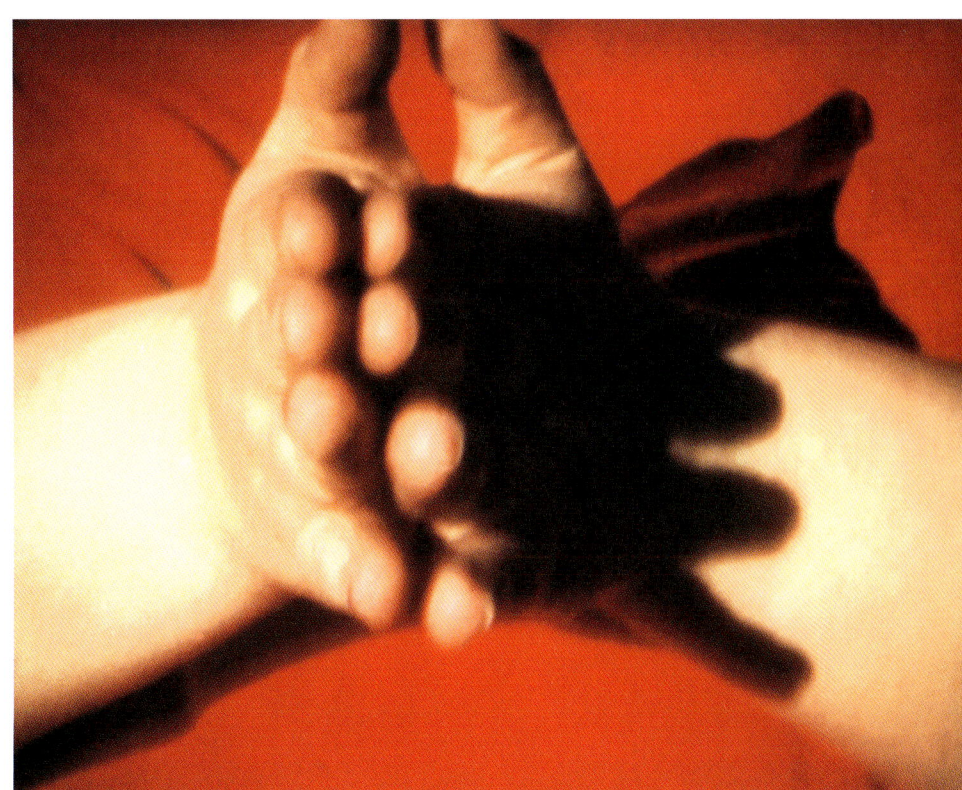

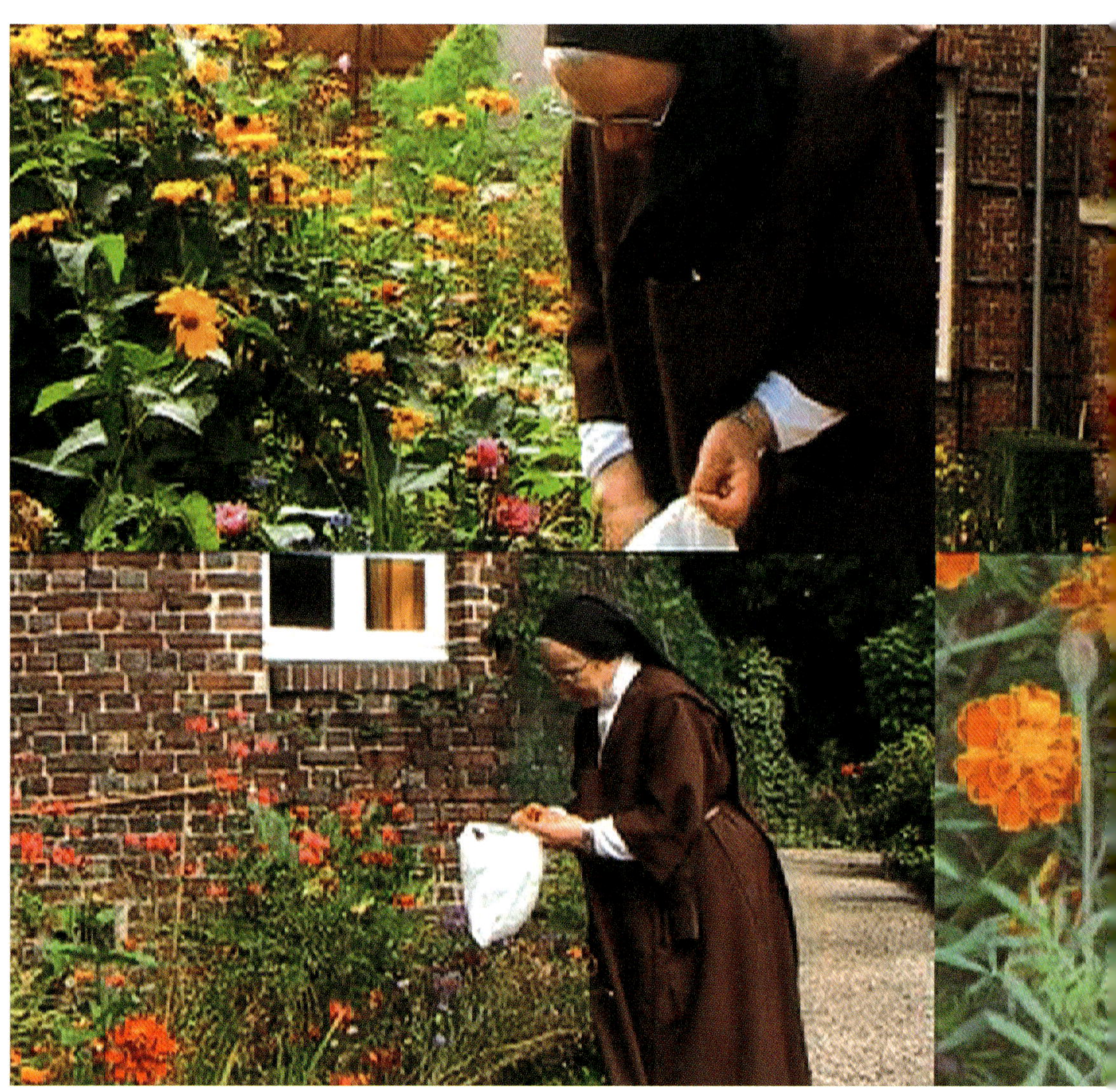

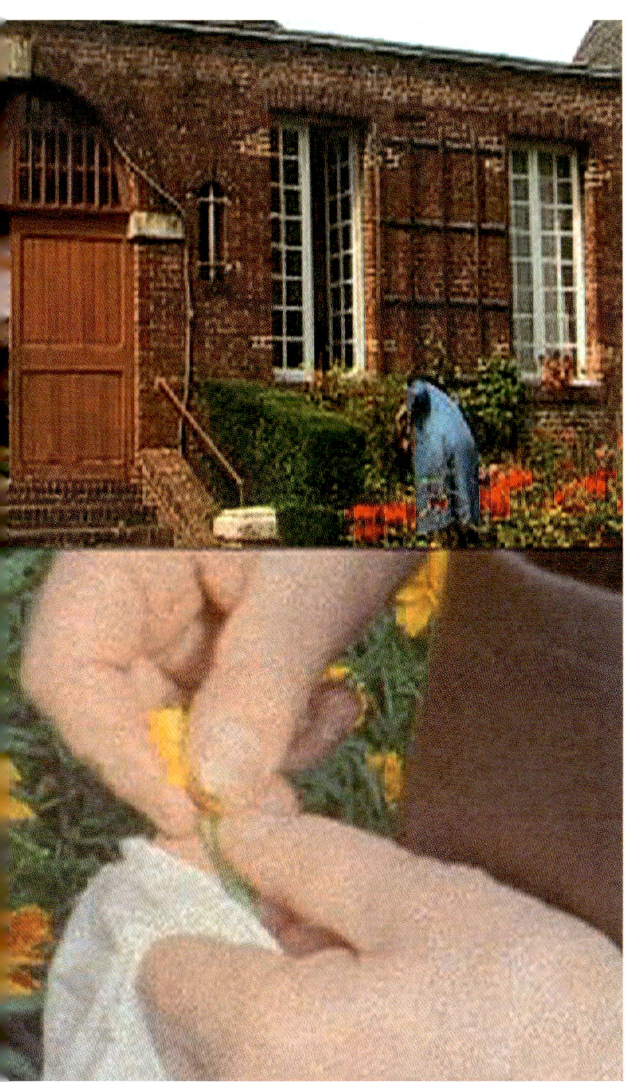

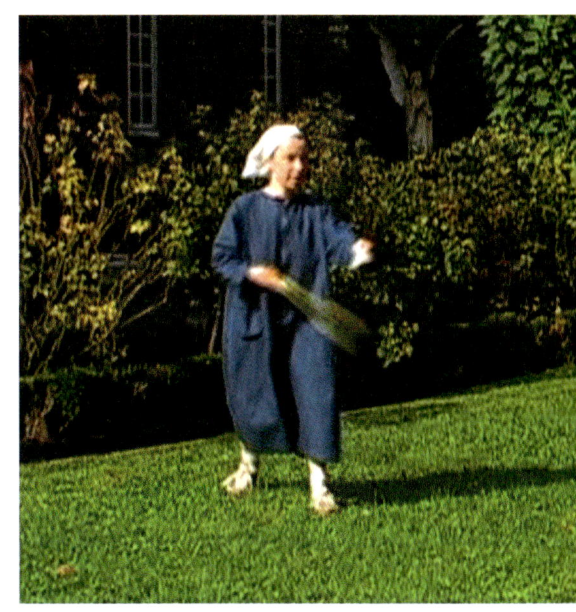

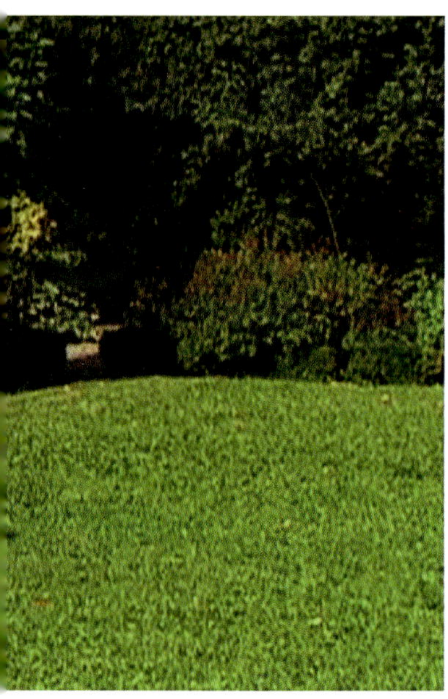

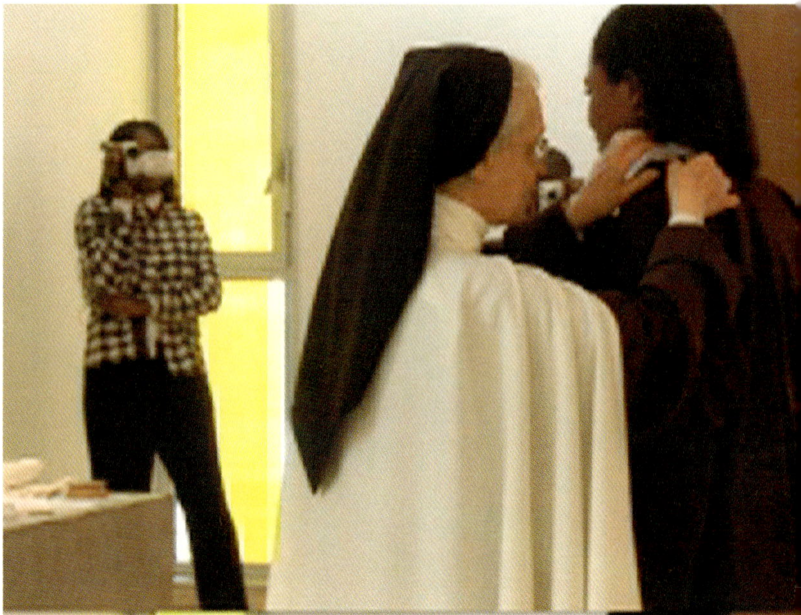

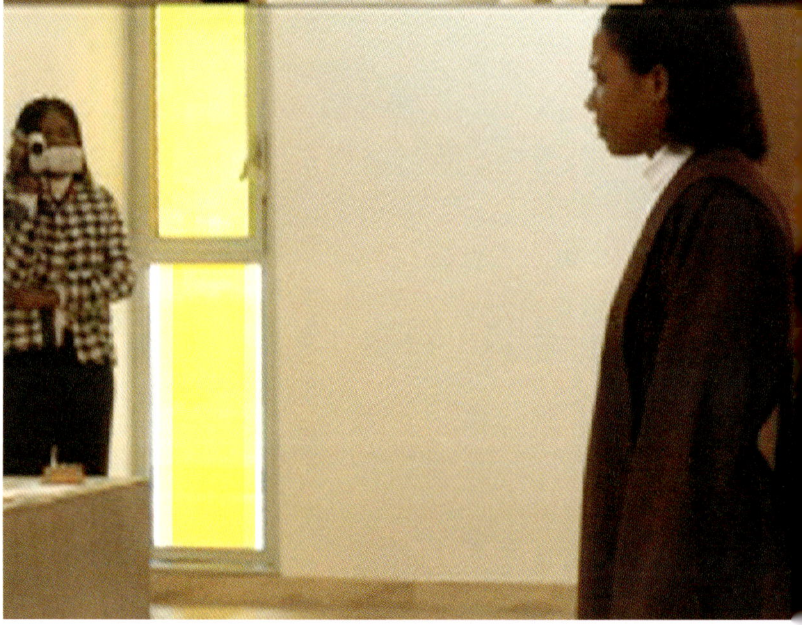

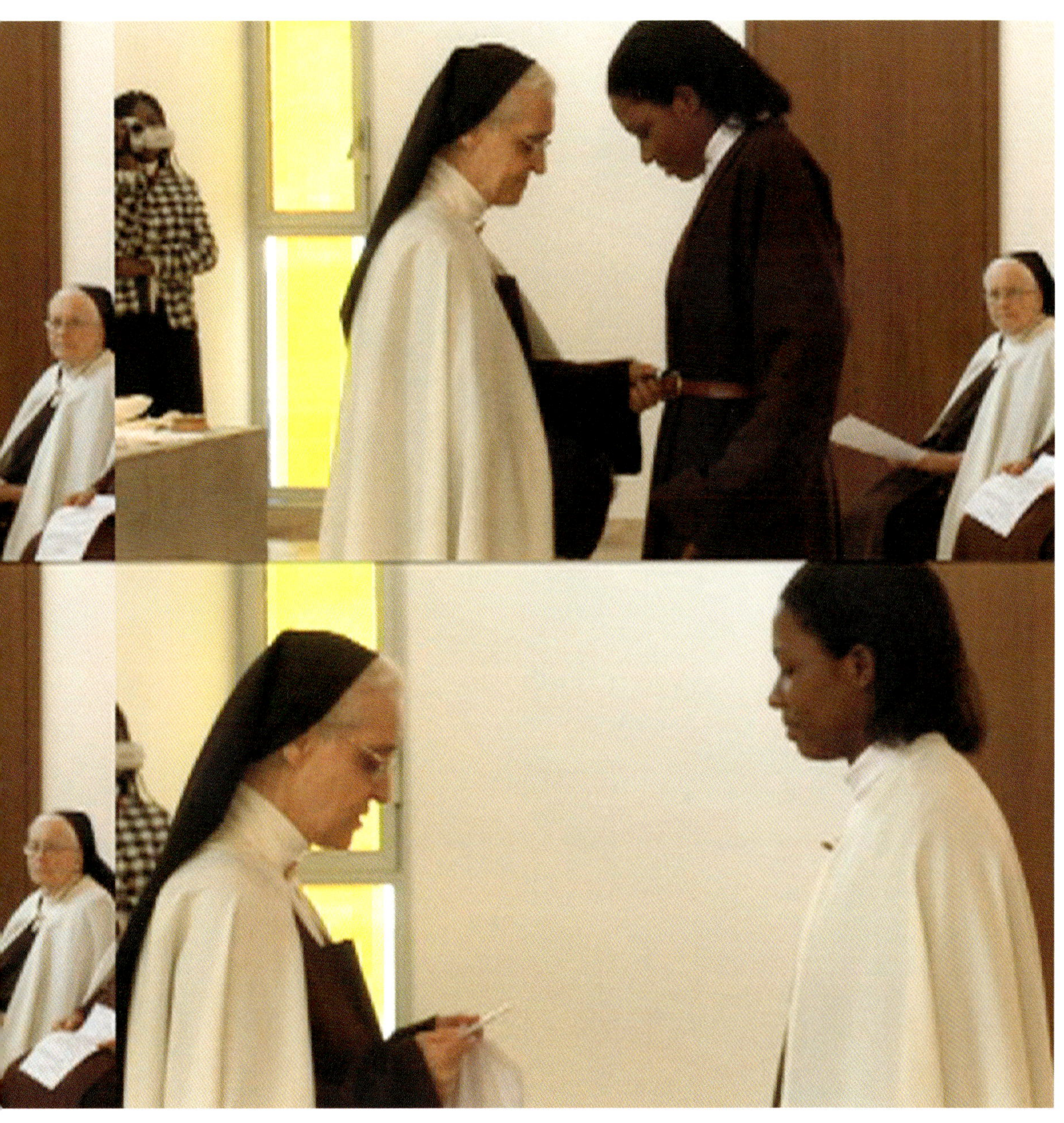

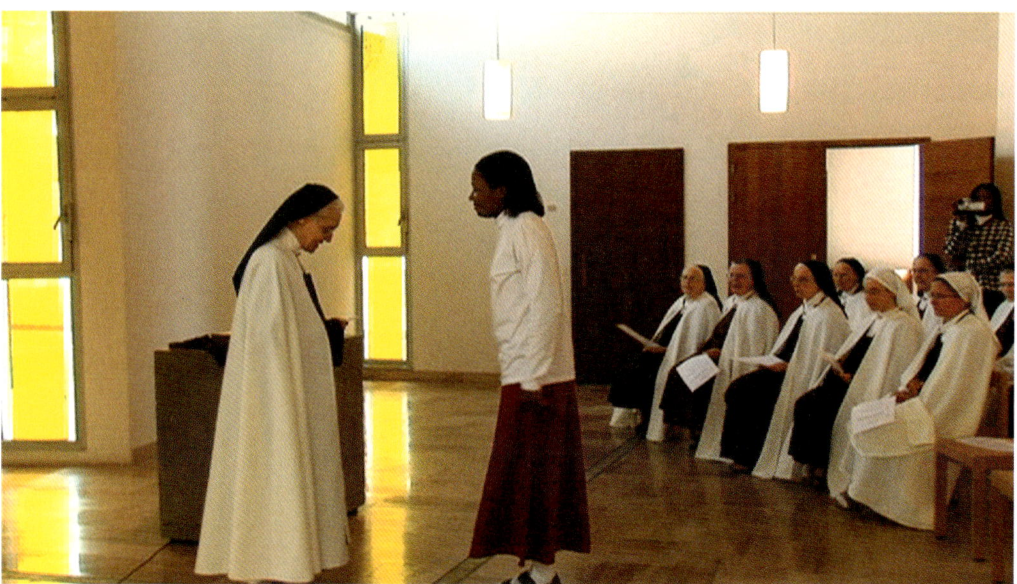

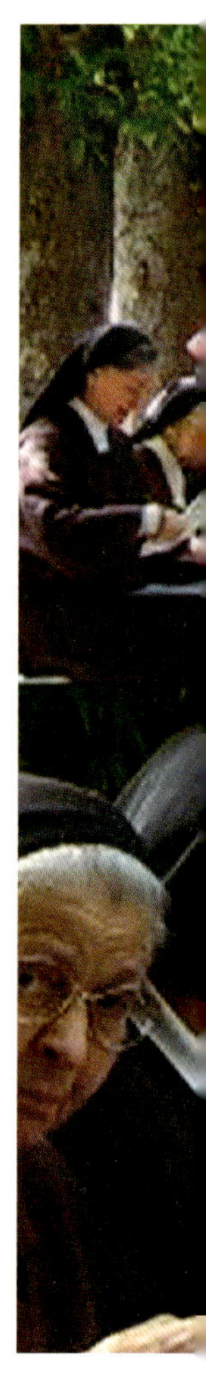

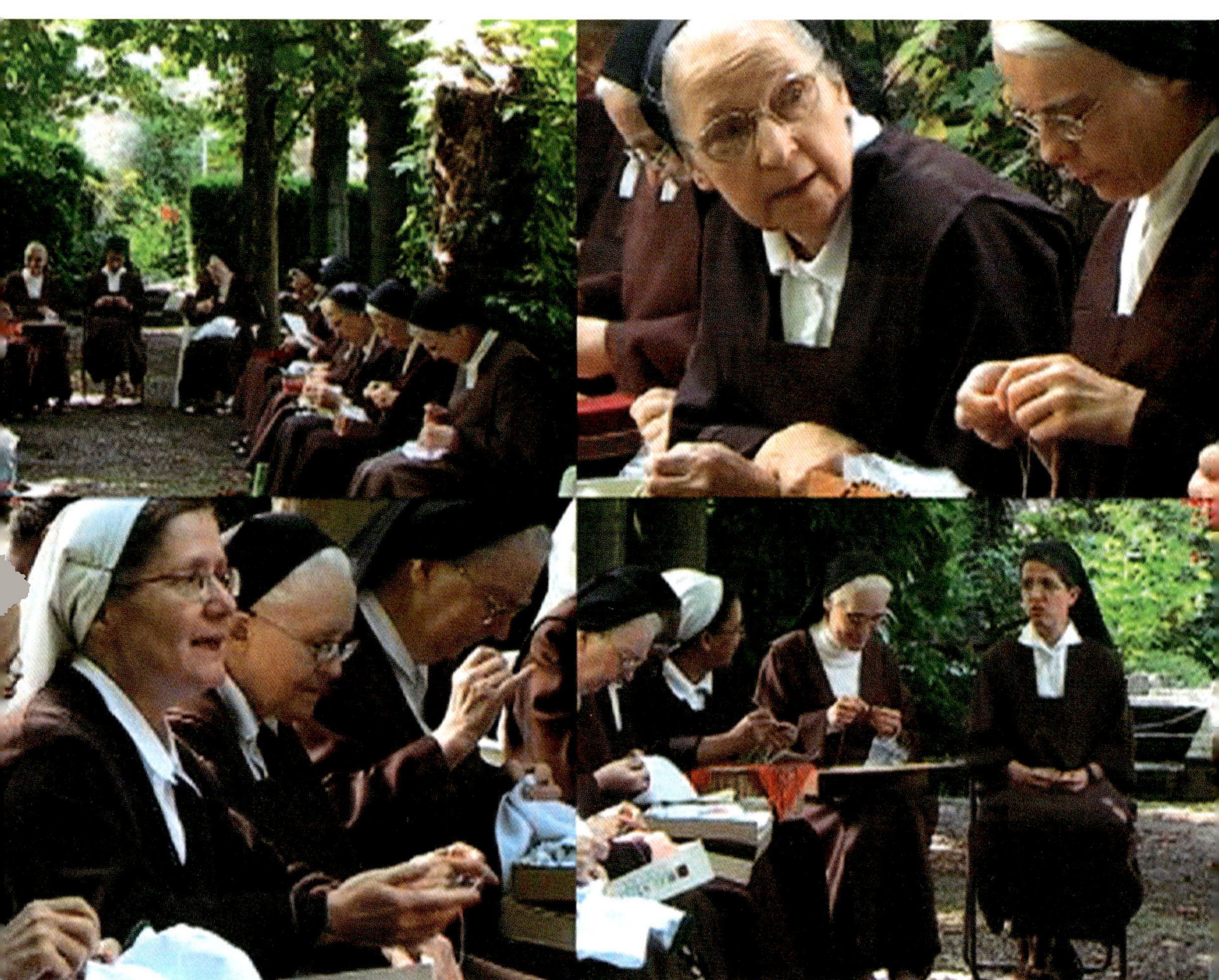

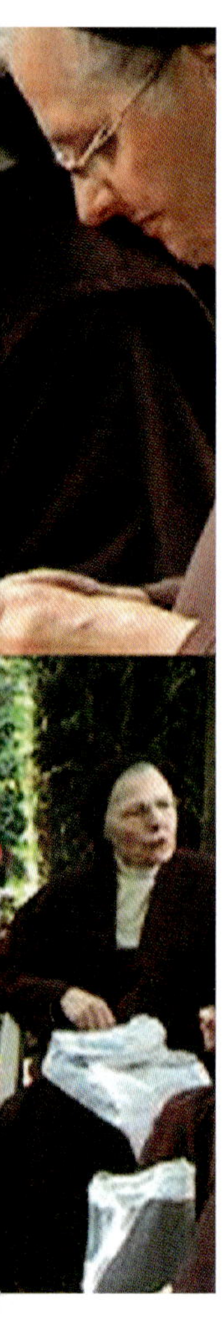

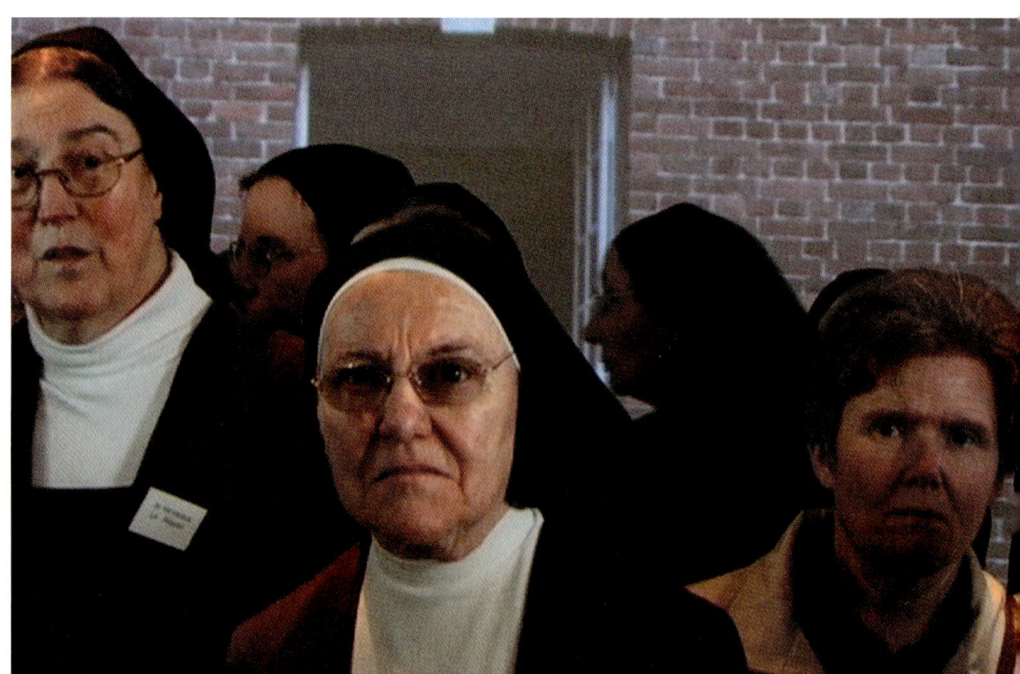

Beck Jee-sook

Andrea, in this Triangular World

Andrea, dans ce monde triangulaire

From our country's point of view, it is to the farthest east, and from Europe's point of view, it is to the farthest west. A person from the farthest east wished to meet someone from the farthest west.
   Park Ji-won[1]

Natacha Nisic's *Andrea* (2012) consists of five videos of different lengths.[2] Screens playing a mix of the videos that she shot in Fischbachau in Bavaria, Germany, and footage from a Bavarian television report[3] were installed throughout the exhibition space where "K. W. Complex"[4] was held [fig.1]. The videos, individually titled *The Encounter*, *The Souls*, *Healing*, *Archives*, and *The Voices*, give an oral narrative conveyed via different video languages of the strange and unfamiliar story of a person. The contrasting landscapes and colors of Germany and Korea, sounds of the wind, popular tunes, silences, and texts that sometimes interrupt and sometimes link the different scenes all provide the backdrop to, and stage for, the drama, and lend a disparate texture to the work. This heterogeneity reveals its full complexity only when we start tracking down *Andrea*'s "family tree."

The "K" in "K. W. Complex," the collaborative project between Natacha Nisic and South Korean artist Park Chan-kyong, stands for the name of the Korean shaman Kim Keum-hwa;[5] the "W" for Norbert Weber, a German Benedictine abbot who visited Korea during the Japanese colonial era at the beginning of the 20th century and who wrote a book titled *Im Lande der Morgenstille, Reise-Erinnerungen an Korea* (*In the Land of Morning Calm*). He also made a film of the same name.[6] The artists divided the book[7] that followed the exhibition into K, the mother chapter, and W, the father chapter, and established Andrea Kalff, Kim Keum-hwa's spiritual daughter, who lives near St. Ottilien, the Benedictine community that sent Norbert Weber to Korea, as K and W's "symbolic" daughter.

The two artists met at a film festival in Japan in 2010. They discovered a common "archival impulse" inspired by an interest in Weber's book and film, and decided to weave Park's longstanding interview work on Kim Keum-hwa into their intellectual and visual exploration of geography and history, to which they also connected *Blue Eyes Possessed by Spirits*,[8] which tells the story of Andrea, who flew from Germany to South Korea to be initiated as a shaman. The word "Complex" expresses the cultural complexity resulting from the geographical and historical influences in the relationship between the three characters.

At the same time, it is a psychoanalytical term that suggests important feelings or thoughts that have long been repressed in many civilizations, as is also the case with family dramas. Park Chan-kyong notes that the complexity touches upon such recurring themes as imperialism, history, and inevitability, which "appear excessively" in the face of individual sickness, death, disaster, and chance in Korea. Faced with the theme, the artists, rather than opting for the easier mode of conversation, chose to focus on a certain silence, a certain opening in-between, in other words, the strong sense of rupture and contrast between the global history of an immense religious organization and the faith of an individual.[9]

When we expand the rhetoric of the "family" further, we discover "sisters." When we put Natacha Nisic's *Carmel* (2008) and *Princess Snow-Flower* (2011) alongside *Andrea* on the family tree, another overtone is created, above the existing vertical composition. *Carmel* is based on the video that the artist made in the course of a year in a Carmelite convent in Lisieux, France. The four smaller screens that fill the screen seem to accentuate the rigor and immaculacy of the lives of the 22 nuns. However, on an occasion when a novice is taking the veil, Nisic's camera enters into this closed space, and temporarily provokes an opening in the austere screen, creating an unexpected sense of rhythm and vitality. *Princess Snow-Flower* is a three-channel video work that the artist produced during her residency in Gyeonggi Province on the outskirts of the South Korean capital, Seoul. It features a young shaman, clearly possessing special powers but appearing extremely tired, gossiping with her followers after performing a somewhat sloppy ceremony at a shambolic outdoor shrine. A montage of *Princess Snow-Flower* and *Carmel* would disrupt modern religious dichotomies that oppose the civilized and the primitive, religion and superstition, worship and trickery, spirituality and capriciousness, and chants and spells. Simultaneously, movements of self-contradiction and negation can be detected within *Princess Snow-Flower* itself. For example, the visual vocabulary of superimposed and dissolving scenes underpinning the oral narrative of the video captures the ghostlike nature of the shaman, and at the same time, renders it volatile. The appearance of the modern specter who, in order to communicate with the spiritual world, places all sorts of shamanistic tools and offerings in a secularized natural setting, and who at the same time yearns for fame, riches, and, above all, the grandness of the city of Seoul, is cut short on the screen when the shaman goes back into the woods led by "a force that she cannot disobey." Meanwhile, Snow-Flower, whose name in Korean culture evokes images of a *gisaeng*[10] more than a shaman, broadens the scope of the "sisterhood" between the postulant in *Carmel* and Andrea. "What use would it be to become an intangible cultural asset or a national shaman? People like me … We don't need men. I will initiate two women, just two, and then I'll be done with it."[11] If the postulant in *Carmel* is a daughter of the Catholic Church and Andrea a daughter of shamanism, Snow-Flower is at the same time the adopted daughter of an anonymous old lady ghost[12] and the jealous surrogate mother of a successful spiritual daughter. She is split between the sacred and the profane, making her the half-sister of the postulant and Andrea.

As such, *Andrea* is at the center of a complex mechanism of exclusion and oppression, or hybridity and syncretism, which crisscrosses the West and the East, colonialism and Orientalism, patriarchy and feminism, and different social classes and peoples. Andrea was initiated in South Korea by Kim Keum-hwa, and currently practices shamanism in Bavaria, Germany. Nisic shows Andrea to be an other in both societies. Through a process of mutual reflection and projection within her work, the two societies, each depicted from a slightly different angle through the artist's lens, unravel the modern boundaries to which they are both tightly bound. Possessed by uncanny spirits, Andrea must certainly be an eccentric character in southern Germany, but she is just as unfamiliar and strange in traditional Korean shamanistic culture. That is because, although spirits of the other world may not have nationalities, in the real world spiritual mediums belong to a pretty solid historical and cultural terrain. During Korea's colonization, shamans were considered to represent the other within society, because they were seen as an obstacle to the country's enlightenment; they were subjected to a history of blatant oppression in colonial Korea, along with feng shui practitioners, begging bonzes, and instigators of riots.[13] In the following era of modernization, on the one hand they were institutionalized into a taxidermized tradition through the intangible cultural assets policy pursued by the military regime, while on the other their practice became established as a religious ritual of subversion with shamanistic spirituality becoming a symbol of political resistance and cultural rebellion against

authority.[14] In this context, Andrea, against the backdrop of Korea's history of colonization and modernization, embodies the Western illusion of Orientalism in its extreme form, and functions as the very rare double other, in other words, "the other from the outside world" or "the other of the other." Her existence restores the suppressed voice of the other within our society and, at the same time, creates a crack in the nationalistic economy of local shamanism that has functioned as a counterbalance to oppression.

The five different video channels of *Andrea*, displayed at a distance from one another and citing, echoing, or confronting each other or just keeping their silence, are "androids" that incarnate the modern spirit. Adopting a conceptual grammar, Nisic's video vocabulary communicates in a physical and emotional way. Already in her earlier works, the artist's video vocabulary was reinforced by diverse hand gestures and facial expressions. In *Andrea*, however, it takes on an organic-mechanical nature. For the androids, headaches, stomach troubles, fractures, and tumors appear as signs of physical illnesses that attack the modernity-disciplined body; the tears and belching of the recovery process are the abjection released by the body. Unlike the working hands, the feet serve as a window that allows the viewer "to read the sadness and the deep concerns for the mother";[15] they are connected to the categories of memory and the family, which constitute the modern body. These two categories are known to form the boundary of normality that comes into play fully when modern rationality rejects the pre-modern ghost in the name of superstition.[16] Andrea puts her Catholic, modern, medicine-revering parents on one side as spokespersons of modern rationality, and on the other, as a force disruptive of that rationality, places her deceased older brother and her daughter Denise, who narrowly escapes being possessed by spirits. In the process of retracing her memory, she talks of her devout Catholic upbringing and her adolescent years in a religious convent run by nuns, of how her parents threatened to cut her off from the family if she became a shaman, and confesses to being shocked when she saw the patients at the psychiatric hospital where her brother was institutionalized and locked up alongside criminals. Andrea's effort at recollection is at its most intense when she comes into contact with her deceased brother's spirit through a male shaman during her initiation ritual in South Korea, and it impels her to criticize her

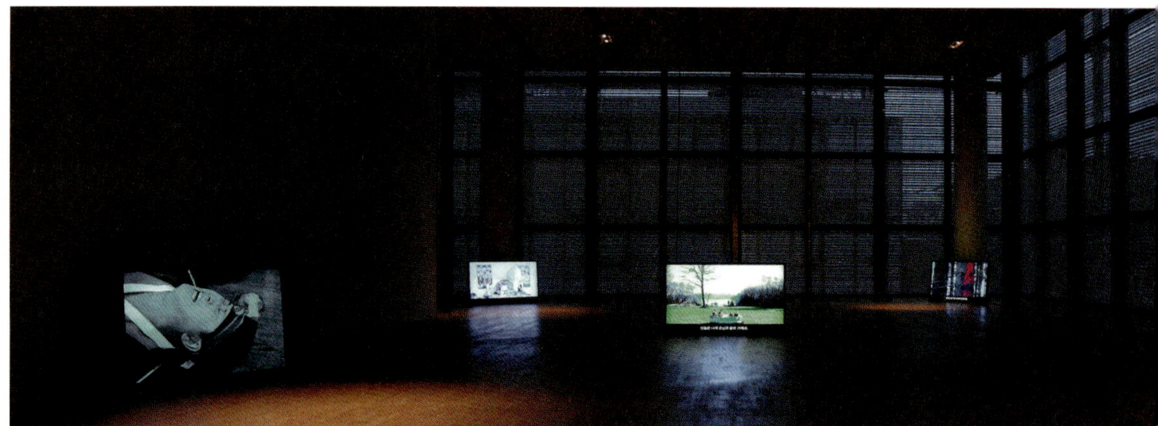

fig.1

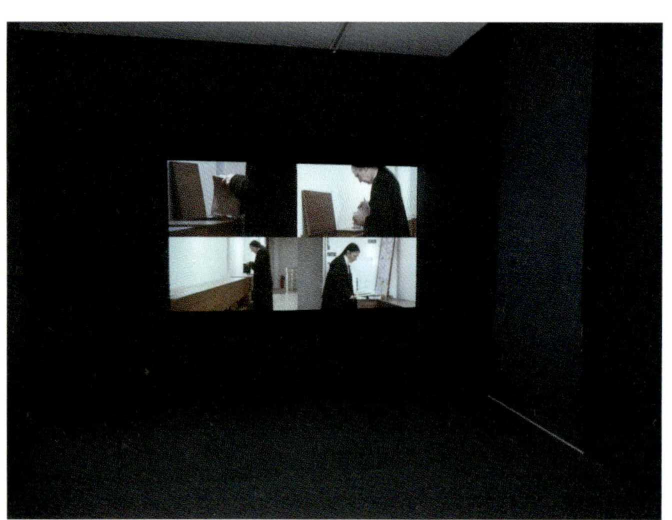

Natacha Nisic, *Carmel*, 2008, 4 rear-projections, HD video,
color, sound, each 25', and 1 HD video projection, color, 3'.
View of the screening room of the "Hello Darkness" series,
K21 Kunstsammlung Nordrhein-Westfalen, Düsseldorf,
2008–2009

fig.2

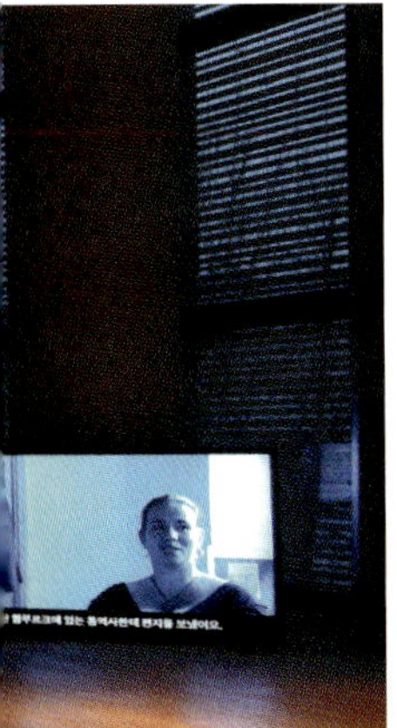

Natacha Nisic, *Andrea*, 2012, 5 HD videos, color, sound, each between 8' 9" and 13' 9".
View of the exhibition "K.W. Complex.
Natacha Nisic / Park Chan-kyong," Atelier Hermès, Seoul, 2012

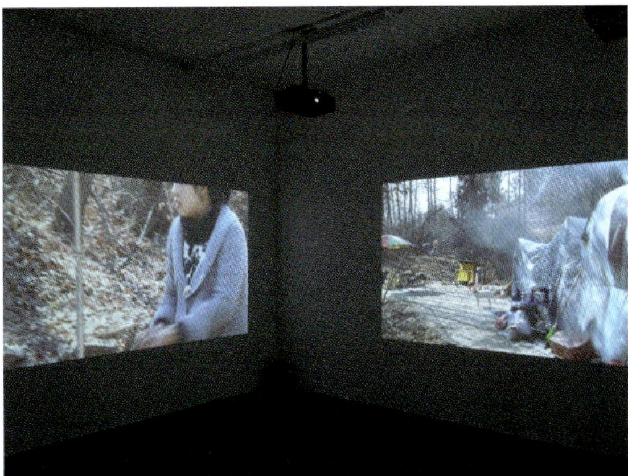

fig. 3

Natacha Nisic, *Princess Snow-Flower*, 2011,
3 HD video projections, color, 5.1 sound, each 19'.
View of the exhibition "Princess Snow-Flower,"
Galerie Florent Tosin, Berlin, 2011

mother's cutting of her coma-stricken brother's hair. Like a tumor that spreads and eats up the host, the process radically and irretrievably changes her entire life by turning everything upside down: interior self and exterior world, mind and body, past and present, flesh and spirit, and the border between life and death.

In fact, in Korean culture, an individual's body is at once an inheritance left by the parents and a "map" that allows a reading of the individual. It is believed that a personological reading – otherwise known as face or character reading – can reveal the past and future of a person, while in traditional Korean medicine, the condition of the internal organs can be diagnosed by examining the outer body. The articulated video screens of the *Andrea* androids extend the physical map of the body, and produce new figures within the terrain of modernity where the map of the imagination and the landscape of representations overlap. First, there are the interior elements in Andrea's shrine, such as the sacrificial table and the shamanistic tools and costumes. Melons, cheese, and cake are set up next to white rice on the table. The "blue-eyed" Andrea dressed in the traditional *hanbok* costume grasps a five-colored flag. The white walls of her shrine even feel cozy compared to a conventional Korean shaman shrine. These same hybrid interior elements, when transposed to the lakes and mountains of Bavaria, the natural setting that inspired German Romantic landscape painting, produce a sense of incongruity. Furthermore, if Nisic's camera explores the image of the sublime in scenes from the artist's walk through the winter forest and views of the snowy mountain peaks, the Bavarian broadcasting company's camera seems to expose the aesthetic territory of terror in the scenes of the strange rock on Seoul's Inwang Mountain that Andrea visits for her initiation, and the snow-covered Ganghwa Island, where Keumhwadang [17] is located. Just like Andrea, who tries to find an analogy between the Berlin Wall and the barbed wire in Ganghwa Island, Snow-Flower, amid a surrealist landscape of English village billboards and bare mountains, and *Carmel*, in a familiar flower- and grass-filled landscape, are yet other forces that cut across the registers of modernity. Moreover, the intrusion of sound that continues to connect and disconnect with the visual imagery and the inclusion of the "hyper" texts that interrupt the scenes completely break down the modern worldview based on a central perspective in which everything returns to the vanishing point. In that sense, the videoscape in *Andrea*, which focuses more on the interrelationship between the subject and the scenery, may be closer to the *sam-won* [18] technique used in traditional Korean painting, with its montage of different time and spatial elements combining close, medium, and distant perspectives.

In the end, *Andrea*'s scenario-roadmap and the resulting scenes seem to go beyond the matrix of modern dichotomies and, at the same time, investigate the capacities of contemporary culture. *Andrea*, by questioning whether we are able to step outside the matrix of modern dichotomies – not by abandoning them, but by regaining our capacity to act on them, and to transform what presents itself as "given" reality – even modifies the layers of meaning in *Carmel* and *Princess Snow-Flower*, and attempts to decolonize the modern colonial imagination. [19]

The *hanbok*-clad Andrea, who wanders the shores of the Bavarian lake like a phantom, reveals the diverse dialectics of an oral history. It would be difficult to claim that an *autogynography*, however dramatic its story, reveals a person, because of the complexity and ambiguity of its narrative mix of the imaginary, the fictive, and fact. Rather, *autogynography* [20] is a unique strategy of camouflage that allows the subject of the story to be anybody – whether Andrea, Snow-Flower, the postulant in *Carmel*, or anybody else – and is triggered by the writing impulse of a split female subject who seeks to establish her self-image as a real existence through words. [21] In her lecture about her initiation, Andrea confesses to feeling cured after listening to the voices inside her and relaying the words of the spirits. In fact, her impressions coincide with the immediate healing effect of the oral narrative. Here, we have an *autogynography* in the form of the drama of Andrea, and an artist who listens to her narrative and interprets it with the camera, someone with a critical view in the Far East who sympathizes with her. If the affect of un-mapping modernity could rise through the flow of energy in the triangle, then who knows? We may, for a short second, be able to reach a state of *mugam*, [22] like the family members of a follower who borrow the shaman's costumes and dance.

1. Park Ji-won, "Written Conversations with Gokjeong," in *The Jehol Journal* (1780), translated from Chinese by Lee Sang-ho, Paju: Bori Publishing, 2004, p. 365 (in Korean).

2. The exhibition "Écho" presents for the first time the work *Andrea en conversation* [p. 41–72], a variation of *Andrea*, which has four additional screens and includes new sequences.

3.   These are archive images from a film report on Andrea Kalff's initiation as a shaman in South Korea, a project that was abandoned.

4.   Atelier Hermès, Seoul, October 11–December 18, 2012.

5.   Listed as an "intangible cultural asset," Kim Keum-hwa is a great shaman and the most famous of Korean shamans both at home and abroad. One of the characteristics of Korean shamanism is that it is almost exclusively made up of women (their male equivalents are very rare).

6.   The book was published for the first time in 1913, while the film, which dated from 1925 (black and white, 117'), included the very first images to be filmed in Korea.

7.   *K.W. Complex. Natacha Nisic, Park Chan-kyong*, Paris: Fondation d'entreprise Hermès, 2013.

8.   *SBS Special: Blue Eyes Possessed by Spirits*, 54' 41", Seoul Broadcasting System, May 13, 2007. Natacha Nisic points out that the fact that such a title for this documentary film by the Korean TV was chosen despite Andrea actually having brown eyes is proof of the stereotype that Asians have about Westerners being blond and blue-eyed.

9.   See *K.W. Complex. Natacha Nisic, Park Chan-kyong*, op. cit.

10.   *Gisaeng* was traditionally a female artist of poetry, calligraphy, painting, and dance who entertained guests on drinking get-togethers. However, with modernization, their role declined into that of sex workers. *Gisaengs* have practically disappeared in Korea today. *Gisaengs* and shamans are both, from the gender point of view, models of the modern subaltern.

11.   Excerpt from an interview with Snow-Flower from Natacha Nisic's *Princess Snow-Flower*.

12.   Snow-Flower keeps up a continuous dialogue with this spirit, whom she calls "Grandmother."

13.   See Park No-ja, "The People's Discourse during the Enlightenment Era and the Others within," in *Acceptance and Transfiguration of the Concept of Knowledge during the Modern Enlightenment Era*, Seoul: Somyong Publishing, 2004 (in Korean).

14.   See the thesis by Chung Yong-nam, *A Study on the Independent Documentary Films about Shamanism: Focusing on "Mudang" and "Between,"* Osan: Graduate School of Han-shin University, Department of Visual Culture Studies, 2007 (in Korean).

15.   Andrea's word, when she is curing a woman in her shrine, from *Andrea*.

16.   See Baek Mun-im, *Girl's Wail in Weolha*, Seoul: Chaeksesang Publishing, 2008 (in Korean).

17.   The shrine where Kim Keum-hwa performs *gut* (the Korean shamanistic ritual).

18.   "*Samwon*, literally 'three perspectives' in Korean, refers to the *gowon* (perspective from the foot of a mountain looking up toward the mountaintop), *simwon* (perspective from right in front of a mountain looking beyond it), and *pyeongwon* (perspective from a mountain in front looking at the scenery that unfolds in the distance between it and the mountain in the background), which constitute the gaze of an artist depicting the natural landscape. Unlike the scientific Western perspective, the *samwon* technique, which formed the basis of traditional oriental landscape paintings, conferred a complex and dynamic movement and unique spatial beauty to the composition of the paintings." *Encyclopedia of Korean Culture*, Seongam, The Academy of Korean Studies (online: http://www.encykorea.com).

19.   See Anselm Franke, "Animism: Notes on an Exhibition," *e-flux Journal*, summer 2012.

20.   Female autobiography.

21.   See Kim Seong-nae, "A Narrative Analysis of a Female Shaman's Oral History," *Korean Women's Study*, vol. 7, 1991.

22.   *Mugam* refers to the act of putting on shamanistic costumes and dancing to the beat of a *gut* (Korean shamanistic ritual) during the short breaks between shamanistic performances by a member or members of the household and/or audience where the

gut is held. Since *mugam* is performed by ordinary people, it does not involve actual shamanistic acts related to *gut*, even if the people are wearing shamanistic costumes and may become agitated and excited. However, there are instances where the inherent special power of a person manifests itself, and he/she has an unusual experience. *Encyclopedia of Korean Folk Culture*, Seoul, The National Folk Museum of Korea, 2011 (online: http://folkency.nfm.go.kr/eng/index.jsp).

—

Translated from Korean by Meeky Song

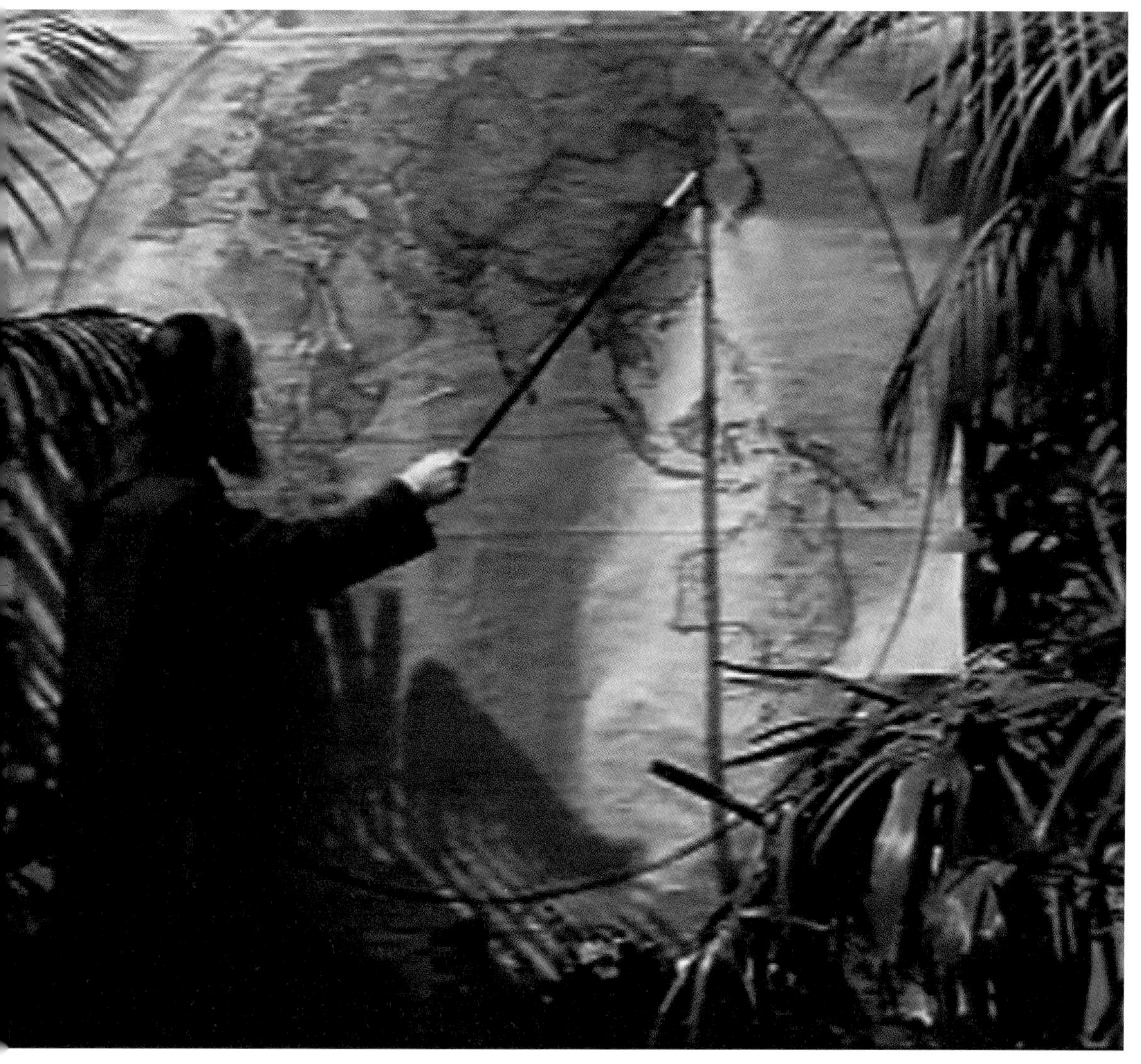

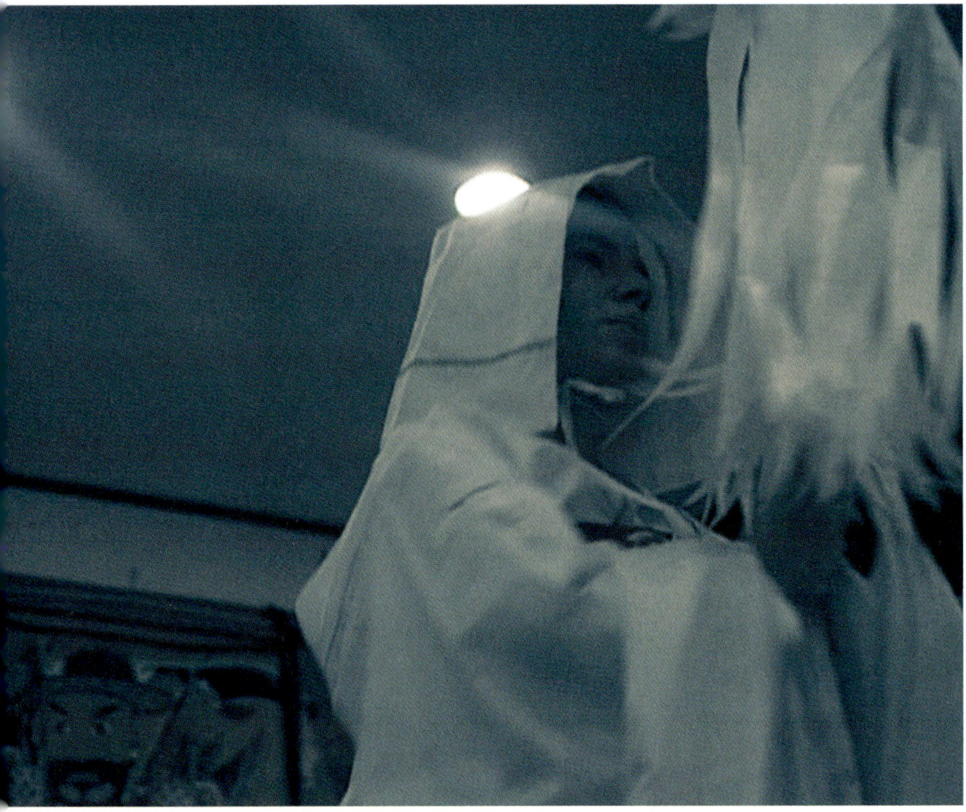

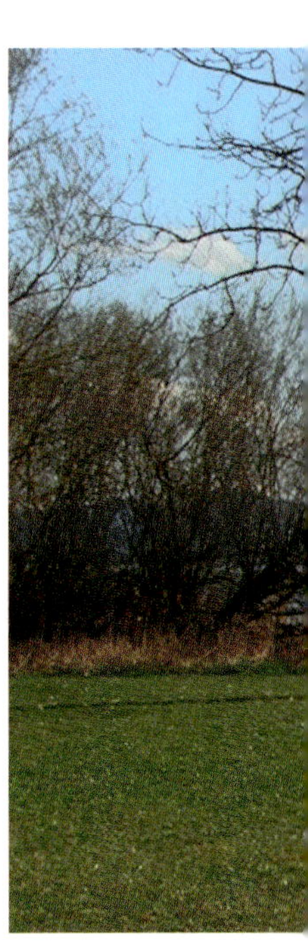

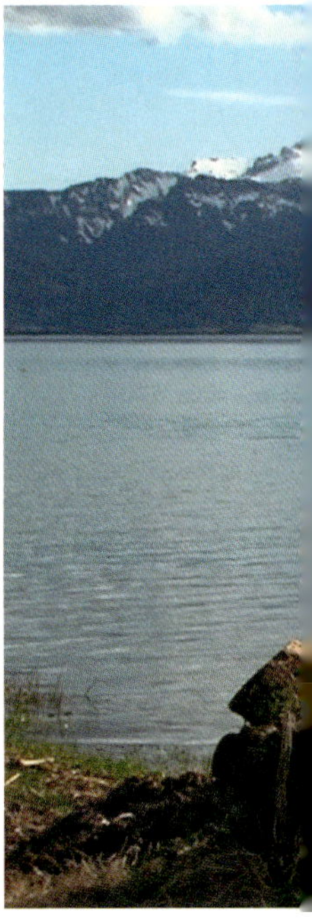

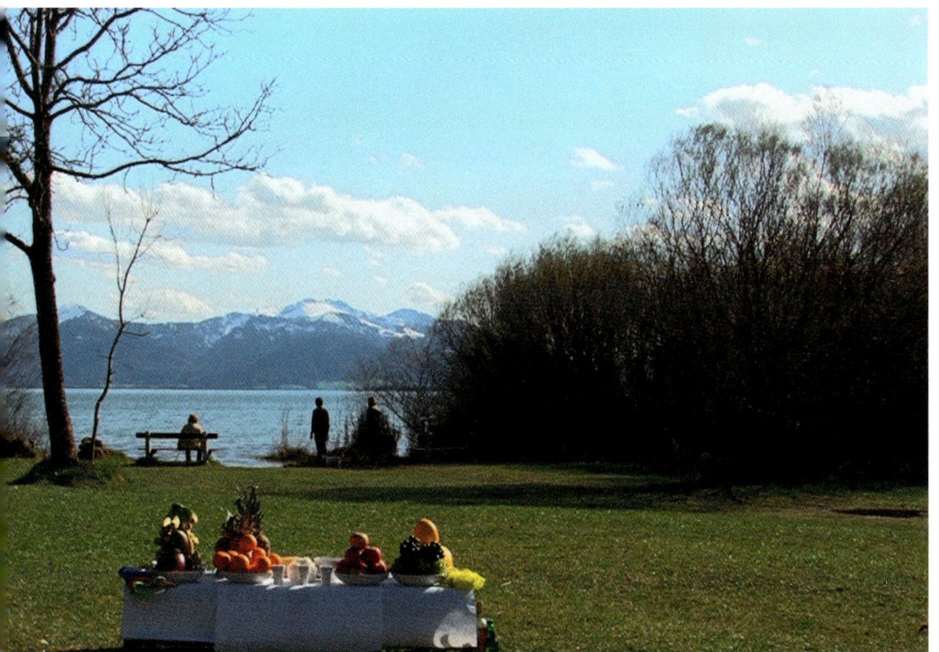

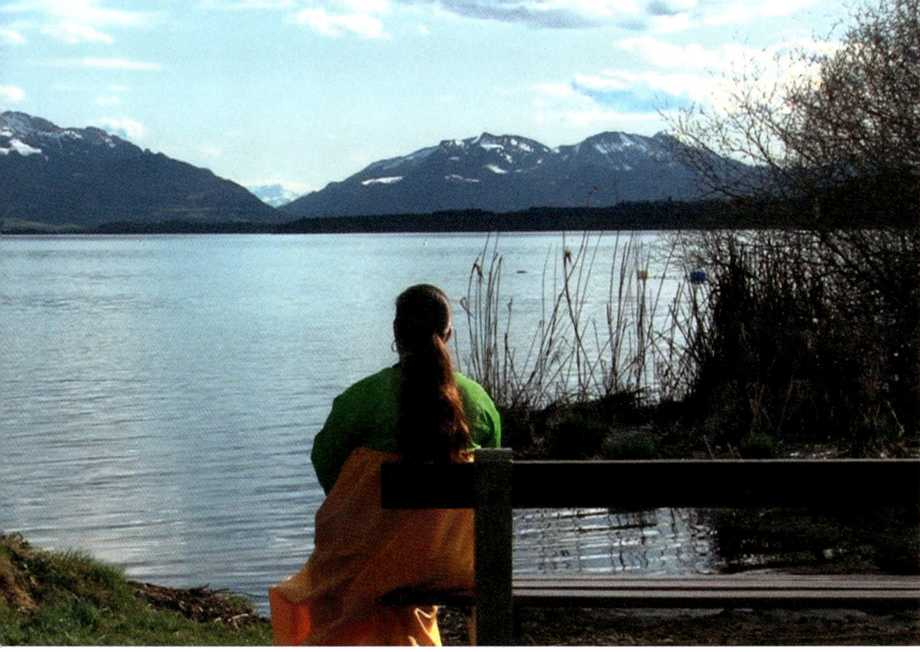

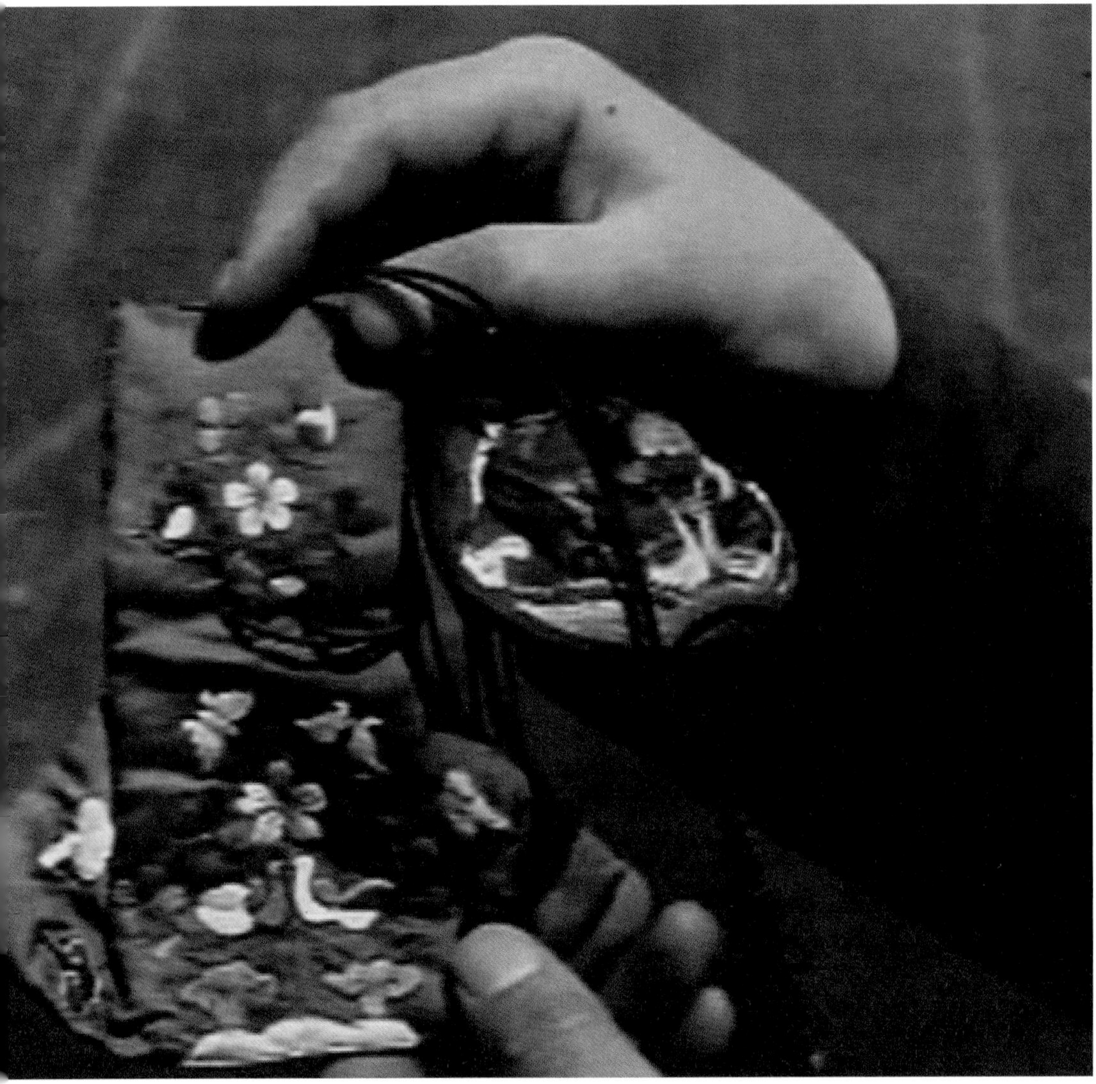

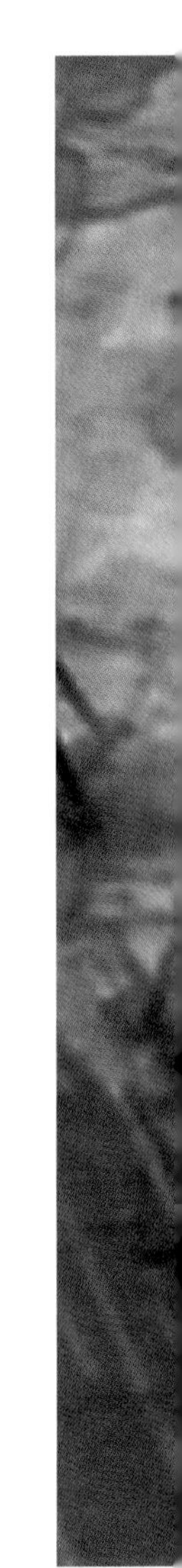

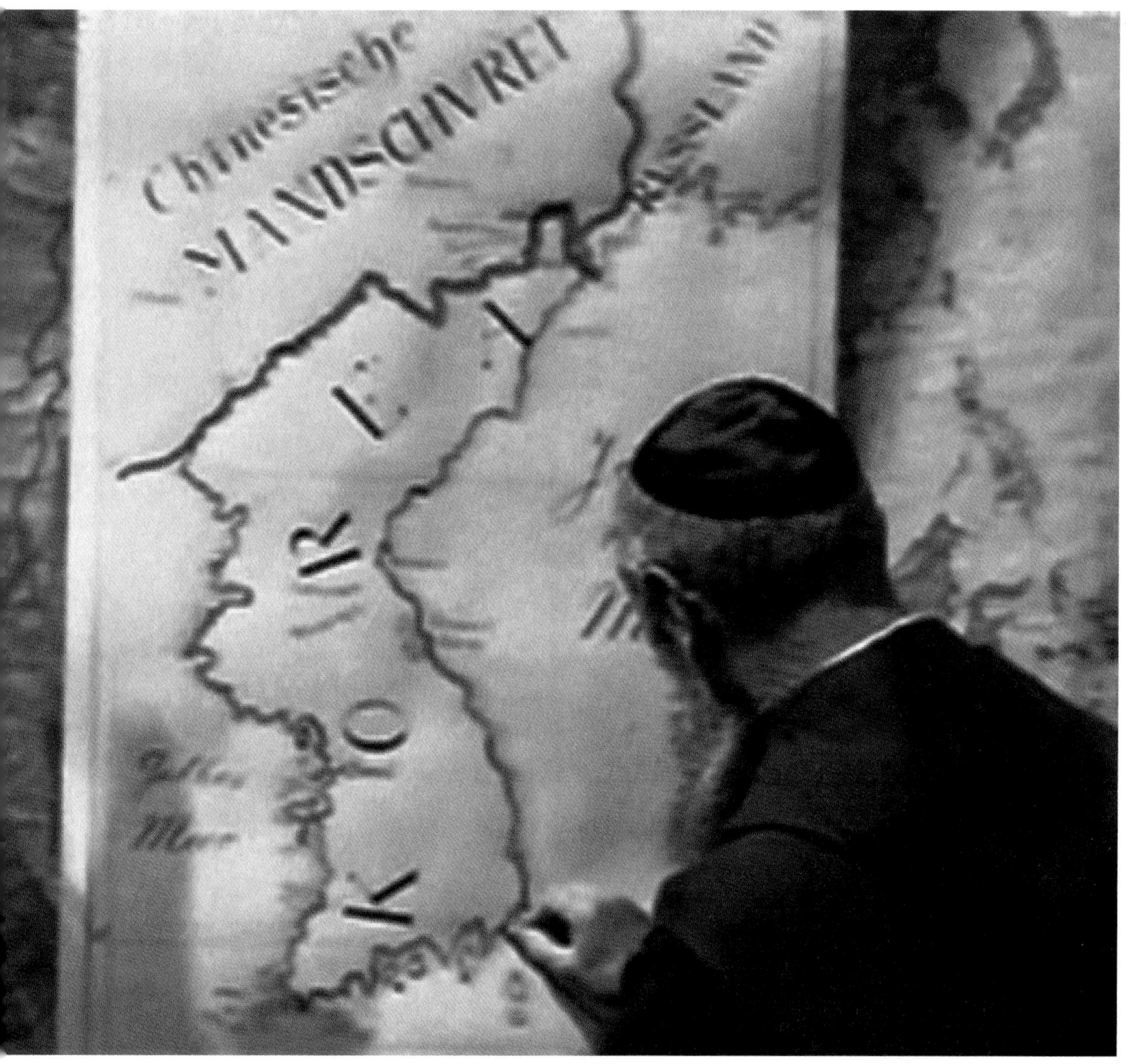
Chinesische
MANDSCHUREI
RUSSLAND

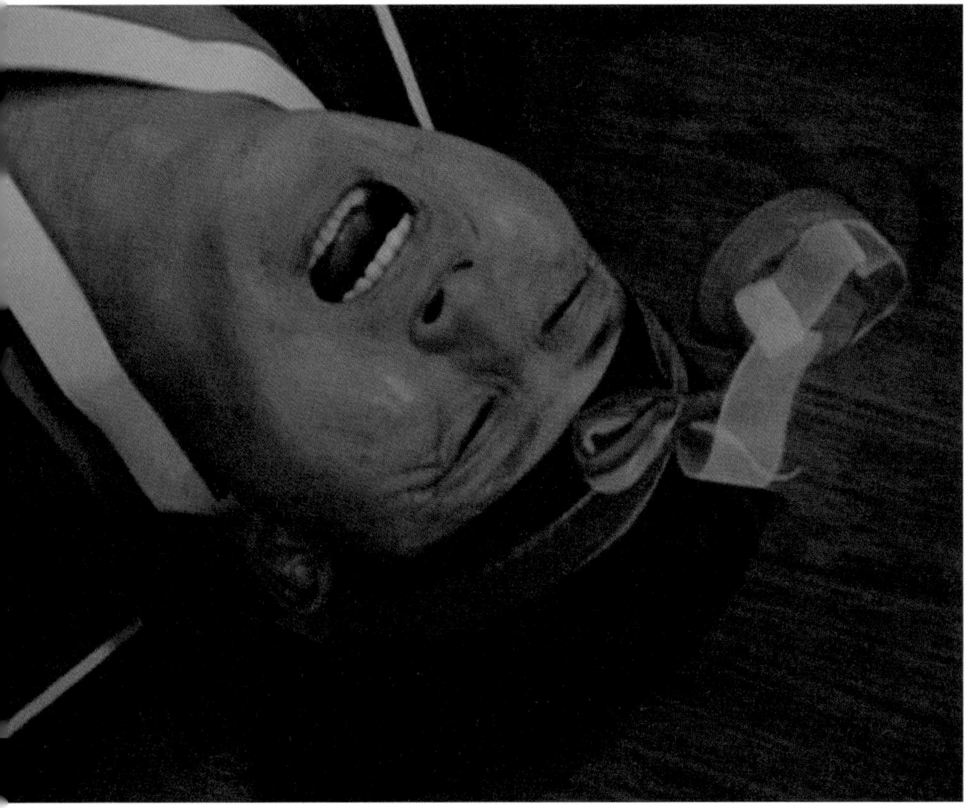

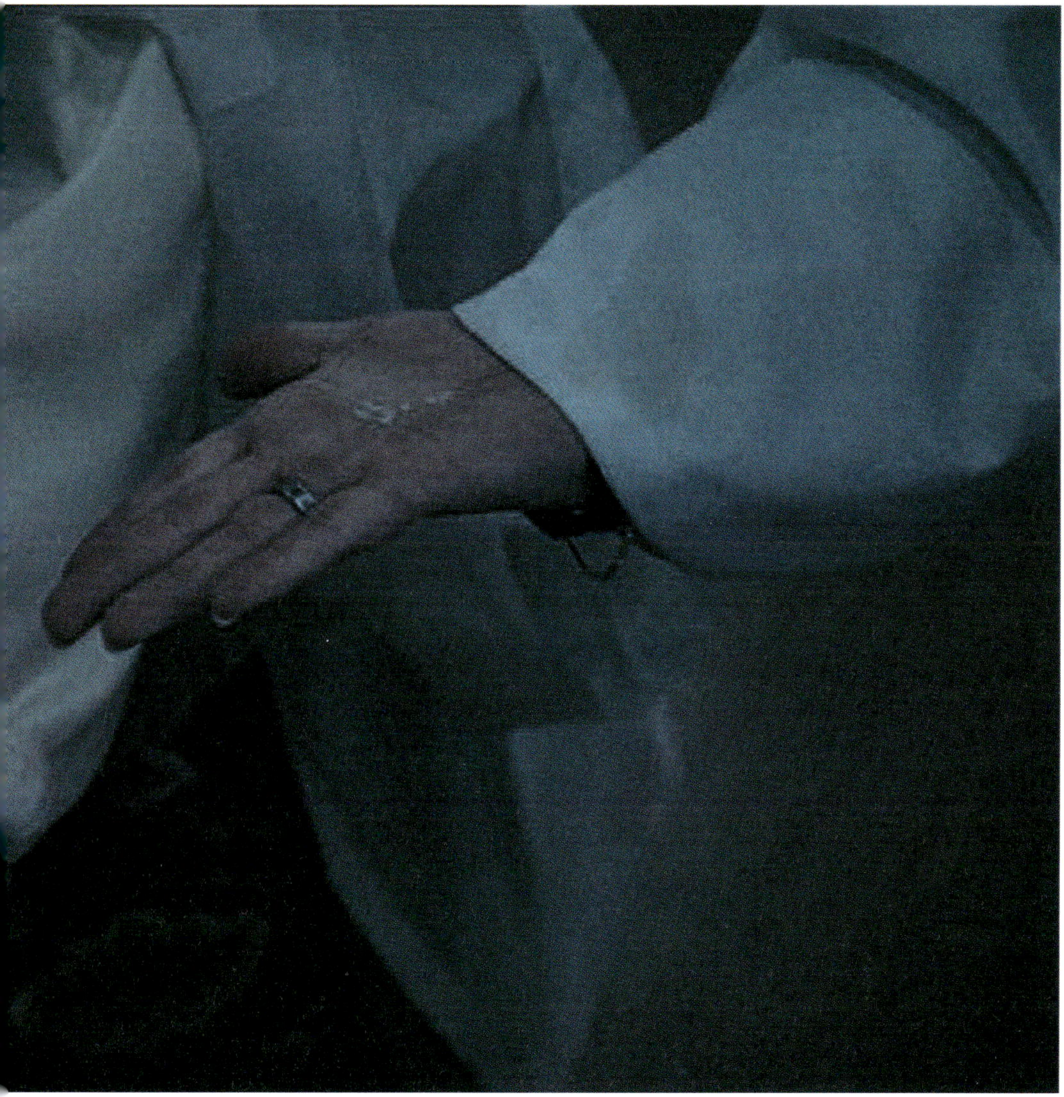

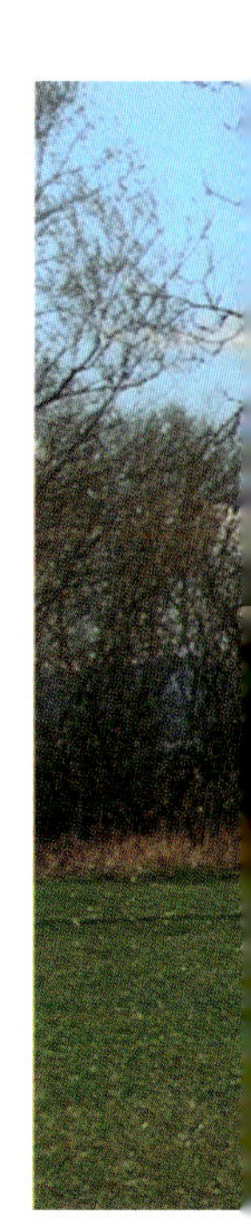

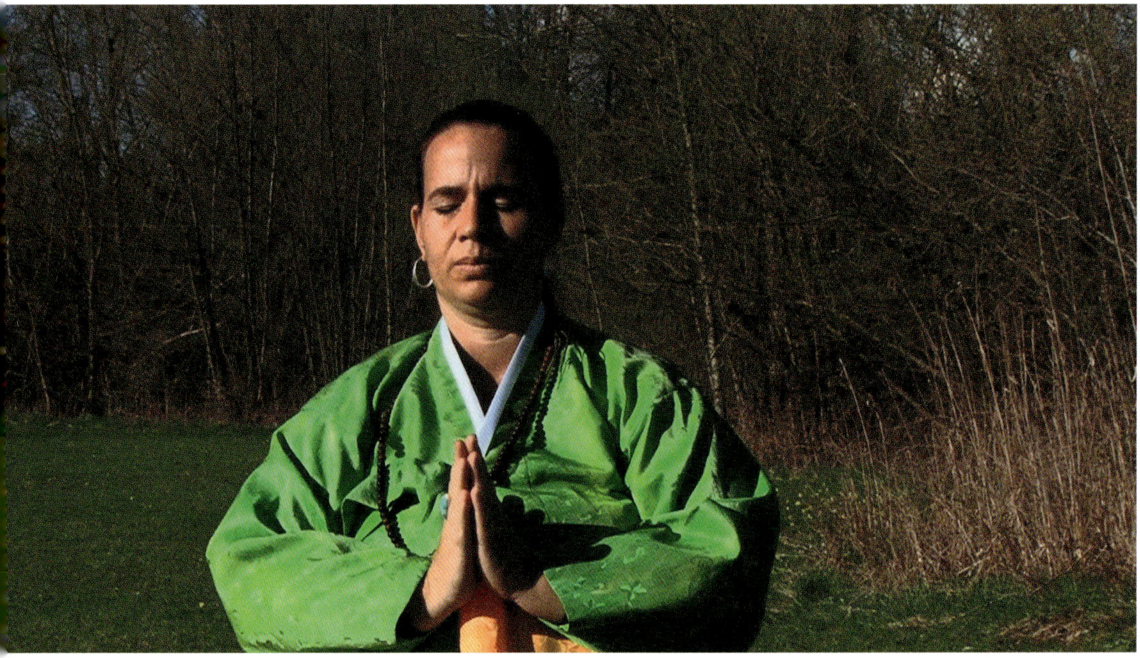

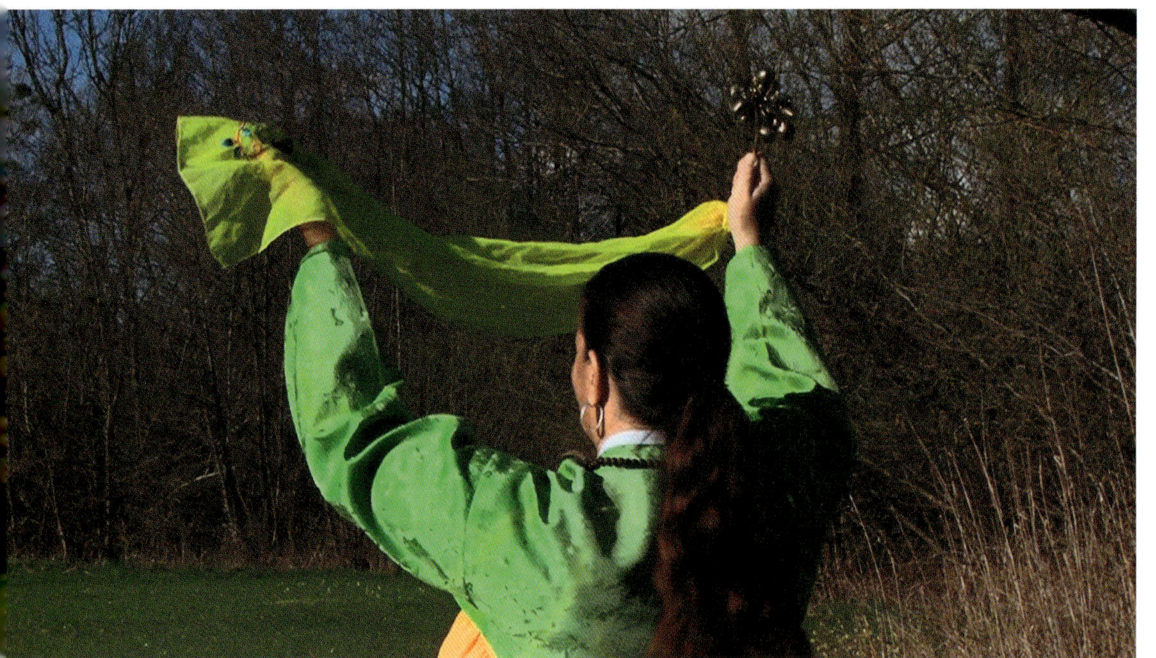

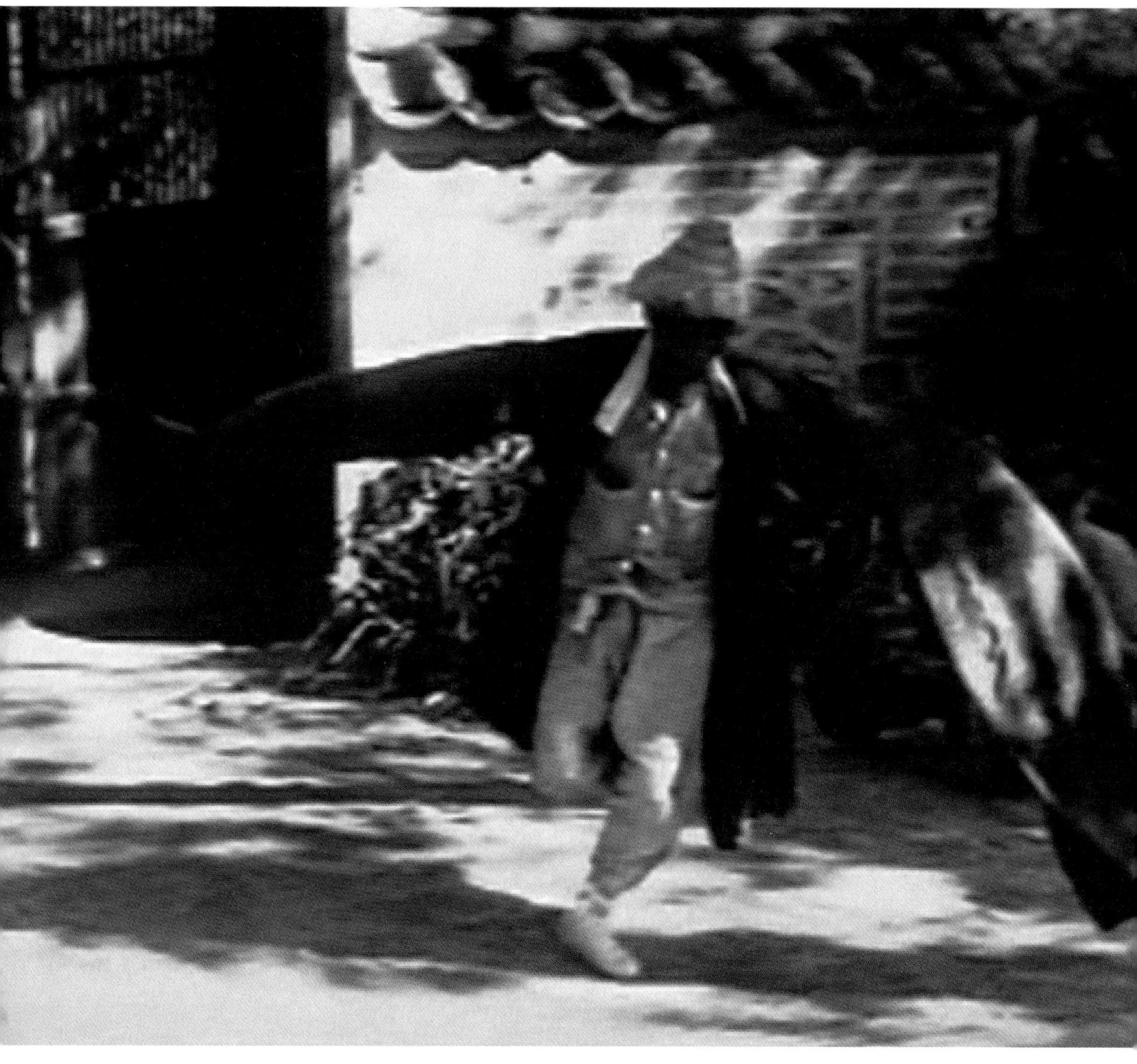

For me, it was like diving into deep water.
I didn't know what to expect.
I had been invited by an acquaintance to a shaman
    conference at Lake Moon,
that was in 2006.
I said I wasn't interested,
that I didn't want to go.
But he insisted I should come.

So I said:
OK, I'll come, but I won't take part in the workshop,
I don't want any contact with a shaman.
I had a strict Catholic upbringing,
went to a convent school for six years.
No, I won't do this.

So we went to the conference,
it was pouring with rain.
And then Ms Kim passed by,
with all the shamans,
in a very colorful *hanbuk*,
and I just said:
"What on earth?"
I was so fascinated by the colors.

Around half past ten,
I went to the restroom
and when I got back a Korean guy taps me
    on the shoulder,
tells me he wants to talk to me
and he'd like my address
and my phone number.
So I said:
I'm married
with three kids.
And he said,
No, you got it wrong. Ms Kim wants to talk to you.
I said,
I don't know Ms Kim
and I won't do this.
And then he said one sentence:
We know what's going on with you.

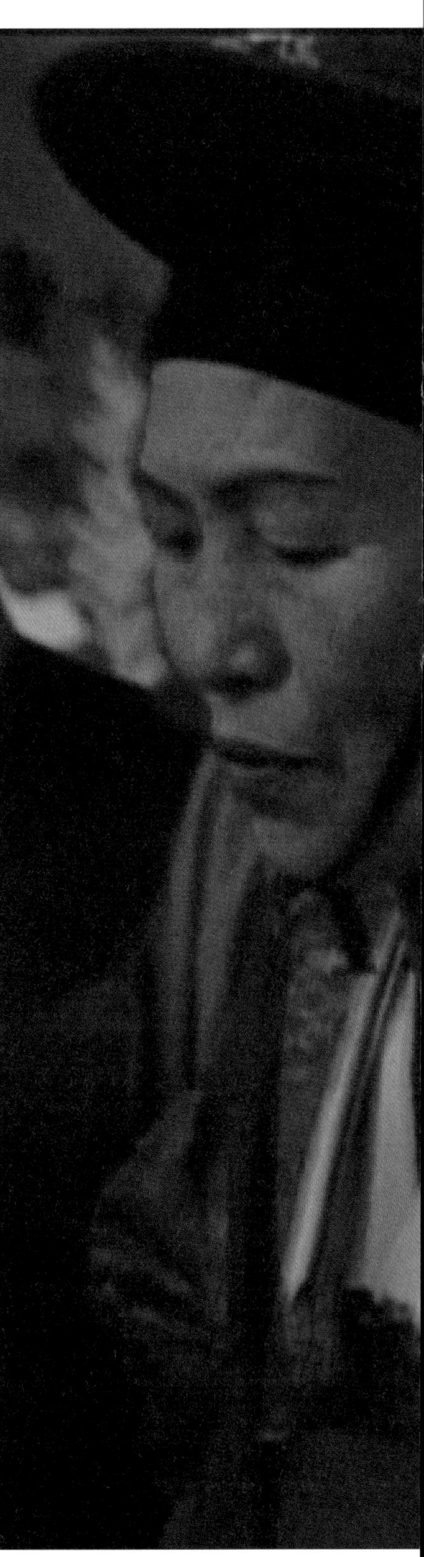

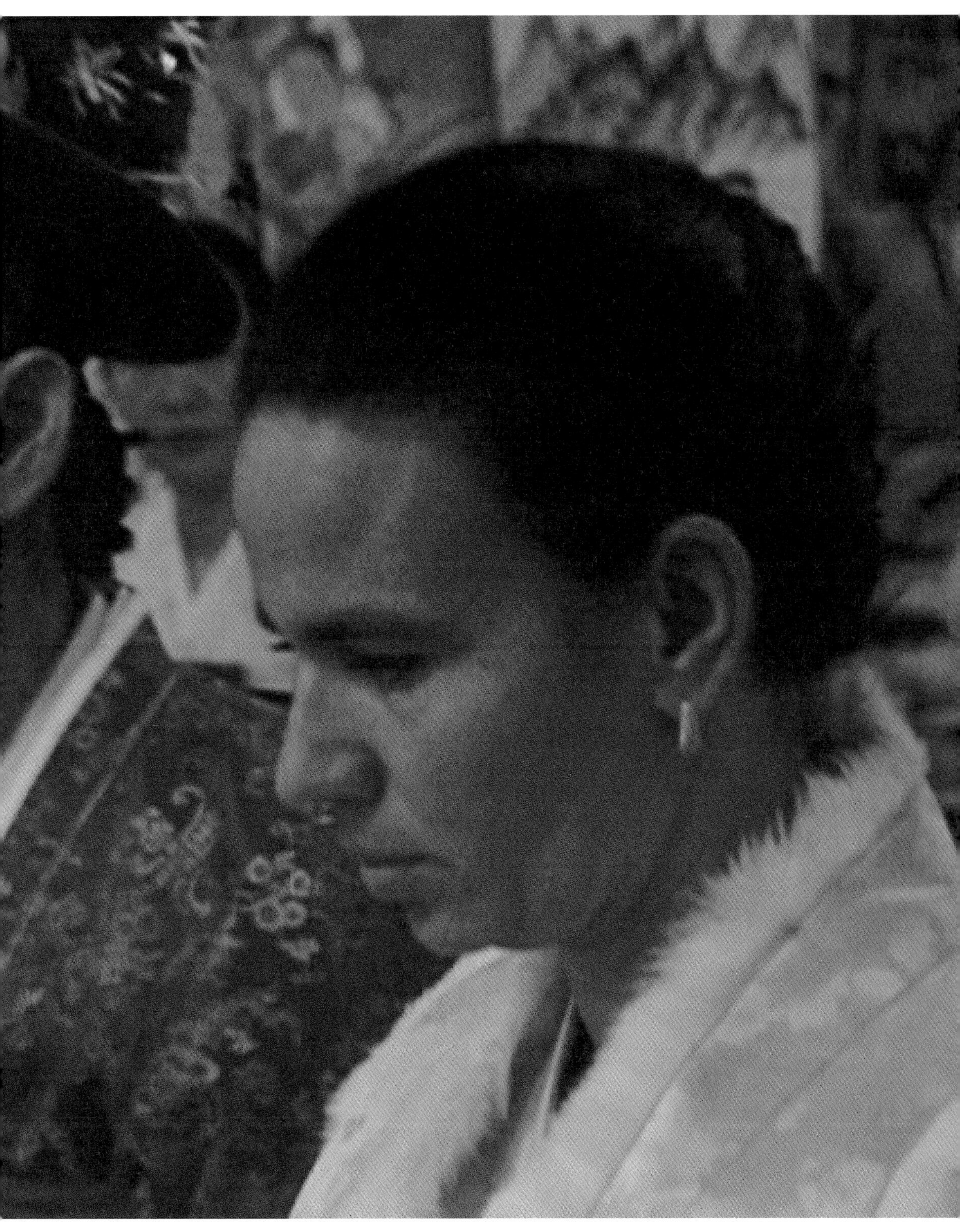

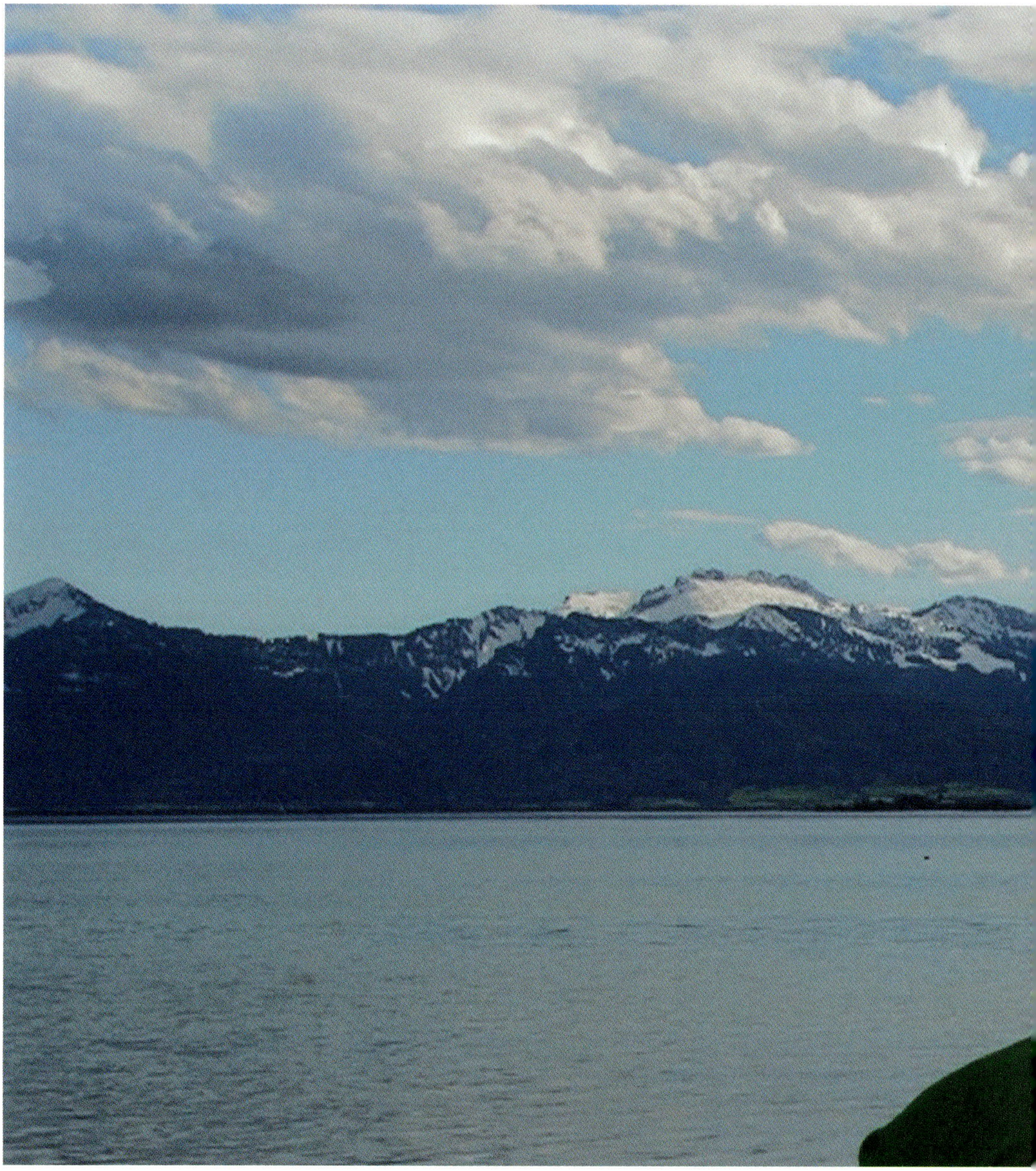

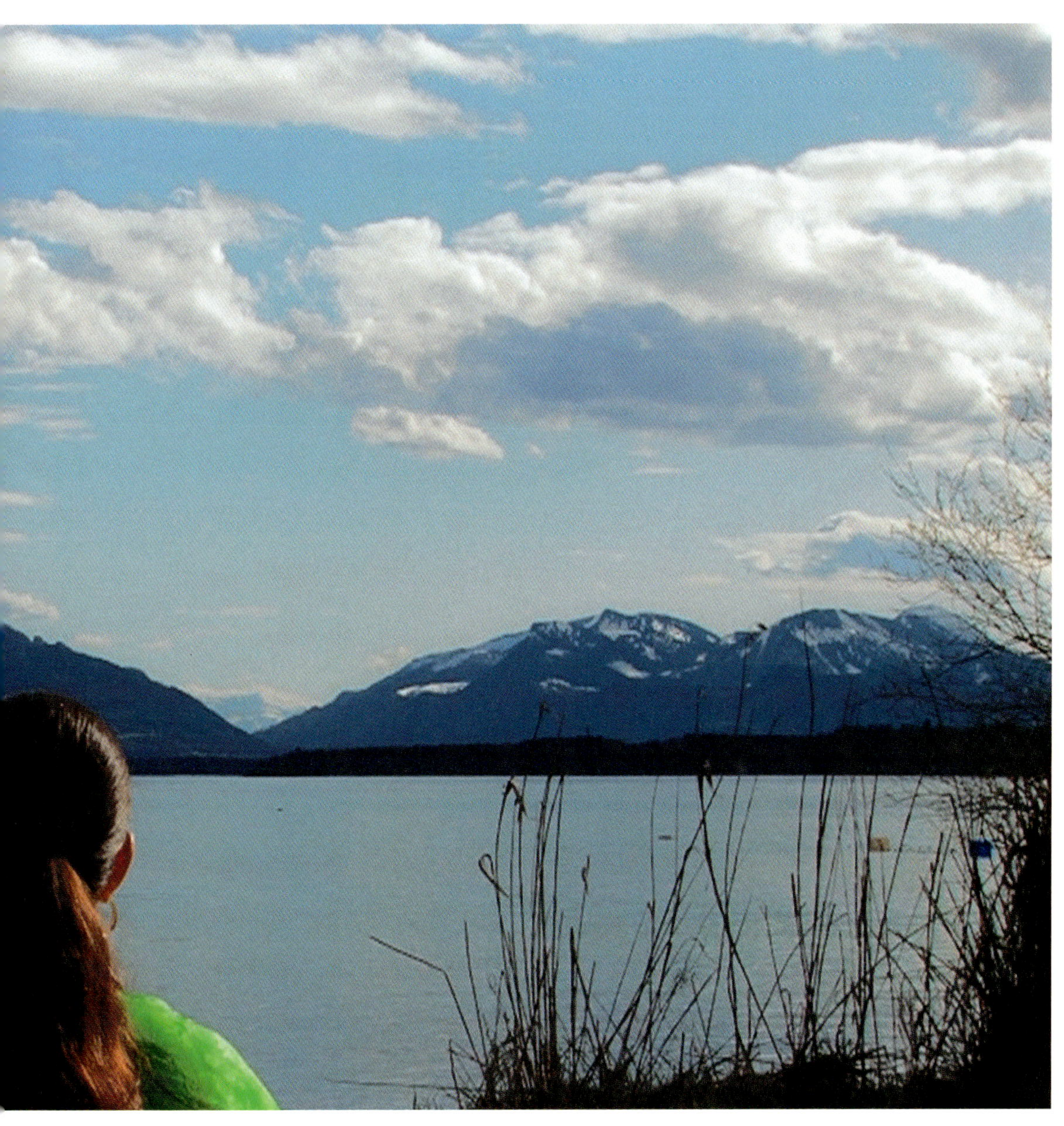

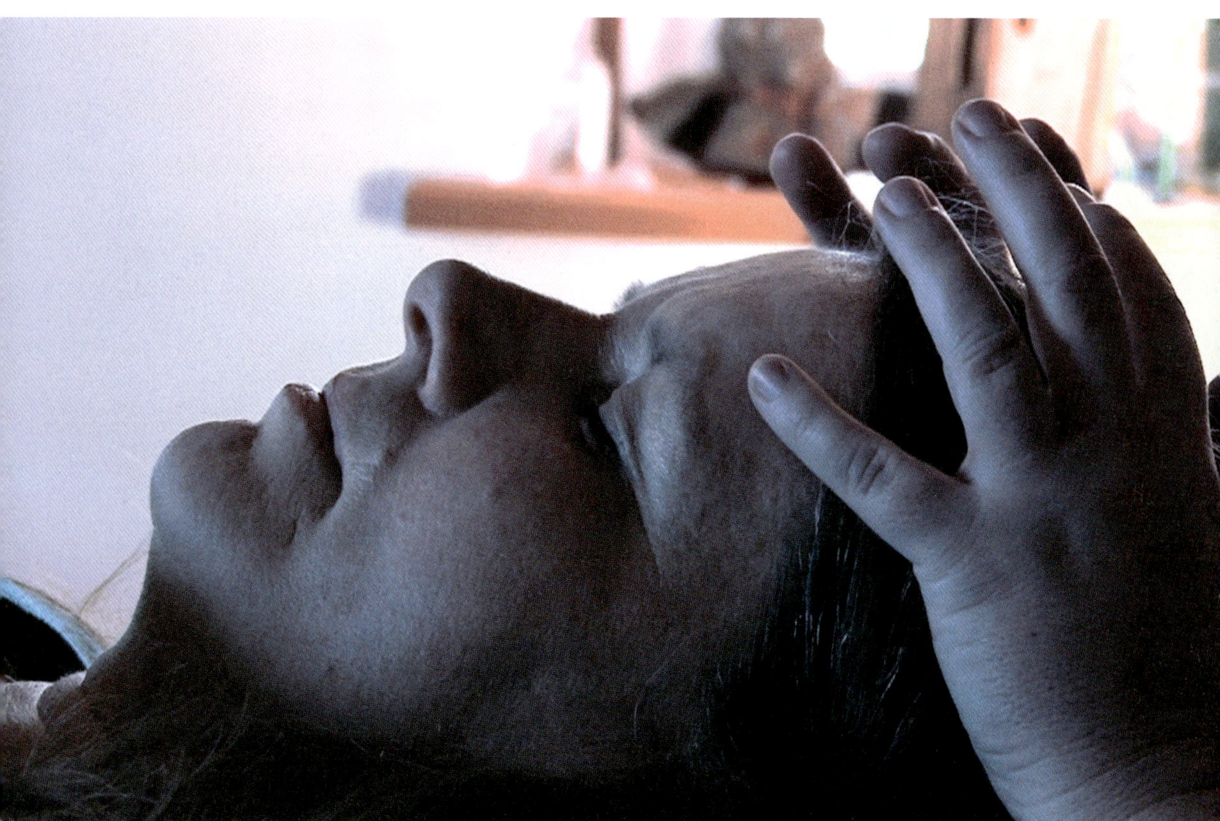

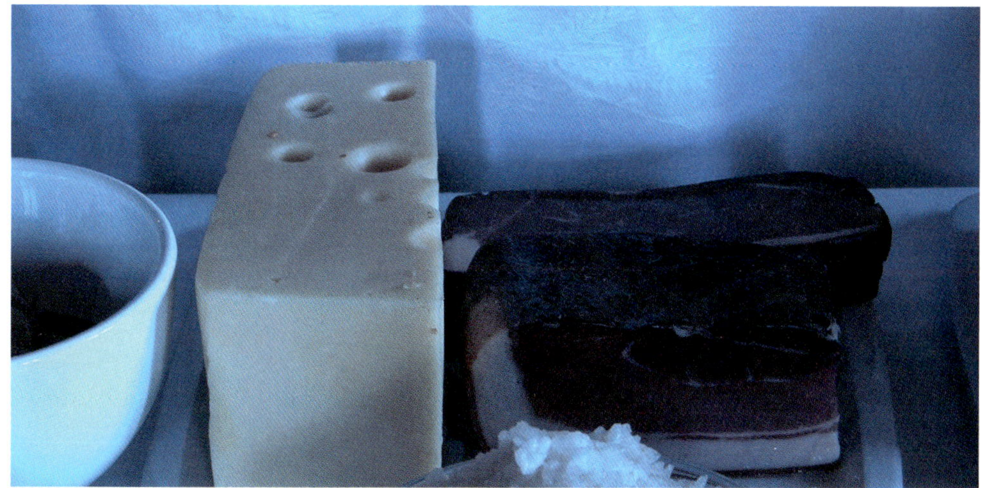

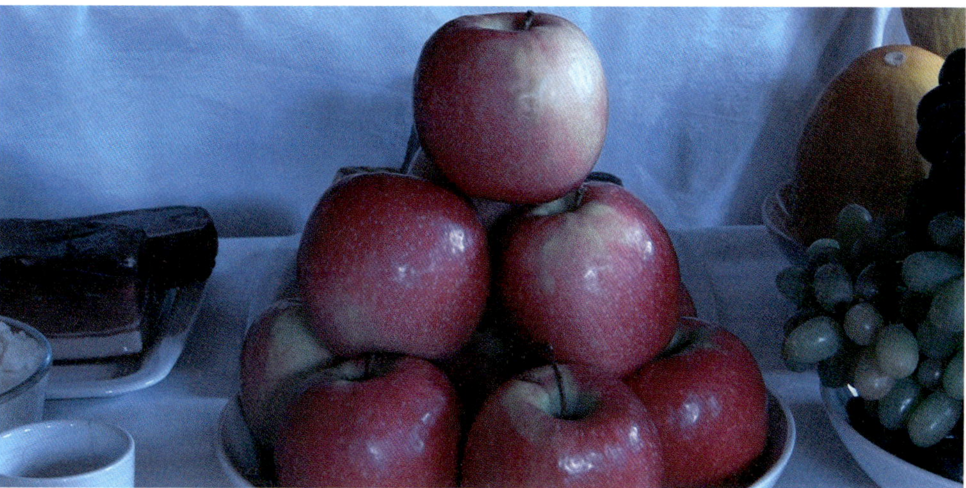

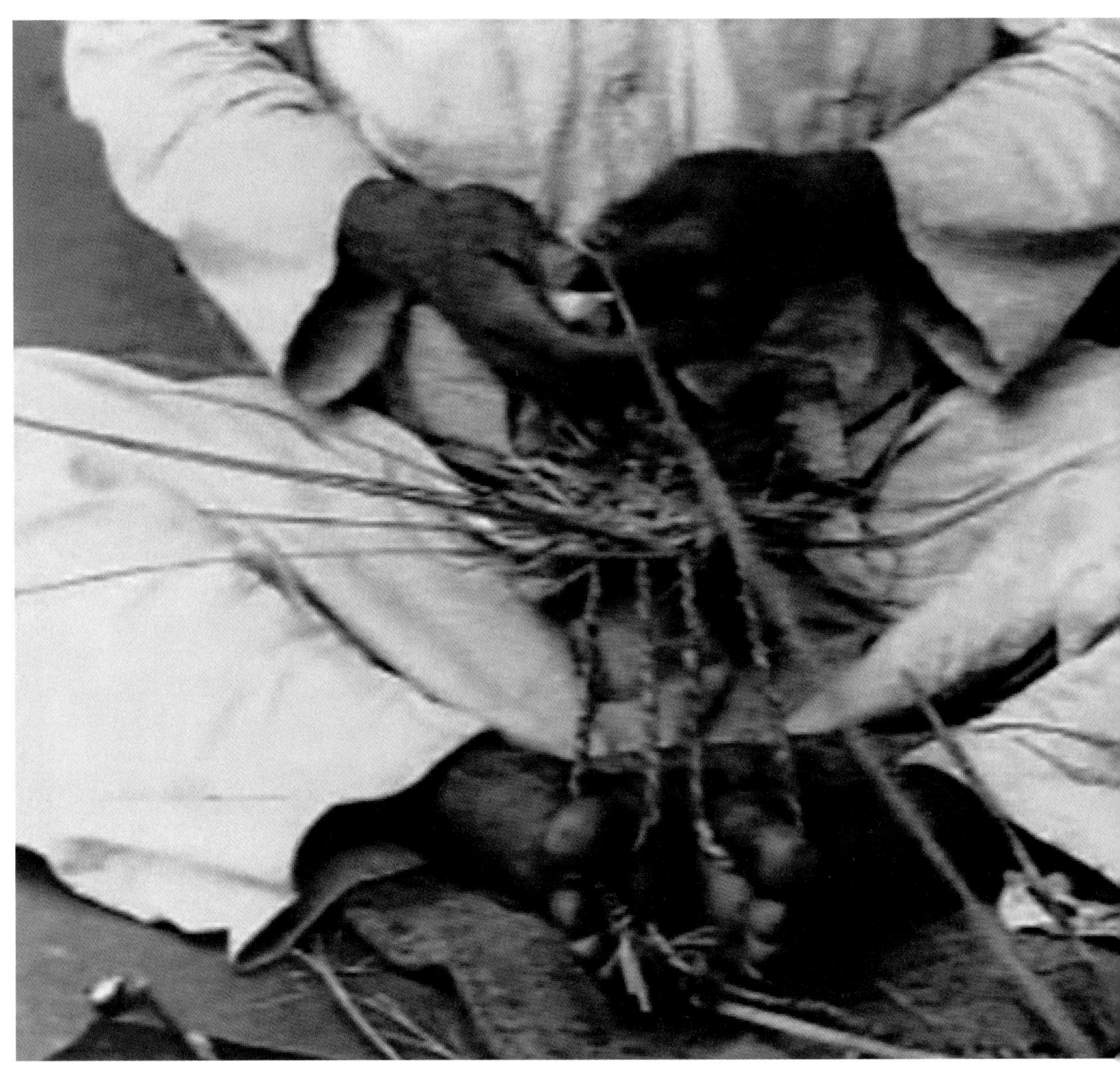

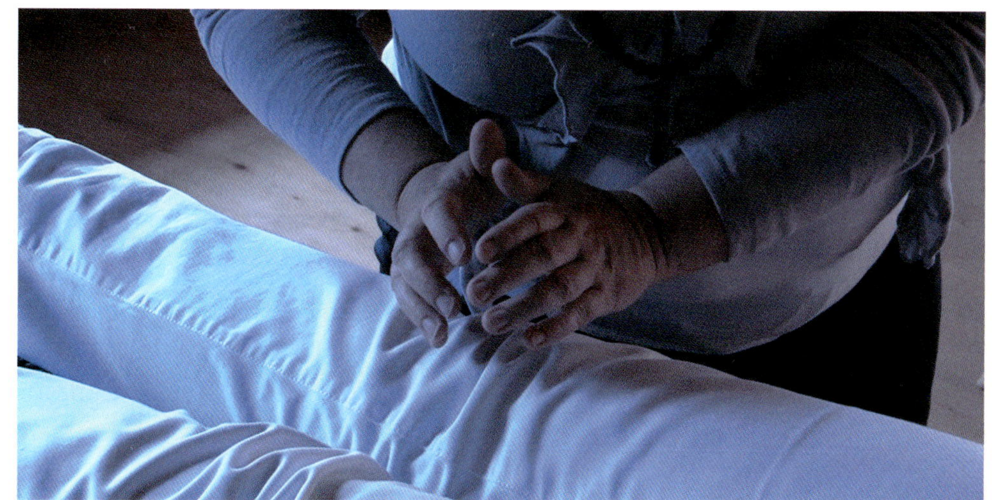

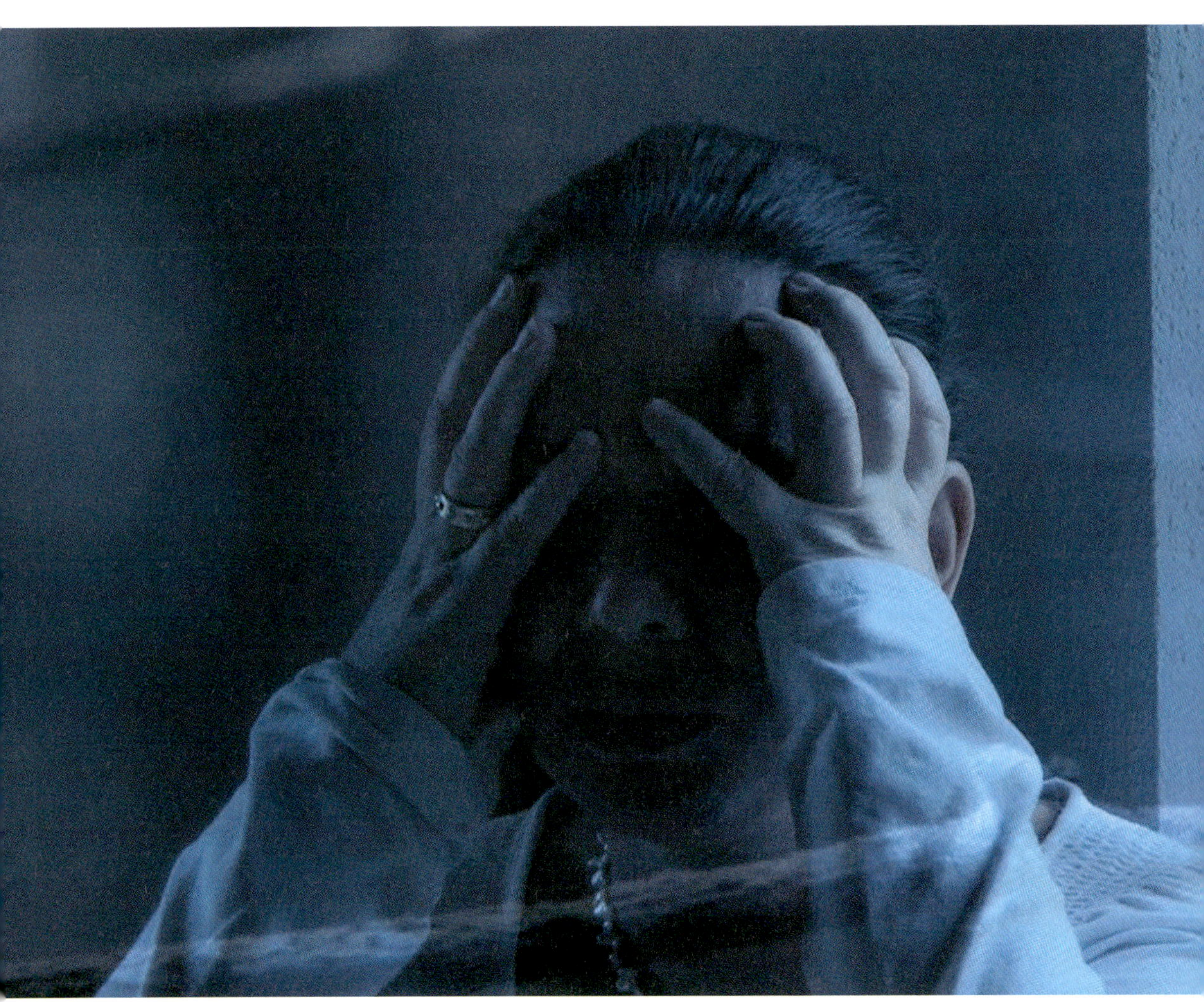

I realize immediately
when I am devoting too little time to them,
for example, when I'm in a plane, or on a trip,
or when I'm pregnant.
I feel unwell,
there is a feeling of dissatisfaction, unfulfillment.
Because they live in me.
I become very restless,
I can't sleep,
I'm sad
and cry a lot.
That is when it is high time that I speak
    only to the gods.
And then everything goes back to normal.
It is an urgent priority.

That's how it is:
we're taking something here,
information and time
and that has to be fed back.
There always has to be a cycle.
I consider my gods as guests
and for guests you also offer food and drink.
It has to be a give and take.

The way you hear the voices of your gods,
what you have to do.
You also hear what the soul needs,
why the soul
is still so wounded
why the soul is so sad
why the soul doesn't want to pass on,
why the soul
still feels it has to take care of the client
and it tells you what it needs to regain balance.
It can be an exchange or a plant . . .

I connect myself.
I sit here,
but my soul and my spirit are elsewhere.
I wouldn't call it different voices,
but various vibrations, different intensities,
forces.
You know how you can tell a child something
    very tenderly,
then a bit more forcefully,
and then really strictly,
like Daishan Grandmother,*
there is no discussion – that's the way it is –
    end of story.

* Goddess of the shamans

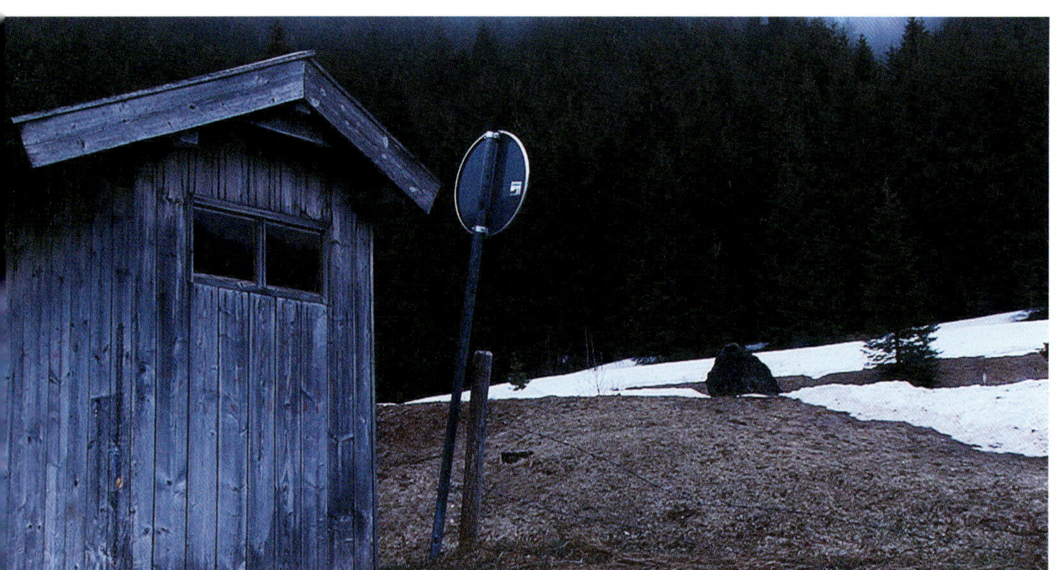

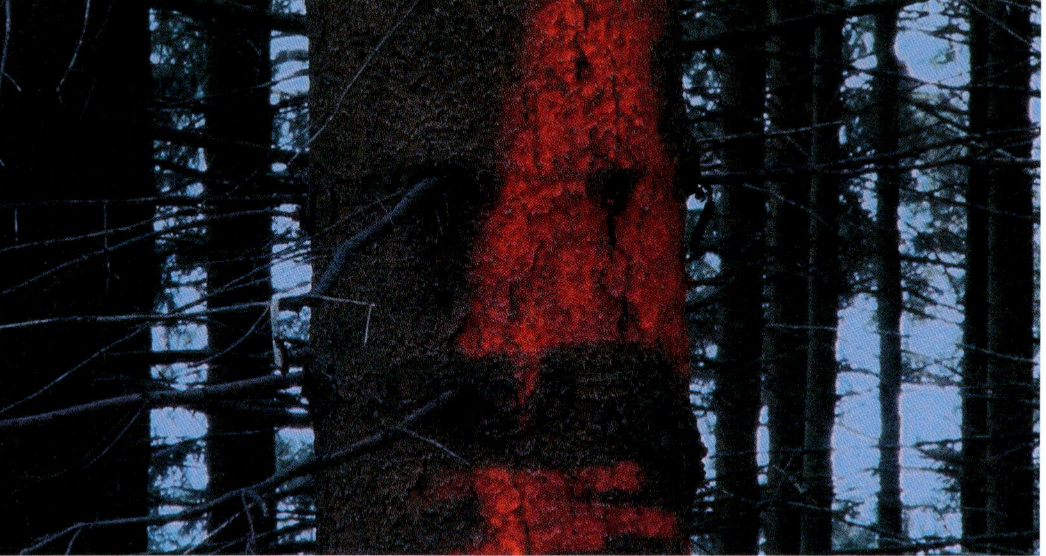

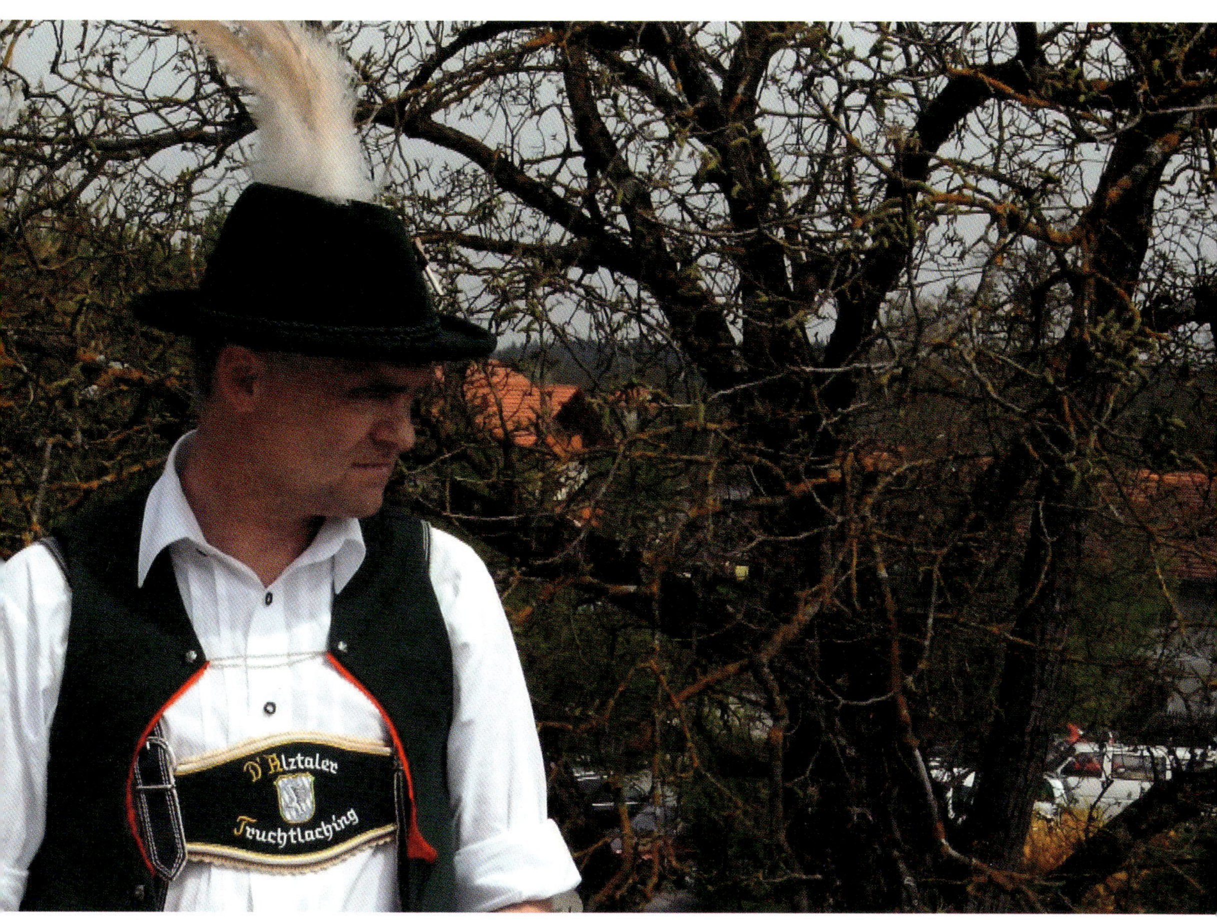

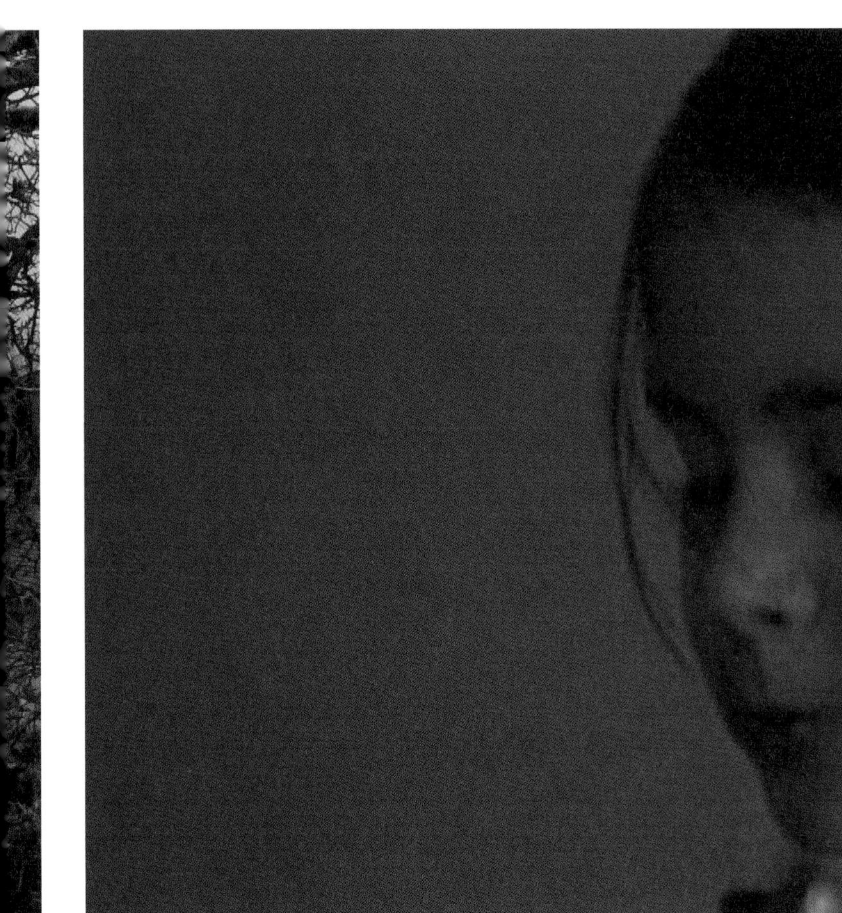

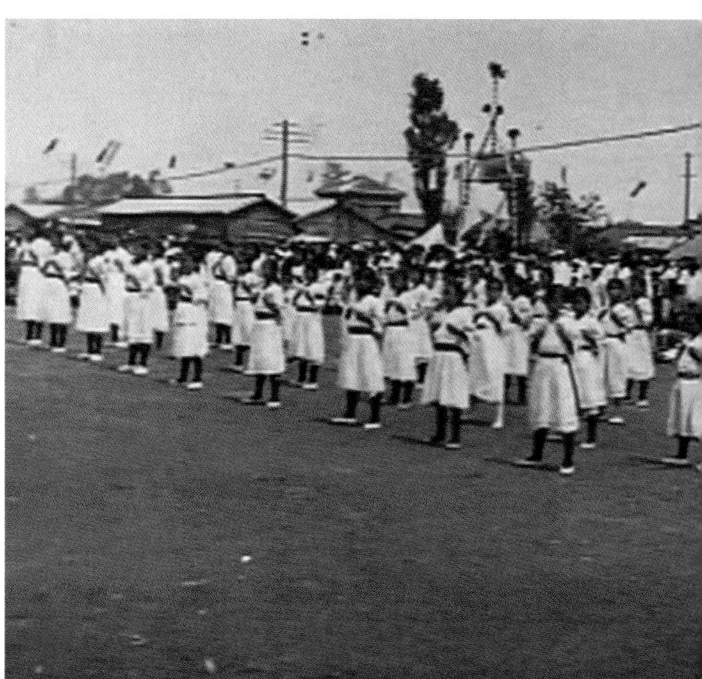

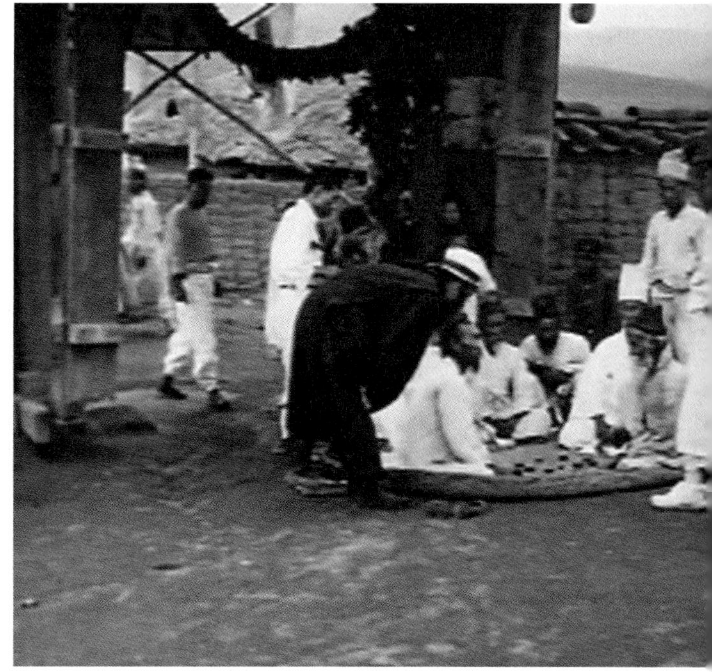

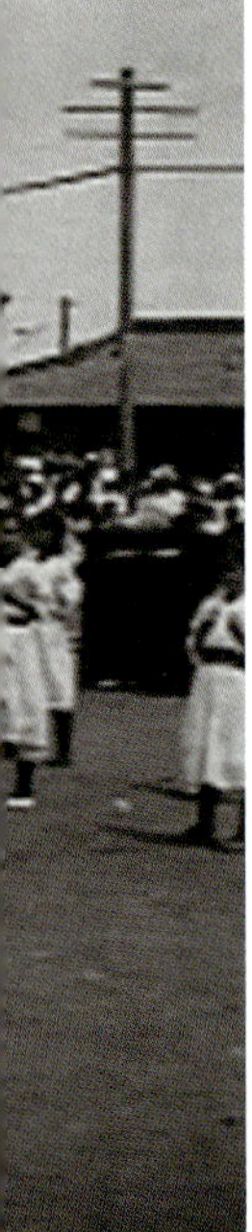

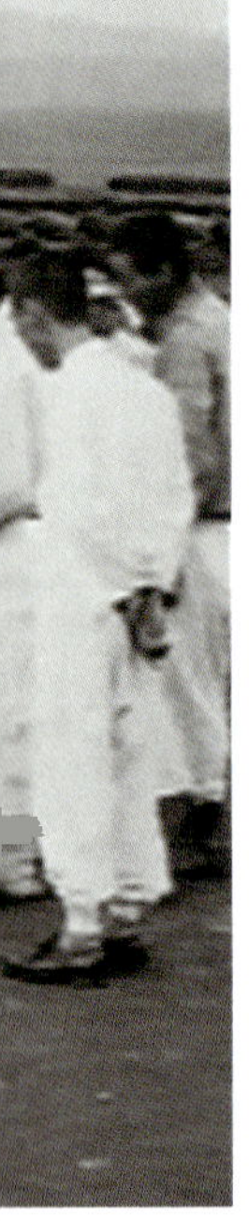

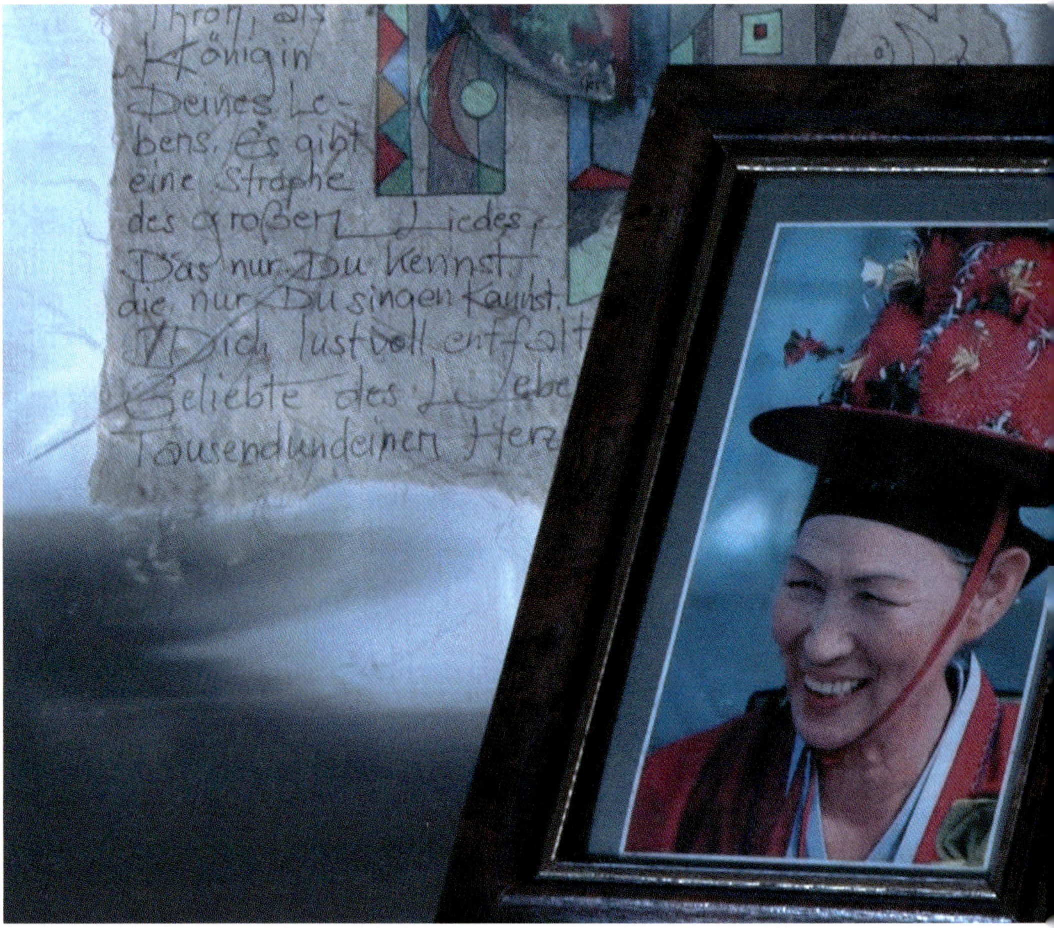

Thron, als
Königin
Deines Le-
bens. Es gibt
eine Strophe
des großen Liedes,
Das nur Du kennst,
die nur Du singen kannst.
Dich lustvoll entfalt
Geliebte des Lebe
Tausendundeinen Herz

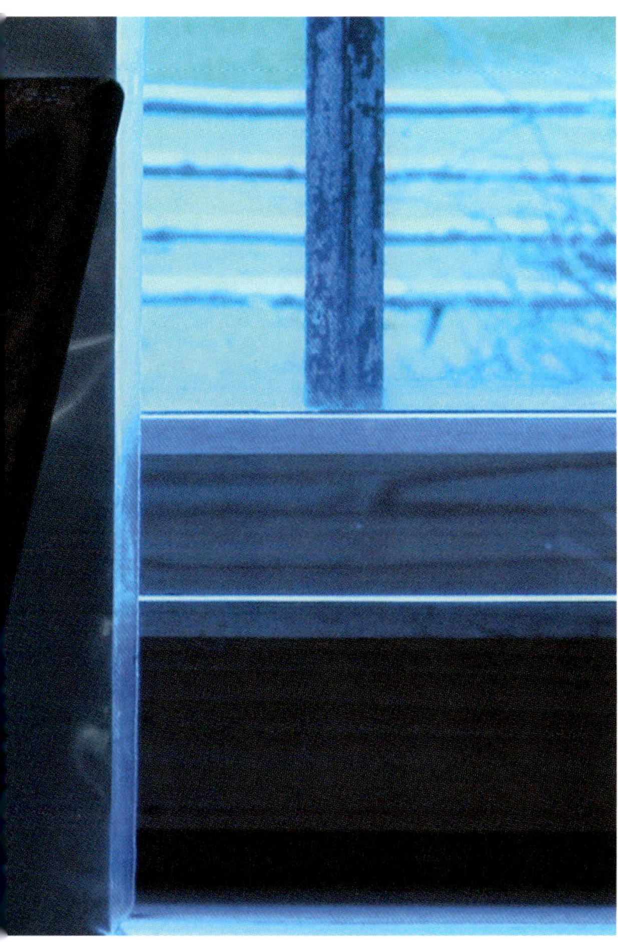

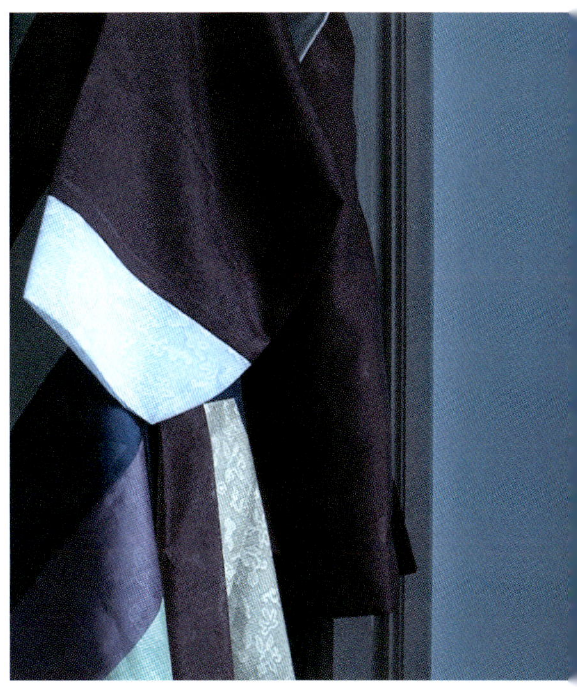

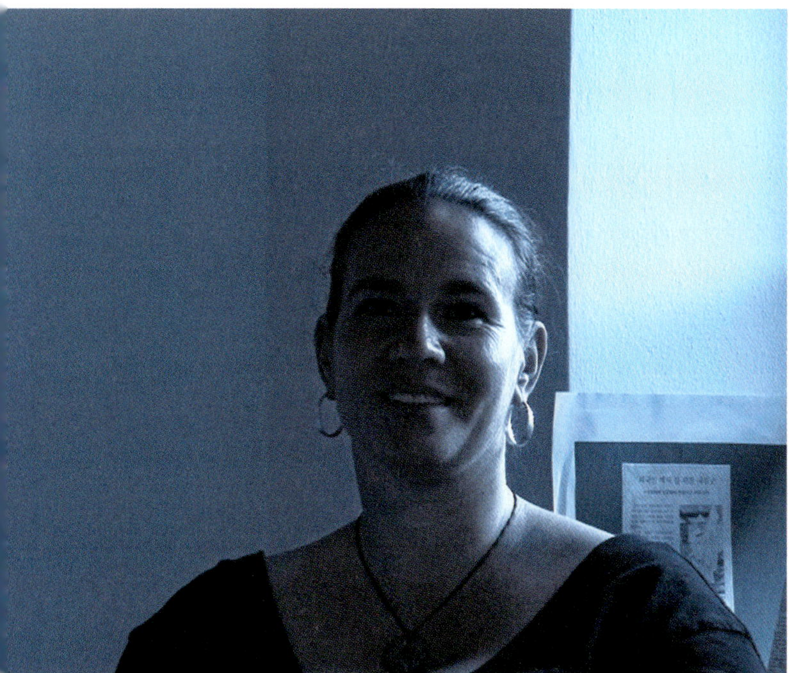

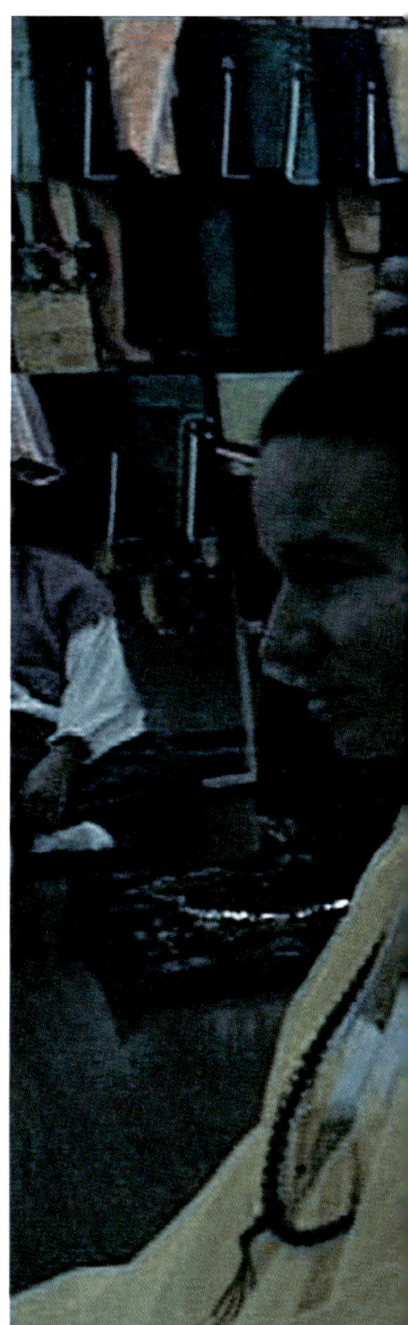

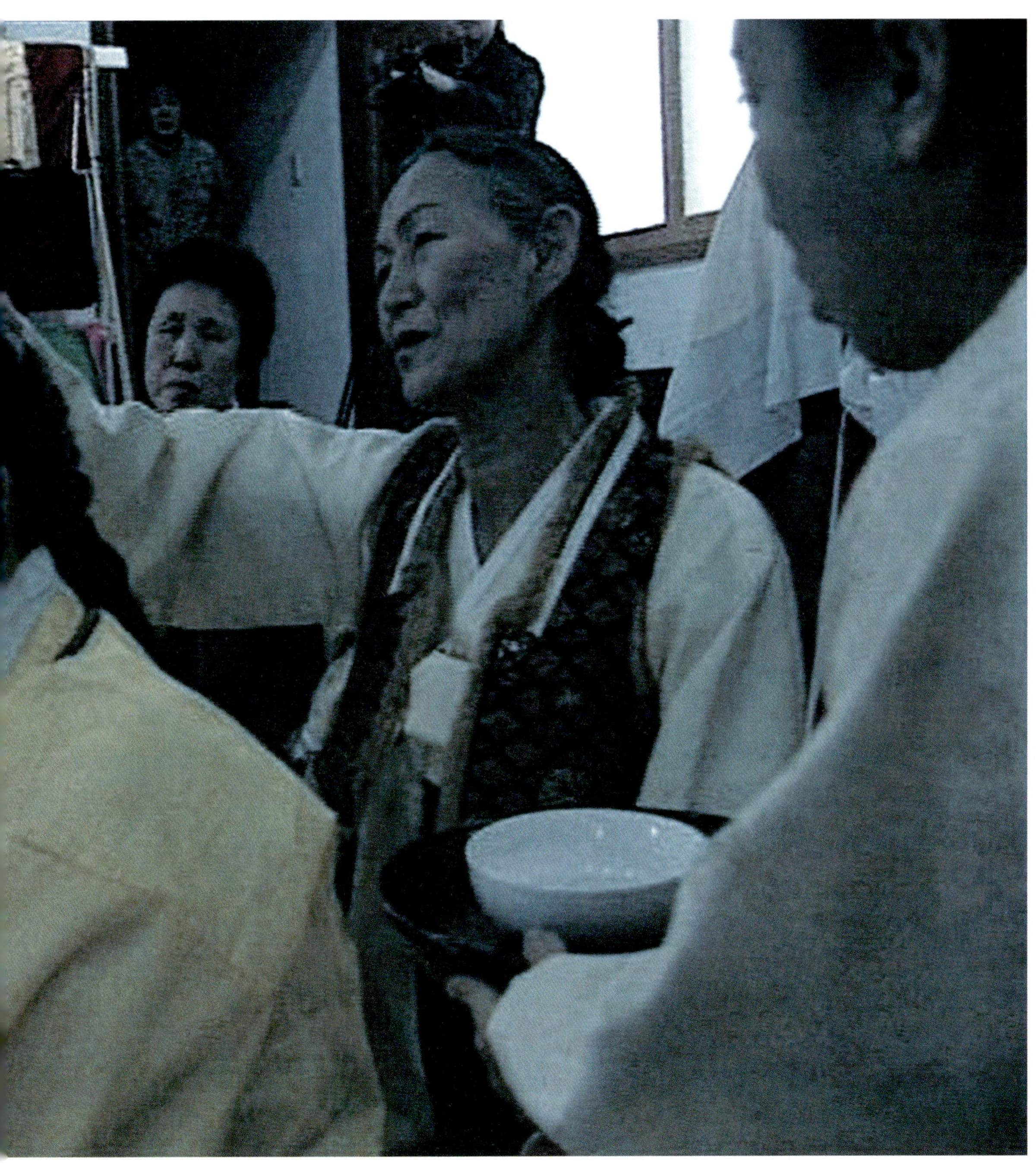

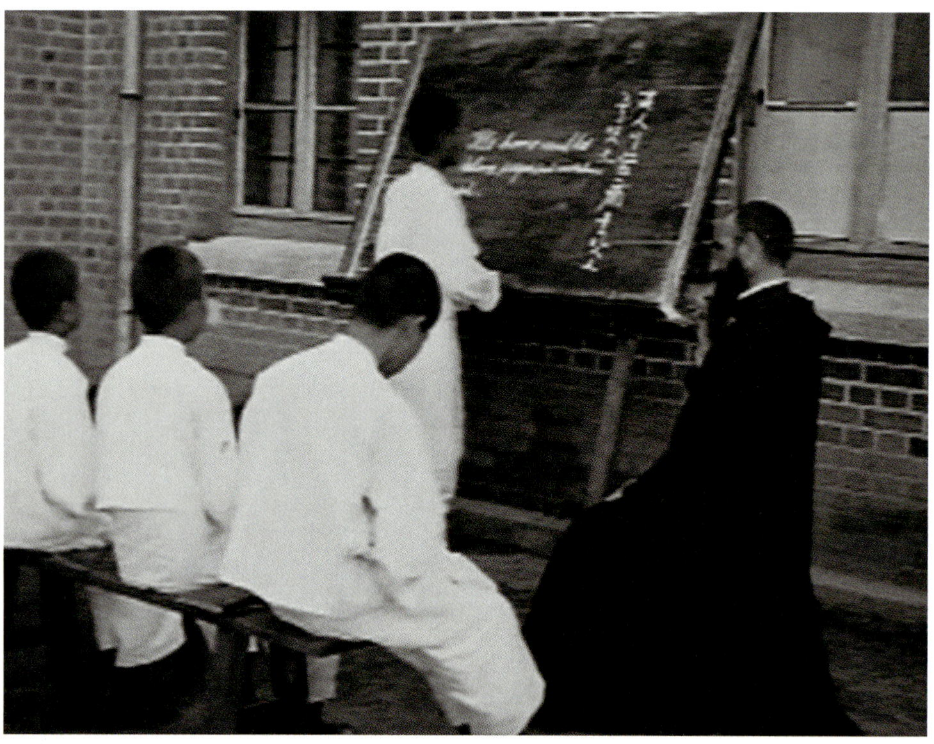

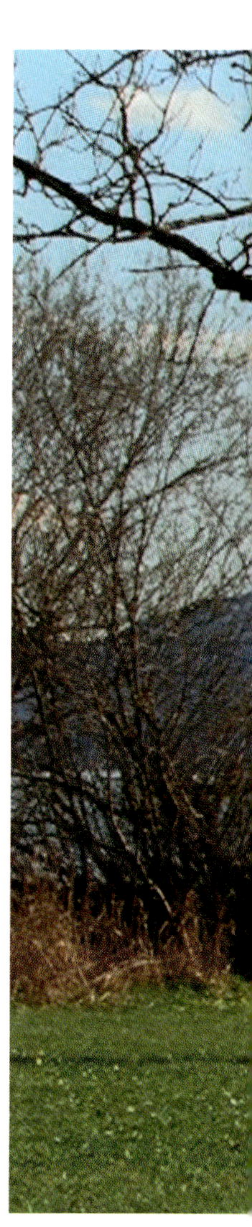

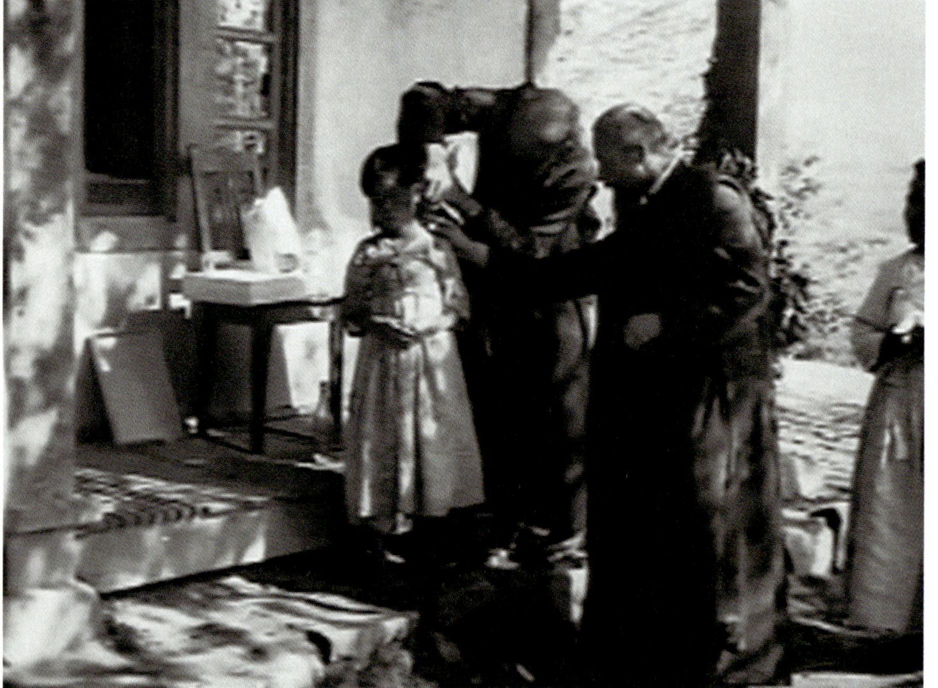

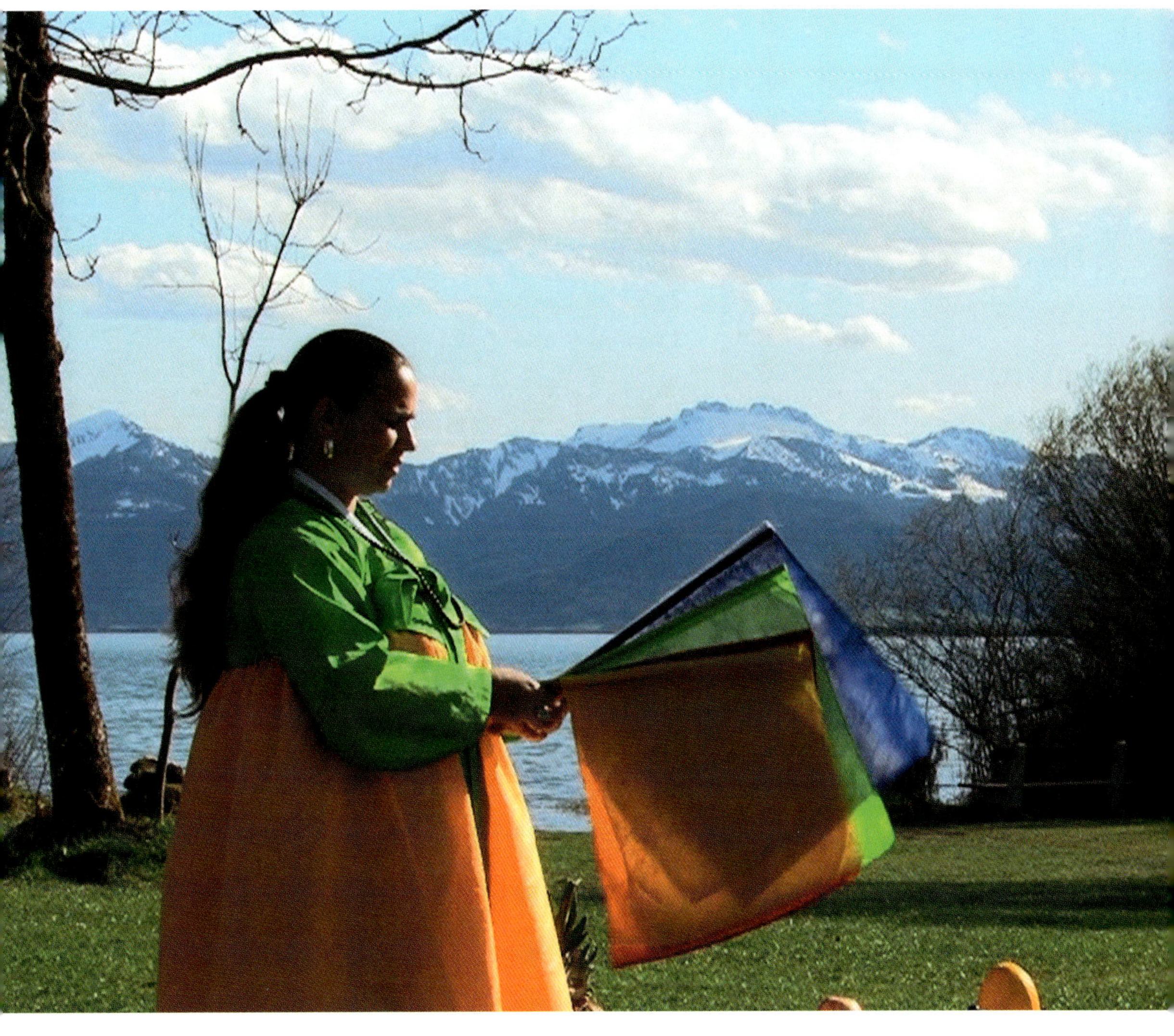

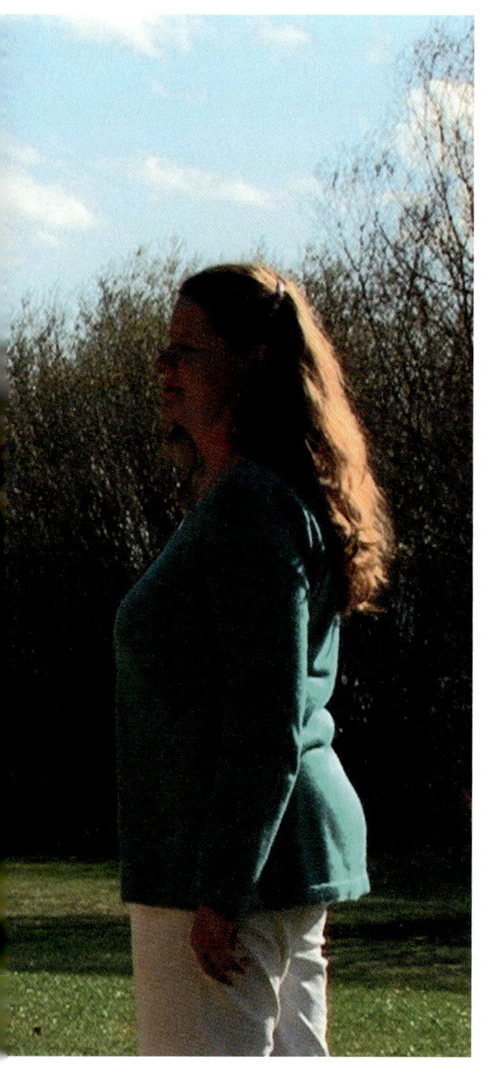

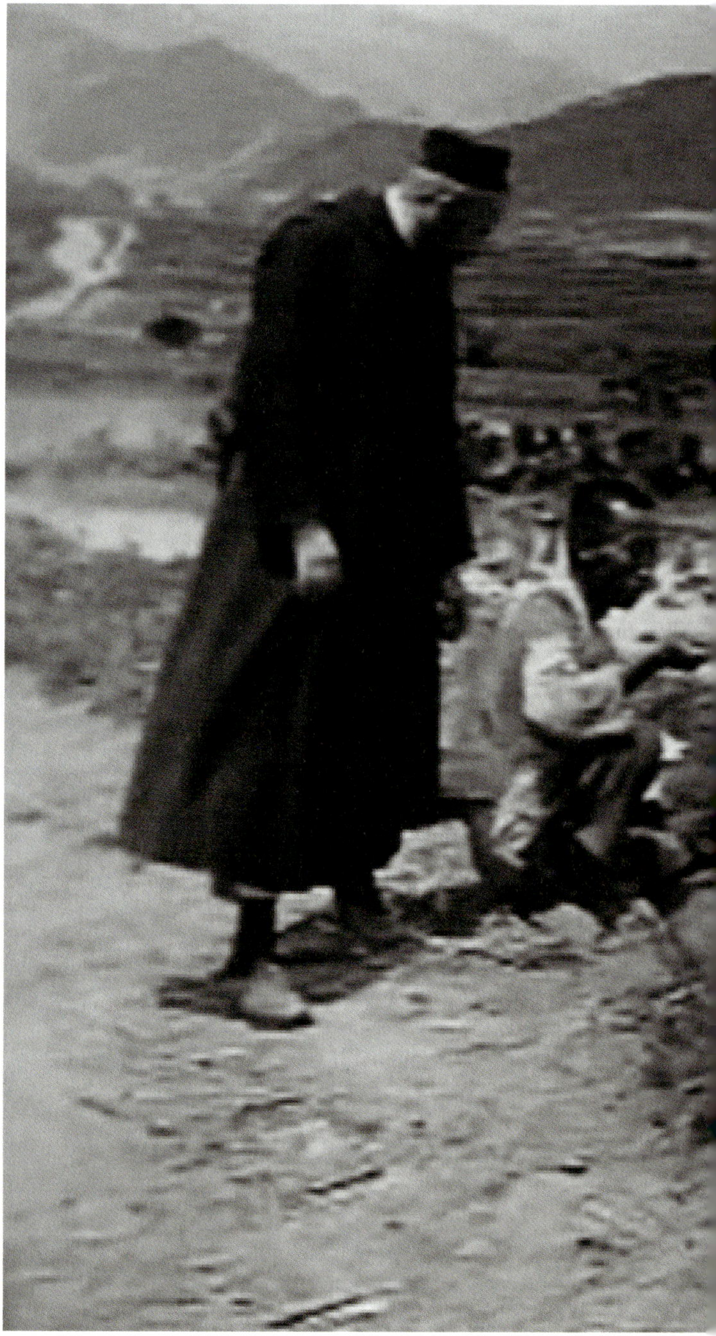

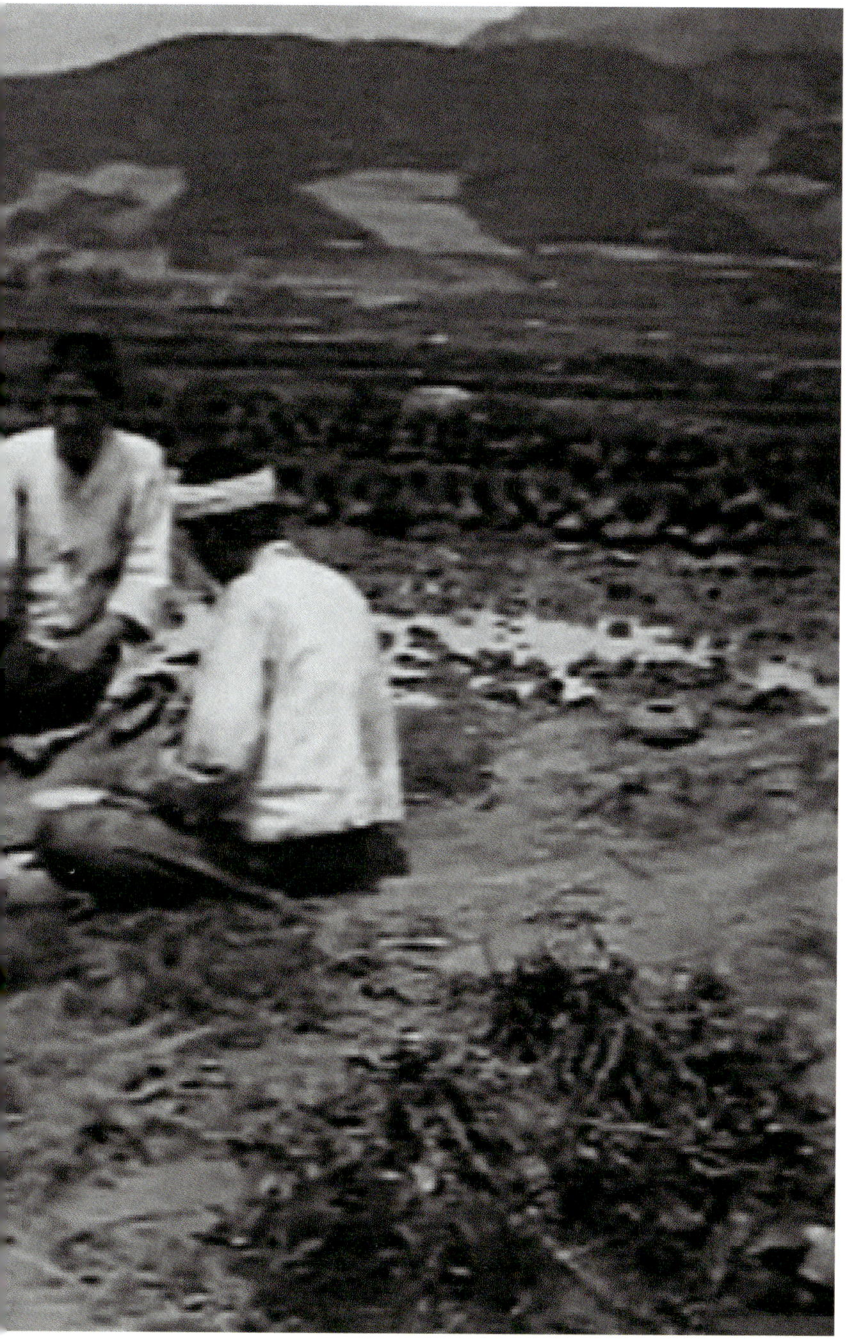

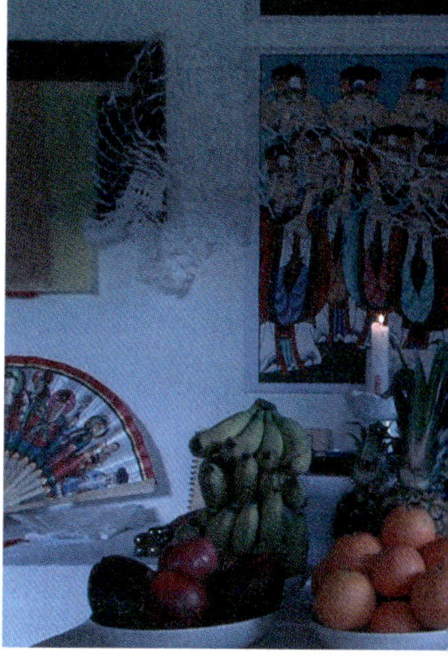

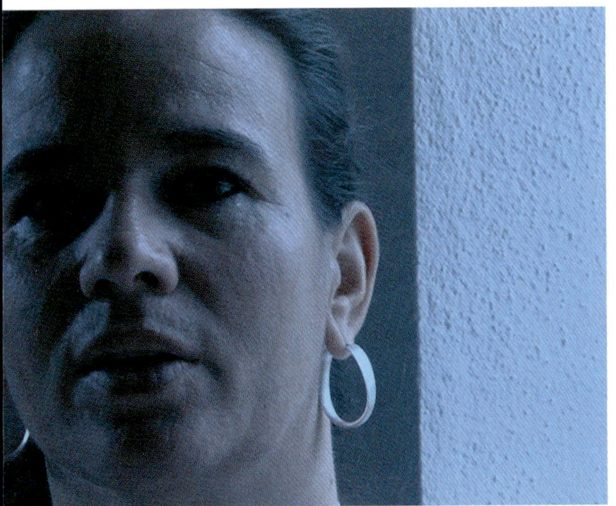

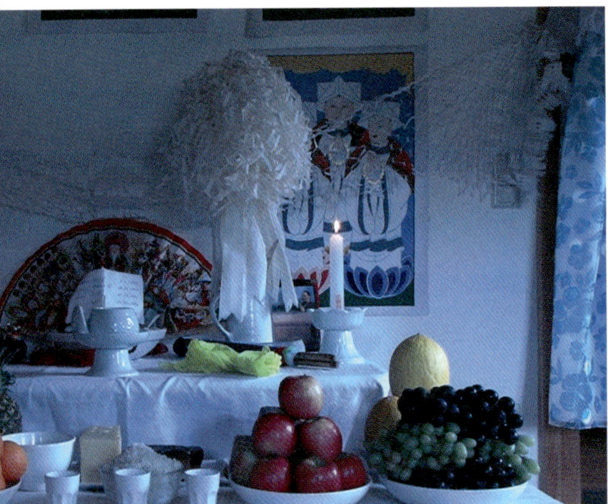

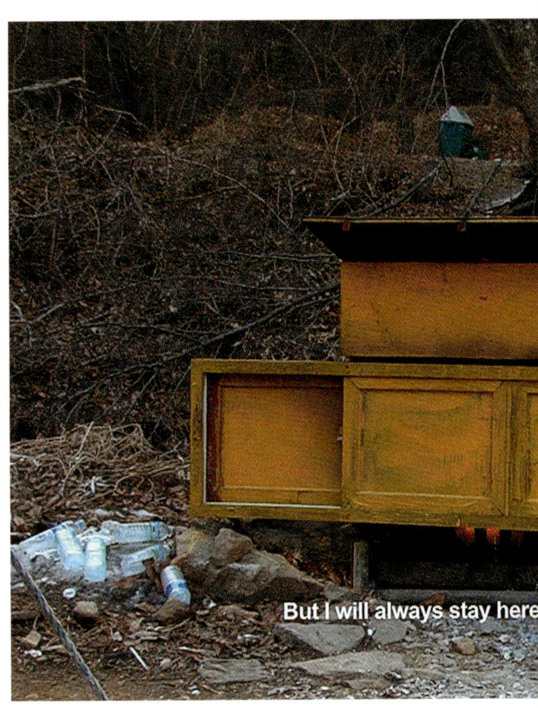
But I will always stay here

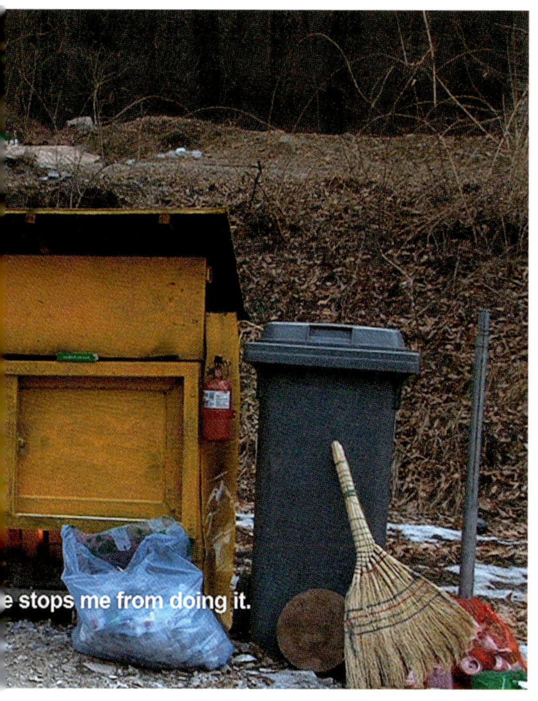
e stops me from doing it.

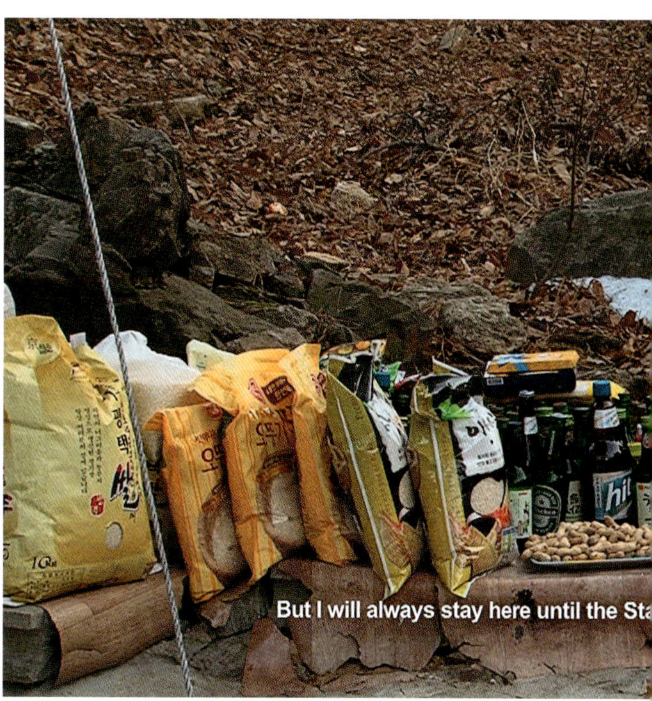
But I will always stay here until the Sta

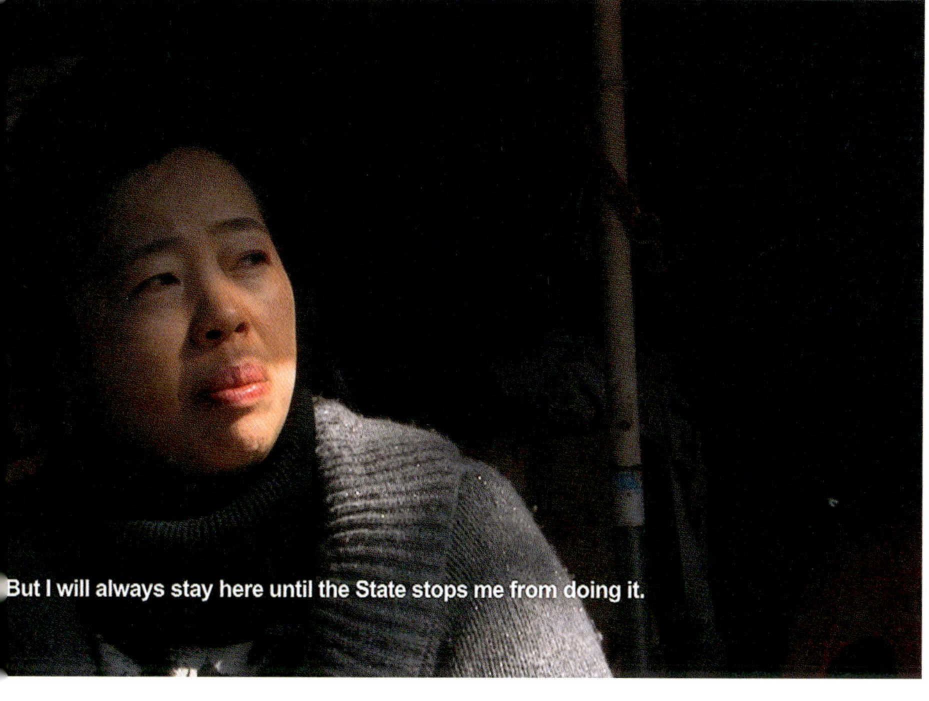
But I will always stay here until the State stops me from doing it.

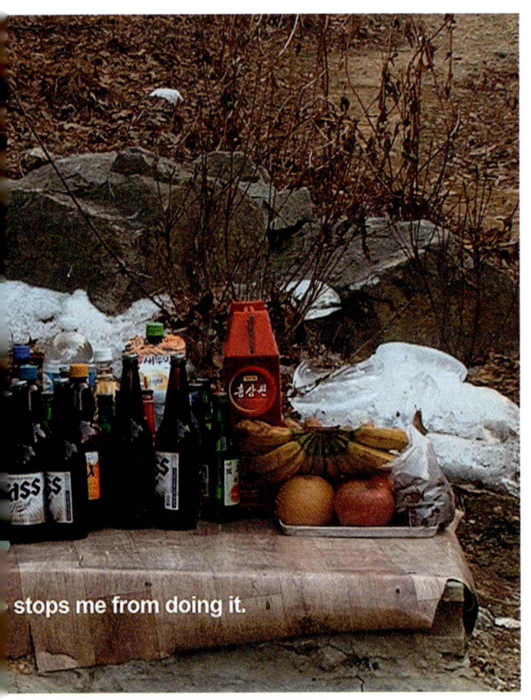
stops me from doing it.

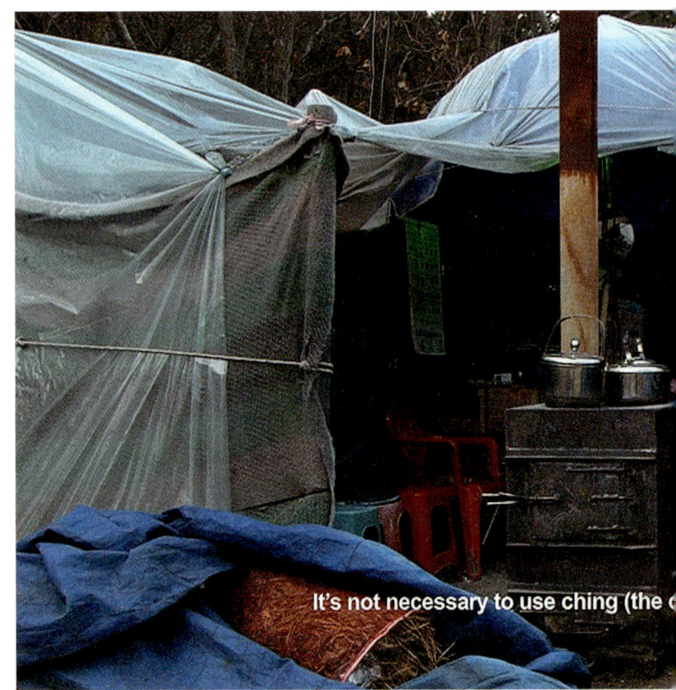
It's not necessary to use ching (the

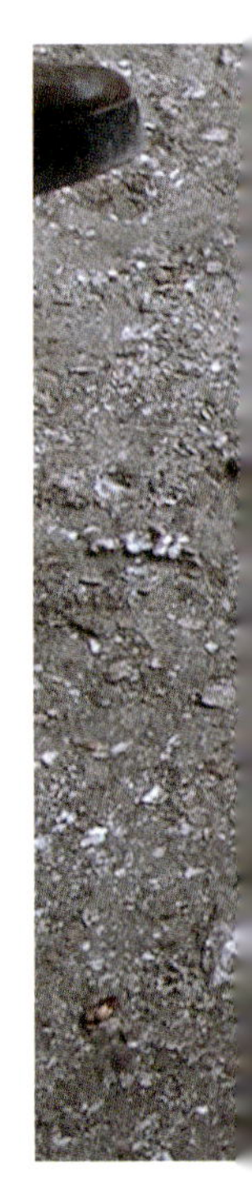

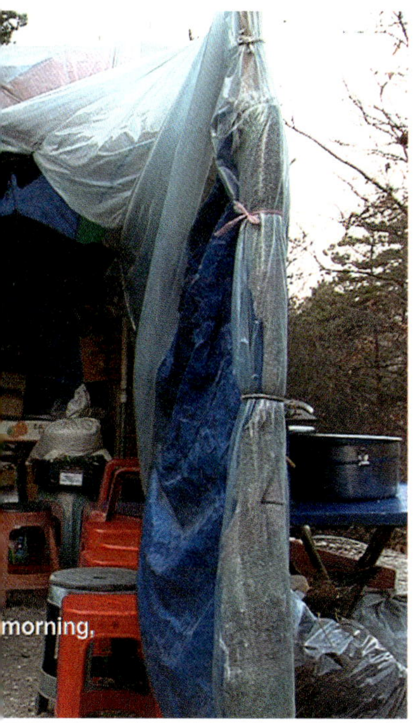

morning,

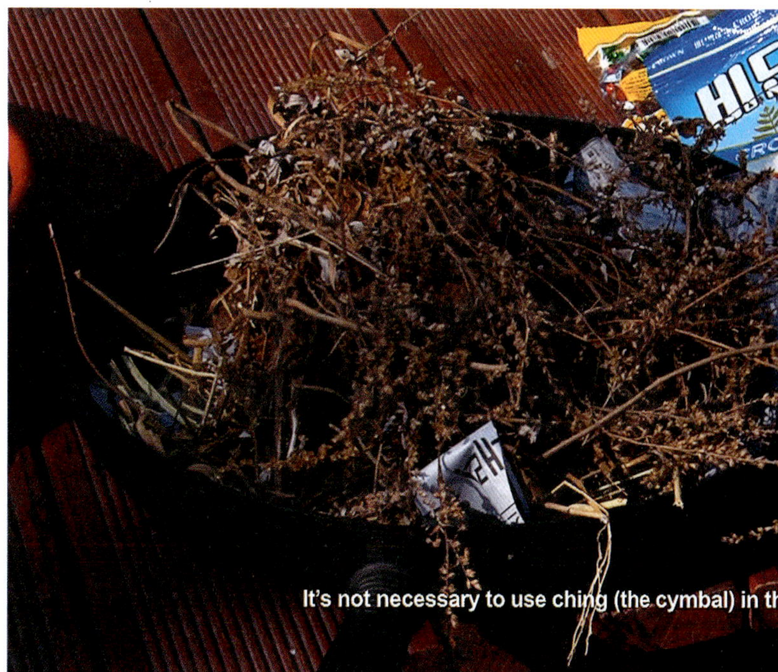

It's not necessary to use ching (the cymbal) in th

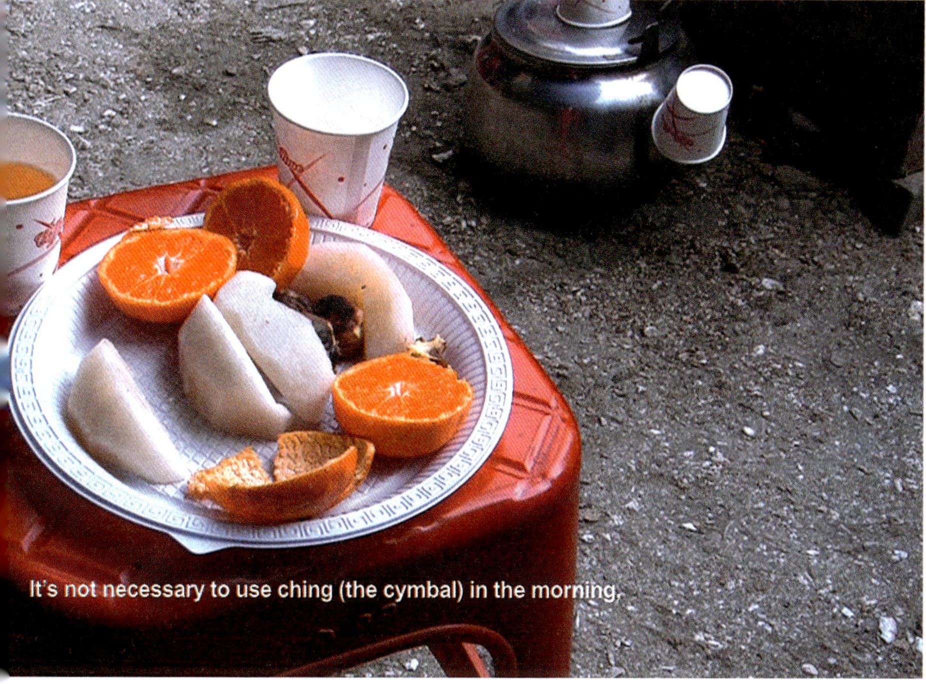

It's not necessary to use ching (the cymbal) in the morning.

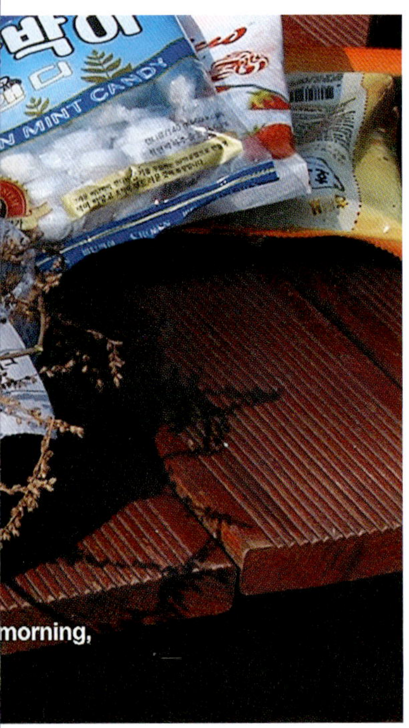
MINT CANDY
morning,

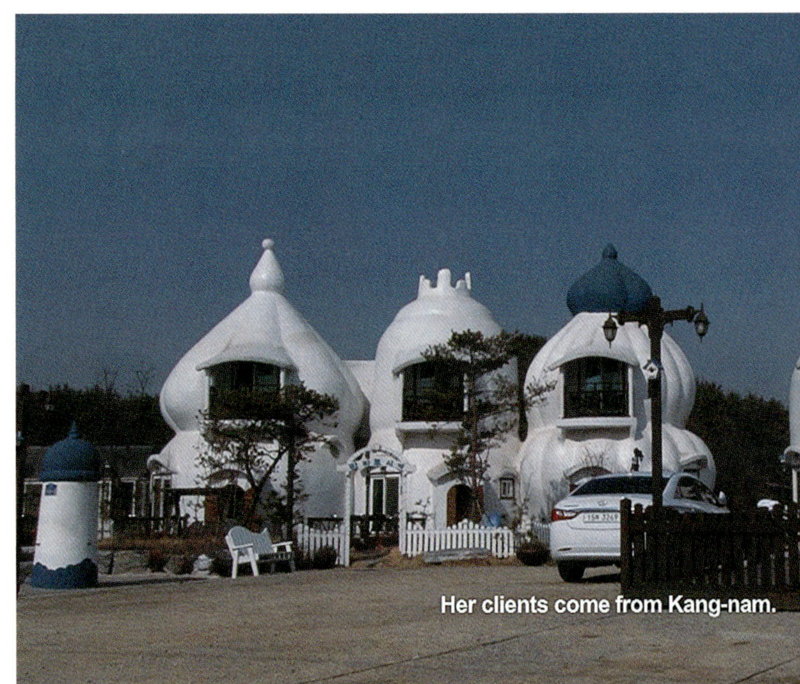
Her clients come from Kang-nam.

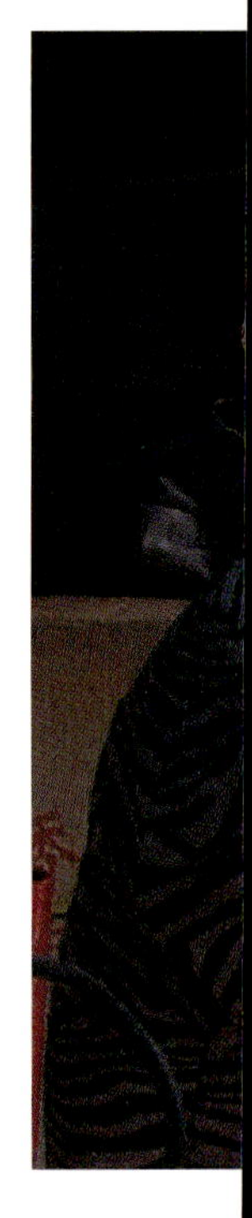

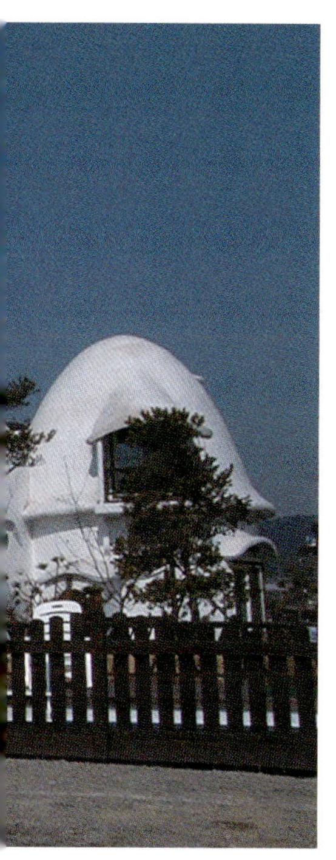

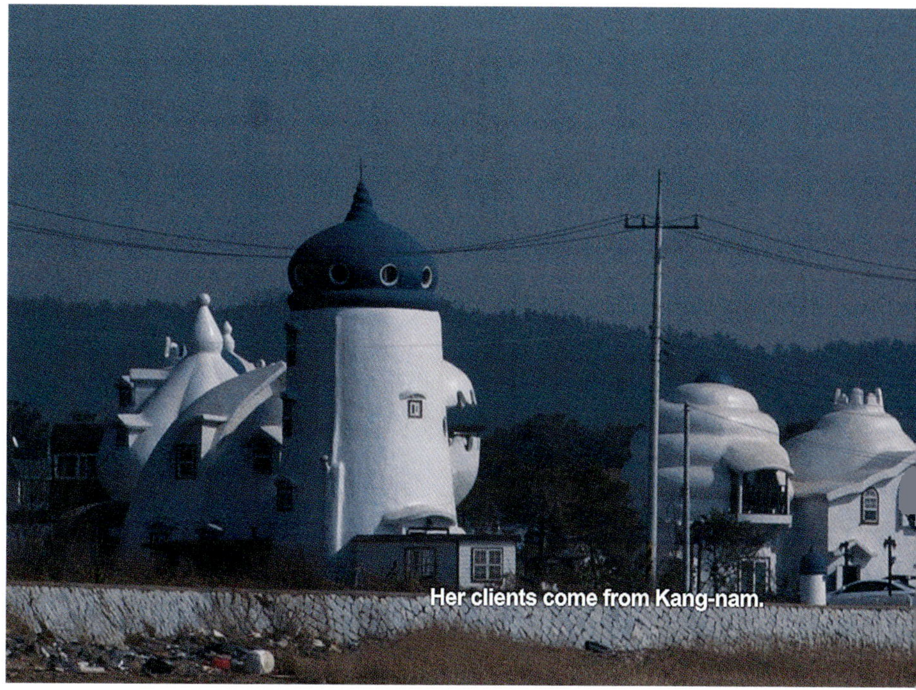
Her clients come from Kang-nam.

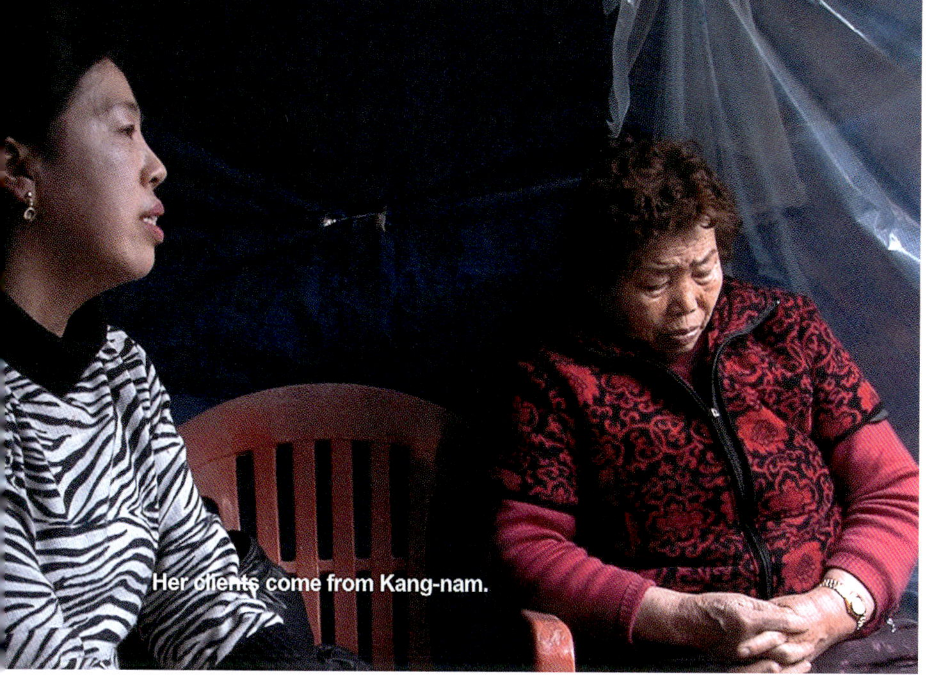
Her clients come from Kang-nam.

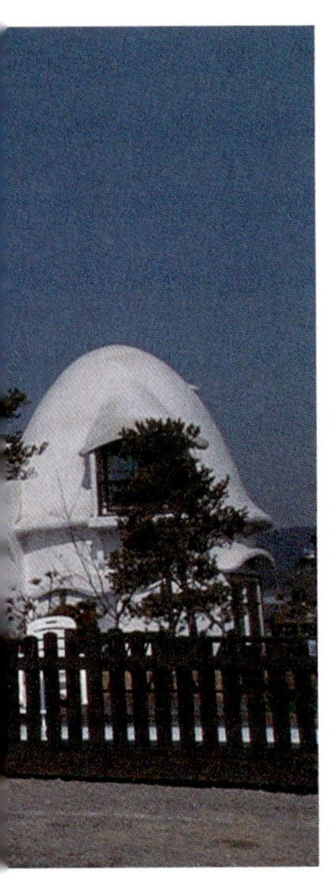

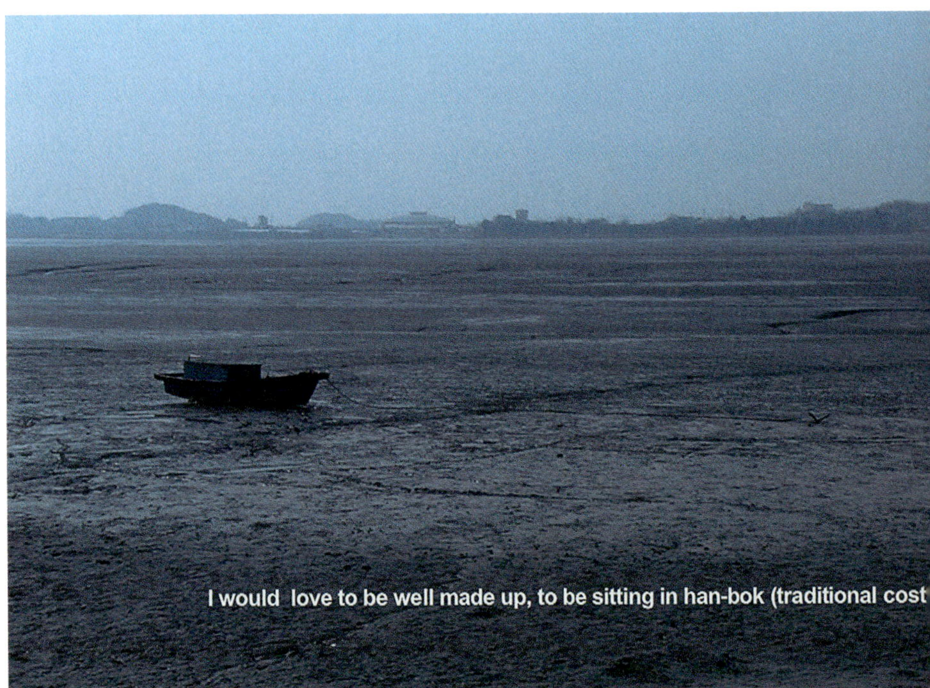
I would love to be well made up, to be sitting in han-bok (traditional cost

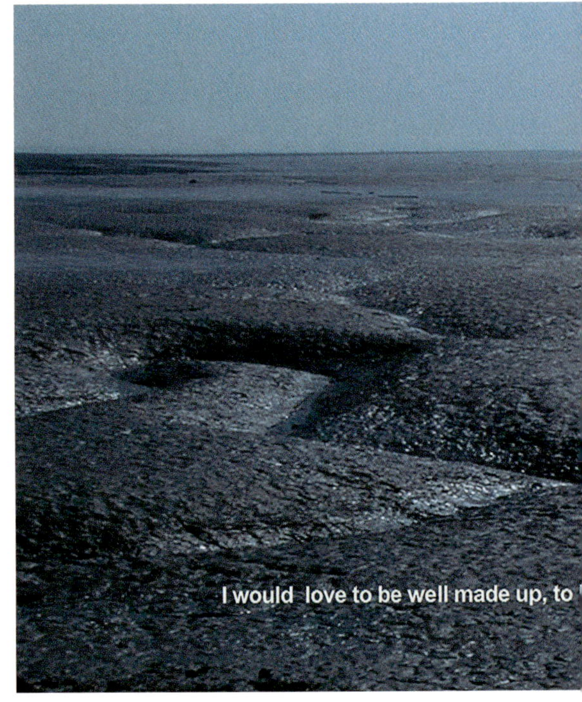
I would love to be well made up, to

AVANT-PROPOS
Marta Gili, directrice du Jeu de Paume

Quelle est la relation entre un geste et un paysage ?
Ou entre un paysage et une voix ? Entre plusieurs voix
et un seul corps ? Existe-t-il un lien entre la Bavière
et la Corée, entre l'indice Nikkei et les esprits, entre une
catastrophe naturelle et des dommages collatéraux ?

Toutes ces questions, en apparence décousues,
trouvent un « écho » dans le travail de Natacha Nisic
à travers des récits sinueux, qui changent sans cesse
de direction et dont les multiples facettes se trouvent
réunies dans cette exposition.

Le travail de Nisic participe de l'intérêt croissant
que certaines pratiques artistiques contemporaines
portent à l'analyse de la tension entre le pouvoir
de fait et le pouvoir diffus, entre le visible et l'invisible.
Dans son cas particulier, l'œuvre de Nisic explore
d'une part les paradoxes de la croyance, de la peur de
l'inconnu ou de la réversibilité / irréversibilité de la
perception. D'autre part, elle oscille de manière subtile
et critique entre l'analyse des effets du colonialisme
et les tentations de l'orientalisme.

C'est ainsi que, depuis son premier *Catalogue de
gestes* jusqu'à ses derniers travaux tels qu'*Indice Nikkei*,
e et, surtout, *f* et *Andrea en conversation*, produits
spécifiquement pour l'exposition, les images de Nisic
appellent une infinité d'associations symboliques,
perceptives et sensorielles, que le spectateur observe
nécessairement de manière kaléidoscopique,
à la lumière du passé et du présent.

Le Jeu de Paume voudrait remercier Natacha Nisic
de s'être investie avec autant d'enthousiasme
pour mener à bien ce projet. Merci également aux
collaborateurs du catalogue, Philippe-Alain Michaud,
Beck Jee-sook et Florent Perrier, pour leurs contributions
pertinentes qui nous éclairent sur le travail de l'artiste.

Enfin, toute notre reconnaissance va au ministère
de la Culture et de la Communication, à Neuflize Vie,
notre mécène principal, à la commission mécénat de
la Fondation Nationale des Arts Graphiques et Plastiques
pour son soutien inestimable, ainsi qu'aux Amis du
Jeu de Paume pour leur aide généreuse au catalogue.

Traduit de l'espagnol par Divina Cabo

MONDE DE ROSÉE
Philippe-Alain Michaud

> Ce monde de rosée
> est un monde de rosée
> et pourtant pourtant…
>
> Kobayashi Issa[1]

I

En 1995, Natacha Nisic commence à travailler à l'élaboration d'un *Catalogue de gestes* qui ne cessera de s'enrichir au fil des années, un catalogue ouvert, constitué d'une série de films tournés en super-8, de la durée d'un chargeur (entre une et deux minutes et demie), cadrant invariablement en plan serré et en légère plongée des mains accomplissant une action simple, réelle ou imaginaire – éplucher, couper, frotter, nettoyer… –, manipulant un objet – une fleur, un fruit, une paire de ciseaux, un couteau… –, ou simplement se frottant l'une l'autre pour esquisser dans l'espace du plan un motif sans commencement ni fin, retourné sur lui-même et sans finalité. Jamais de recadrage sur les visages : si les mains, pour la plupart des mains de femmes, sont marquées par le temps et révèlent quelque chose de leur histoire – ridées, tavelées ou tachées, parfois ornées d'une alliance ou d'une bague –, elles ne sont jamais rapportées à un corps et accomplissent par elles-mêmes une fonction détachée de tout sujet. D'abord projetés en pellicule, les films, désormais numérisés et diffusés sur des écrans plats, défilent en boucle, installés dans les espaces d'exposition en nombre variable, selon des compositions ouvertes et indéfiniment permutables.

Le *Catalogue de gestes* qui, dans l'œuvre de Natacha Nisic, prendra un caractère toujours plus ouvertement inaugural, éveille le souvenir d'autres films consacrés au mouvement des mains. En 1934, Ralph Steiner et Willard Van Dyke, membres du groupe de documentaristes radicaux de la Film and Photo League, réalisaient *Hands*, un film silencieux produit par la Works Progress Administration (WPA) et montrant des mains de chômeurs, d'artisans et d'employés d'usine, désœuvrées ou au travail. Les deux documentaristes entendaient décrire sur un mode expérimental, eux aussi sans jamais filmer les visages mais en utilisant des effets de montage, des cadrages et des éclairages

[fig. 1, p. 10]   Natacha Nisic, *Catalogue de gestes* (extraits), 1995-…, films super-8 numérisés, couleur, entre 1' et 2'30" chacun. Vue de l'exposition «elles@centrepompidou», Centre Pompidou, Musée national d'art moderne, Paris, 2009-2010
+
[p. 15-25]

[fig. 2, p. 10]   Ralph Steiner et Willard Van Dyke, *Hands*, 1934, film 16 mm, noir et blanc, 4'

[fig. 3, p. 10]   Natacha Nisic,
Nord, 2007, installation,
5 projections de films 16 mm
transférés en vidéo, couleur,
son stéréo, 5'50" chacune

[fig. 4, p. 10]   Yvonne Rainer,
Hand Movie, 1966,
film 8 mm, noir et blanc, 5'

[fig. 5, p. 11]   Richard Serra,
Hand Catching Lead, 1968,
film 16 mm, noir et blanc, 3',
Centre Pompidou, Musée
national d'art moderne,
Paris

hyper-expressifs, les gestes des travailleurs pour en révéler la beauté. Le *Catalogue de gestes* de Natacha Nisic présente la même préoccupation sociale et culturelle que *Hands* de Steiner et Van Dyke mais, pas plus qu'il ne constitue un simple répertoire de formes, il ne peut se réduire à un projet conservatoire ou archivistique. Il ne s'agit pas seulement de conjurer l'oubli en lui opposant la pérennité des images, de conserver, au moyen de la photo-impression, la trace de gestes fugitifs et désormais sans effectivité, que l'histoire efface irrémédiablement, mais bien de représenter, en tant que tel, le travail du temps : les mains anonymes répétant en boucle, inlassablement, la même opération, dessinent dans l'espace des tresses de durée, à la manière de celles des Parques déroulant et tranchant le fil des destins. C'est ainsi que dans *Nord*, un film réalisé en 2007, présenté en projection simple ou en installation, l'artiste se concentre, en donnant à ses images une orientation apparemment documentaire, sur les gestes des organisateurs de combats de coqs nouant méticuleusement les ardillons aux pattes de leurs animaux, puis sur les gestes des anciens ouvriers des usines de filature réduits au chômage, répétant, face à la caméra, leurs gestes désormais fantômes et reproduisant mimétiquement, alignés les uns à côté des autres, la chaîne de production dans laquelle ils s'inscrivaient. Les filatures comme les combats de coqs ne sont plus que des survivances : les habitants du Nord devenus les figurants de *Nord* reproduisent les gestes qu'ils ont toujours accomplis, avant de les laisser se perdre dans l'oubli. Le film, dans sa dimension performative, fonctionne à la fois comme description et comme symptôme : il protège le geste d'une disparition dont simultanément il entérine l'accomplissement, il noue le fil et en même temps le coupe.

Mais le *Catalogue de gestes* éveille un autre écho, à la fois plus proche et plus énigmatique : en 1966, après une opération chirurgicale qui devait l'empêcher de danser pendant de longs mois, Yvonne Rainer décide de tourner un film dans lequel, défiant l'immobilité, elle continue de danser avec les doigts de sa main droite : dans son *Hand Movie*, dont Richard Serra s'inspirera à son tour, à partir de 1968, pour réaliser la série de ses *Hand Films*, le mouvement de la main, en remplaçant celui du corps, prend une signification discrètement prophylactique ou conjuratoire et rejoint cette fonction magique accordée au geste, que la tradition anthropologique a scrutée dans les sociétés antiques, dans les traditions populaires et dans les cultures

extra-occidentales[2]. Le geste est une façon de nouer
les choses entre elles, de manière invisible,
en contournant le régime des causalités réelles :
avançons qu'il est devenu, pour Natacha Nisic, avec le
catalogue qu'elle inaugure en 1995, une manière
de concevoir le film comme une opération chamanique,
à partir de la toute-puissance de la manipulation.

II

En mai 1889, Wassily Kandinsky, alors étudiant en droit,
faisait, sous l'égide de la société ethnographique russe,
un voyage de près de six semaines dans la région
de Vologda, pour étudier les conceptions religieuses et
les structures juridiques des populations zyrianes.
Deux décennies plus tard, en 1913, il se souvient ainsi
de son voyage : « Les impressions ultérieures
particulièrement fortes que j'ai connues quand j'étais
étudiant et qui ont agi de façon décisive sur plusieurs
années de ma vie furent Rembrandt à l'Ermitage de
Saint-Pétersbourg et mon voyage dans le gouvernement
de Vologda, où je fus envoyé [en tant qu'ethnographe
et juriste] par la Société [impériale] de sciences
naturelles, d'anthropologie et d'ethnographie. Ma tâche
était double : étudier le droit criminel [paysan] dans
la population russe (chercher à dégager les principes
du droit primitif) et recueillir les survivances de religion
païenne qui subsistaient chez la peuplade zyriane de
paysans et de chasseurs en lente voie de disparition[3]. »
Étudiant les catégories de pensée de cette communauté
finno-ougrienne, le jeune Kandinsky allait découvrir
une forme d'âme particulière nommée *ort*, qui avait une
présence palpable dans la vie quotidienne des hommes :
donné à chacun à sa naissance, « l'*ort* apparaît aux
proches d'un sujet à l'approche de la mort, et toujours
la nuit, sous la forme de la personne qui va bientôt
mourir[4] ». À ce moment, il était réputé infliger
un pincement si sévère qu'il laissait une marque bleue
sur la peau, une preuve manifeste de sa nature réelle.
Ainsi s'explique la coutume, chez les Finno-Ougriens,
de laisser à l'extérieur des maisons, posés dans
l'embrasure des fenêtres, une cruche remplie d'eau
et un linge afin que l'*ort* puisse se laver le visage.
Les conceptions des Zyrianes entourant le mystère de
la mort allaient fissurer les catégories de pensée juridiques
de Kandinsky et lui faire comprendre l'existence
de formes de pensée chamaniques capables de détecter,
sous la surface stable du visible, la présence de forces
contradictoires à l'œuvre – une expérience

[p. 26-32 + 36]

[p. 37 + 72-78]

[p. 36-37]

qui allait s'avérer essentielle dans la genèse de sa recherche picturale autour de la fragmentation du plan et de la dissociation de la forme et de la couleur.

En 2007, Natacha Nisic est autorisée à filmer la vie quotidienne des carmélites de Lisieux *(Carmel)* : elle enregistre les gestes des recluses, la préparation des repas, les travaux de couture et de jardinage, les récréations, la prière, dans l'espace terne et sans apprêt de leurs cellules et des lieux communautaires, loin de la clarté étincelante dans laquelle baignait le couvent où Robert Bresson avait filmé les carmélites transfigurées par la grâce des *Anges du péché*. Les religieuses de Natacha Nisic ne changent pas le monde, elles en reproduisent la réalité prosaïque en glissant à sa surface, comme en l'effleurant de leurs gestes. De même, la chamane coréenne de *Princess Snow-Flower* (2011), installée au milieu de la campagne, dans un lieu propice à la manifestation des forces bénéfiques ou maléfiques qui gouvernent le monde, depuis sa cabane de fortune au milieu d'une montagne de produits de consommation, accomplit les gestes rituels comme on fait la cuisine, et se met en contact avec les morts (« peut-être l'esprit d'un suicidé fait-il sentir sa présence dans mon corps », dit-elle, ou encore : « Tu es enterré si profond que tu es devenu transparent »), secouée par les frissons de la transe sans cesser de se plaindre du manque d'argent et rêvant de refaire sa vie à Séoul. Comme l'a noté Mircea Eliade, les maladies, les rêves et les extases plus ou moins pathogènes sont autant de moyens d'accès à la condition de chaman : « [Ils] parviennent à transformer l'homme profane d'avant "le choix" en un technicien du sacré [5]. » C'est ainsi que la jeune Bavaroise à laquelle Natacha Nisic demande de raconter son histoire (*Andrea*, 2012) se trouve initiée malgré elle, sans même l'avoir imaginé, au terme d'une série d'épreuves qui affectent sa santé et sa raison [6]. Le pouvoir chamanique se transmet à distance, de génération en génération, comme une prédestination : la chamane est l'héritière de la sorcière que Jules Michelet décrivait renaissant de ses cendres au fil de l'histoire, sous des noms différents, comme l'incarnation d'un principe de vitalité : « La sorcière a fini pour toujours mais non pas la fée. Elle réapparaîtra sous cette forme, qui est immortelle [7]. »

III

« Si le bombardement atomique d'Hiroshima et de Nagasaki, les 6 et 9 août 1945 respectivement, constitue

un désastre démesuré, alors par-delà non seulement
le nombre de morts et la destruction manifeste
de bâtiments, dont des musées, des bibliothèques
et des temples, et diverses autres traces physiques,
ainsi que les effets matériels de long terme cachés
dans des cellules affectées par la radioactivité au "fond"
du corps et les traumatismes latents qui peuvent
se manifester après coup, il y aurait également un retrait
immatériel des textes littéraires, philosophiques et
de pensée ainsi que de certains films, vidéos et œuvres
musicales – alors même qu'il en subsiste des éléments
physiquement disponibles –, de peintures ou de
bâtiments qui n'ont pas été physiquement détruits, ainsi
que de guides spirituels, ou du caractère sacré / spécial
de certains espaces[8]. »

Les œuvres de Natacha Nisic visent de manière
systématique à manifester cet effacement dont Jalal
Toufic fait à la fois l'effet et le symptôme d'un
désastre qu'il nomme « démesuré » parce qu'il échappe
à la quantification, et par suite à la description, une
démesure que l'œuvre artistique ou littéraire ne peut
que reproduire mimétiquement, en s'inscrivant

[p. 138 + 156-184]

dans le retrait. *e* (« image » en japonais ; 2009) est composé
de séquences montées sur trois écrans ; explorant
une région du Nord de l'île de Honshu ravagée, en 2008,
par un tremblement de terre. Un habitant de l'île confie
avoir éprouvé, au moment de la catastrophe, une
sensation de vertige, comme si la terre, sous ses pieds,
était traversée par des forces contradictoires :
« Les étagères et les objets bougeaient en sens contraire. »
Il rejoue sa terreur au moment de la secousse et
sa course à l'extérieur de la maison : il ne peut en réalité
que montrer l'impossibilité de répéter le désastre
(à un certain point de son récit, l'image devient noire).
Des plans pris d'avion, reproduits sur trois écrans,
effleurent alors le paysage ravagé, montrant la terre
retournée par une puissance viscérale dont l'image ne
peut recueillir après coup que les signes de surface.

[p. 143-156]

f a été tourné, en 2013, également au Japon, sur le site
contaminé de Fukushima, un paysage d'affliction
à la surface duquel la caméra glisse en une série de
travellings continus qui ne « fictionnalisent » pas le réel,
mais au contraire marquent son opacité. Des miroirs
installés dans l'espace et qui traversent le cadre bord
à bord accentuent le caractère d'inaccessibilité de
l'arrière-plan, ce pan de réalité à la fois visible et effacé,
situé au-delà des miroirs, où des hommes continuent
de vivre et de travailler. La surface de l'image se retourne
et devient réfléchissante : en se refusant à la prospection,

elle introduit dans la spatialité imaginaire de ce plan
retourné un moment d'irréalité. Les éléments du paysage
et les êtres relégués qui l'habitent se dissolvent dans
les limbes de l'image, engendrant une vacuité spatiale où,
peut-être, il faut reconnaître un écho des peintures
de paysage que les artistes de l'ère Edo présentaient
scindées sur des panneaux de paravent.

IV

« L'image porte en elle sa propre contradiction » :
c'est ainsi que Natacha Nisic a pu décrire la manière
dont elle construit ses dispositifs de représentation face
aux objets, aux corps, aux paysages qu'elle filme
ou qu'elle photographie ; l'image, fixe ou en mouvement,
n'est pas description, mais révélation d'un état de
tension qui traverse les choses, une démonologie dont
le « travelling compensé » pourrait bien être l'opération
modélisante ou la figure ultime. Associant un zoom
avant et un travelling arrière (ou, à l'inverse, un zoom
arrière et un travelling avant), le travelling compensé
produit un mouvement contradictoire né de la rencontre
de deux forces, l'une optique (celle de l'objectif) et
l'autre physique (celle de la caméra), qui s'exercent l'une
à l'inverse de l'autre, sans solution de continuité ni
résolution. De cette figure de style, Alfred Hitchcock
a donné la construction pure dans la séquence finale
de *Vertigo* (1958), comme une représentation de l'origine
du vertige : une cage d'escalier, reproduite en maquette
et cadrée en plongée à 90 degrés, se creuse sous
l'effet d'un zoom avant comme un puits sans fond où
le regard est inexorablement attiré, tandis qu'il est
simultanément ramené vers la surface de l'image par
la force régrédiente d'un travelling arrière. L'image
devient à la fois élastique et statique, sa surface se dilate
sans se rompre à la manière d'un pont secoué
par une secousse sismique, sous l'effet des forces qui
se déploient et se composent en elle sans s'annuler.

[p. 137] En 2005, avec *La Porte de Birkenau*, une œuvre
aujourd'hui installée à Paris au Mémorial de la Shoah,
Natacha Nisic réinvente cette figure d'immobilité pour
produire une image de ce qui ne peut pas se montrer :
la caméra, fixée sur les rails, se rapproche physiquement
(et imperceptiblement) de la porte du camp
d'extermination dont la forme se détache toujours plus
nettement au fond du plan et résiste optiquement
au mouvement mécanique qui l'entraîne vers l'avant.
Cette construction dialectique est une réponse
transparente au célèbre travelling du *Kapo* de Gilles

Pontecorvo (1959), dont Jacques Rivette dans les *Cahiers du cinéma* a fait le commentaire cinglant : « Voyez, dans *Kapo*, le plan où [Emmanuelle] Riva se suicide, en se jetant sur les barbelés électrifiés : l'homme qui décide, à ce moment, de faire un travelling avant pour recadrer le cadavre en contre-plongée, en prenant soin d'inscrire exactement la main levée dans un angle de son cadrage final, cet homme n'a droit qu'au plus profond mépris [9]. » Représentant l'impossibilité du franchissement en même temps que son caractère inéluctable, le travelling compensé devient la figure même de la résistance à la mise en scène. En empêchant la résolution lyrique du plan, c'est-à-dire sa transformation en fiction, Natacha Nisic utilise l'image non dans son pouvoir de révélation, mais comme le symptôme de puissances qui, pour s'être retirées du visible, continuent d'agir en celui-ci.

La surface n'est pas ce qui révèle, mais ce qui recouvre l'abîme : elle est le lieu de son oubli et celui-ci ne se manifeste en elle que sous la forme du surgissement. « La première fois où j'ai pris le temps d'errer dans le camp, j'ai trouvé cette errance très étrange puisqu'il s'est soudain mis à faire très beau, les oiseaux chantaient… L'image était très pittoresque. Je me suis alors demandé si j'avais le droit d'éprouver une émotion proche de la joie, de l'allégresse. Je me suis approchée d'un réservoir situé juste à côté des rails et dont je n'avais jamais entendu parler. Il ne correspondait absolument pas à l'image que j'avais d'Auschwitz. La surface de ce réservoir rempli d'eau formait une image parfaite, une réflexion du monde presque archétypale, comme un tableau du XIXe siècle… L'image était très troublante. Lorsque je me suis rapprochée j'ai entendu un bruit très étrange, c'était celui d'un crapaud qui était assis sur les marches du réservoir. Je l'ai photographié [10]… » Dans *Effroi* (2005), le travelling compensé s'est pour ainsi dire vitrifié dans l'image : sur la nappe d'eau grise à la fois inquiétante et calme, réfléchissante comme un miroir de métal, le paysage se redouble et s'inverse dans l'éclat d'une réfraction claire interdisant au regard de s'aventurer dans sa profondeur, tandis qu'en bas de l'image, au fil de l'eau grise affleure la forme ectoplasmique d'un crapaud, comme le signe hallucinatoire que dans l'image qui flotte à la surface du monde sans le toucher quelque chose, obstinément, ne cessera de faire retour.

1 — *Mon année de printemps* (1819),
trad. Brigitte Allioux, Nantes,
Cécile Defaut, 2006, p. 66.
2 — Dans la littérature ancienne,
voir par exemple Andrea de Jorio,
*La Mimica degli antichi investigata
nel gestire napoletano* (Naples, Dalla
Stamperia e Cartiera del Fibreno,
1832) ou encore Garrick Mallery, « Sign
Language among North American
Indians Compared with That among
Other Peoples and Deaf-Mutes »
(dans *First Annual Report of the Bureau
of Ethnology to the Secretary of
the Smithsonian Institution, 1879-1880*,
Washington, Government Printing
Office, 1881, p. 263-552).
3 — Wassily Kandinsky, *Regards
sur le passé et autres textes
(1912-1922)*, Paris, Hermann, 2009,
p. 102.
4 — Wassily Kandinsky, « Carnet
de voyage en Vologda » (1889), cité
par Peg Weiss, *Kandinsky and Old
Russia. The Artist as Ethnographer
and Shaman*, New Haven et Londres,
Yale University Press, 1985, p. 23.
5 — Mircea Eliade, *Mythes, rêves
et mystères*, Paris, Gallimard, 1957,
p. 106 *sq*.
6 — À l'occasion de l'exposition
du Jeu de Paume en 2013, l'artiste
a produit une seconde version
de l'œuvre, intitulée *Andrea en
conversation*, sous forme d'installation
pour neuf moniteurs, où peut-être
la démultiplication et la redistribution
des images reproduisent
le déplacement chamanique de
la fonction du sujet.
7 — Jules Michelet, *La Sorcière* (1862),
Paris, Garnier-Flammarion, 1966,
p. 258.
8 — Jalal Toufic, *Le Retrait de la
tradition suite au désastre démesuré*,
trad. Omar Berrada et Ninon
Vinsonneau, Paris, Les Prairies
ordinaires, 2011, p. 11.
9 — Jacques Rivette,
« De l'abjection », *Cahiers du cinéma*,
n° 120, juin 1961, p. 54-55, repris dans
Antoine de Baecque (dir.), *Théories
du cinéma*, Paris, Cahiers du cinéma,
2001, p. 37-40.
10 — « Le réservoir se situe sur
le côté gauche des rails (en regardant
vers les fosses dos à la porte) :
au milieu de la distance qui sépare
la porte du camp des chambres à gaz,
rasées par les nazis. Il y a peu de
littérature sur ces réservoirs. On peut
penser qu'ils servaient à nettoyer
les latrines et en cas d'incendie.
Une image m'a longtemps hantée
et quasi retenue de publier la mienne :
celle de jeunes gens, des soldats
en train de se baigner dans un
de ces réservoirs. Une photographie
légère et gaie utilisée par les
révisionnistes pour prouver que
le camp d'Auschwitz était un camp
de vacances. Je n'ai pas trouvé
d'autres images de ces réservoirs. »
Natacha Nisic, courriel du 4 mai 2013.

[p. 41-72]

ANDREA,
DANS CE MONDE TRIANGULAIRE
Beck Jee-sook

> Notre pays se dit à l'orient le plus extrême et l'Europe à l'occident le plus extrême. Une personne de l'orient le plus extrême souhaitait rencontrer quelqu'un de l'occident le plus extrême.
>
> Park Ji-won[1]

Andrea (2012) de Natacha Nisic se compose de cinq vidéos de longueurs variables[2]. Dans l'exposition « K. W. Complex[3] », l'œuvre, qui mêle des séquences tournées par l'artiste à Fischbachau en Bavière et des images d'archives de la télévision bavaroise[4], se déployait sur des écrans répartis dans l'espace d'une salle entière. Intitulées *La Rencontre*, *Les Âmes*, *Les Soins*, *Archives* et *Les Voix*, les vidéos exposent, à travers des « langages » différents, l'histoire étrange et insolite d'un personnage. Paysages et couleurs contrastés de l'Allemagne et de la Corée du Sud, silence et bruit du vent, chansons populaires et textes des sous-titres, qui tour à tour interrompent et lient le flux d'images, constituent la toile de fond de ce drame et confèrent à l'ensemble de l'installation une texture extrêmement disparate. Cette hétérogénéité ne révèle toute sa complexité que lorsque l'on entreprend de retracer « l'arbre généalogique » d'*Andrea*.

Dans le titre « K. W. Complex », projet collaboratif de Natacha Nisic et de l'artiste sud-coréen Park Chan-kyong, le « K » renvoie au nom de la chamane coréenne Kim Keum-hwa[5] et le « W » à l'abbé bénédictin allemand Norbert Weber, qui visita la Corée à l'époque de la colonisation japonaise, au début du XXe siècle, avant de publier l'ouvrage *Im Lande der Morgenstille, Reise-Erinnerungen an Korea (Au pays du Matin calme, souvenirs de voyage en Corée)* et de réaliser le film éponyme[6]. Organisé par les artistes en un chapitre K – la mère – et un chapitre W – le père –, le livre[7] conçu à l'issue de leur exposition présente l'héritière spirituelle de Kim Keum-hwa, Andrea Kalff, comme la fille « symbolique » de K et de W. Cette dernière vit d'ailleurs non loin de Sainte-Odile, la communauté bénédictine qui envoya Weber en Corée.

Les deux artistes se sont rencontrés lors d'un festival de cinéma au Japon en 2010. Saisis d'un « élan d'archivistes » suscité par leur intérêt commun pour le livre et le film de Weber, ils ont entrepris d'articuler le travail d'interviews de la grande chamane Kim Keum-hwa, mené de longue date par Park Chan-kyong, à un processus d'exploration visuelle et intellectuelle à travers la géographie et l'histoire, qu'ils ont aussi croisé avec *Blue Eyes Possessed by Spirits*[8], l'histoire du voyage d'Andrea jusqu'en Corée du Sud afin de s'initier au chamanisme. Le mot « Complex » exprime la complexité culturelle inhérente aux influences géographiques et historiques qui traversent les relations entre les trois personnages. En même temps, il s'agit d'un terme psychanalytique désignant des émotions ou des pensées fondamentales qui ont été longtemps refoulées, aussi bien à l'échelle de civilisations que d'histoires familiales. Park Chan-kyong note que cette complexité touche à des notions telles que l'impérialisme, l'histoire et la fatalité qui, en Corée, « entrent démesurément en jeu » dans les situations individuelles de maladie, de mort, de catastrophe, de hasard. Confrontés à ce thème, les artistes, plutôt que de choisir la facilité du dialogue, ont préféré privilégier un certain silence, un certain entre-deux afin de souligner la rupture marquante et le contraste entre l'histoire générale d'une immense organisation religieuse et la foi d'un individu[9].

Si l'on pousse plus loin l'analogie avec la « famille », apparaissent des « sœurs ». En plaçant horizontalement *Carmel* (2008) et *Princess Snow-Flower* (2011) de Natacha Nisic aux côtés d'*Andrea* sur l'arbre généalogique, la composition verticale préexistante se teinte d'une autre tonalité. *Carmel* a été réalisé à partir de la vidéo tournée par l'artiste en l'espace d'un an dans un couvent de carmélites à Lisieux, en France. Les quatre petits écrans juxtaposés soulignent la vie saine et réglée des vingt-deux nonnes. Mais à l'occasion de la prise de voile d'une novice, la caméra de Natacha Nisic pénètre au sein de cet univers clos et provoque une déchirure temporaire dans cet espace austère, créant un rythme et une vitalité inattendus. Triple projection vidéo, *Princess Snow-Flower* a été conçue par l'artiste au cours de sa résidence dans la province du Gyeonggi, à la périphérie de Séoul. Elle met en scène une jeune chamane qui, manifestement douée de pouvoirs exceptionnels mais indéniablement fatiguée, bavarde librement avec des adeptes à l'issue d'une cérémonie maladroite, célébrée dans un sanctuaire de plein air désordonné. Un montage de *Princess Snow-Flower* et de *Carmel* confronterait les dichotomies religieuses modernes, la civilisation et la barbarie, la croyance et la superstition, le culte et la supercherie, la spiritualité et l'inconstance, les chants et les incantations. En même temps, *Princess Snow-Flower* est marquée par des mouvements de contradiction interne et de négation. Par exemple, le vocabulaire visuel des scènes en surimpression et en fondu enchaîné, bien qu'en retrait de la narration orale, évoque étroitement la nature fantomale du personnage, tout en le rendant volatil. La modernité de ce spectre, qui dispose au sein d'une nature profane les objets de culte et les offrandes pour communiquer avec le monde des esprits et qui, tout à la fois, rêve de renommée, de richesse et, plus que tout, de la grande ville de Séoul, semble soudain révolue quand survient une scène où la chamane retourne dans les bois, mue par une « force à laquelle elle ne peut désobéir ». Par ailleurs, Snow-Flower, dont le nom dans la culture orale coréenne évoque davantage l'image d'une *kisaeng* [10] que celle d'une chamane, élargit la portée de la « sororité » qui lie de façon évidente la postulante de *Carmel* et Andrea. « Pourquoi devenir un bien culturel vivant ou une chamane nationale… Les gens comme moi… Nous n'avons pas besoin d'hommes, je compte initier deux femmes, seulement deux, et j'en aurai terminé [11]. » Si la postulante de *Carmel* est fille de l'Église catholique et Andrea fille du chamanisme, Snow-Flower est à la fois la fille adoptive du spectre d'une vieille dame anonyme [12] et la mère spirituelle jalouse d'une disciple brillante. En tant que sujet divisé entre le sacré et le profane, elle apparaît, en quelque sorte, comme la demi-sœur de la postulante carmélite et d'Andrea.

Ainsi, Andrea se trouve au centre d'un mécanisme complexe d'exclusion et d'oppression, d'hybridité et de syncrétisme, qui lie en tous sens l'Occident et l'Orient, le colonialisme et l'orientalisme, le patriarcat et le féminisme, les classes et les peuples. Initiée par Kim Keum-hwa en Corée, Andrea vit et pratique aujourd'hui le chamanisme en Bavière. Elle est une Autre dans les deux sociétés. À travers un processus de réflexion et de projection mutuelles au sein de l'œuvre de Natacha Nisic, ces sociétés, dépeintes chacune sous un angle légèrement différent par l'objectif de l'artiste, se disloquent et se révèlent par la fluctuation des frontières modernes auxquelles elles sont toutes deux solidement arrimées. Possédée par des esprits mystérieux, Andrea apparaît certainement comme excentrique en Allemagne du Sud, mais elle demeure tout aussi étrange et singulière au regard de la culture chamanique coréenne traditionnelle.

Car bien que les esprits de l'autre monde n'aient pas de nationalité, ici-bas les médiums spirituels appartiennent à un substrat historique et culturel très solide.
Au cours de la colonisation de la Corée, les chamanes, considérées comme les « Autres de l'intérieur », étaient rejetées en tant qu'obstacle à l'édification du pays ; elles subirent une cruelle oppression, au même titre que les praticiens du *feng shui*, les bonzes mendiants et les instigateurs d'émeutes [13]. Dans la période de modernisation qui s'ensuivit, le régime dictatorial institutionnalisa leur tradition à travers la politique des biens culturels intangibles, tandis que leur pratique finit par devenir une sorte de rite religieux de subversion – l'esprit chamanique étant désormais perçu comme un symbole de résistance politique et de rébellion culturelle contre le pouvoir [14]. Dans ce contexte, Andrea, sur l'arrière-plan de l'histoire de la colonisation et de la modernisation de la Corée, incarne à l'extrême l'illusion orientaliste du monde occidental et occupe la fonction, très rare, du double – en d'autres termes, de « l'Autre du monde extérieur » ou de « l'Autre de l'Autre ». Son existence restaure la voix intérieure étouffée de l'Autre autant qu'elle ouvre une brèche dans l'économie nationale du chamanisme qui, autrefois, fonctionnait en tant que contrepoids à l'oppression.

Les cinq écrans vidéo d'*Andrea* qui, placés à une certaine distance les uns des autres, se citent, se font écho, s'opposent ou observent simplement le silence, sont des « androïdes » de l'âme moderne. Soumis à une grammaire conceptuelle, le vocabulaire vidéo de Natacha Nisic, qui joue sur un registre physique et émotionnel, était déjà renforcé, dans ses travaux antérieurs, par des gestes manuels et des expressions faciales. Dans *Andrea*, cependant, il prend un tour organique et mécanique. Pour les androïdes, maux de tête, brûlures d'estomac, fractures, tumeurs apparaissent comme des signes de maladies physiques qui agressent le corps discipliné par la modernité. Les larmes et les éructations qui surviennent lors du processus de convalescence sont « l'abject » produit par le corps. À la différence des mains au travail, les pieds sont une voie pour « lire la tristesse et la profonde sollicitude envers la mère [15] » ; ils sont liés à la mémoire et à la famille, deux entités constitutives de l'identité moderne. Ces entités, on le sait, forment la frontière de la normalité quand la rationalité moderne rejette le spectre prémoderne sous le nom de superstition [16]. Andrea fait de ses parents, catholiques et adeptes de la médecine occidentale, les porte-parole de la rationalité moderne et, comme pour troubler cette rationalité, elle pose en contrepoint son frère aîné décédé et sa fille Denise, laquelle échappe de peu à une possession par les esprits. En retraçant ses souvenirs, elle parle à cœur ouvert de son éducation de catholique fervente et de ses années d'adolescence dans une institution tenue par des sœurs, des menaces parentales de la couper de la famille si elle recevait l'initiation chamanique ; elle avoue aussi avoir été bouleversée devant les patients de l'hôpital psychiatrique où son frère avait été interné aux côtés de criminels. La remémoration d'Andrea atteint son paroxysme quand, lors de son rituel d'initiation en Corée du Sud, elle entre en contact, à travers une chamane, avec l'esprit de son frère décédé, ce qui la pousse à critiquer sa mère pour avoir coupé les cheveux de celui-ci alors qu'il était plongé dans le coma. Telle une tumeur incontrôlable qui se répand et ronge son hôte, ce processus, qui lui permet de relire à rebours le scénario de sa vie, va changer radicalement son existence en chamboulant ses limites de façon irrémédiable : moi intérieur et monde extérieur, esprit et corps, passé et présent, chair et esprit, frontières entre vie et mort.

Dans la culture traditionnelle coréenne, le corps est à la fois un héritage laissé par ses parents et une « carte » qui permet de décrypter un individu. La croyance veut que la lecture personnologique – dite aussi lecture du visage ou du caractère – puisse révéler le passé et l'avenir d'une personne, tandis qu'en médecine coréenne l'état des organes internes peut être diagnostiqué en examinant l'apparence extérieure du corps. Les écrans vidéo articulés formant les androïdes d'*Andrea* élargissent la carte physique de ce corps et produisent de nouvelles « figures » sur le terrain de la modernité, où la carte de l'imagination et le paysage des représentations se chevauchent. D'abord, il y a les éléments intérieurs du sanctuaire d'Andrea, tels que la table sacrificielle et les ustensiles et costumes chamaniques. Des melons, du fromage et des gâteaux sont disposés sur la table à côté du riz blanc. Andrea, la « femme aux yeux bleus », vêtue du *hanbok*, le costume traditionnel coréen, serre un drapeau à cinq couleurs. Son sanctuaire aux murs blancs est calme en comparaison du sanctuaire chamanique classique. Ces éléments intérieurs disparates, transposés dans le décor naturel des lacs et des montagnes de Bavière – qui inspira les peintres de paysage de l'Allemagne romantique –, produisent un sentiment d'incohérence. En outre, si la caméra de l'artiste explore l'image du sublime en parcourant la forêt hivernale et les pics enneigés, celle de la télévision bavaroise semble dévoiler le territoire esthétique de la terreur à travers des scènes de l'étrange rocher du mont Inwang à Séoul, qu'Andrea visite pour recevoir son initiation, et de l'île, enneigée, de Ganghwa, où se trouve Keumhwadang [17]. Tout comme Andrea, qui cherche une analogie entre le mur de Berlin et les barbelés de l'île de Ganghwa, Snow-Flower, au milieu d'un paysage surréaliste de panneaux publicitaires de villages anglais et de montagnes dénudées, et la postulante de *Carmel*, dans un paysage familier de fleurs et de pelouses, constituent d'autres forces qui traversent les registres de la modernité. Aussi l'intrusion du « paysage sonore » qui, tout au long des vidéos, est tantôt synchrone, tantôt en rupture avec le paysage visuel, et l'insertion d'« hyper »-textes, qui interrompent soudainement le déroulement des scènes, décomposent-elles tous les aspects de la vision du monde basée sur la perspective occidentale à point de fuite unique. En ce sens, le « vidéopaysage » d'*Andrea*, qui se concentre davantage sur l'interrelation entre l'individu et le paysage, semble plus proche de la technique picturale du *samwon* [18], qui effectue un montage de différents temps et espaces mêlant premier plan, plan moyen et arrière-plan.

Au final, le scénario « cartographique » d'*Andrea* sort du carcan des dichotomies modernes autant qu'il explore les moyens de la culture contemporaine. En interrogeant notre capacité à dépasser ce carcan – non pour abandonner ces dichotomies mais pour être à nouveau à même d'agir sur elles et de transformer ce qui se donne pour la réalité –, *Andrea* va jusqu'à modifier les strates de signification de *Carmel* et de *Princess Snow-Flower* et s'offre comme une tentative de décolonisation de l'imaginaire colonial moderne [19].

Andrea qui, vêtue du *hanbok*, erre sur les rives d'un lac bavarois comme un spectre, met au jour, à travers l'œuvre de Natacha Nisic, les diverses stratégies rhétoriques d'une tradition orale. Dans une autogynographie [20], quelle que soit sa dramaturgie, il est difficile de déceler un « moi » spécifique en raison de la complexité et de l'ambiguïté du récit, où se mêlent imaginaire, fiction et réalité. L'autogynographie est plutôt une stratégie de camouflage originale, qui autorise le sujet de l'histoire à être n'importe qui – Andrea, Snow-Flower, la postulante de *Carmel* ou toute autre personne. Cette forme de récit a pour origine l'impulsion narrative émanant d'un sujet féminin divisé qui cherche, à travers les mots, à constituer l'image de son moi comme une existence réelle[21]. Évoquant son initiation, Andrea déclare s'être sentie guérie après avoir prêté l'oreille à ses voix intérieures et relayé la parole des esprits. En fait, ce sentiment coïncide avec les effets thérapeutiques immédiats du récit oral. Ici, nous sommes en présence d'une autogynographie sous la forme du drame d'Andrea, d'une artiste qui le revit en tendant l'oreille et l'interprète en se saisissant de sa caméra, et d'un regard critique d'Extrême-Orient qui entre en empathie avec cette dernière. Si l'affect engendré par la « décartographie » de la modernité atteint son maximum au travers du flux d'énergie dégagé par ce triangle, qui sait si nous ne pourrons pas entrevoir, l'espace d'un instant, l'état de *mugam*[22], comme les membres de la famille d'un disciple qui emprunte la danse et le costume de la chamane ?

Traduit du coréen par Patrick Maurus

1 — Park Ji-won, « Conversations écrites avec Gokjeong », dans *Journal du Jehol* (1780), trad. du chinois par Lee Sang-ho, Paju, éditions Bori, 2004, p. 365 (en coréen).

2 — L'exposition « Écho » présente la pièce inédite *Andrea en conversation*, variante d'*Andrea* augmentée de quatre écrans, qui inclut de nouvelles séquences.

3 — Atelier Hermès, Séoul, 11 octobre - 18 décembre 2012.

4 — Il s'agit des archives d'un reportage filmique sur l'initiation chamanique d'Andrea Kalff en Corée du Sud, dont le projet a été abandonné.

5 — Classée « bien culturel intangible » en Corée du Sud, Kim Keum-hwa est la plus célèbre chamane, tant dans son pays qu'à l'étranger. L'une des particularités du chamanisme coréen est d'être presque exclusivement le fait des femmes (leur équivalent masculin est extrêmement rare).

6 — L'ouvrage paraît pour la première fois en 1913, tandis que le film, datant de 1925 (noir et blanc, 117'), livre les toutes premières images cinématographiques de la Corée.

7 — *K. W. Complex. Natacha Nisic, Park Chan-kyong*, Paris, Fondation d'entreprise Hermès, 2013.

8 — *SBS Special : Blue Eyes Possessed by Spirits* (*Des yeux bleus possédés par les esprits*), 54' 41", Séoul, Seoul Broadcasting System, 13 mai 2007. Natacha Nisic signale que le choix, bien qu'Andrea ait les yeux bruns, du titre de ce documentaire réalisé par la télévision coréenne témoigne de la vision stéréotypée des Asiatiques, qui voient dans les Occidentaux des blonds aux yeux bleus.

9 — Cf. *K. W. Complex. Natacha Nisic, Park Chan-kyong, op. cit.*

10 — Dans la tradition, la *kisaeng*, artiste versée dans la poésie, la calligraphie, la peinture et la danse, divertissait les invités lors des beuveries. Avec la modernisation, son rôle s'est réduit à celui de travailleuse sexuelle. Les *kisaeng* ont pratiquement disparu de la Corée moderne. *Kisaeng* et chamane sont toutes deux, du point de vue du genre, des modèles de subalternes modernes.

11 — Extrait d'une interview de Snow-Flower, tiré de *Princess Snow-Flower*.

12 — Snow-Flower entretient un dialogue constant avec cet esprit qu'elle nomme « Grand-Mère ».

13 — Cf. Park No-ja, « Le discours du peuple pendant l'époque des Lumières et l'Autre de l'intérieur », dans *Acceptation et transfiguration du concept de savoir pendant les Lumières*, Séoul, éditions Somyong, 2004 (en coréen).

14 — Cf. la thèse de Chung Yong-nam, *A Study on the Independent Documentary Films about Shamanism : Focusing on "Mudang" and "Between"*, Osan, Graduate School of Han-shin University, Department of Visual Culture Studies, 2007 (en coréen).

15 — Propos d'Andrea soignant une femme dans son sanctuaire, tirés d'*Andrea*.

16 — Cf. Baek Mun-im, *Lamentation d'une fille à Weolha*, Séoul, éditions Chaeksesang, 2008 (en coréen).

[p. 41-72]

17 — Sanctuaire où Kim Keum-hwa pratique le *kut* (le rituel chamanique coréen).

18 — *Samwon*, qui signifie littéralement « trois perspectives » en coréen, renvoie au *kowon* (vue depuis le pied d'une montagne vers le sommet), au *simwon* (vue d'une montagne de face englobant son arrière-plan) et au *pyŏngwon* (vue depuis une montagne sur le paysage qui s'étend au loin entre celle-ci et la montagne située en arrière-plan) et correspond au regard d'un artiste peignant le paysage naturel. À la différence de la perspective scientifique occidentale, la technique du *samwon*, fondement de la peinture de paysage orientale traditionnelle, confère un mouvement dynamique complexe et une beauté spatiale unique à la composition des peintures. *Encyclopedia of Korean Culture*, Seongam, The Academy of Korean Studies (en ligne : http://www.encykorea.com).

19 — Cf. Anselm Franke, « Animism : Notes on an Exhibition », *e-flux Journal*, été 2012.

20 — Récit autobiographique féminin.

21 — Cf. Kim Seong-nae, « A Narrative Analysis of Female Shaman's Oral History », *Korean Women's Study*, vol. 7, 1991.

22 — *Mugam* désigne, pour un ou plusieurs membres du foyer et/ou de l'assistance où se tient un rituel chamanique coréen *(kut)*, le fait de revêtir des costumes chamaniques et de danser au rythme de la cérémonie durant les courts intervalles qui séparent les prestations chamaniques. Puisque le *mugam* est exécuté par des gens ordinaires, il ne comporte pas d'actes réellement chamaniques obéissant à un *kut*, même si ces personnes portent des costumes de chaman et peuvent être en proie à une agitation et à une excitation. Toutefois, il arrive que le pouvoir intérieur propre à un individu s'exprime et que celui-ci vive une expérience hors du commun. *Encyclopedia of Korean Folk Culture*, Séoul, The National Folk Museum of Korea, 2011 (en ligne : http://folkency.nfm.go.kr/eng/index.jsp).

Florent Perrier

> Les poètes, les artistes et toute la race humaine
> seraient bien malheureux, si l'idéal, cette absurdité,
> cette impossibilité, était trouvé. Qu'est-ce
> que chacun ferait désormais de son pauvre moi,
> – de sa ligne brisée?
>
> Charles Baudelaire [1]

De traverser ou subir une catastrophe, on sort aussi
peu indemne que du paradis ; on ne quitte d'ailleurs l'un
que déchu comme on ne réchappe de l'autre qu'en
miraculé.

Il en va de même en matière de représentation.
Figurer un lieu édénique, dépeindre une catastrophe
– des biais, des approches latérales sont nécessaires.
Il faut dévier la frontalité même de l'indescriptible,
faire un pas de côté, s'ouvrir à une voie oblique qui
relève en réalité du sujet traité en ce qu'il nous oblige
à détourner le regard.

La réfraction – *refringere* : briser, casser – appartiendrait
ainsi en propre à la représentation de la catastrophe :
une brisure nécessaire qui offre au regard un
changement de direction, à notre vision du monde une
remise en question : une échappée critique qui, comme
s'y emploie Natacha Nisic, nous laisse voir décalé,
à l'écart, ce qu'un strict reflet laisserait insoutenable,
irreprésentable.

Réfracté, l'implacable de la catastrophe est retardé,
ralenti, troublé ou détourné par une forme d'après-coup
qui lui ôte son autoritaire violence et la dispose
à l'appréhension, à la saisie par l'entendement que
l'imagination soutiendra pour recomposer ce qu'une
image brute aurait de trop obscène, de suffocant.

Redoublé par ses moyens d'expression, cet après-
coup est geste de l'artiste : passage à un milieu
de réfringence, de résistance différente qui déplace
la vision première et réoriente le regard – décollement
de la représentation de l'événement même qui ménage
dès lors, avec d'autres œuvres, en d'autres temps
ou d'autres lieux, des possibilités de dialogues libérés
de l'emprise étouffante de l'actualité.

Ainsi ce lavis de Denis-Auguste-Marie Raffet,
où l'après-coup se fait mise en série de corps mutilés,
tronçons d'êtres humains brûlés recueillis après

la première catastrophe de l'histoire du chemin de fer, le 8 mai 1842. Réfracté, le montage de « corps sans histoire » devient annonciateur de désastres à venir, sidérante esquisse où l'événement inaugural des noces mortelles entre techniques et transports de masse contient ses plus funestes prolongements[2].

« Des corps sans histoire », tels furent aussi pour Paul Gauguin les hommes et femmes peints sur les toiles rêches de son ultime séjour aux Marquises quand, après avoir quitté l'île encore trop policée de Tahiti, il s'y réfugia en septembre 1901. Dix années plus tôt, il affirmait partir en Polynésie « pour être tranquille, pour être débarrassé de l'influence de la civilisation » et ne s'adonner qu'à « de l'art simple » au milieu d'une nature vierge[3].

Là, il multiplia les œuvres dédiées à l'Ève exotique, les évocations paradisiaques de *jours délicieux*. La figure classique de la décadence de l'Occident s'accompagne d'un retrait dans une île du bonheur et, lorsqu'il colle sous la reliure de son manuscrit *L'Esprit moderne et le catholicisme* la gravure sur bois intitulée *Paradis perdu*, il identifie sans détour « la colonisation et le péché originel, l'Occident et l'arbre de science corrupteur[4] ».

L'échange acerbe avec August Strindberg en fut une confirmation : « Vous avez créé une nouvelle terre, et un nouveau ciel, mais je ne me plais pas au milieu de votre création [...] et dans votre paradis habite une Ève qui n'est pas mon idéal » – à quoi Gauguin répondit que le rejet de sa peinture trahissait « tout un choc entre votre civilisation et ma barbarie. Civilisation dont vous souffrez, barbarie qui est pour moi un rajeunissement[5]. »

Un mois avant sa mort, isolé et malade, il revendiquait toujours son éloignement volontaire de la civilisation comme la nécessité de désapprendre en sauvage une histoire devenue trop lourde[6], grevée d'entraves à la saisie instinctive d'une grâce supérieure qu'il percevait chez ses hôtes insulaires.

Ceci explique pourquoi les corps peints par Gauguin lui semblaient d'or, ceux d'un âge d'or rêvé, mais cependant encore tangible pour lui, trace vive d'un Éden vécu et dont le titre du tableau de 1901, *Et l'or de leur corps*, forme la cristallisation.

Du « corps doré presque nu[7] » de la petite Vaitauni à la peau « jaune doré[8] » des insulaires, Gauguin exalte la pudique sensualité des Polynésiens, dont l'innocence parfois espiègle contraste avec toute la pourriture civilisée qu'il exècre et fustige. Ce rapport à l'impureté, il l'entretint pourtant à sa manière lorsqu'il fut d'abord un agent parmi d'autres de la colonisation [9], mais il la portait surtout sur lui, cette pourriture, à la fin de sa vie, les plaies de ses jambes rongées par l'eczéma et marquées par une syphilis ramenée d'Europe qui le donnait pour lépreux. Pire encore, ce qui était visible sur lui à son corps défendant, cette catastrophe appelée « civilisation » dont il ne pouvait s'abstraire, il la savait violemment présente dans cette culture qu'il fantasmait vierge de tous les maux occidentaux :

> Bientôt le Marquisien sera incapable de monter à un cocotier, incapable d'aller dans la montagne chercher les bananes sauvages qui peuvent le nourrir. L'enfant retenu à l'école, privé d'exercices corporels, le corps (histoire de décence) toujours vêtu, devient délicat, incapable de supporter la nuit dans la montagne. Ils commencent à porter tous des souliers, et leurs pieds, désormais fragiles, ne pourront courir dans les rudes sentiers, traverser les torrents sur des cailloux. Aussi nous assistons à ce triste spectacle qui est l'extinction de la race en grande partie poitrinaire, les reins inféconds et les ovaires détruits par le mercure [10].

Sous l'or de leur corps, une pourriture à l'œuvre donc, un peuple voué à la disparition, une catastrophe sans mesure pour des êtres passés depuis lors à l'imaginaire.

Aussitôt découvert, le dessin de Natacha Nisic fut associé dans mon esprit au titre du tableau de Gauguin *Et l'or de leur corps*.

Intuition d'une même pourriture qui couve sous des dehors intacts ? Relation immédiate entre la sous-jacence d'un mal invisible au travail et une représentation exempte de toute violence directe ? Ou bien l'or, l'or de leur corps, des corps eux aussi sans histoire, abstraits, désindividualisés, sauf à considérer le titre de cette pièce – *Fukushima* [11].

Un dessin associé au titre d'un tableau qui lui est antérieur de plus d'un siècle mais aussi, hasard objectif, le titre du premier intimement lié au contenu du second, une histoire de réfraction en somme, de regards déviés, voire l'effraction intempestive d'une œuvre au cœur d'une autre : résonance ou constellation, hospitalité ou corps étranger – une rencontre.

Sur un fort papier Canson d'un blanc immaculé travaillé en rouleau – la vision du dessin en cours d'exécution était donc toujours parcellaire, fragmentée, masquée par les retours du papier sur lui-même – subsistent de rares traits d'esquisses au crayon

[p. 127-132]
+
[fig. 4, p. 137] Natacha Nisic, *Fukushima*, 2011, crayon de couleur sur papier Canson, 75 × 315 cm

maigre : formes générales, contours partiellement effacés, repentirs ici ou là. Ces traits d'esquisses sont les seules lignes prolongées du dessin, les seules lignes tenues (mais vouées à disparaître), car le dessin n'est en lui-même composé que de stries ou de raies, de traits suspendus aussitôt après avoir été entamés, des bâtons si l'on veut, non pas des touches, mais les marques scrupuleuses d'un retour régulier du crayon sur la feuille, un battement ou une pulsation, la dispersion de traces parallèles organisées en aires successives et déposées selon un rythme immuable, implacable – se propageant, contaminant par taches toute l'étendue assignée au motif.

Cette texture sans fond sinon le blanc du papier, une texture sans trame donc, flottement ou émergence, vibration d'un miroitement, a ceci de singulier qu'elle est exclusivement faite avec des crayons métalliques luminescents dans le noir – ainsi les lucioles, luminescentes elles aussi.

Dans la boîte de douze crayons, de l'étain, du cuivre ou de l'argent côtoient l'or et l'or antique, l'usage de ces dernières teintes ayant suscité l'association avec *Et l'or de leur corps*.

Comprendre pourquoi Natacha Nisic a choisi ces crayons pour représenter la catastrophe de Fukushima survenue depuis le 11 mars 2011, c'est d'abord faire retour sur un parcours où la catastrophe et ses modes de représentation sont interrogés avec une rigueur grande.

En 2005, Natacha Nisic se rend au camp d'extermination d'Auschwitz où elle filme *La Porte de Birkenau* avec un travelling compensé qui laisse une impression de trouble, de tension irrésolue, comme si l'étale avait été saisi dans l'impossibilité même de son mouvement et avant et après tout déferlement de violence, impression renforcée au Mémorial de la Shoah, où l'œuvre est projetée en permanence, par l'utilisation de deux écrans séparés par un passage, ligne brisée où s'immisce la vie, le mouvement : matérialisation d'une réfraction, progression entre milieux de réfringence différente.

Dans le même lieu, l'artiste a mis en espace le *Mémorial des enfants* à partir des archives photographiques patiemment recueillies par Serge Klarsfeld. Natacha Nisic avait alors souhaité créer une pulsation lumineuse imperceptible, détail non réalisé mais qui consonne avec l'utilisation de crayons luminescents pour *Fukushima*, soit un travail minutieux sur la luminosité, la différence de densité lumineuse propre à toute réfraction.

[fig. 5, p. 137]   Natacha Nisic, *La Porte de Birkenau*, 2005, projection vidéo HD, couleur, 3'

[fig. 6, p. 137]   Natacha Nisic, *Mémorial des enfants*, 2005, 3 500 impressions numériques sur lais de papier Arche contrecollés sur panneaux de Macrolife rétro-éclairés sur structure acier, 120 m², Mémorial de la Shoah, Paris

Avec *La Porte de Birkenau*, Natacha Nisic tourne
et photographie en outre à Auschwitz ce qui deviendra
Effroi, marche d'exorcisme aux abords et à l'intérieur
du camp d'extermination, ses vestiges, et où le choc entre
le cadre apaisé des lieux et le savoir comme le souvenir
de ce dont ils furent le théâtre, et restent le réceptacle,
prend forme sous l'espèce d'un masque mortuaire
émergeant à la surface d'une étendue d'eau artificielle,
informe chimère, spectre effroyable que la réfraction,
encore ici au travail, le trouble des plans mêlés rend plus
encore énigmatique. Si l'artiste a photographié une
surface de réflexion – « les surfaces d'eau où le ciel
et le paysage se reflètent dans une quiétude, une beauté
indécente. La mare entourée de bouleaux ressemble
à un paysage serein, une nature paisible. La mare est
située au pied de la chambre à gaz. Pas d'eau pure,
elle contient les cendres des corps, c'est pourtant un
miroir parfait du monde [12] » –, sa volonté de « saisir plus
encore la densité de l'eau » comme le surgissement
du masque mortuaire, mi-émergé mi-englouti, et la
distorsion visuelle qui en résulte, déplacent son geste du
domaine de la réflexion à celui de la réfraction : de la
ligne droite, l'insoutenable ligne droite, à la ligne brisée.

Un détail l'indique dans le catalogue *Effroi* lorsque
l'artiste précise qu'après la découverte du spectre
aqueux, elle revint à Auschwitz pour « tenter d'exorciser
ce jeu du sort », songeant d'abord à filmer l'action :

> L'action consiste à retourner près du réservoir
> (au départ, j'imagine porter une sorte de masque
> translucide garantissant l'anonymat et l'universalité
> du geste, une surface, une distance entre le corps
> et les éléments), et plonger mon visage recouvert
> du masque dans cette eau. De la vie rendue
> à la surface de l'eau et à ce qu'elle contient [13].

Entre la tête masquée plongée sous la surface de l'eau
et le corps extérieur à l'élément liquide, la réalité
est déviée, la réfraction à l'œuvre, la vision bouleversée.

Et comment ne pas associer ici le masque mortuaire
du réservoir d'Auschwitz à celui, translucide, qu'aurait
voulu porter l'artiste en réponse à l'effroi, comment
ne pas associer ces masques confondus et se mêlant
– la mort anonyme, la mort effroyable – à ceux qu'arborent
les hommes du dessin *Fukushima* ?

En juin 2008, Natacha Nisic se rend précisément
dans cette région du Japon où un tremblement de
terre très puissant vient de bouleverser de somptueux
paysages de montagne. Avec cette catastrophe

103

[fig. 8, p. 138]   Natacha Nisic, *e*,
2009, 3 projections vidéo HD,
couleur, son 5.1, 19' chacune.
Vue de l'exposition « Big Picture
(Orte / Projektionen) »,
K21 Kunstsammlung Nordrhein-
Westfalen, Düsseldorf, 2011
+
[p. 156-184]

[fig. 9, p. 138]   Jean-Luc Godard
et Anne-Marie Miéville,
De l'origine du XXIe siècle, 2000,
vidéo, couleur, 16'

[p. 143-156]

aujourd'hui oubliée, déjà dépassée, c'est la nature vierge évoquée par Gauguin qui est atteinte en son cœur même. *e* – image en japonais –, l'installation de l'artiste, revient après coup sur ce qui eut lieu comme en secret, non sans affecter les hommes, leurs structures ou modes de vie, mais avec un éloignement tel des zones fortement habitées que le désastre passa presque inaperçu, ne laissant ici et là que quelques lignes brisées, traces tangibles d'une réfraction sismique dans les profondeurs. *Le Monde* notait alors que, « selon des déclarations officielles, les activités des centrales nucléaires n'ont pas été affectées. Néanmoins, dans la province de Fukushima, une *"petite quantité d'eau radioactive"* s'est échappée d'un centre de stockage d'un site nucléaire à la suite du séisme, *"mais sans danger pour la population"*, a annoncé la compagnie d'électricité Tepco qui gère la centrale nucléaire de Fukushima [14]. »

Des crayons métalliques pour représenter la catastrophe de mars 2011, des teintes dorées, mordorées ou moirées, un miroitement, une pulsation lumineuse cernés par un contour sans bords véritables, mais nul épanchement ni débordement, aucune inquiétude sensible – l'éblouissement seul de traits sans histoire ?

Fukushima réfracte pourtant notre regard vers l'immense archive d'images de catastrophes antérieures : du sublime éclat du soleil nucléaire aux champs colorés d'explosions de napalm, Natacha Nisic recueille la trace d'éblouissements passés devenus ici fragmentés, émaillés en une infinité de stridences visuelles – échardes du souvenir entées sur l'œil ouvert, sur la pupille interdite [15].

Si, elle le souligne au sujet de la représentation de la Shoah, sa sensibilité lui fait aborder « les choses de biais plutôt que frontalement [16] », c'est bien que la catastrophe ne peut être regardée en face, il faut en dévier l'incidence, lui opposer un milieu réfringent plus dense, d'une épaisseur historique ou sensible qui n'en relativise pas la singularité présente, mais la rend au contraire absolument distincte par la confrontation, la traversée des époques comme des événements.

Le dispositif retenu pour *f* en est en creux l'illustration. Pour cette pièce tournée dans la région de Fukushima en 2013, Natacha Nisic nous expose, par un jeu de miroirs d'apparence élémentaire, à une suite de confrontations moins avec le paysage de la catastrophe qu'avec le monde évidé d'après la catastrophe. De renvois en répercussions – boucles visuelles parcourues tel un ruban de Möbius, éternel retour –, l'écho du monde ne se livre que dos tourné à son mouvement : sens de lecture perturbé, visions décalées, présent maintenu en énigme ou flottement de l'espace comme du temps, à l'image de ces fils, ces cordes sans pendus qui errent au gré du vent.

La réfraction se fait ici l'écho du reflet, soit ce vers quoi, hors champ, l'artiste déplace notre regard et l'ouvre par l'écart ainsi ménagé – non pas un regard pétrifié par le strict reflet (de la catastrophe), mais son autre inquiété, mouvementé par ce décentrement, cette disjointure.

Source d'erreurs, la réfraction a ses vices qui faussent l'observation [17], déforment la vision [18] et provoquent des déviations latérales [19] trompeuses en topographie. Dans *Le Problème de la réfraction dans l'histoire du cartésianisme*, l'auteur note que « la connaissance de la loi fondamentale de la réfraction » permit seule d'améliorer « la fabrication des lentilles employées dans les télescopes. L'enjeu du problème, du point de vue spéculatif, [étant] la confirmation triomphante de l'héliocentrisme par l'observation [20]. »

À travers la détection de ces erreurs ou vices de réfraction qui séparent le normal du pathologique, le droit du déviant, c'est notre vision du monde qui est donc en jeu.

Mais l'art est résistant comme l'artiste est réfractaire, ils jouent de l'écart ou de la ligne brisée pour renverser tout héliocentrisme triomphant comme ici le soleil nucléaire auquel rien ni personne, à en croire la vulgate contemporaine, ne devrait pouvoir se soustraire.

Pourtant Fukushima, Fukushima répété : un affairement d'hommes en combinaison, vraie danse macabre d'êtres en sursis sous leurs maigres protections. Comme au XIVe siècle, la chaîne des morts et des vifs ne s'interrompt pas ; ce ne sont cependant pas les membres qui assurent le contact, mais l'organisation même de la matière graphique que la couleur seule comme la densité, l'intensité du trait, distinguent en formes et figures. Le dessin s'apparente à un bas-relief [21], interprétation renforcée par la rectitude des poses, leur hiératisme. À le scruter, cette compacité-là se délite pourtant, mais dans le fond seul qui passe d'un assemblage de formes dures, géométriques, à leur dissolution progressive, formes archipéliques progressivement absorbées par le blanc de la feuille. De même, si les formes arrêtées sont rendues par des traits orientés avec ordre, celles plus organiques le sont selon un tressage plus changeant, miroitement ou grouillement plutôt qu'alignement.

Les figures ne connaissent, elles, guère de variation, les corps sont presque tous à la même hauteur, comme nivelés par le format du dessin que leur verticalité étaie. Cette égalité symbolique n'est toutefois que factice ; les masques arborés protègent ceux qui restent vivants, debout pour un temps peut-être limité, les moins lotis étant déjà à terre, morts sans doute. Quand le cataclysme produit une forme d'égalité parfaite, nul ne pouvant obvier à sa soudaineté, la catastrophe industrielle ou technologique renforce à l'inverse les hiérarchies sociales et économiques. À Fukushima, où l'on dénombra d'abord près de trente mille morts, les populations eurent seules la responsabilité de fuir les zones sinistrées, les gouvernants ne leur laissant que la liberté d'être riches pour évacuer ou pauvres pour mourir sans histoire. Les liquidateurs y proviennent en outre d'un sous-prolétariat séculaire issu « des castes les plus méprisées du Japon. Descendant des communautés *eta* – littéralement "plein de souillures" – et *hinin* – "non humains" –, les *burakumin* [...] sont traditionnellement tenus à l'écart et remplissent les tâches liées à la mort, au sang, à l'impureté[22]. »

Derrière ces six masques aux vibrations chatoyantes, derrière ces figures engoncées, ces yeux que l'on ne voit pas et ces regards aux directions incertaines, il y aurait donc le savoir, le savoir doublé du pouvoir, en position de surplomb, spectres défilant à l'orée d'une moderne caverne platonicienne où au soleil des idées se seraient substitués le feu nucléaire et sa réalité – morbide –, sa vérité – mensongère.

Ce mirage généralisé orchestré par Tepco et relayé par le pouvoir narcotique de médias complices d'un État défaillant, le dessin de Natacha Nisic ne le traite pas seulement sous l'espèce du mutisme, mais d'un autisme, un aveuglement qui n'est pas sans rappeler le nom de l'atoll polynésien où furent expérimentées les armes de la dissuasion nucléaire française – Mururoa, « le grand secret » en maori[23].

Paul Gauguin est précisément en Polynésie française lorsque Marie Curie, à Paris, invente le terme de « radioactivité » (1898) et c'est au moment même où Jean Perrin imagine une représentation des atomes comme des systèmes solaires en miniature qu'il peint *Et l'or de leur corps*.

Réfractions *Fukushima* ?

Fukushima, en japonais : « l'île du bonheur ».

1 — « Salon de 1846 », dans *Curiosités esthétiques*, Paris, Garnier, 1962, p. 147.

2 — Cf. mon article « Des corps sans histoire – théâtres de l'imprévisible », *Recherches en esthétique*, n° 15, octobre 2009, p. 29-40.

3 — Entretien à *L'Écho de Paris*, cité par Bengt Danielsson, « Gauguin à la recherche de la Polynésie d'autrefois », dans *Gauguin*, actes du colloque du musée d'Orsay (11-13 janvier 1989), Paris, La Documentation française, 1989, p. 245.

4 — Françoise Cachin, *Gauguin*, Paris, Flammarion, 1988, p. 233.

5 — Cité par Françoise Cachin, *ibid.*, p. 210.

6 — Cf. Paul Gauguin, *Lettres à sa femme et à ses amis*, Paris, Grasset, 1992, p. 339.

7 — Paul Gauguin, *Avant et après*, Papeete, Avant et après, 2003, p. 12.

8 — *Ibid.*, p. 76.

9 — Vêtu d'habits coloniaux blancs immaculés, fréquentant le Cercle militaire de Papeete, refusant d'être admis à l'hôpital avec les indigents, il fut aussi un temps dessinateur au Bureau des travaux publics.

10 — Paul Gauguin, *Avant et après*, *op. cit.*, p. 77.

11 — Ce dessin mesure 75 × 315 centimètres et fut montré pour la première fois en avril 2012 à la galerie Dominique Fiat, Paris.

12 — Natacha Nisic, « Ce qui reste », dans Annette Becker, Octave Debary (dir.), *Montrer les violences extrêmes*, Paris, Créaphis, 2012, p. 147-148.

13 — Natacha Nisic dans le catalogue de son exposition « Effroi », Paris, musée Zadkine / Paris-Musées, 2005, n. p.

14 — Édition du 14 juin 2008.

15 — Ici remanié, cet article fut d'abord une contribution au colloque « Penser la catastrophe », organisé par Alain Fleischer et Jean-Claude Conésa (que je remercie) au Fresnoy – Studio national des arts contemporains en janvier 2013. Celle-ci comportait une section où la place de l'or dans certaines œuvres contemporaines était mise en relation avec le dessin de Natacha Nisic ; citons seulement les noms d'Alain Resnais et Marguerite Duras, d'Yves Klein et Robert Rauschenberg, de Gérard Deschamps et Jean-Luc Godard.

16 — Natacha Nisic, « Spectre », entretien avec Nathan Réra, dans N. Réra (dir.), *De Paris à Drancy ou les Possibilités de l'art après Auschwitz*, Pertuis, Rouge profond, 2009, p. 71.

17 — Ils furent en cela objet d'études pour comprendre l'originalité des peintres. Cf. la thèse d'Aron Polack, *Rôle de l'état de réfraction de l'œil dans l'éducation et dans l'œuvre du peintre* (Paris, Librairie Ollier-Henry, 1900), qui a notamment observé les yeux d'Émile Bernard, Eugène Carrière ou Jean-Léon Gérôme.

18 — Cf. la thèse de Denis-Félix Bodet, *Des vices de réfraction, de l'acuité visuelle, du sens chromatique et du sens visuel dans l'armée et la marine*, Bordeaux, Paul Cassignol, 1905.

19 — Charles Lallemand, « L'erreur de réfraction dans le nivellement géométrique », *Rivista di topografia e catasto*, Turin, Bona, 1897, vol. 9, p. 5.

20 — Marie-Claire Macris-L'Hoest, *Le Problème de la réfraction dans l'histoire du cartésianisme*, thèse dirigée par Suzanne Bachelard, université Paris-I Panthéon-Sorbonne, 1983-1984, p. 18.

21 — On sait l'influence des photographies de frises classiques, grecques ou indiennes, chez Gauguin.

22 — Arkadi Filine, *Oublier Fukushima. Textes et documents*, Le Mas-d'Azil, Les Éditions du bout de la ville, 2012, p. 57-58.

23 — L'étymologie première est « grande nasse », mais l'on comprend que, par extension, « ce qui retient en grand dans ses filets », associé au règne du « secret-défense », ait pu signifier « le grand secret ».

ENTRETIEN AVEC NATACHA NISIC
Marta Gili

M. G. : D'après Héraclite, la vraie nature des choses
est occulte. Pourtant, nous nous efforçons en permanence
de comprendre et de « déchiffrer » ce qui sépare l'occulte
du visible. La science et la religion tentent aussi
d'apporter des réponses à certaines de ces questions.
Mais quel est, selon toi, le rôle du discours artistique ?

N. N. : Comme tu le soulignes, nous nous efforçons de
comprendre le monde : j'aime beaucoup cette expression
car elle contient en elle sa propre négation. Cela peut
être pris avec humour, humilité ou profond désespoir,
mais c'est une donnée, celle du manque. L'art est
lacunaire, il ne professe pas, ne démontre pas, n'inscrit
ni pensée ni geste dans un mouvement globalisateur.
Lorsque j'ai commencé le *Catalogue de gestes* en 1995,
j'avais en tête les visions à tentation exhaustive
de registres nosographiques ou les photographies
des planches d'Eadweard Muybridge, mais aussi l'*Atlas*
de Gerhard Richter : un mélange d'admiration et de
recul à l'idée même du projet d'exhaustivité des formes,
de complétude des savoirs. Le *Catalogue de gestes*
devait ainsi contenir en sa conception un principe
contradictoire : la promesse d'une sorte d'exhaustivité,
comme dans « cataloguer », « faire l'inventaire »,
et son impossibilité même en décidant d'en faire une
œuvre ouverte, potentiellement incomplète. La forme
conceptuelle de cette œuvre constitue comme
un paradigme de ce que je conçois comme activité
artistique : un *double bind* entre la volonté de figer,
de marquer dans un temps précis, et cette impossibilité
même car fugitive, éphémère, simple et vaine.

M. G. : Dans la plupart de tes œuvres, la recherche de
spiritualité ou de forces occultes se présente non comme
une forme de détachement ou une fuite de la réalité,
mais comme une immanence, une affirmation de
l'indissociabilité du visible et de l'invisible. Si cette
dimension, me semble-t-il, est présente dès le *Catalogue
de gestes*, elle devient plus évidente encore dans
tes derniers travaux.

N. N. : Dans le cas de mes œuvres plus récentes,
qui mettent en jeu la représentation de mondes religieux,
l'ensemble de ces questionnements prend une valeur
supplémentaire. Giorgio Agamben note que le rite

[p. 10 + 15-25]

[p. 37 + 72-78]

[fig. 1, p. 188]   Natacha Nisic,
« Attitudes », la salle d'attente n° 1,
1997, 16 sièges en toile
et aluminium, 5 projections vidéo,
couleur, 10' chacune.
Vue de l'exposition « Remise
en forme », galerie Xippas, Paris,
1997-1998

[fig. 2, p. 188]   Natacha Nisic,
« Attitudes », la salle de projection,
1999, 20 fauteuils de cinéma,
3 projections vidéo, couleur,
42' chacune, moniteur et caméra
de surveillance.
Vue de l'exposition « La salle
de projection », L'atelier, Centre
national de la photographie,
Paris, 1999

est le lieu de l'association d'un récit et d'un geste ; sans ce lien fondamental, le geste perd tout sens et toute raison d'être. Or que ce soit pour *Carmel* (2008), *Princess Snow-Flower* (2011) ou plus récemment *Andrea* (2012), j'ai filmé des situations pour lesquelles je n'avais pas ou peu d'accès au récit liturgique, au corps sémantique du rite. Par exemple, en Corée du Sud, sur une île située à cinquante kilomètres de Séoul, j'ai filmé une femme dont on m'avait dit qu'elle était chamane (*Princess Snow-Flower*). Elle était très volubile mais je ne comprenais ni ses actes ni ses paroles ; je ne voyais que son corps soumis à des tensions violentes. J'ai filmé sans savoir, comme si les gestes allaient m'apporter une réponse à l'inintelligibilité de la situation, des gestes sans récit, pris tels quels dans l'intensité de leur mouvement. J'avais par ailleurs vécu une situation quasi similaire dans le couvent des carmélites de Lisieux. Mon peu d'éducation chrétienne inscrivait l'ensemble du déploiement des gestes rituels des sœurs dans une histoire qui me rattache à celle de la peinture ou du cinéma. Je pense à Alain Cavalier ou à Robert Bresson. Cette mise à nu d'un « en-soi du corps », sans récit, muet, a été une ligne de conduite dans l'élaboration du *Catalogue de gestes*, mais aussi de nombreuses pièces qui ont immédiatement suivi comme *« Attitudes », la salle d'attente n° 1* (1997) et *« Attitudes », la salle de projection* (1999). Dans ces deux pièces, les corps de personnes en situation d'attente ou d'attention devant un film invisible sont projetés sur des sièges. Le visiteur peut s'associer à cette communauté fictive en s'asseyant sur le siège, mais il s'agit avant tout d'opérer un montage d'associations de gestes sans récit, réduits à leurs fonctions « pures », désolidarisés de tout contexte explicite.

Ainsi, que ce soit dans mes pièces anciennes ou plus récentes, deux mouvements tendent, paradoxalement, vers le même souci de défragmentation du réel. Le premier se sert des formes du langage sacré et rituel, dont il s'agit de dissocier une première strate de récit, et le second s'attache au quotidien le plus banal, décontextualisant les gestes et attitudes qui nous entourent, pour les rendre accessibles à une nouvelle forme de récit. Ils se sacralisent ainsi, non pas dans une forme religieuse figée, mais dans un nouveau registre d'association, comme une émergence, une fracture de l'inconscient.

M. G. : Une sorte de rupture s'opère très nettement dans ta démarche avec le dispositif de narration de tes

[p. 138 + 156-184]

dernières installations, où le récit se présente en plusieurs temps et instants.

N. N. : Ce qui s'affirme dans mes dernières œuvres – depuis *e* en particulier, réalisée en 2009 – est la tentation d'une forme de récit qui associerait la parole aux êtres et aux paysages. Dans le cas de *e* se déploient trois temps de ce récit, l'avant de la catastrophe qui contient une part d'insouciance, le temps suspendu où « cela » se passe, qui est un temps subjectif paradoxal car les quelques secondes du tremblement de terre sont vécues comme une éternité par ceux qui le subissent, et l'après, qui est un temps qui porte les stigmates visibles ou invisibles de l'événement et doit se redéfinir, se réinventer. La linéarité de ce récit en trois temps n'est qu'un effet de surface, une construction abstraite qui ne peut se produire qu'avec une distance extérieure ou lointaine comme celle du témoin, de l'étranger, ou avec une distance temporelle suffisante. C'est un effet de perspective, c'est-à-dire une construction du récit où des lignes de fuite et des axes peuvent se réunir en un ou plusieurs points, quelque chose de la diffraction et de la brisure peut ainsi se reconstruire. Le dispositif de l'installation en trois écrans simultanés demande au spectateur de se saisir des sens multiples, de choisir et d'associer les éléments d'un montage subjectif dans une situation de seuil : à l'incomplétude inhérente au dispositif s'associent des éléments englobants tels que le son, mêlant des ambiances de nature, avec oiseaux et insectes stridents, et des fréquences graves quasi telluriques. Le mouvement de retrait par rapport à l'incomplétude du sens est compensé par d'autres éléments du langage des formes et des sons.

M. G. : Dans « Notes sur le geste[1] », Giorgio Agamben, que tu as cité, décrit l'invention du cinéma comme un acte de sauvegarde et d'enregistrement de gestes qui, autrement, seraient perdus. Est-ce que tu te considères aussi comme une archéologue du geste ?

[p. 10]

N. N. : À partir de 2007, j'ai réalisé *Nord*, un travail dans le Nord de la France, dans la région de Lille-Roubaix, qui porte les stigmates d'une grandeur économique désormais disparue. De façon intuitive, il m'a semblé que les corps résistaient à la ruine. Les gestes, en se greffant à un rituel, à une tradition, comme dans le cas des combats de coqs, ou dans une relation étroite avec le travail, notamment celui du textile, échafauderaient un récit singulier qui s'affirmerait comme une résistance.

[p. 170-171]

[p. 11 + p. 138]

Dans la pièce *e*, j'ai également filmé le geste suspendu d'un très grand maître de kabuki, Ichikawa Danjûrô XII, dans un temps suspendu de l'action qui se nomme *mie*. Ce geste semblait signifier le point paroxystique de la catastrophe, mais aussi la mémoire des gestes passés et à venir.

M. G. : Qu'est-ce que la « mémoire suggestive », dont tu as fait mention lors de ton exposition intitulée « Effroi » au musée Zadkine, en 2005 ?

N. N. : Le mot « effroi » est celui qui m'est venu à l'esprit lorsque j'ai découvert, après agrandissement, la figure qui se trouve au centre de la photographie d'un réservoir situé le long des rails du camp de Birkenau. C'est une figure sans visage, un spectre dont je n'ai pu expliquer ni la présence ni la forme et qui agit, un peu comme dans le film *Blow-Up* de Michelangelo Antonioni, comme un point de non-retour, un point mort de la vision tel que « derrière chaque image se cache un meurtre ». À Auschwitz, dans chaque morceau de terre, dans chaque goutte d'eau se cache la cendre. L'image dans ce réservoir n'a pas de corps ni de nom, elle se trouve à fleur de perception, de réflexion.

M. G. : Tu appartiens à une génération d'artistes contemporains qui interrogent les problématiques de la représentation à travers une grande variété de supports, les images fixes et en mouvement, le langage et la narration… Comment situes-tu ton travail par rapport aux artistes de cette génération ?

N. N. : Je suis née un an avant 1968, je pense que les années de mon enfance ont été baignées dans un monde de profondes transitions : un monde conservateur en train de s'effriter, comme par exemple les modèles familiaux, les codes des valeurs morales, éducatives, culturelles, et un mouvement utopique, ou tout au moins une aspiration à une forme de liberté, dans lequel mes parents ont été impliqués à titre personnel, comme dans une vague, le *Zeitgeist* auquel on n'échappe pas. Puis, dans le courant des années 1980, mon père a été un des précurseurs en France des expérimentations faites avec la vidéo, ce que l'on nomme à présent « art vidéo », il a réalisé ensuite des documentaires. Je retiens de ce temps un double mouvement : celui d'une diffraction libératrice, mue par un désir utopique fort, qui contient dans le même temps un éclatement auquel sont liées séparations, ruptures.

Un double mouvement que j'ai retrouvé lors de situations et d'événements historiques fondateurs pour moi : la chute du mur de Berlin, où je me trouvais pour faire une partie de mes études, puis la guerre de Yougoslavie que nous avons subie très fortement malgré la distance géographique. Ce sont des passages, de la guerre froide au monde « globalisé », d'un monde d'information et de production d'images binaires à une pléthore de modes et de possibilités de représentation, de diffusion. À cela se sont greffées très naturellement les questions théoriques sur la notion de représentation, sachant qu'il n'y avait pas d'« a-idéologie » des images. J'ai ainsi partagé les œuvres et préoccupations de réalisateurs ou d'artistes comme Harun Farocki, Hartmut Bitomsky, Aurelia Mihai et Maja Bajevic, ou encore Gillian Wearing et Eija-Liisa Ahtila.

Puis il y eut le Japon, rencontre qui a été décisive dès 1999. Je n'ai cessé depuis de tisser toutes sortes de liens, que cela soit par les séjours ou les collaborations artistiques, comme avec le compositeur Jean-Luc Hervé, la chorégraphe Mié Coquempot. C'est aussi au Japon que j'ai rencontré Park Chan-kyong. J'ai partagé son regard sur les rapports de forces historiques et idéologiques, la frontière, la guerre, la religion, autant de sujets importants et qui me parlent d'un monde qui n'a pas vraiment fait la transition avec la guerre froide, où plusieurs temporalités historiques cohabitent encore.

M. G. : J'ai eu l'occasion d'exposer le travail, au Jeu de Paume et ailleurs, de plusieurs des artistes dont tu dis te sentir proche : Maja Bajevic, Harun Farocki, Gillian Wearing, Eija-Liisa Ahtila. Je vois des problématiques qui te rapprochent en particulier de ces deux dernières artistes, comme les échanges d'identités (par exemple dans *10-16*, que Wearing a réalisé en 1997) ou les rituels de réparation à travers plusieurs temporalités (je pense à la pièce *Where is Where?* d'Ahtila de 2008)…

[fig. 3, p. 188]   Gillian Wearing, *10-16*, 1997, projection vidéo, couleur, son, 15'

N. N. : Le dispositif de *10-16* permute les genres et les âges. Wearing invente les modalités du rituel de passage à la parole et crée un écart qui ressemble au travail de la psychanalyse ; il y a révélation, trouble et peut-être réparation. Ce qui est caché, inavouable, se déclare. Je pense aux sœurs du Carmel qui *a contrario* ont fait vœu de silence. Silence qui habite mon regard sur les lieux de *Princess Snow-Flower*. Les objets hétéroclites, les paysages où se côtoient ruines agricoles et constructions modernes kitsch sont les seuls

[fig. 4, p. 188]   Eija-Liisa Ahtila,
Where is Where ?, 2008,
6 projections vidéo HD, 16/9,
couleur, son DD 7.1, 52'

[p. 36-37]

[p. 41-72]

[fig. 5, p. 189]   Natacha Nisic,
Le Ciel d'Andrea, photographie
de tournage, juillet 2013

« vestiges » d'une parole qui ne peut pas émerger : que cela soit par la « clôture » du monastère ou celle de la langue. Dans *Where is Where ?*, Eija-Liisa Ahtila met en scène des éléments de la culture historique refoulée de la France. Elle porte un regard de l'autre sur l'autre, cette distance lui permet un discours critique qui a difficilement sa place en France ; c'est une position dans laquelle je me reconnais.

M. G. : Qui est Andrea, cette femme aux multiples histoires qui se tissent de l'Occident à l'Orient, du visible à l'invisible, du descriptible à l'indescriptible ?

N. N. : Andrea est la fille spirituelle de Kim Keum-hwa, une chamane célèbre mais aussi un « bien culturel vivant » en Corée. Andrea est allemande et vit en Bavière, je l'ai rencontrée à la suite de mes voyages en Corée, où Park Chan-kyong m'a parlé d'elle. Après une première installation, *Andrea*, j'ai décidé en 2013 de compléter et d'étendre le récit de sa vie et des forces étranges qui l'entourent dans la pièce *Andrea en conversation* et dans un long métrage documentaire, *Le Ciel d'Andrea*. Ces différentes œuvres mettent en scène et en espace les circonstances hors du commun qui ont conduit Andrea à devenir une chamane coréenne. Une révolution personnelle et culturelle dont l'enjeu est celui de la vie ou de la mort.

Andrea est une figure centrale, entre deux mondes qui se font face : l'Europe occidentale, héritière d'une pensée rationaliste des Lumières, qui n'a de cesse de tenter de consolider le concept de civilisation, socle d'une société aux frontières plus ou moins poreuses avec ce qu'elle a désigné comme barbare depuis la Grèce antique. Et l'Orient, figure lointaine masquée par les tentations de l'orientalisme, une lecture de l'Autre, inaccessible, parfois effrayant, mais séduisant d'exotisme. Le chemin d'Andrea est inédit, il fait se côtoyer notre panthéon classique, son propre héritage catholique ainsi qu'une cosmologie complexe et riche venue de Chine et de Corée.

En Corée du Sud, le chamanisme est une poche de résistance face aux violences de l'histoire. Les chamanes sont avant tout des figures de femmes. Être chamane est un ostracisme, mais c'est aussi une place, un rôle social reconnu, une force dans un monde patrilinéaire dessiné par les hommes.

Filmer Andrea est une façon de penser la place du couple filmeur-filmé, et par là même celle du spectateur. Une part de la vie d'Andrea reste inexpliquée, mystérieuse, hors du commun. Cette part de mystère ne doit pas faire l'objet d'une spectacularisation. Au contraire, la caméra est fidèle à une tradition objectiviste, elle pourrait être envisagée dans une position analogue à l'écriture poétique. Je pense à Charles Reznikoff et aux objectivistes américains pour qui l'énoncé, dans sa structure même, est déjà un déplacement du langage. En effet, la pratique d'Andrea en Bavière n'a rien d'exotique, elle est parfaitement lisible, intégrée dans le paysage quotidien. Pour Andrea, il semble plus familier de vêtir un *hanbok* coréen qu'un costume traditionnel bavarois, mais pour un œil extérieur les deux vêtements sont à la fois attrayants et étranges.

Par ailleurs, l'extrême singularité du récit d'Andrea tient au fait qu'il semble hanté par autant de personnes *réelles* que de présences *virtuelles*. Comment représenter ces mondes des absents et des vivants ? Comment faire cohabiter le visible et l'invisible ? J'ai en mémoire André Bazin pour qui la question ontologique du passage de la photographie au cinéma se traduit au-delà d'un progrès purement mécanique [2]. L'illusion n'est pas une grammaire de cinéma, mais sa fonction même, sa nature ontologique qui engendre les plaisirs scopiques du spectateur. Faire cohabiter les mondes d'Andrea, réels et virtuels, est simplement parler de cinéma. Parler de perceptions, du réel ou des réalités. Il ne s'agit pas de construire une vision illusionniste, voire naïve. Les choix de mise en scène se construisent dans cet interstice entre présence, absence et mémoire.

M. G. : Quelle mise en scène envisages-tu pour *Andrea en conversation*, nouvelle version d'*Andrea* à neuf écrans, conçue spécifiquement pour l'exposition du Jeu de Paume ?

N. N. : Deux dispositifs de perception et de narration vont dialoguer : le film et l'installation. L'installation stipule, par sa mise en forme, une déambulation, un espace élargi aux corps en mouvement. Dans ce dispositif, les images, les sons, les paroles d'Andrea sont inclus dans un ensemble physique et mental ouvert. Le visiteur de l'exposition est un spectateur parfois inattentif, il crée un montage singulier, intérieur, des signes et images mis à sa disposition. L'espace de l'exposition fait la part belle à l'éclatement du récit, à la perte d'un sens univoque, linéaire, au profit d'une construction non autoritaire, parcellaire, du récit. L'installation propose une indiscipline du regard. Le film quant à lui garde une structure hétérogène, et la linéarité du récit est fragmentée par les différentes sources d'images, correspondances visuelles et sonores, passages complexes de temporalités.

M. G. : Toutes ces forces invisibles ou ces spectres de nature insaisissable, tu les explores également dans des situations d'une réalité aussi accablante qu'incompréhensible, comme dans *Indice Nikkei*. Quelle est l'histoire de cette pièce ?

N. N. : La première version d'*Indice Nikkei* a été réalisée en 2003 pour mon exposition personnelle « Haus / raus-aus » au Plateau – Frac Île-de-France. Il me semblait alors que la Bourse et les systèmes financiers étaient au cœur de notre fragilité, fragilité au sens d'un monde opaque que nous, citoyens, ne pouvions saisir, comprendre et par là même influencer, ne serait-ce que par la puissance de la pensée. Dix ans plus tard, cette analyse est devenue un poncif et « la crise » de 2008 a marqué une nouvelle étape dans la perception de l'idée de catastrophe. La structure en écho de la pièce, les murs peints en rouge et la craie sur les murs sont des mises en scène des effets de saturation et de vertige provoqués, entre autres, par un profond sentiment d'incapacité à agir. Les courbes ressemblent étonnamment aux fractures de la roche dans la montagne de Kurihara à la suite du séisme de 2008. Les formes de ces courbes ont ensuite été « interprétées » comme un acte de résistance par la chanteuse soprano Donatienne Michel-Dansac, que j'ai invitée à participer au projet.

M. G. : Cette part d'inconnu, que ce soit le mystère qui caractérise *Andrea* ou l'opacité des systèmes financiers d'*Indice Nikkei*, semble se manifester sous d'autres formes dans *e* et *f*.

N. N. : Il y a des forces « naturelles », imprévisibles, comme celles qui provoquent les tremblements de terre. J'ai conçu *e* après avoir pris connaissance d'une légende fameuse au Japon, celle de Namazu, le poisson-chat. Le Japon serait posé sur un poisson-chat géant dont les agitations créent les tremblements de terre. Il est retenu par le dieu Kashima. Mais Kashima est un dieu volage, et à chacune de ses échappées le poisson-chat se réveille. Ce qui m'a frappée, ce sont les nombreuses gravures représentant Namazu invité à dîner à la table des charpentiers qui festoient en son honneur. Grâce à lui, le travail et l'opulence reprennent alors que les habitants des villes pleurent sous les

[fig. 6, p. 189]   Natacha Nisic, *Indice Nikkei*, 2003, bande sonore, 5', 14 dessins au crayon sur papier, fauteuils. Vue de l'exposition « Haus / raus-aus », Le Plateau – Frac Île-de-France, Paris, 2003 + [p. 193-196]

[fig. 7, p. 189]   Namazu invité à la table des charpentiers (artiste anonyme), vers 1855 (?), estampe. Musée préfectoral d'Histoire et de Folklore de Saïtama, Omiya

décombres. Namazu n'est pas une figure tragique car il est aussi la promesse d'un renouveau.

Ces forces imprédictibles nous permettent de forger notre relation adaptative au monde et replacent l'homme dans un tout, un ensemble dont il est une force agissante tout autant que passive, soumise. En revanche, lorsqu'il s'agit de « forces » telles que le danger nucléaire ou les jeux des finances mondiales, ces forces trouvent leurs sources dans une idée de toute-puissance de l'homme. Qu'il asservisse l'énergie ou les calculs vertigineux par des machines ou des ordinateurs, l'homme « civilisé » rivalise avec les forces imprévisibles, les domine et croit les contrôler. Cette démesure engendre un vertige, une peur qui porte en elle la négation de l'homme. Face à cela, je ne peux proposer que des gestes d'une grande simplicité : la création vocale de Donatienne Michel-Dansac pour *Indice Nikkei* ou, pour *f*, l'utilisation de miroirs qui, trouvés sur le lieu même du tsunami, ont vu le désastre de la grande vague et lui ont survécu.

[p. 143-156]

1 — *Trafic*, n° 1, hiver 1991,
p. 33-34.
2 — Voir André Bazin,
Qu'est-ce que le cinéma ?, Paris,
Éditions du Cerf, 1990.

BIOGRAPHIE

Née à La Tronche, France, en 1967

Vit et travaille à Malakoff, France

Formation

2004
— Atelier scénario, La fémis,
École nationale supérieure des métiers
de l'image et du son, Paris

1989
— Deutsche Film- und Fernsehakademie,
Berlin

1986
— École nationale supérieure des arts
décoratifs, Paris

Bourses et résidences

2007
— Villa Médicis, Rome

2006
— RIAA – Residencia Internacional
de Artistas en Argentina

2002
— Cité internationale des arts, Paris

2001
— Villa Kujoyama, Kyoto

2000
— Senatsverwaltung für Bildung,
Wissenschaft und Forschung, Berlin

1997
— FIACRE – Fonds d'incitation
à la création, ministère de la Culture
et de la Communication, France

Expositions personnelles

2013
— « Natacha Nisic. Écho »,
Jeu de Paume, Paris

2012
— « K. W. Complex. Natacha Nisic /
Park Chan-kyong », Atelier Hermès,
Séoul
— « Aurélie Sement / Natacha Nisic »,
Grandes Galeries de l'ESADHaR,
aître Saint-Maclou, Rouen
— « Chantal Akerman, Natacha Nisic,
Marguerite Duras », galerie Florent
Tosin, Berlin

2011
— « My Corean Dream », Maison
des arts de Malakoff
— « Princess Snow-Flower », galerie
Florent Tosin, Berlin

2010
— « (s'entretenir)² », Atelier de création
radiophonique, France Culture, Paris
— LOOP Barcelona, Barcelone,
stand de la galerie Dominique Fiat

2009
— « e », galerie Dominique Fiat,
Paris

2007
— « Nord », villa Médicis, Rome
— « Forget me not », Domaine
départemental de Chamarande

2005
— « Effroi », musée Zadkine, Paris

2004
— « Hand-Made », galerie Xippas,
Paris

2003
— « Haus / raus-aus », Le Plateau –
Frac Île-de-France, Paris

2002
— « Fill-Île », Iteza Gallery, Kyoto
— « La Méthode B », Tokyorama,
palais de Tokyo, Paris

2001
— « 3 × 36 aide-mémoire », Sai Gallery,
Osaka

2000
— « Natacha Nisic », Kunstbank, Berlin
— « Zu vermieten », galerie Karlheinz
Meyer, Karlsruhe

1999
— « La salle de projection », L'atelier,
Centre national de la photographie,
Paris
— « Le S. C. sans peine », galerie
Anton Weller, Paris

1995
— « Pleine campagne », Galerie d'art
contemporain, Auvers-sur-Oise
— « Natacha Nisic / Gilles Picouet »,
galerie ART'O, Aubervilliers

Projections

2012
— *Le textile est mort mais les gens vivent encore*, « D comme documentaire », Gaîté lyrique, Paris

2011
— « Kunstabend », K21 Kunstsammlung Nordrhein-Westfalen, Düsseldorf
— *e*, Festival video_dumbo, New York
— *e*, Rencontres internationales Paris / Berlin / Madrid, Centre Pompidou, Paris, Museo Nacional Centro de Arte Reina Sofía, Madrid, Haus der Kulturen der Welt, Berlin
— *Catalogue de gestes*, « Un dimanche, une œuvre », Centre Pompidou, Paris

2009
— *En découverte*, Festival Remise, Bludenz

2008
— *Carmel*, « Hello Darkness », K21 Kunstsammlung Nordrhein-Westfalen, Düsseldorf
— *Nord* et *Carmel*, Centre Pompidou, Paris

2007
— *La Porte de Birkenau*, concert de la pièce *Different Trains* de Steve Reich, Parco della Musica, Rome
— « Le Regard ordinaire », rétrospective des films de Natacha Nisic, villa Médicis, Rome
— *En découverte*, villa Médicis, Rome
— *Le textile est mort mais les gens vivent encore*, « Cinem'art », Auditorium dell'arte, Rome
— *La Porte de Birkenau* et *Effroi*, « Trying to Land », MACRO – Museo d'Arte contemporanea di Roma, Rome
— *Effroi*, Paris Tout Court, Festival international du film court de Paris

2006
— *Catalogue de gestes*, « S.8 », Centre Pompidou, Paris
— *Le Suicide des objets*, « Vidéo club », MAC / VAL, Vitry-sur-Seine
— *En découverte*, Festival Manca, Nice
— *Hand-Made*, 5e EMAP – Ewha Media Art Presentation, Séoul

2005
— *En découverte*, « Objets parallèles », Festival Némo, Auditorium de la vidéothèque de Paris
— « Rétrospective Natacha Nisic », galerie Remparts, Toulon

Expositions collectives

2012
— « Le Plateau : 10 ans ! », Le Plateau – Frac Île-de-France, Paris

2011
— « Big Picture (Orte / Projektionen) », K21 Kunstsammlung Nordrhein-Westfalen, Düsseldorf
— « Fragmentations : trajectoires contre nature », Domaine départemental de la Garenne-Lemot, Gétigné-Clisson / musée d'Art et d'Histoire, Saint-Brieuc
— « Bien à vous », Red Brick House, Yokohama

2010
— « The Yvonne Rainer Project », British Film Institute, Londres
— « Between me and you », Rencontres internationales Paris / Berlin / Madrid, La Tabacalera, Madrid
— « Yebisu International Festival for Art & Alternative Visions », Metropolitan Museum of Photography, Tokyo

2009
— « elles@centrepompidou. Artistes femmes dans les collections du Musée national d'art moderne », Centre Pompidou, Musée national d'art moderne, Paris
— « Art et territoires », hospice d'Havré, Le Fresnoy – Studio national des arts contemporains, Tourcoing
— « Là où je ne connais personne », Centre du Vieux-Colombier, Frac Bretagne, Rennes

2008
— « FEW », Wattwiller
— « Yokohama collection 08 », Yokohama

2007
— « Spazi aperti », Accademia di Romania, Rome

2006
— « Paris-Belgrade », Centre culturel français, Belgrade

2005
— « À table(s) », Domaine
départemental de Chamarande

2004
— « Territoire et déplacement », Centre
Arc-en-Ciel, Liévin
— « Fenster zum Hof », NGBK, Berlin
— « Tempered Ground », Museum
of Garden History, Londres

2003
— « Flambant vu. Corps, spectacles »,
galerie Séquence, Chicoutimi
— « Une sélection 1998-2003 », Frac
Bretagne, Rennes
— « Histoire de gestes », Le Quai,
Mulhouse
— « Para ver de otra manera », Festival
Huesca Imagen, musée de Huesca

2001
— « Contemporary Utopia », Centre
d'art contemporain letton, Riga
— « Plan B », avec Herbert Schwarze,
hARTwareprojekt, Dortmund

1999
— « Zauber*haft », Waldschlösschen,
Dresde
— « Kyushu Contemporary Art
Adventure », Inter Media Station,
Fukuoka
— « Extra*et*Ordinaire », Le Printemps
de Cahors

1998-1999
— « Aller-retour », Bonner Kunstverein,
Bonn ; Stadtgalerie Saarbrücken,
Sarrebruck ; Stadtgalerie im
Kulturviertel, Kiel

1998
— « Élizabeth Creseveur, Rose Gibbs,
Natacha Nisic, Mélik Ohanian,
Jana Simpson », galerie Jennifer Flay,
Paris
— « Regard fatigué », avec Christophe
Marchand-Kiss, Akademie Schloss
Solitude, Stuttgart

1997
— « Remise en forme », galerie Xippas,
Paris

1994
— « Chez l'un l'autre », galerie Anton
Weller, Paris

BIBLIOGRAPHIE SÉLECTIVE

Entretiens

— « Natacha Nisic / L'art au risque de
la mémoire », entretien avec Catherine
Francblin, avec la participation
de Philippe Forest, *Entretiens sur l'art*,
Fondation d'entreprise Ricard,
20 septembre 2005 (compte rendu
en ligne : http://fondation-entreprise-
ricard.com/conferences/entretiens/
art/natacha-nisic/).

— *Natacha Nisic*, entretien avec Éric
Corne et Maëlle Dault, compte rendu
de la rencontre du 3 avril 2003 autour
de l'exposition « Haus / raus-aus », Paris,
Le Plateau – Frac Île-de-France, 2004.
— « Spectre. Natacha Nisic », dans
Nathan Réra (dir.), *De Paris à Drancy ou
les Possibilités de l'art après Auschwitz*,
Pertuis, Rouge profond, 2009, p. 57-71.

Études et catalogues
d'expositions monographiques

— Galdo, Luisa, *Natacha Nisic, "Come
l'invisibile diventa visibile". La Shoah
– I Gesti*, thèse d'histoire de l'art
contemporain sous la dir. de Simonetta
Lux, Sapienza – Università di Roma,
Facoltà di Lettere e Filosofia, 2011.
— *Haus / raus-aus. Natacha Nisic*,
Bruxelles, La Lettre volée / Paris,
Le Plateau – Frac Île-de-France, 2003 ;
textes d'Éric Corne et Christophe
Marchand-Kiss.
— *K. W. Complex, Natacha Nisic /
Park Chan-kyong*, Paris, Fondation
Hermès, 2013 ; textes de Natacha Nisic
et Park Chan-kyong.

— *Natacha Nisic. Écho*, Paris,
Jeu de Paume / Arles, Actes Sud, 2013 ;
textes de Beck Jee-sook,
Philippe-Alain Michaud, Florent Perrier,
entretien de l'artiste avec Marta Gili.
— *Natacha Nisic. Effroi*, Paris,
musée Zadkine / Paris-Musées, 2005 ;
texte d'Annette Becker, préface
de Noëlle Chabert, note d'intention
de Natacha Nisic.
— *Natacha Nisic. Pleine campagne*,
Auvers-sur-Oise, Office
municipal de la culture, 1995 ;
textes de Christophe Domino
et Véronique Pittolo.

Catalogues d'expositions
collectives

—*À table(s)*, Chamarande, Domaine
départemental de Chamarande, 2005 ;
texte de Christophe Domino.
—*Aller et retour : 35 Jahre Deutsch-
Französisches Jugendwerk*, Bonn,
Bonner Kunstverein / Sarrebruck,
Stadtgalerie Saarbrücken / Kiel,
Stadtgalerie im Kulturviertel, 1999 ;
texte d'Annelie Pohlen.
—*Ateliers 1997-2002. Centre national
de la photographie*, Paris, Centre
national de la photographie, 2002 ;
sous la dir. de Régis Durand et
Claire Jacquet ; texte de Christophe
Marchand-Kiss.
—*Big Picture. Orte / Projektionen :
zwölf kinematographische
Installationen*, Berlin, Kerber, 2011 ;
sous la dir. de Doris Krystof.
—*Contemporary Utopia – Mūsdienu
Utopija*, Riga, Laikmetīgās mākslas
centrs (Centre d'art contemporain
letton), 2001 ; sous la dir. de Frank
Wagner.
—*Dynasty*, Paris, ARC – musée
d'Art moderne de la Ville de Paris /
Paris-Musées, 2010 ; sous la dir. de
Patrice Hergott et Christian Wahler ;
texte de Doris Krystof.
—*Elles@centrepompidou : pionnières,
feu à volonté, corps slogan, eccentric
abstraction, une chambre à soi, le mot
à l'œuvre, immatérielles, elles@design,
architecture et féminisme ? Artistes
femmes dans la collection du Musée
national d'art moderne-Centre
de création industrielle*, Paris,
Centre Pompidou, 2009 ; textes de
Quentin Bajac et Camille Morineau.

—*ExtraetOrdinaire. Le Printemps
de Cahors. Photographies & arts visuels*,
Arles, Actes Sud, 1999 ; textes de
Christine Macel *et al.*
—*Flambant vu. Corps, spectacles*,
Chicoutimi, galerie Séquence, 2002 ;
texte de Sylvain Campeau.
—*Huesca Imagen. Para ver de otra
manera*, Huesca, Diputación
provincial de Huesca, 2003 ; sous la dir.
de Liliana Albertazzi.
—*Le Plateau, 10 ans, Frac Île-de-France*,
Paris, Le Plateau – Frac Île-de-France,
2012.
—*Ossip's studio : mémoires d'atelier,
expérience de production*, Paris,
musée Zadkine / Paris-Musées, 2008 ;
textes de Noëlle Chabert, Hubert Lucot,
Jérôme Mauche *et al.*
—*Plan B – Kunst Raum Stadt*,
Dortmund, Hartware
MedienKunstVerein, 2001 ; textes
de Hans D. Christ, Iris Dressler,
Diana Ebster *et al.*
—*Remise en forme*, Paris, galerie
Xippas, 1997 ; texte de Liliana
Albertazzi.
—*Temper Ground*, Londres, Museum
of Garden History / Parabola, 2004 ;
sous la dir. d'Eliza Williams.
—*Yebisu International Festival
for Art & Alternative Visions 2010 :
Searching Songs*, Tokyo, Metropolitan
Museum of Photography, 2010 ;
sous la dir. de Keiko Okamura,
Hiroko Tasaka, Masako Immaki
et Jiro Iio.

Essais

—Becker, Annette, et Debary, Octave
(dir.), *Montrer les violences extrêmes*,
Paris, Créaphis, 2012.
—Brenez, Nicole, et Lebrat, Christian
(dir.), *Une histoire du cinéma d'avant-
garde et expérimental en France*,
Paris, La Cinémathèque française /
Hazan, 2000.

—Parfait, Françoise, *Vidéo, un art
contemporain*, Paris, Éditions du Regard,
2002.

Articles

—Ackermann, Tim, « Bilder
der gezähmten Welt », *TAZ Berlin*,
31 juillet 2004, p. 29.
—Bach, Jana J., « C. Akerman,
M. Duras, N. Nisic », *Zitty Berlin*,
février 2013, p. 132.
—Benhamou-Huet, Judith, « Trois
galeries dans le vent. De jeunes artistes
français et allemands à découvrir »,
Les Échos week-end, n° 19177,
11-12 juin 2004, p. 6.
—Benhamou-Huet, Judith,
« Les tabous de Natacha », *Les Échos
week-end*, n° 18903, 9 mai 2003, p. 4.
—Berelowitch, Irène, « Vidéolettres »,
Télérama, n° 2371, 21 juin 1995, p. 72.

—Blazevic, Dunja, « Destruction
de l'image, image de la destruction »,
Art press, n° 192, juin 1994,
p. 46-50.
—Brignone, Patricia, « L'image-geste »,
Omnibus, n° 30, octobre 1999, p. 12.
—Campeau, Sylvain, « Opsis mobile »,
Papel Alpha, n° 6, 2002-2003, p. 51.
—Champagne, Aurélie, « Vision
de l'indicible, Natacha Nisic, "Effroi" »,
Zurban Paris, n° 260, 17-23 août 2005,
p. 76.
—Colard, Jean-Max, « Natacha Nisic »,
Les Inrockuptibles, spécial « Printemps
de Cahors », supplément au n° 203,
16 juin 1999, p. 9.

— Corne, Éric, « Pariz / Beograd, srodnost po izboru », *Danas* (Belgrade), 15-16 avril 2006, p. 3.
— Cosar, Sascha, « Wenn das Schaf zum Telephon Hörer greift », *Bonner Kultur*, n° 304, 31 décembre 1998, p. 24.
— Couturier, Élisabeth, « Les hommes au placard, les femmes au musée ! », *Paris Match*, n° 3131, 25 mai-3 juin 2009, p. 30-31.
— Delaporte, Ixchel, « Supermarché, objet d'art », *L'Humanité hebdo, la semaine télé*, 11 décembre 2004, p. 23.
— Dhellemmes, Bertram, « "Effroi" de Natacha Nisic, musée Zadkine, Paris », *L'Architecture d'aujourd'hui*, n° 361, novembre-décembre 2005, p. 12-13.
— Douaire, Pierre-Évariste, « Natacha Nisic », *ParisART*, juin 2004 (en ligne : http://www.paris-art.com/galerie-photo/Natacha%20Nisic/Natacha%20Nisic/4388.html).
— Escalle, Clotilde, « Les traces de la mort », *Tageblatt* (Luxembourg), n° 142, 21 juin 2005, p. 17.
— Farine, Manou, « Femmes. "Elles" envahissent Beaubourg », *L'Œil*, n° 614, juin 2009, p. 36-43.
— Fau, Alexandra, « Les artistes et l'Holocauste », *(Art absolument)*, n° 16, printemps 2006, p. 62-68.
— Francblin, Catherine, « Natacha Nisic. Musée Zadkine », *Art press*, n° 316, octobre 2005, p. 88.
— Gamba, Mario, « Come interpretare quest'altro Reich », *Il manifesto*, 5 avril 2008.
— Jarton, Cyril, « Natacha Nisic, pour la vie », *Beaux Arts magazine*, décembre 1996, n° 151, p. 37.
— Ko, Miseok, « Rencontre de croyances entre tradition et modernité, Orient et Occident », *Dong-a Ilbo*, 20 novembre 2012, p. 22 (en coréen).
— Kröner, Magdalena, « In der Wollfaden-Metropole », *Die Tageszeitung*, 28 juin 2000, p. 15.
— Krystof, Doris, « *Catalogue de gestes* », Centre Pompidou, Musée national d'art moderne, collection des films (notice en ligne : http://collection.centrepompidou.fr/mediaNavigart/oeudoc/fra/GE/NE/GENERATION-AUTO-15000000005910000309.htm), 2009.
— Lamy, Frank, et Lavrador, Judicaël, « Le tour des galeries », *Beaux Arts magazine*, n° 241, juin 2004, p. 42.
— Lee, Doeun, « Chosun Seen by a German Monk, and + α », *JoongAng Sunday*, 4 novembre 2012, p. 25.
— Lee, Mihye, « House of Healing », *Vogue Korea*, décembre 2012, p. 234 (en coréen).
— Lee, Seulbi, « K. W. Complex », *Monthly Art*, décembre 2012, p. 140-145 (en coréen).
— Lemaître, Isabelle, « Domaine départemental de Chamarande, ou un centre d'art contemporain arrivé à son rythme de croisière », *Flux News*, juillet 2005, p. 23.
— Lequeux, Emmanuelle, « Le Centre Pompidou glorifie les femmes au risque de les placer dans un ghetto », *Le Monde*, 29 mai 2009, p. 20.
— Lequeux, Emmanuelle, « Natacha Nisic. Plongée dans les eaux troubles de la mémoire », *Beaux Arts magazine*, n° 255, septembre 2005, p. 124.
— Lequeux, Emmanuelle, « Un instant de mémoire révélé », *En ville*, n° 7, juin 2005, p. 49.
— Lequeux, Emmanuelle, « Natacha Nisic. Aide-mémoire », *Beaux Arts magazine*, n° 228, mai 2003, p. 35.
— Lesauvage, Magali, « La loi du genre, elles@centrepompidou », *Fluctuat*, 8 juin 2009 (en ligne : www.fluctuat.net/6853-elles-centrepompidou).
— Marcelis, Bernard, « extra et ordinaire, le printemps de cahors », *Art press*, n° 249, septembre 1999, p. 90.
— Marchand-Kiss, Christophe, « Et compagnie », *Action poétique*, n° 182, décembre 2005, p. 82.
— Martínez, Beatriz, « La distorsión líquida », *Cahiers du cinéma España*, n° 45, mai 2011, p. 10-12.
— Mauche, Jérôme, « Hand-Made / Fait main : Natacha Nisic », *Synesthésie*, 2004 (en ligne).
— Moulène, Claire, « Natacha Nisic, *Haus / raus-aus* », *Les Inrockuptibles*, 26 mars 2003, p. 70.
— Müller, Michael-Georg, « Wiederaufstehen nach dem Beben », *NRZ*, 19 mars 2011.
— Müller, Michael-Georg, « Kunst : Japaner glauben an eine neue Àra », *WAZ-NRZ*, 18 mars 2011.
— Mura, Giannina, « Bambini tra le ceneri e il mare », *Il manifesto*, 14 septembre 2005, p. 15.
— « "My Corean Dream". Natacha Nisic », *Libération*, cahier spécial, 19 septembre 2011, n. p.
— Naphegyi, Caroline, « Natacha Nisic », *Le Journal des expositions*, n° 40, novembre 1996, p. 6.
— Nisic, Natacha, « Projet d'investissement de la salle de projection du CNP », *Journal du CNP*, n° 6, janvier 1999, p. 11.
— Nowak, Ewa Isabella, « Haus / raus-aus », *Arteon*, n° 10, juillet 2003, p. 10-11.
— Nuridsany, Michel, « Vidéo, appartements et chambres d'hôtel. La jeune création passe à l'attaque », *Le Figaro*, 3 septembre 1996, p. 23.
— Pittolo, Véronique, « Natacha Nisic : The Time of the Movement », *Katalog*, vol. 9, n° 4, automne 1997, p. 58.
— Ramade, Bénédicte, « Natacha Nisic, hors de la maison », *L'Œil*, n° 545, mars 2003, p. 99.
— Rebischung, Jean-François, « Souvenirs d'ouvriers entre mains d'artistes », *Nord Éclair*, 12 juin 2009, p. 17.

— Reneau, Olivier, « De la vidéo chez les impressionnistes », *Technikart*, n° 3, décembre 1996, p. 94.
— Sardá, Juan, « Cita con la vanguardia », *El Mundo*, 20 mai 2011.
— Schaeffer, Ute, « Experimente in Labor Europa », *General Auzenger*, 16 décembre 1998.
— Sipp, Thomas, « Le mois du film documentaire », *Bref*, n° 75, novembre-décembre 2006, p. 2.
— Soyer, Carine, « Aller-retour : les pérégrinations créatrices de quatre artistes », *Jalouse*, n° 61, juin 2003, p. 84-87.
— Thély, Nicolas, « Natacha Nisic, artiste en construction », *Aden*, 12-20 mars 2003, p. 27.
— Vanbremeersch, Sandra, « Natacha Nisic. Haus / raus-aus », *ParisART*, juin 2003 (en ligne : http://www.paris-art.com/graff/haus--raus-aus/nisic-natacha/4077.html).

— Viau, René, « Natacha Nisic… VIVRE ? », *ETC*, n° 63, septembre-octobre-novembre 2003, p. 69-71.
— Villeneuve, Mathilde, « Natacha Nisic », *02*, n° 35, automne 2005, p. 43.
— Wanzelius, Rainer, « Schluchzende Töne aus alter und neuer Welt », *Westdeutsche allgemeine Zeitung*, 25 mai 2000.
— Yánez, Jara, « "Extranjero" y "valor trabajo". A través de la frontera », *Cahiers du cinéma España*, n° 33, avril 2010, p. 19.

Radio

— France Culture, *Direct*, 23 mars 2009 ; « Journée Claude Lanzmann ».
— France Culture, *Ultra contemporain*, 2 juillet 2005 ; exposition « Effroi », musée Zadkine.
— France Culture, *In situ*, 17 avril 2002 ; autour de la question de l'atelier d'artiste.
— France Culture, *Trans / Formes*, 20 octobre 1999 ; exposition « Extra*et*Ordinaire », Le Printemps de Cahors.

— France Culture, *Peinture fraîche*, 21 juin 1999 ; exposition « Extra*et*Ordinaire », Le Printemps de Cahors.
— Radio Aligre, janvier 1998 ; exposition « Remise en forme », galerie Xippas, Paris.
— Radio FG, janvier 1996 ; exposition « Natacha Nisic / Gilles Picouet », galerie ART'O, Aubervilliers.

Télévision

— Arte Vidéo Night, octobre 2011 ; entretien entre Dominique Fiat et Natacha Nisic.
— TV Belgrade, avril 2006 ; exposition « Paris-Belgrade », Centre culturel français, Belgrade.

— Direct TV 8, 21 juillet 2005 ; exposition « À table(s) », Domaine départemental de Chamarande.
— Arte, *Exhibition, la chute*, avril 2004 ; interview de Natacha Nisic autour de son œuvre *Le Suicide des objets*.

Filmographie

— *Des témoins racontent, le Titanic*, vidéo, couleur, son, 22', Paris, Arte France Développement / Cherbourg, musée de la Mer, 2012.
— *Les Carriers*, vidéo, couleur, son, 16', Tercé, La Carrière de Normandoux, 2008.
— *L'important est que cela soit mis en eaux*, vidéo, couleur, son, 17', Domaine départemental de Chamarande, 2007.
— *Une histoire de topinambours*, vidéo, couleur, son, 16', Domaine départemental de Chamarande, 2007.
— *Christoph Hein. À mi-mots*, vidéo, couleur, son, 41', Paris, MK2 TV / Arte, 2006.

— *Maternelles. Dominique*, vidéo, couleur, son, 13', Paris, La Cinquième / MK2 TV, 2003.
— *Histoires d'écrivains, Hélène Lenoir, Jacques Roubaud*, vidéo, couleur, son, 2 × 13', Paris, La Cinquième / MK2 TV, 2002.
— *Kyoto, voyages, voyages*, vidéo, couleur, son, 41', Paris, MK2 TV / Arte, 2002.
— *Le Dessous des cartes*, vidéo, couleur, son, Paris, Arte, 1995-2013.
— *Au sujet d'un secret entre vous et moi*, couleur, son, 8', Paris, Télérencontres, 1992.
— *Durable*, 16 mm, couleur, son, 19', Berlin, DFFB / Paris, ENSAD / Ex Nihilo, 1991.

Les œuvres présentées dans l'exposition du Jeu de Paume sont signalées d'un astérisque.

[p. 10 + 15-25]
— *Catalogue de gestes* (extraits)*,
1995-…
Films super-8 numérisés, couleur,
entre 1' et 2' 30" chacun
Centre Pompidou, Musée
national d'art moderne / Centre
de création industrielle, Paris
(don de l'artiste)

[p. 188]
— *« Attitudes », la salle d'attente n° 1*,
1997
Installation, 16 sièges en toile
et aluminium, 5 projections vidéo,
couleur, 10' chacune
Production : La Sept Vidéo,
Paris, Centre national des arts
plastiques, Paris, galerie
Renos Xippas, Paris
Fonds national d'art contemporain

[p. 188]
— *« Attitudes », la salle de projection*,
1999
Installation, 20 fauteuils de cinéma,
3 projections vidéo, couleur,
42' chacune, moniteur et caméra
de surveillance
Assistant réalisation : Vincent Royer
Production : La Sept Vidéo,
Paris, Centre national
de la photographie, Paris
Collection de l'artiste

[p. 189]
— *Indice Nikkei*, 2003
Installation, bande sonore, 5',
14 dessins au crayon sur papier,
fauteuils
Production : Le Plateau –
Frac Île-de-France
Collection de l'artiste

[p. 193-196]
— *Indice Nikkei**, 2003-2013
Installation, 2 bandes sonores,
10' chacune, dessins à la craie
sur peinture rouge, 2 fauteuils
Écriture sonore : Donatienne
Michel-Dansac
Son : Jean-Yves Pouyat,
Éric Marciszewer
Collection de l'artiste

[p. 137]
— *La Porte de Birkenau*, 2005
Projection vidéo HD, couleur, 3'
Chef opératrice : Muriel Coulin
Production : Mémorial de
la Shoah, Paris, MK2 TV, Paris
Installation permanente
au Mémorial de la Shoah,
Paris

[p. 137]
— *Mémorial des enfants*, 2005
Installation, 3 500 impressions
numériques sur lais de papier
Arche contrecollés sur panneaux
de Macrolife rétro-éclairés sur
structure acier, 120 m²
Production : Mémorial de la Shoah,
Paris, Fin avril, Paris
Installation permanente au Mémorial
de la Shoah, Paris

[p. 11]
— *Effroi*, 2005
Vidéo, couleur, 7' 30"
Caméra : Natacha Nisic
Son : Thomas Bauer
Production : musée Zadkine, Paris,
Fin avril, Paris
Collection de l'artiste

[p. 138]
— *Effroi – La Vistule*, 2005
Photographie couleur, 110 × 80 cm
Production : musée Zadkine, Paris
Collection de l'artiste

[p. 11]
— *Effroi – Réservoir*, 2005
Photographie couleur, 200 × 135 cm
Production : musée Zadkine, Paris
Fonds national d'art contemporain

[p. 10]
— *Nord*, 2007
Installation, 5 projections de films
16 mm transférés en vidéo, couleur,
son stéréo, 5' 50" chacune
Chef opérateur : Sébastien Buchmann
Assistante opératrice : Lou Vernin
Caméra vidéo : Olivier Menanteau
Montage : Natacha Nisic
Son : Cyrille Lauwerier,
Nicolas Verhaeghe
Mixage : Hugues Petit
Assistantes réalisation :
Émilie Dudognon, Christine Crutel
Production : Centre national de
la cinématographie, Paris, Le Fresnoy –
Studio national des arts contemporains,
direction régionale des Affaires
culturelles Nord-Pas-de-Calais,
Tourcoing, Image / mouvement – Centre
national des arts plastiques, Paris,
La Mondiale, Paris, villa Médicis, Rome
Collection de l'artiste

[p. 26-32 + 36]
— *Carmel*, 2008
4 rétroprojections, vidéo HD,
couleur, son, 25' chacune,
et 1 projection vidéo HD, couleur, 3'
Caméra : Natacha Nisic
Chef opérateur : Sébastien Buchmann
Assistante opératrice : Lou Vernin
Chef machiniste : Richard De Vadder
Machinistes : Valéry Lhomme,
Frédéric Oliver
Montage et son : Natacha Nisic
Post-production : Bertrand Sart
Production : musée du Carmel, Lisieux
Installation permanente au musée
du Carmel, Lisieux

[p. 138 + 156-184]
— *e**, 2009
Installation, 3 projections vidéo HD,
couleur, son 5.1, 19' chacune
Caméra vidéo : Natacha Nisic,
Olivier Menanteau
Montage : Natacha Nisic
Post-production : Bertrand Sart
Son : Ikeno Tekeaki
Assistant : Jeffrey Lebeau
Mixage : Cyrille Lauwerier
Traduction : Sekiguchi Ryoko
Production exécutive : Akatsu Hiroko
– Synapse Ent., Tokyo
Production : Image / mouvement –
Centre national des arts plastiques,
Le Fresnoy – Studio national
des arts contemporains, Tourcoing,
Institut français du Japon, Paris,
galerie Dominique Fiat, Paris,
Arte France Développement
Collection Fonds régional d'art
contemporain Bretagne

[p. 37 + 72-78]
— *Princess Snow-Flower*, 2011
Installation, 3 projections vidéo HD,
couleur, son, 19' chacune
Caméra, montage et son :
Natacha Nisic
Assistant : Vincent Royer
Production : GCC – Gyeonggi
Art Center, Corée, galerie Florent
Tosin, Berlin
Collection de l'artiste

[p. 127-132 + 137]
— *Fukushima**, 2011
Crayon de couleur sur papier Canson,
75 × 315 cm
Collection de l'artiste

[p. 36-37]
— *Andrea*, 2012
Installation, 5 vidéo HD, couleur, son,
La Rencontre : 13' 9", *Les Âmes* : 8' 9",
Les Soins : 9' 27", *Archives* : 10' 32",
Les Voix : 8' 55"
Caméra et montage : Natacha Nisic
Son : Jean-Yves Pouyat
Production : Fondation Hermès, Paris,
Fondation Nationale des Arts
Graphiques et Plastiques, Paris
Collection de l'artiste

[p. 41-72]
— *Andrea en conversation**, 2013
Installation, 9 vidéos HD, couleur, son,
env. 10' chacune
Caméra : Natacha Nisic
Chef opératrice : Nathalie Durand
Son : Jean-Yves Pouyat
Assistante réalisation :
Charlotte Lessana
Montage : Natacha Nisic
Mixage : Jean-Yves Pouyat
Production : Jeu de Paume, Paris,
Seconde Vague Productions, Paris
Avec le soutien de la Fondation
Nationale des Arts Graphiques
et Plastiques, Paris
Collection de l'artiste

[p. 143-156]
— *f**, 2013
Projection vidéo HD, couleur, son, 20'
Caméra : Nathalie Durand
Chef machiniste : Kenichi Watanabe
Assistants : Sugeeta Kajuto,
Otake Nobu
Montage : Natacha Nisic
Son : Natacha Nisic, Philippe Langlois
Production exécutive :
Annick Lemonnier – Epileptic Films,
Akatsu Hiroko – Synapse Ent., Tokyo
Production : Jeu de Paume, Paris
Collection de l'artiste

[non reproduit]
— *Fukushima**, 2013
Crayon de couleur sur papier Canson,
75 × 315 cm
Collection de l'artiste

[p. 189]
— *Le Ciel d'Andrea*, 2013
Vidéo HD, couleur, son, 65'
Caméra : Natacha Nisic,
Nathalie Durand
Montage : Natacha Nisic
Son : Jean-Yves Pouyat
Assistante réalisation :
Charlotte Lessana
Production : Seconde Vague
Productions, Paris, Centre national
du cinéma et de l'image animée,
Paris, Arte, Paris

JEU DE PAUME

Ce catalogue est publié à l'occasion
de l'exposition « Natacha Nisic. Écho »,
présentée au Jeu de Paume, Paris,
du 15 octobre 2013 au 26 janvier 2014.

Commissaires de l'exposition :
Natacha Nisic et Marta Gili

— Direction :
Marta Gili
— Secrétariat général :
Maryline Dunaud

— Administration et comptabilité :
Claude Bocage
— Communication et mécénat :
Anne Racine
— Éditions :
Muriel Rausch
— Expositions :
Véronique Dabin
— Librairie :
Pascal Priest
— Projets artistiques et action
culturelle : Marta Ponsa
— Projets éducatifs :
Sabine Thiriot
— Régie :
Pierre-Yves Horel

Exposition
— Coordination de l'exposition :
Véronique Dabin
— Régie des œuvres :
Maddy Cougouluègnes
— Régie technique :
Olivier Filippi

Catalogue
— Coordination éditoriale :
Lætitia Moukouri

Le Jeu de Paume est subventionné
par le ministère de la Culture
et de la Communication.

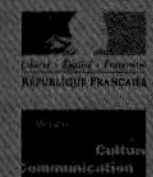

Il bénéficie du soutien de
NEUFLIZE VIE, mécène principal.

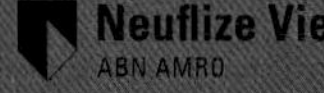

Cet ouvrage est publié avec le soutien
des Amis du Jeu de Paume.

Andrea (2012) et *Andrea en conversation*
(2013) ont été sélectionnées par
la commission mécénat de la Fondation
Nationale des Arts Graphiques
et Plastiques, qui leur a apporté
son soutien.

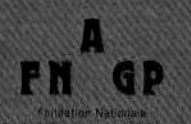

Remerciements

Le Jeu de Paume adresse ses plus
vifs remerciements à Natacha Nisic
pour son implication dans ce projet
d'exposition et de livre.

Sa reconnaissance la plus sincère
va aussi à l'ensemble des prêteurs
ayant accepté de participer
à cette exposition :
— Centre Pompidou, Musée
national d'art moderne / Centre
de création industrielle, Paris
— Fonds régional d'art
contemporain Bretagne
— Galerie Florent Tosin, Berlin

Pour leur précieuse collaboration
dans la préparation de ce projet,
l'institution témoigne aussi toute
sa gratitude à :
— Dominique Fiat, galerie
Dominique Fiat, Paris
— Philippe-Alain Michaud,
Centre Pompidou, Musée national
d'art moderne, Paris
— Sandra Richard

ainsi qu'aux personnes
et institutions suivantes :
Eija-Liisa Ahtila, Clotilde Escalle,
Yumi Kang, Doris Krystof,
Anne-Marie Miéville, Philippe Mothe,
Dominique Palmé, Ahran Sohn,
Ruth Waldburger, Gillian Wearing,
Le Fresnoy – Studio national
des arts contemporains, Tourcoing,
galerie Xippas, Paris, galerie
Marian Goodman, New York et Paris,
K21 Kunstsammlung Nordrhein-
Westfalen, Düsseldorf, Maureen
Paley, Londres, Mémorial de la Shoah,
Paris, Le Plateau – Frac Île-de-France,
Paris, Vega Film, Zurich,
et Video Data Bank, Chicago

Que la galerie Florent Tosin, Berlin,
soit enfin tout particulièrement
remerciée, notamment pour
son généreux soutien au catalogue.

—

Natacha Nisic exprime sa profonde
reconnaissance envers ses producteurs
et partenaires pour leur confiance
et leur engagement :
— Gérard Alaux, Fondation Nationale
des Arts Graphiques et Plastiques,
Paris
— Régis Durand
— Dominique Fiat, galerie Dominique
Fiat, Paris
— Akatsu Hiroko, Synapse Ent., Tokyo
— Yvonnic Le Fustec, Arte France
Développement, Paris
— Annick Lemonnier, Epileptic Films,
Paris
— Caroline Naphegyi, Tomorrow Land,
Paris

— Luciano Rigolini, La Lucarne, Paris
— Martine Saada, Arte France, Paris
— Paul Saadoun, Seconde Vague
Productions, Paris
— Florent Tosin, galerie Florent Tosin,
Berlin

L'artiste tient également à remercier
chaleureusement tous ceux qui
l'ont soutenue et aidée tout au long
de l'élaboration des œuvres :
— Claire Aubret
— Benjamin Cordero
— Andrea Kalff-Cordero
— Hendrikje Lange
— Charlotte Lessana
— Julia Marchand-Nisic
— Park Chan-kyong
— Delphine Pellereau
— Sandra Richard
— Merryl Roche
— Vincent Royer
— Pascal Sottovia
— Han Sunhee
— Frank Tétart

ainsi que :
— Maître Kim Keum-hwa
— La communauté des bénédictins
de Sainte-Odile, Bavière
— La communauté des bénédictins
de Waegwan, Corée du Sud
— Les habitants et le maire
de la ville d'Hisanohama, région
de Fukushima
— Sugeeta Kajuto, www.j-one21.jp

ACTES SUD

Coordination éditoriale :
Arnaud Bizalion

Responsable des partenariats :
Anne-Sylvie Bameule

Fabrication :
Géraldine Lay

—

Correction :
Aité Bresson (français),
Bernard Wooding (anglais)

Conception graphique :
Maquette & Mise en page
– Hugo Anglade, Thomas Petitjean,
Antoine Stevenot

Photogravure :
Quat'coul

Actes Sud
Le Méjan, place Nina-Berberova
13200 Arles, France
www.actes-sud.fr

Jeu de Paume
1, place de la Concorde
75008 Paris, France
www.jeudepaume.org

—

Achevé d'imprimer en août 2013
par l'imprimerie Castelli Bodis,
en Italie, pour le compte
des éditions Actes Sud

ISBN : 978-2-330-02379-9

Dépôt légal 1re édition :
novembre 2013

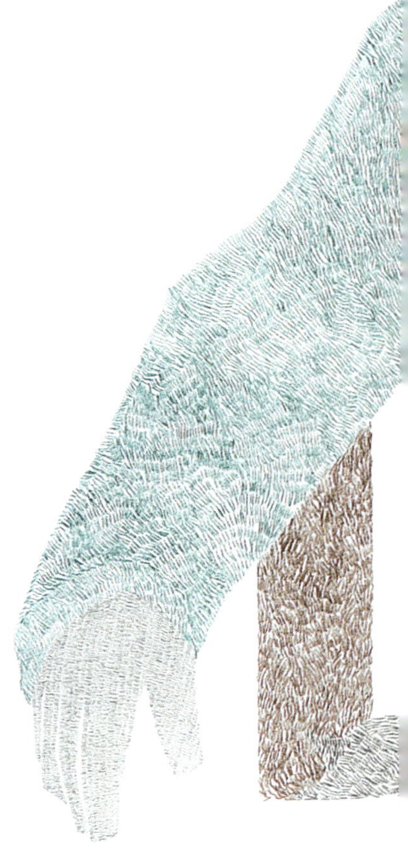

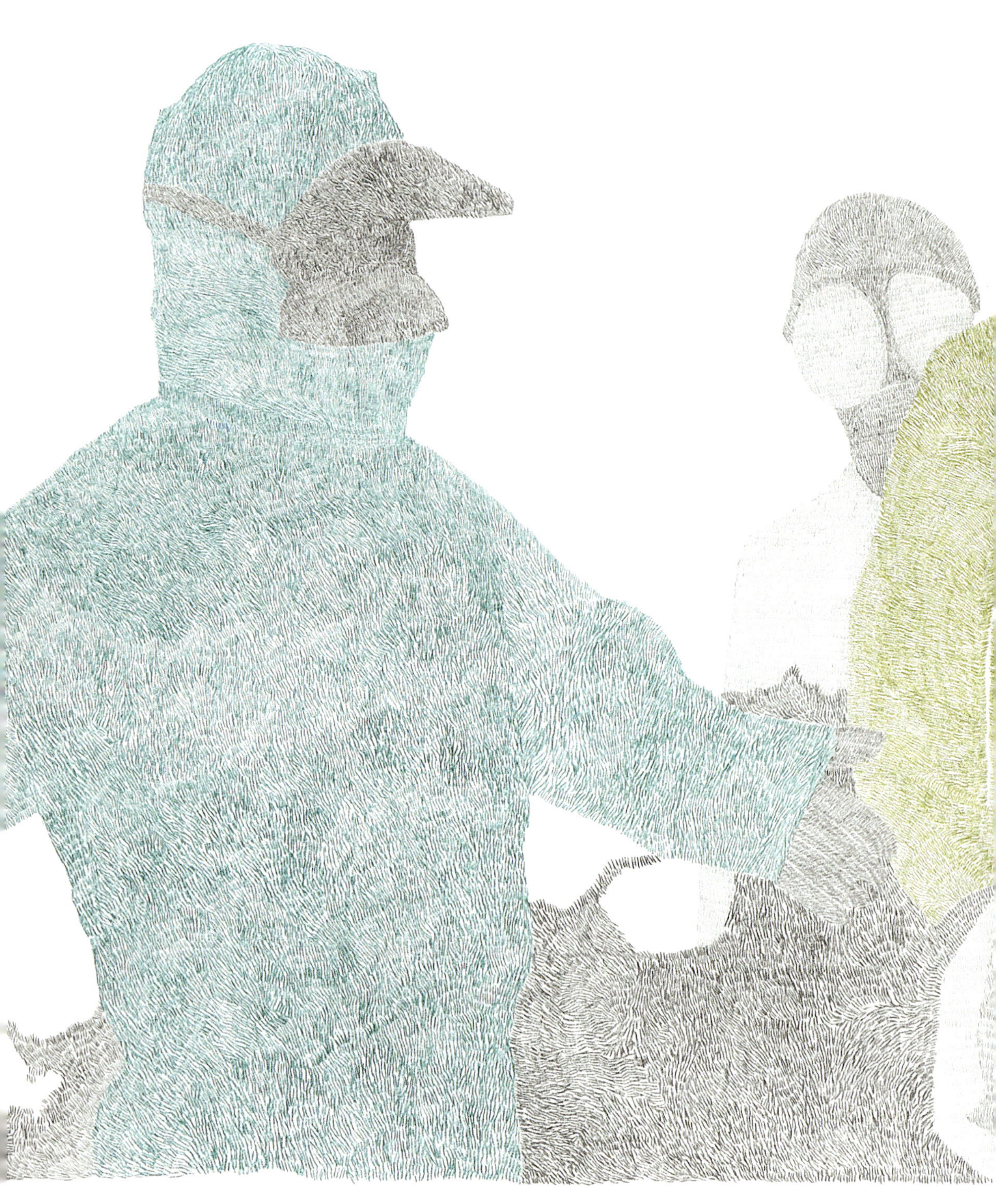

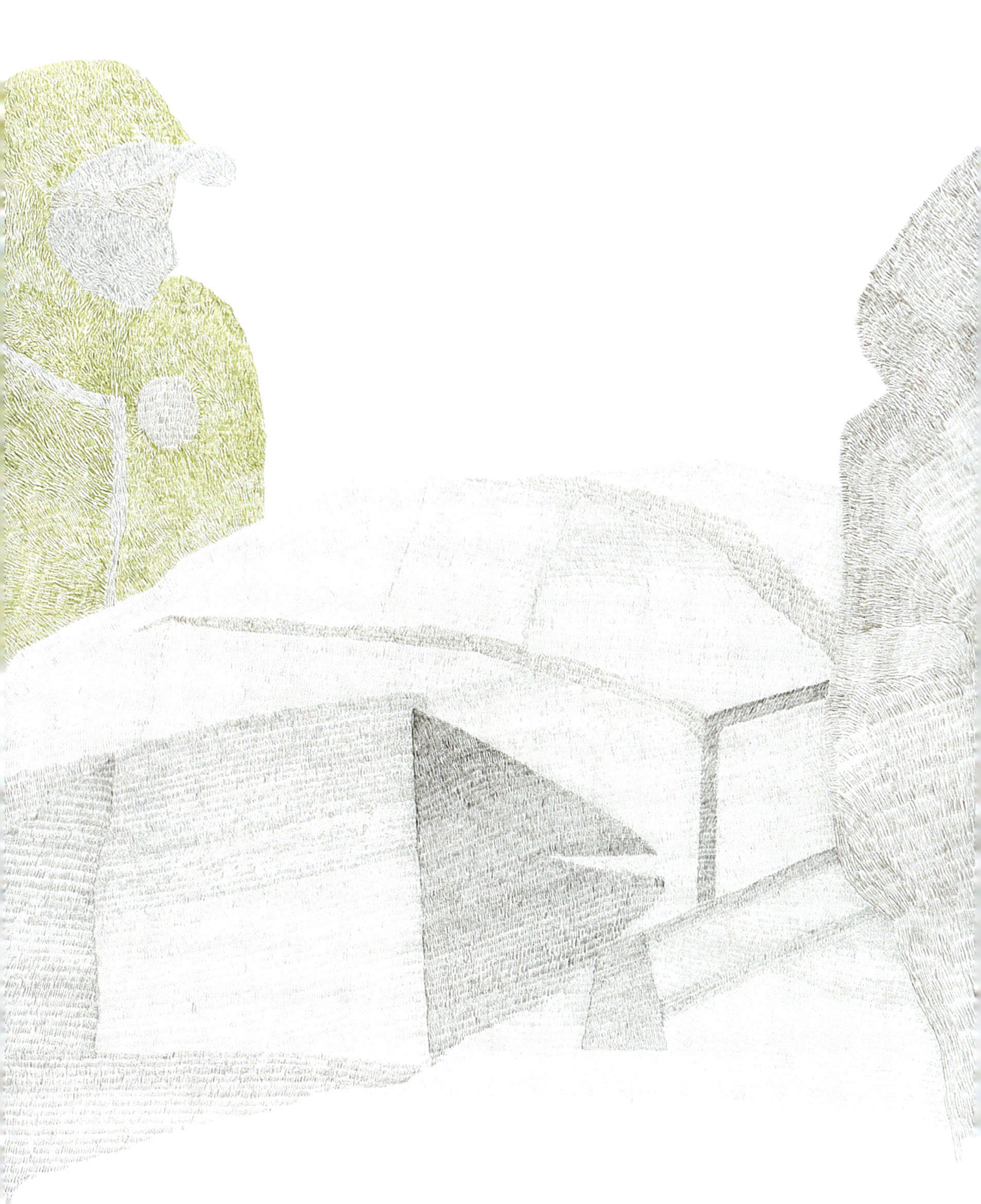

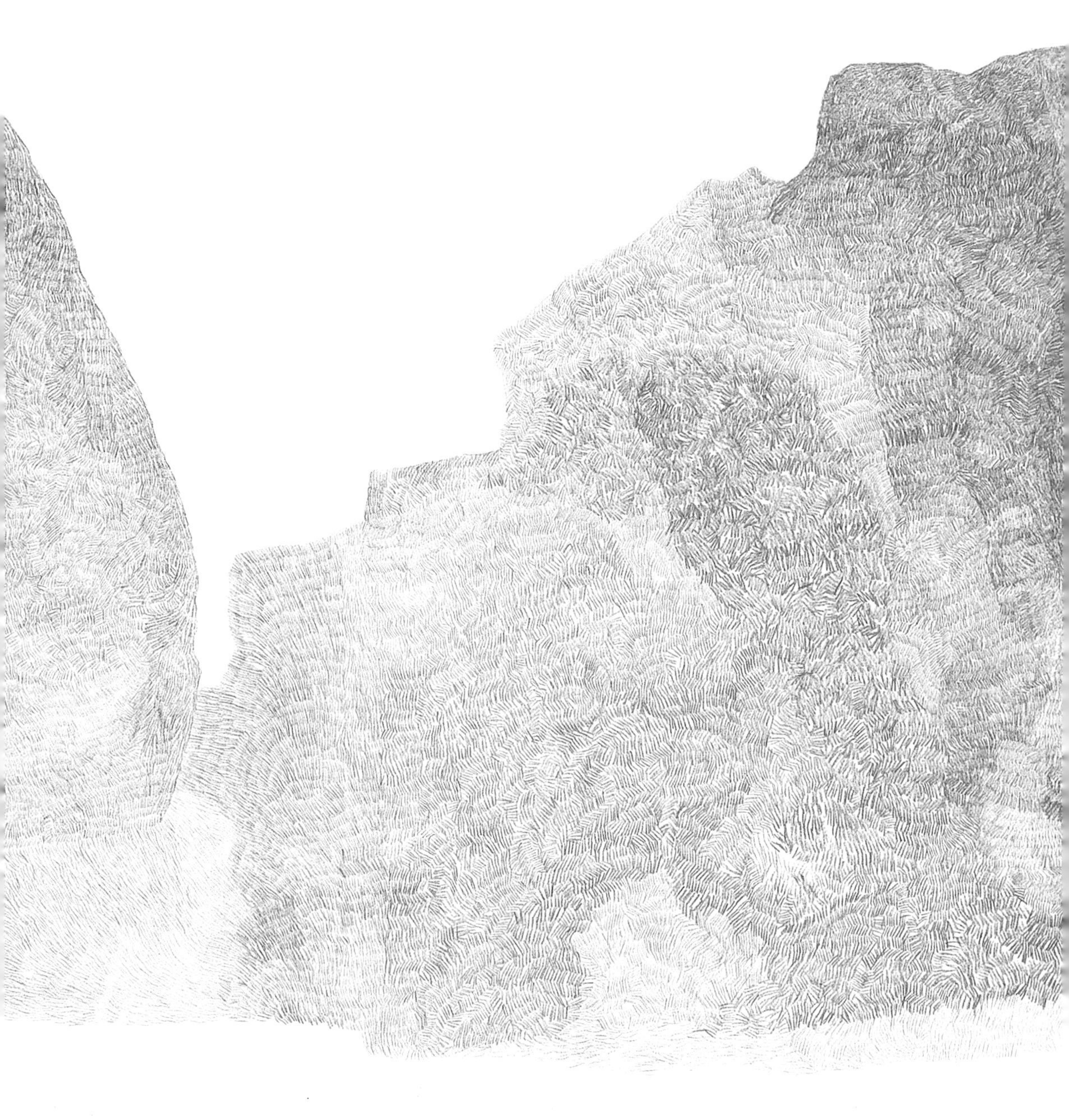

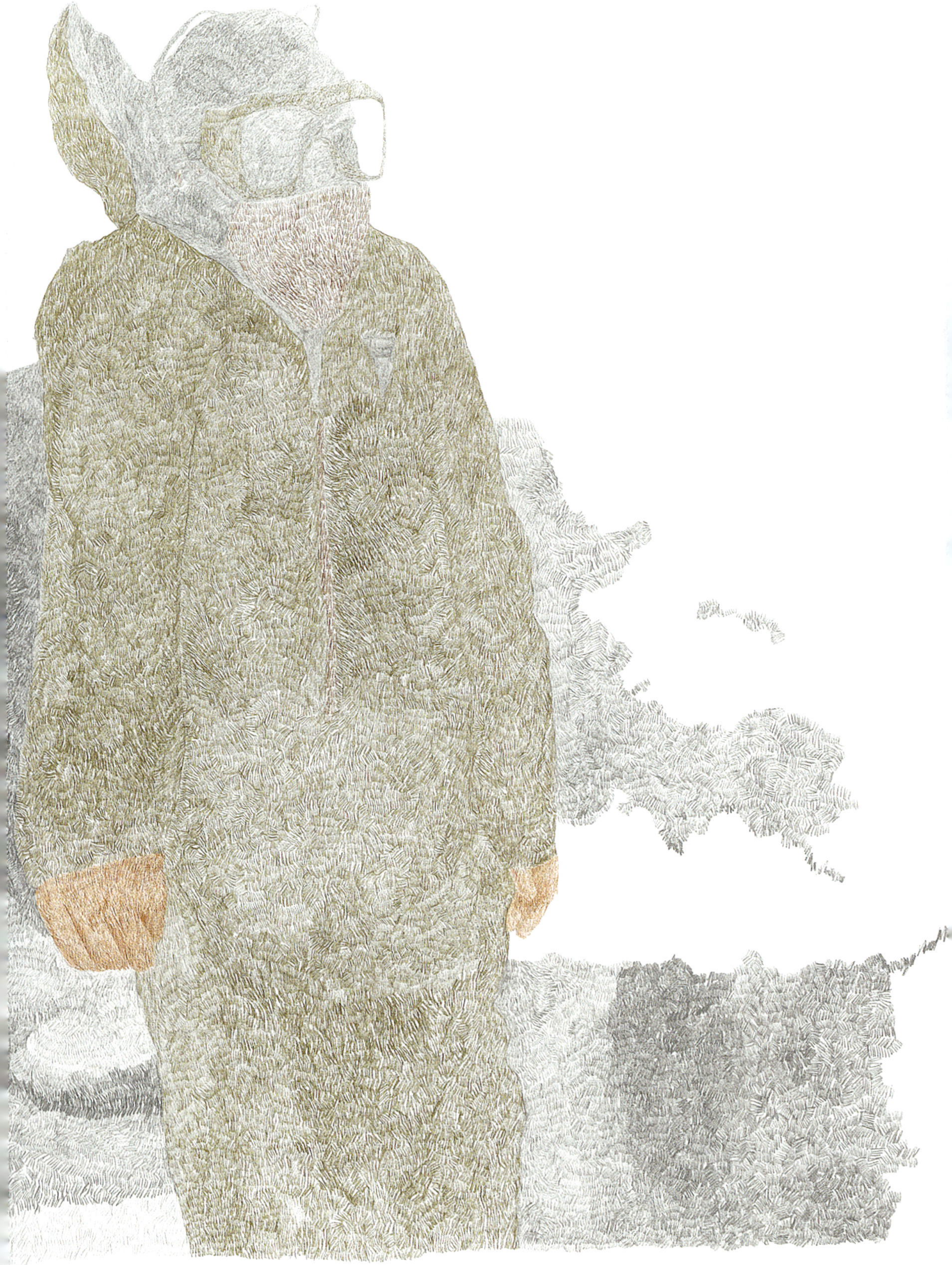

Florent
Perrier

And the Gold of Their Bodies

—

Refractions of Fukushima

p. 98

Et l'or de leur corps

—

Réfractions Fukushima

Poets, artists and the entire human race would be most unhappy if that absurdity, the ideal, were to be discovered. What would each of us do thereafter with his poor ego, his broken line?

Charles Baudelaire [1]

After living through or undergoing catastrophe, we can no more emerge unscathed than we can leave paradise undiminished: from the latter we emerge fallen, from the former as a miraculous survivor.

It is the same in matters of representation. To represent an Edenic place, to depict a catastrophe, you have to come at it from the side, to shift the frontality of the indescribable, take a step to one side, open up to an oblique approach that in fact stems from the subject itself, in that it forces us to look aside.

Refraction – *refringere*: to shatter or break – would thus be inherent in the representation of catastrophe: a necessary shattering that offers the gaze a change of direction, that calls into question our vision of the world: a critical escape that, as Natacha Nisic engineers it, allows us to see from an odd angle, from the margins, what a strict reflection would leave as unbearable, un-representable.

When refracted, the implacable nature of catastrophe is delayed, slowed down, disrupted or deviated by a kind of latency that removes its authoritarian violence and readies it for apprehending, for the grasp of the understanding which, with the support of the imagination, recomposes what in a raw image would be obscene, suffocating.

Redoubled by means of expression, this capture after-the-event is the act of the artist, a passage into a medium of refringency, of different resistance, which displaces the original vision and reorients the gaze: representation is peeled away from the event itself, allowing, with other works, at other times, and in other places, for possibilities of dialogue freed from the smothering grip of topicality.

Witness this wash showing Denis-Auguste-Marie Raffet [fig. 1], where aftermath becomes a series of mutilated bodies, chunks of burned human beings assembled after the first ever railway disaster on 8 May 1842. Refracted, the montage of "uneventful bodies" becomes the foretelling of future disasters, a mind-twisting sketch in which the inaugural event of the mortal marriage of technology and mass transport already contains its most fatal prolongations. [2]

"Uneventful bodies" – bodies without history – is what Paul Gauguin saw in the men and women

he painted on the rough canvases of his last stay in the Marquesas, when he left what, for him, was the overly controlled island of Tahiti and took refuge there in September 1901. Ten years earlier, he said he was leaving for Polynesia "in order to have peace and quiet, to be rid of the influence of civilization" and "to do simple, very simple art" in the midst of virgin nature. [3]

There he depicted exotic Eves and paradisiacal evocations of "delicious days" [fig. 2]. The standard trope of the decline of the West is accompanied here by a withdrawal to an island of happiness, and in gluing under the binding of his manuscript on "The Modern Spirit and Catholicism" a woodcut titled *Paradise Lost* he was directly identifying "colonization with original sin, the West and the corrupting tree of knowledge." [4]

This was confirmed in his acerbic exchange with August Strindberg, who told him: "You have created a new earth and a new heaven, but I don't feel at home in this world of yours . . . And your paradise contains an Eve who isn't my ideal." [5] Gauguin replied that the rejection of his painting revealed "the conflict between your civilization and my barbarism. Civilization from which you suffer; barbarism which is for me a rejuvenation." [6]

One month before his death, isolated and sick, he still insisted on his voluntary remoteness from civilization as meeting the need to unlearn, as a savage, a history that had become burdensome, [7] constantly hindering him from instinctively grasping the superior grace that he observed in his insular hosts.

This would explain why the bodies painted by Gauguin were so precious to him, why they were the bodies of a golden age that he dreamed about, but even more tangible than that: the living trace of a lived Eden summed up in the title of a painting from 1901: *And the Gold of Their Bodies* [fig. 3].

From the "golden, almost naked body" [8] of the young Vaitauni to the "golden yellow" [9] skin of the island people, Gauguin magnified the modest sensuality of the Polynesians, whose sometimes playful innocence contrasted with the civilized rottenness that he execrated and denounced. And yet, in his way, the artist himself maintained a link with this impurity as an agent of colonization. [10] Above all, he carried it in himself, this rottenness, up to the end of his life, in the form of the wounds on his legs, corroded by eczema and marked by the syphilis he brought with him from Europe, marking him out as a kind of leper. Even worse, what was visible on him, however much he rejected it – this catastrophe called "civilization" which he could not avoid – he also knew to be violently present in this culture that he fantasized as being free of all Western ills:

"Soon the Marquesan will be incapable of climbing a cocoanut-tree, incapable of going up the mountain after the wild bananas that are so nourishing to him. The child who is kept in school, deprived of physical exercise, his body always clad (for the sake of decency) becomes delicate and incapable of enduring a night in the mountains. They are all beginning to wear shoes and their feet, which are tender now, cannot run over the rough paths and cross the torrents on stones. Thus we are witnessing the spectacle of the extinction of the race, a large part of which is tubercular, with barren loins and ovaries destroyed by mercury." [11]

Under the gold of their bodies, therefore, rot was at work. A whole people was doomed to extinction, a measureless catastrophe for beings who could now exist only in the imagination.

The first time I saw it, Natacha Nisic's drawing reminded me of the title of that Gauguin painting, *And the Gold of Their Bodies.*

Was it the sense of a similar decay at work behind the immaculate exterior? An immediate relation between the subjacency of an invisible evil and a representation devoid of direct violence? Or the gold, the gold of their bodies, bodies that are also unhistorical, abstract, and disindividualized – unless we bear in mind the work's title: *Fukushima* [p. 127–132 + fig. 4].[12]

This drawing is associated with the title of a painting that is over a century older, but in addition, by objective chance, the title of the earlier work is intimately linked to the contents of the later one: it is, then, a matter of refraction, of the deviated gaze, or even of the untimely refraction of one work through another: resonance or constellation, hospitality or foreign body. An encounter, in any case.

On strong, immaculate white Canson paper, worked on as a roll – the vision of the drawing being executed was thus always sectioned, fragmentary, masked by the paper as it wrapped back over itself – remain only scant marks sketched in pencil: general forms, contours partially erased, corrections here or there. These sketchy forms are the only lines that continue the drawing, the only slender (and soon to disappear) lines, for the drawing itself is made up only of striations and creases, of marks no sooner begun than suspended, stick drawings you might say, not touches, but the scrupulous marks of the pencil returning regularly over the sheet in a beat or pulse, the scattering of parallel traces organized in successive zones and laid out to a changeless, implacable rhythm, propagating and contaminating with its marks the whole expanse assigned to the motif.

This texture with no backing other than the white of the paper, a texture without a weft, therefore, like something floating or emerging, the vibration of a shimmer, is distinctive in that it is made exclusively with luminescent metal pencils amidst the darkness – like fireflies, which are also luminescent.

In the box of twelve pencils, pewter, copper, and silver sit with gold and antique gold. It was the use of the latter that prompted the association with *And the Gold of Their Bodies.*

To understand why Natacha Nisic chose to represent the disaster that occurred at Fukushima on 11 March 2011 we must first look back over a career in which catastrophe and its modes of representation are probed with extreme rigor.

In 2005, Natacha Nisic went to the extermination camp at Auschwitz, where she filmed *La Porte de Birkenau* [fig. 5] using a tracking and zoom shot which leaves an impression of unease, of unresolved tension, as if the stillness had been captured in the very impossibility of its movement and before and after any unleashing of violence. This impression is heightened at the Shoah Memorial in Paris, where the work is on permanent display, projected on two screens separated by a passage, a broken line where life and movement intervene, in the materialization of a refraction, a progression between media of differing refringency.

In this same place, the artist has set out the *Mémorial des enfants* [fig. 6] based on photographic archives patiently collected by Serge Klarsfeld. Nisic wanted to create a subtle luminous pulsation, a detail that in the end could not be achieved but which resonates with the use of luminous pencils for *Fukushima* in terms of the meticulous work on light, on the difference in luminous density characteristic of all refraction.

Along with *La Porte de Birkenau*, at Auschwitz Nisic also shot and photographed what would become *Effroi* [p. 11 + fig. 7], a cathartic walk along the edges and on the inside of the extermination camp, among its ruins, where the violent contrast between the peaceful setting and the knowledge and memory of what happened there, of what the

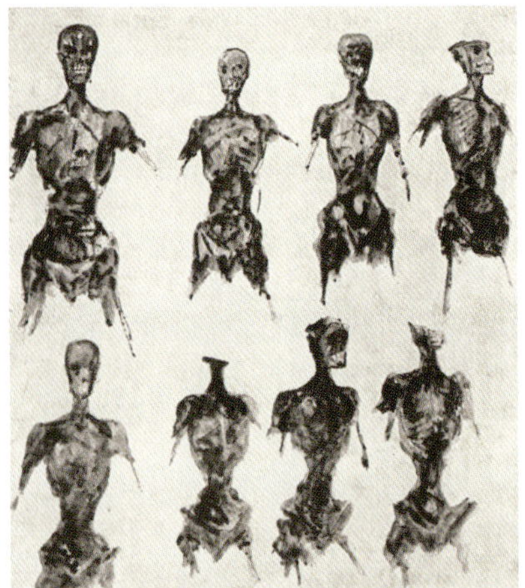

Denis-Auguste-Marie Raffet, *8 mai 1842. Victimes de l'accident de chemin de fer de la rive gauche*, 1842, reproduction of the original drawing, 12.4 × 13.7 cm. Bibliothèque Nationale de France, Département des Estampes et de la Photographie, Paris (Qb1-1841-1842/M113016)

fig. 1

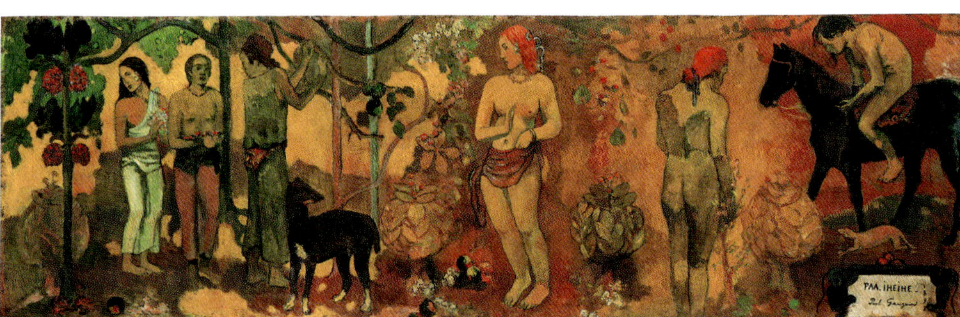

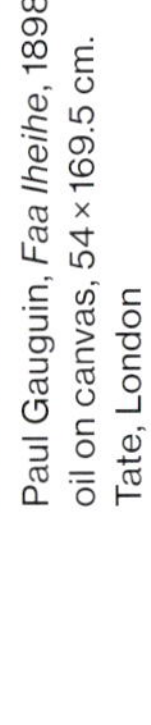

Paul Gauguin, *Faa Iheihe*, 1898, oil on canvas, 54 × 169.5 cm. Tate, London

fig. 2

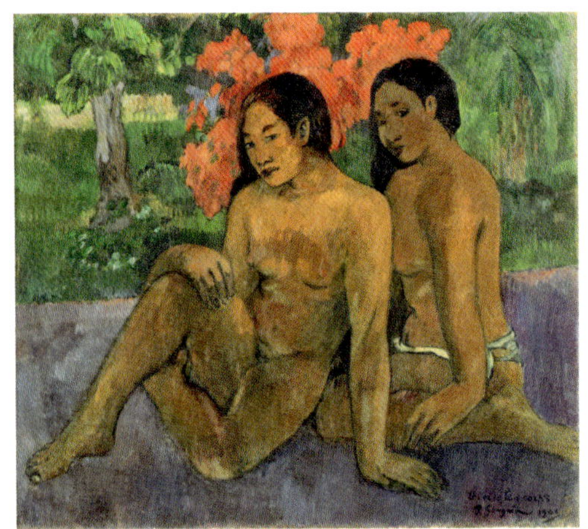

Paul Gauguin, *Et l'or de leur corps*, 1901, oil on canvas, 67 × 76.5 cm. Musée d'Orsay, Paris

fig. 3

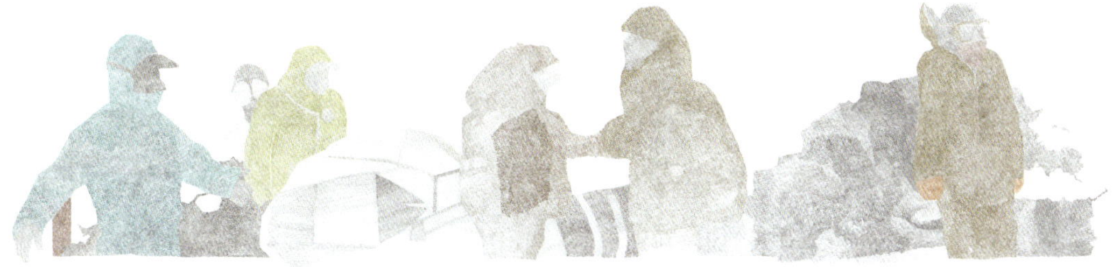

fig. 4

Natacha Nisic, *Fukushima*, 2011, color pencil on Canson paper, 75 × 315 cm

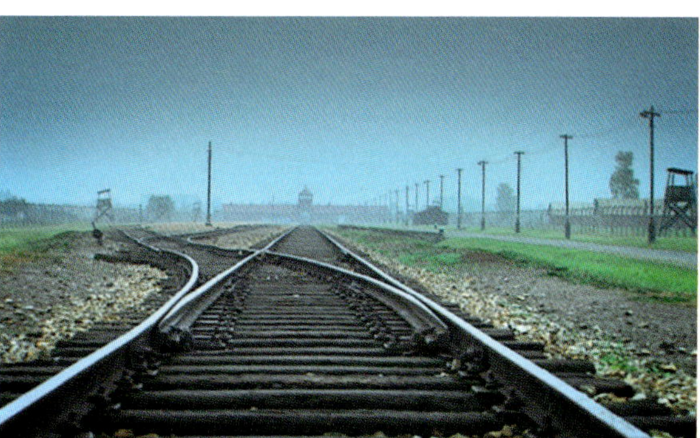

fig. 5

Natacha Nisic, *La Porte de Birkenau*, 2005, HD video projection, color, 3'

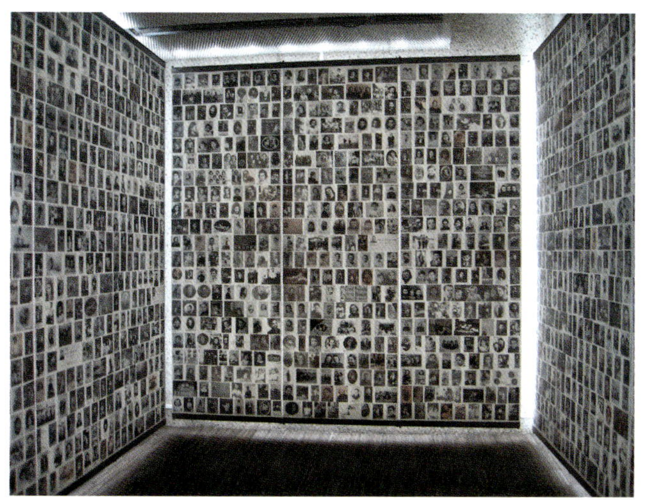

fig. 6

Natacha Nisic, *Mémorial des enfants*, 2005, 3,500 digital prints on strips of Arche mounted on Macrolife panels lit from behind on a steel structure, 120 m². Mémorial de la Shoah, Paris

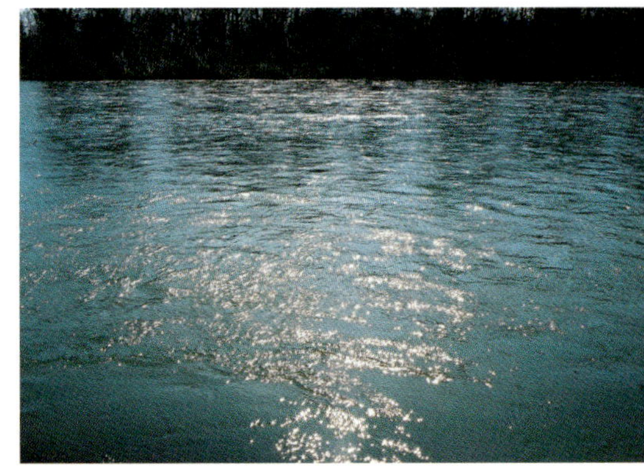

fig. 7

Natacha Nisic, *Effroi – La Vistule*, 2005, color photograph, 110 × 80 cm

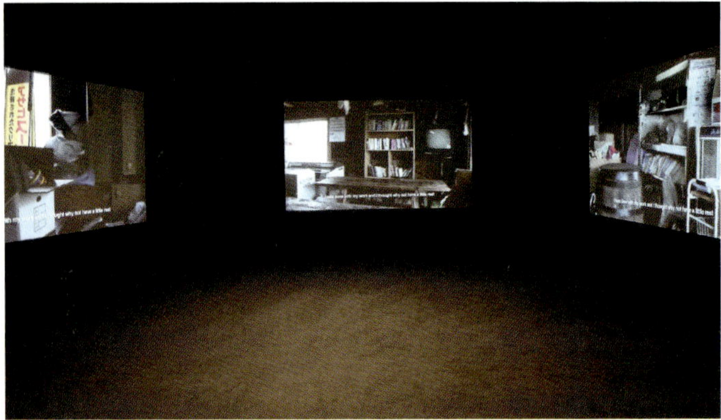

fig. 8

Natacha Nisic, e, 2009, 3 HD video projections, color, 5.1 sound, each 19'. View of the exhibition "Big Picture (Orte / Projektionen)," K21 Kunstsammlung Nordrhein-Westfalen, Düsseldorf, 2011

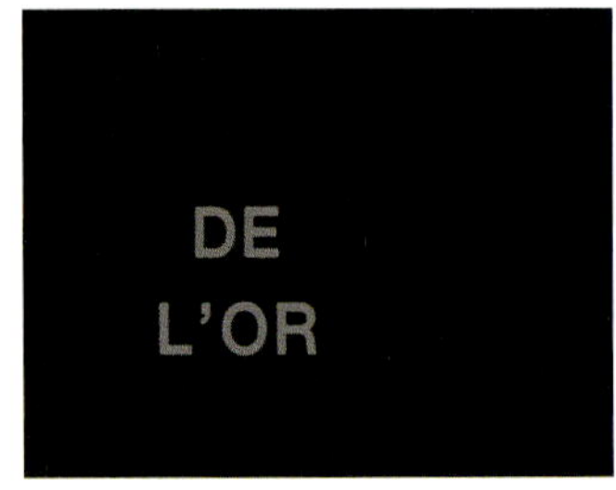

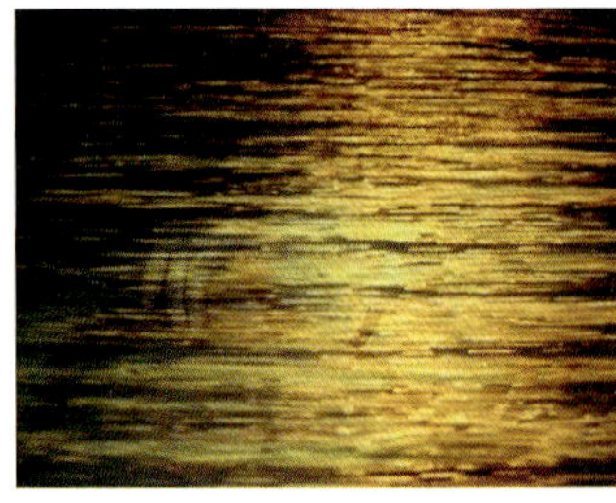

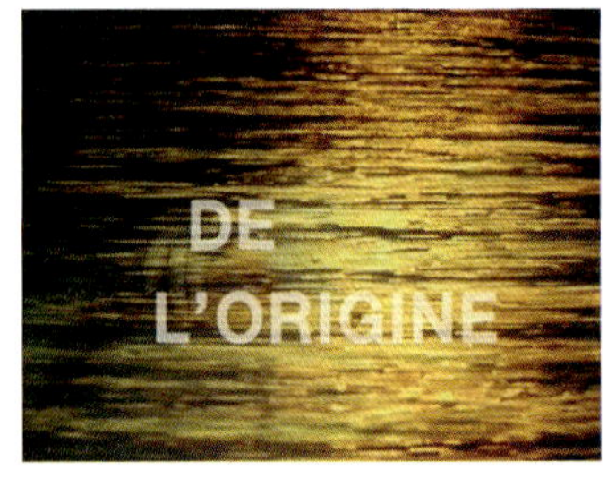

Jean-Luc Godard and Anne-Marie Miéville, *De l'origine du XXIe siècle*, 2000, video, color, 16'

place continues to contain, takes the form of a kind of death mask emerging on the surface of an artificial pond, an amorphous chimera, a dreadful specter that refraction – at work here once again – and the disorientation of the juxtaposed shots make even more enigmatic. Although the artist photographed a reflective surface – "a watery surface where the sky and scenery are tranquilly reflected with an indecent beauty. The pond surrounded by birch trees has the appearance of a serene landscape, a peaceful natural setting. The pond is located just below the gas chamber. Not pure water. It contains the ashes of bodies, and yet it is a perfect mirror of the world"[13] – her desire to "capture even more intensely the density of the water" as the sudden appearance of a death mask, half-emerging and half-drowned, and the visual distortion that results from it, displace her action from the field of reflection to that of refraction: from the straight line, the unbearable straight line, to the broken line.

A detail in the *Effroi* catalogue indicates this, when the artist points out that, after the discovery of that aqueous specter, she returned to Auschwitz to "attempt to exorcise the play of fate," and originally thought of filming the action:

"The action consists in going back close to the reservoir (I originally thought of wearing a kind of translucent mask guaranteeing the anonymity and universality of the action, a surface, a distance between the body and the elements), and immersing my face, covered by the mask, in the water. Life restored to the surface of the water and to what it contains."[14]

Between the masked head plunged underwater and the body remaining outside the liquid element, reality is deviated, refraction is at work, vision overturned.

And how can we not associate the death mask of the Auschwitz reservoir with the translucent one that the artist wanted to wear in response to the fear, how can we not associate these confounded and commingling masks – anonymous death, dreadful death – with the ones worn by the men in the drawing *Fukushima*?

In June 2008, Nisic travelled to that same region in Japan where a violent earthquake had wrought havoc among the superb mountain scenery. With that now forgotten, already exceeded catastrophe, it was the virgin nature evoked by Gauguin that was impacted at its very heart. The artist's installation *e* (image in Japanese)

returns after the event to what occurred as if in secret, not without affecting men, their structures and ways of life, but at such a distance from the densely populated zones that the disaster went almost unnoticed, leaving here and there only a few broken lines, tangible traces of a seismic refraction deep down [fig. 8 + p. 156–184]. As *Le Monde* noted at the time, "according to official statements, the activities of the nuclear power stations have not been affected. Nevertheless, in Fukushima Province, a 'small quantity of radioactive water' did escape from the storage tanks of a nuclear site after the seism, 'but with no danger to the population,' announced the Tepco electricity company, which manages the nuclear reactor at Fukushima."[15]

Metallic pencils to represent the catastrophe of March 2011, golden, bronze, or moiré tints, a shimmering, a luminous pulsation surrounded by an outline with no real edges, but no spreading or overflowing, no tangible distress – the simple brightness of uneventful, unhistorical lines?

And yet *Fukushima* refracts our gaze toward the great archive of images of past catastrophes: from the sublime brightness of the nuclear sun to the colored fields of exploding napalm, Nisic gathers the trace of past dazzlements, which here have become fragments, beaded in an infinity of visual stridencies – shards of memory grafted onto the open eye, onto the prohibited pupil [fig. 9].[16]

If, as she points out with regard to representation of the Shoah, her sensibility leads her to approach things "from the side rather than frontally,"[17] that is also because the catastrophe cannot be contemplated face-on, because its incidence must be deviated, placed against a denser refringent medium, with a historical or sensorial density that does not relativize its present singularity but, on the contrary, makes it absolutely distinct by confrontation, by the traversal of epochs and events.

The apparatus chosen for *f* implicitly illustrates this [p. 143–156]. In this piece shot in the Fukushima region in 2013, Nisic uses a seemingly elementary play of mirrors to expose us to a series of confrontations, less with the landscape of catastrophe than with the world that it has hollowed out. Cross references and repercussions – visual loops like Moebius strips leading to an eternal return – the echo of the world comes to us only when we turn our backs on its movement: the direction of our reading is disrupted, visions are off-kilter, the present is suspended like an enigma, and both time and space hover, like those threads, those ropes with nothing hanging from them swaying in the wind.

Here, refraction echoes reflection, or that toward which, outside the frame, the artist displaces our gaze and opens it via the gap thus created – not a gaze petrified by strict reflection (of the catastrophe), but its other, disquieted, agitated by this un-centring, this disjoining.

A source of errors, refraction has its vices that distort observation,[18] deform vision, and provoke lateral deviations [19] that are topographically deceptive. In *Le Problème de la réfraction dans l'histoire du cartésianisme*, the author notes that "knowledge of the fundamental law of refraction" alone was enough to allow improvement "of the manufacture of the lenses used in telescopes. At stake here, from a speculative viewpoint [was] the triumphant confirmation of heliocentrism by means of observation."[20]

By observing these errors or flaws of refraction separating the normal from the pathological, the direct from the deviant, what is at stake is thus our vision of the world.

But art resists, just as artists are refractory. They play on gaps and broken lines in order to overturn triumphant heliocentrism or, here, the nuclear sun that nothing and no one, if we are to believe the contemporary doctrine, should be able to avoid.

And yet, Fukushima, Fukushima repeated: a bustle of men in boiler suits, a genuine *danse macabre* of reprieved beings beneath their meager projections. As in the 14th century, the chain of the living and dead is unbroken. But it is not limbs that ensure the contact, but the very organization of the graphic material that color and the density and intensity of the line distinguish as forms and figures. The drawing is like a bas-relief,[21] an interpretation reinforced by the uprightness of the hieratic poses. Looking closely, though, we see that this compactness is crumbling, but only in the background, which goes from an assemblage of hard, geometrical forms to their gradual dissolution, archipelagic forms gradually absorbed by the white of the sheet. Likewise, if the fixed forms are rendered by orderly lines, the more organic ones are woven by more shifting strokes, a shimmering or teeming rather than an alignment.

As for the figures, they hardly vary. The bodies are nearly all of the same height, as if leveled by the format of the drawing propped by their verticality. Nevertheless, this symbolic equality is factitious: the masks worn here protect those who are still alive, standing for what may be a limited time, the least fortunate being already on the ground, no doubt dead. Whereas a cataclysm produces a form of perfect equality, when none can obviate its suddenness, industrial or technological disaster reinforces social and economic hierarchies. At Fukushima, where the initial death count was 30,000, the populations were left alone to escape the disaster zone, with government leaving them only the liberty to be rich and evacuate or poor to die without a fuss. The liquidators, indeed, came from an ancient sub-proletariat, that of "Japan's most despised castes. Descendants of the *eta* – literally 'dirt-ridden' – and *hinin* – 'non-human' communities, the *burakumin* . . . are traditionally outsiders who perform tasks related to death, blood, and impurity."[22]

Behind these six vibrant, shimmering masks, behind these cramped figures, these eyes that we cannot see and these stares aimed we know not where, there is, then, a knowledge, knowledge redoubled by power, overhanging it, specters flitting by at the mouth of a modern Platonic cave, where the sun of ideas seems to have been replaced by nuclear fire and its morbid reality, its mendacious truth.

This general mirage orchestrated by Tepco and passed on by the narcotic power of the media, the accomplices of a failing state, is addressed by Nisic's drawing not only in the form of a silence, but also as an autism, a blindness in some ways reminiscent of the name of the Polynesian atoll where the French nuclear deterrent was tested – Moruroa: "great secret" in Maori.[23]

Paul Gauguin was in French Polynesia when, in Paris, Marie Curie coined the term "radioactivity" (1898), and it was exactly when Jean Perrin pictured atoms as solar systems that the artist painted *And the Gold of Their Bodies*.

Refractions, *Fukushima*?

Fukushima, Japanese for "island of happiness."

1.   "The Salon of 1846" in *Baudelaire: Selected Writings on Art and Artists*, Cambridge University Press, 1981, p. 77.

2.   Cf. my article "Des corps sans histoire – théâtres de l'imprévisible," *Recherches en esthétique*, no. 15, October 2009, p. 29–40.

3.   Interview with *L'Écho de Paris*, cited in *The Writings of a Savage*, New York: Vintage, 1978, reprint Cambridge, Mass.: Da Capo Press, 1996, p. 48.

4.   Françoise Cachin, *Gauguin*, Paris: Flammarion, 1988, p. 233.

5.   *Strindberg, Letters,* vol. 2, selected and edited by Michael Robinson, London: Athlone Press, 1992, p. 348.

6.   Letter to Strindberg, quoted in. Herschel B. Chipp, *Theories of Modern Art*, Berkeley: University of California Press, 1968, p. 82

7.   Cf. Paul Gauguin, *Lettres à sa femme et à ses amis*, Paris: Grasset, 1992, p. 339.

8.   Paul Gauguin, *Intimate Journals*, New York: Dover, p. 2.

9.   Paul Gauguin, *Intimate Journals*, New York: Dover, p. 39.

10.   He wore the spotless white garb of the colonizer, frequented the Cercle Militaire in Papeete, refused to be hospitalized with the poor, and for a while worked as a draftsman for the Office of Public Works.

11.   Paul Gauguin, *Intimate Journals*, New York: Dover, p. 39.

12.   The drawing measures 75 × 315 centimeters and was first exhibited at the Galerie Dominique Fiat, Paris, in April 2012.

13.   Natacha Nisic, "Ce qui reste," in Annette Becker and Octave Debary (eds.), *Montrer les violences extrêmes,* Paris: Créaphis, 2012, p. 147–148.

14.   Natacha Nisic in the catalogue to her exhibition *Effroi*, Paris: Musée Zadkine / Paris-Musées, 2005, n.p.

15.   Newspaper dated June 14, 2008.

16.   Reworked for this text, this article was originally a contribution to the symposium "Penser la catastrophe," organized by Alain Fleischer and Jean-Claude Conésa (whom I thank) at Le Fresnoy – Studio National des Arts Contemporains in January 2013. It comprised a passage in which the use of gold in certain contemporary works was related to Nisic's drawing. Here I will simply mention the names Alain Resnais and Marguerite Duras, Yves Klein, Robert Rauschenberg, Gérard Deschamps and Jean-Luc Godard.

17.   Natacha Nisic, "Spectre," interview with Nathan Réra in N. Réra, *De Paris à Drancy ou les Possibilités de l'art après Auschwitz*, Pertuis: Rouge profond, 2009, p. 71.

18.   Studies have considered the role in defining the originality of certain painters. Cf. the thesis by Aron Polack, *Rôle de l'état de réfraction de l'œil dans l'éducation et dans l'œuvre du peintre* (Paris: Librairie Ollier-Henry, 1900), which considers the vision of Émile Bernard, Eugène Carrière, and Jean-Léon Gérôme.

19.   Charles Lallemand, "L'erreur de réfraction dans le nivellement géométrique," *Rivista di topografia e catasto*, vol. 9, Turin: Bona, 1897, p. 5.

20.   Marie-Claire Macris-L'Hoest, *Le Problème de la réfraction dans l'histoire du cartésianisme*, thesis supervised by Suzanne Bachelard, Université Paris-I Panthéon-Sorbonne, 1983–1984, p. 18.

21.   We know that Gauguin was influenced by photographs of Greek and Indian friezes.

22.   Arkadi Filine, *Oublier Fukushima. Textes et documents*, Le Mas-d'Azil: Les Éditions du bout de la ville, 2012, p. 57–58.

23.   The basic etymological meaning is "big net," but by extension that which is captured therein. Linked with the idea of defense department secrecy, that gives us "the big secret."

—

Translated from French by Charles Penwarden

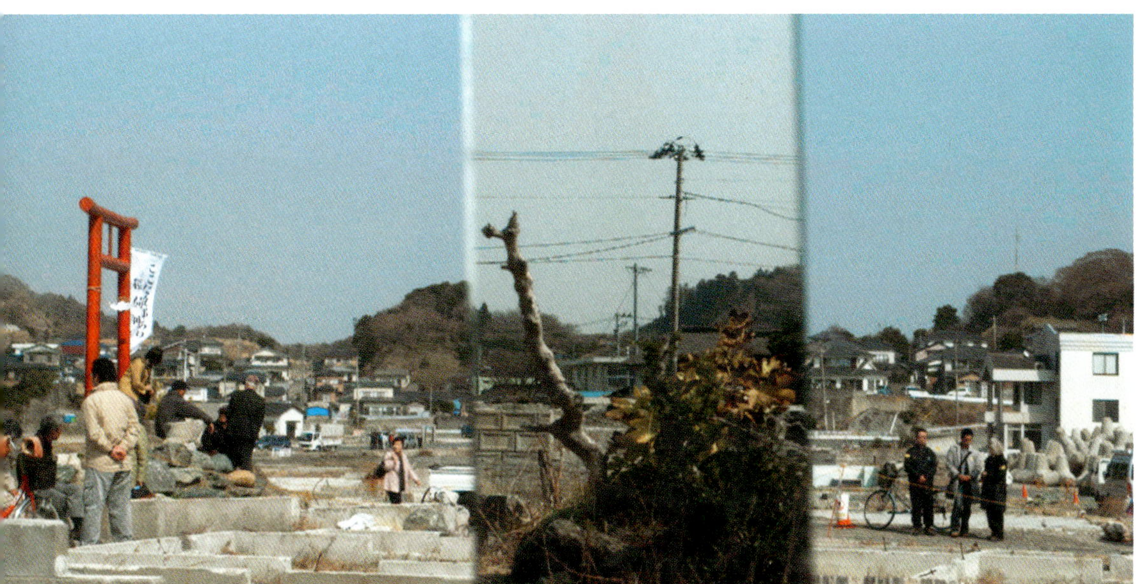

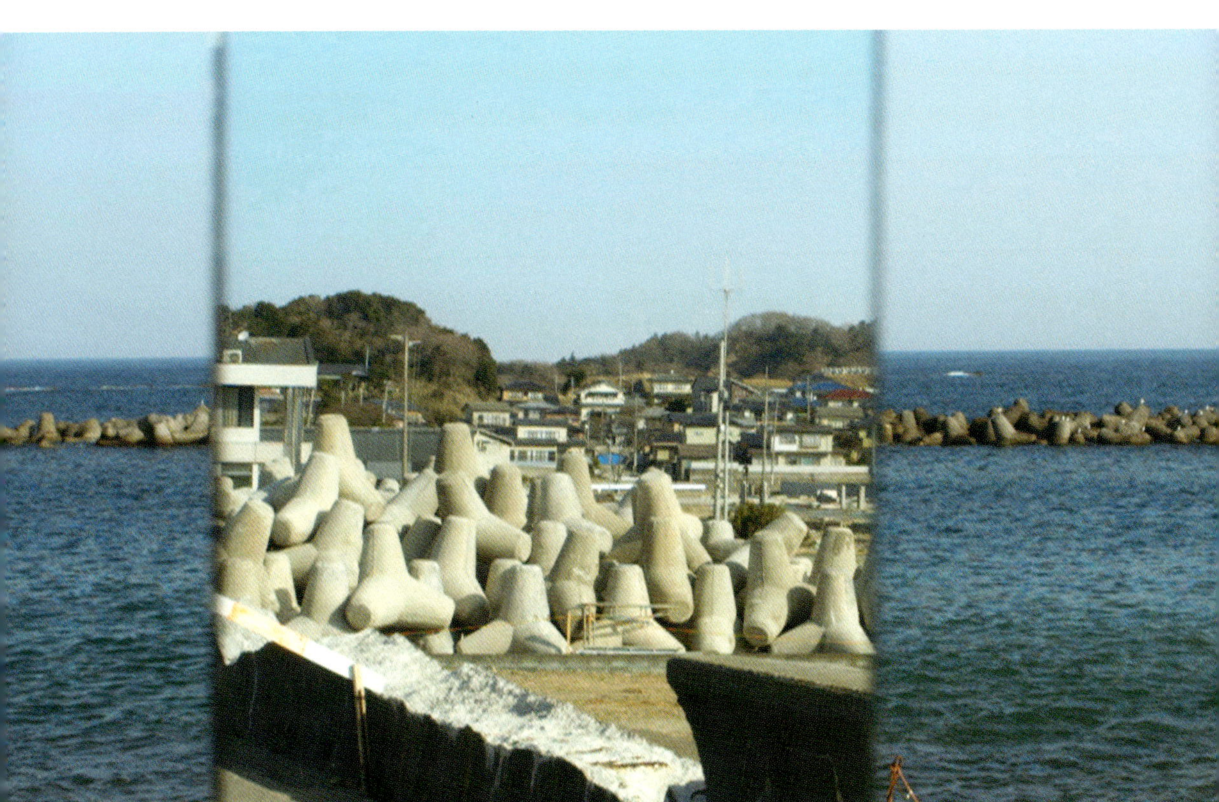

f

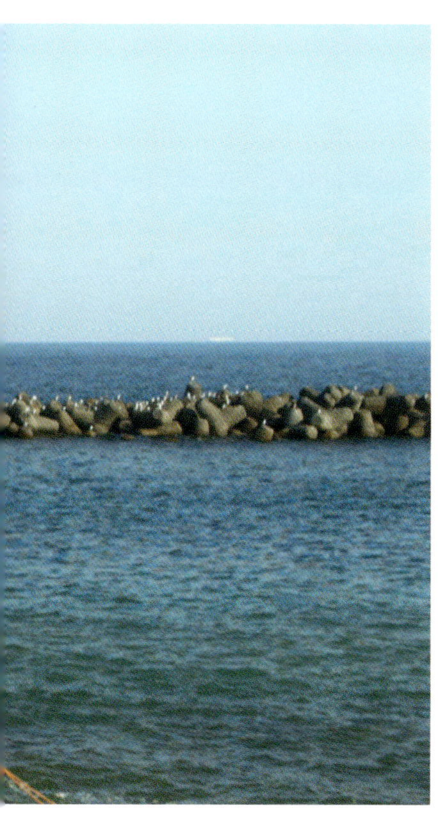

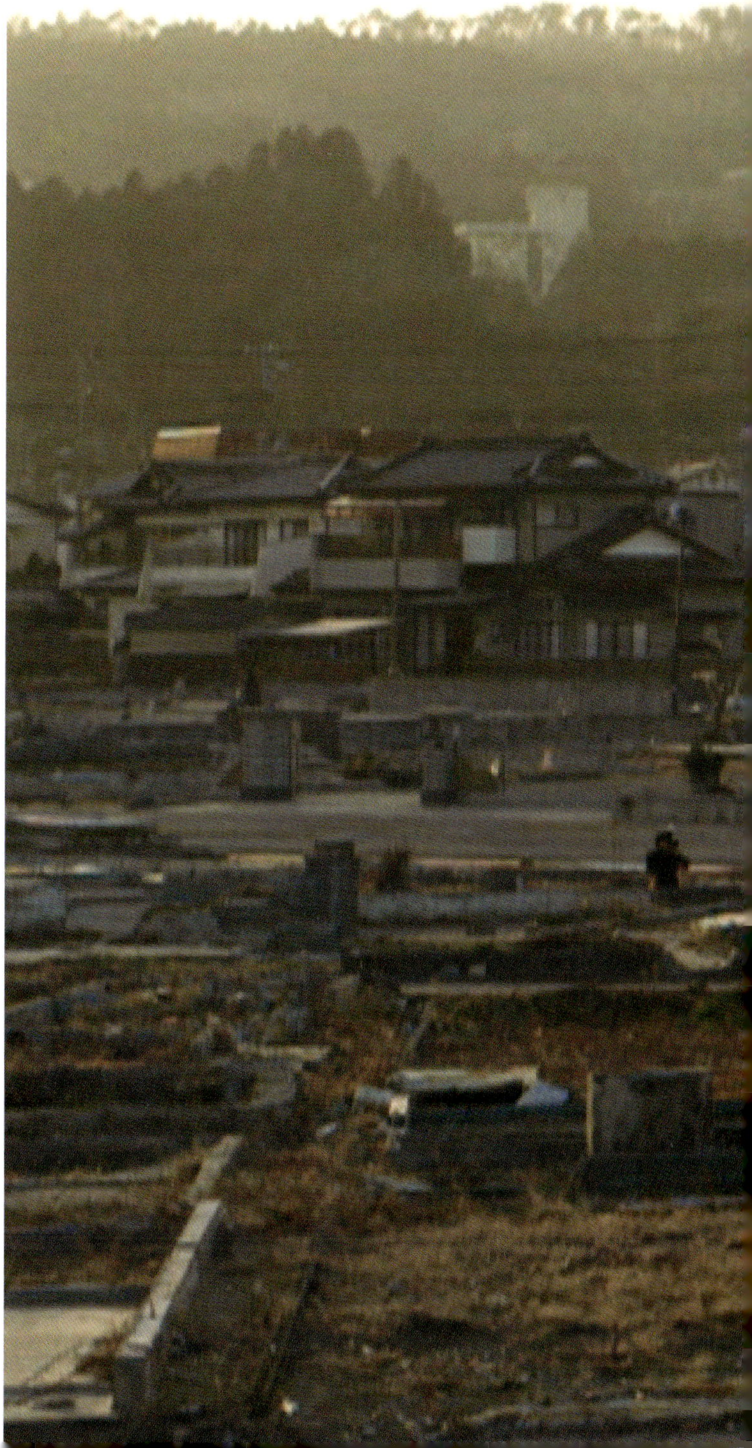

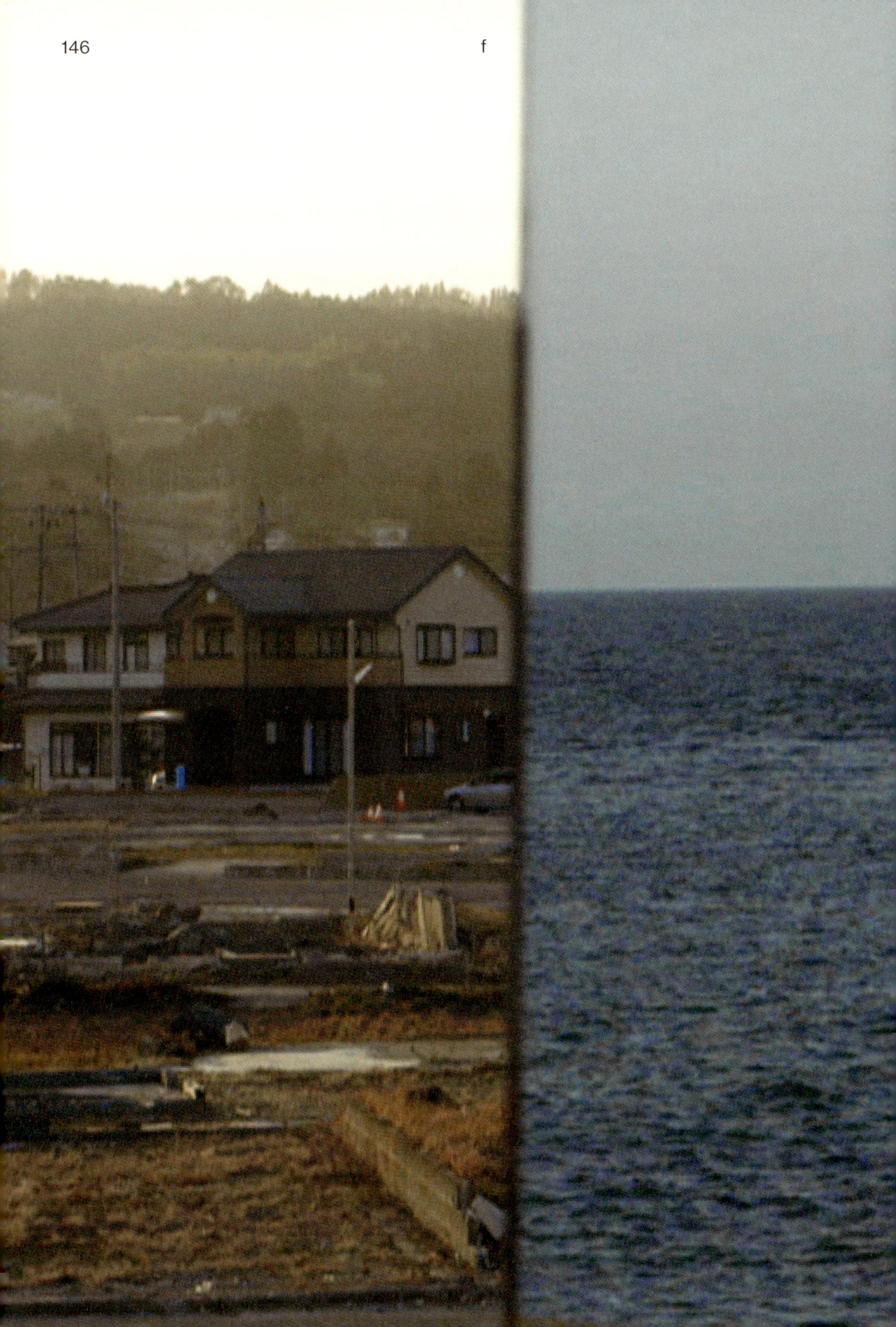

f

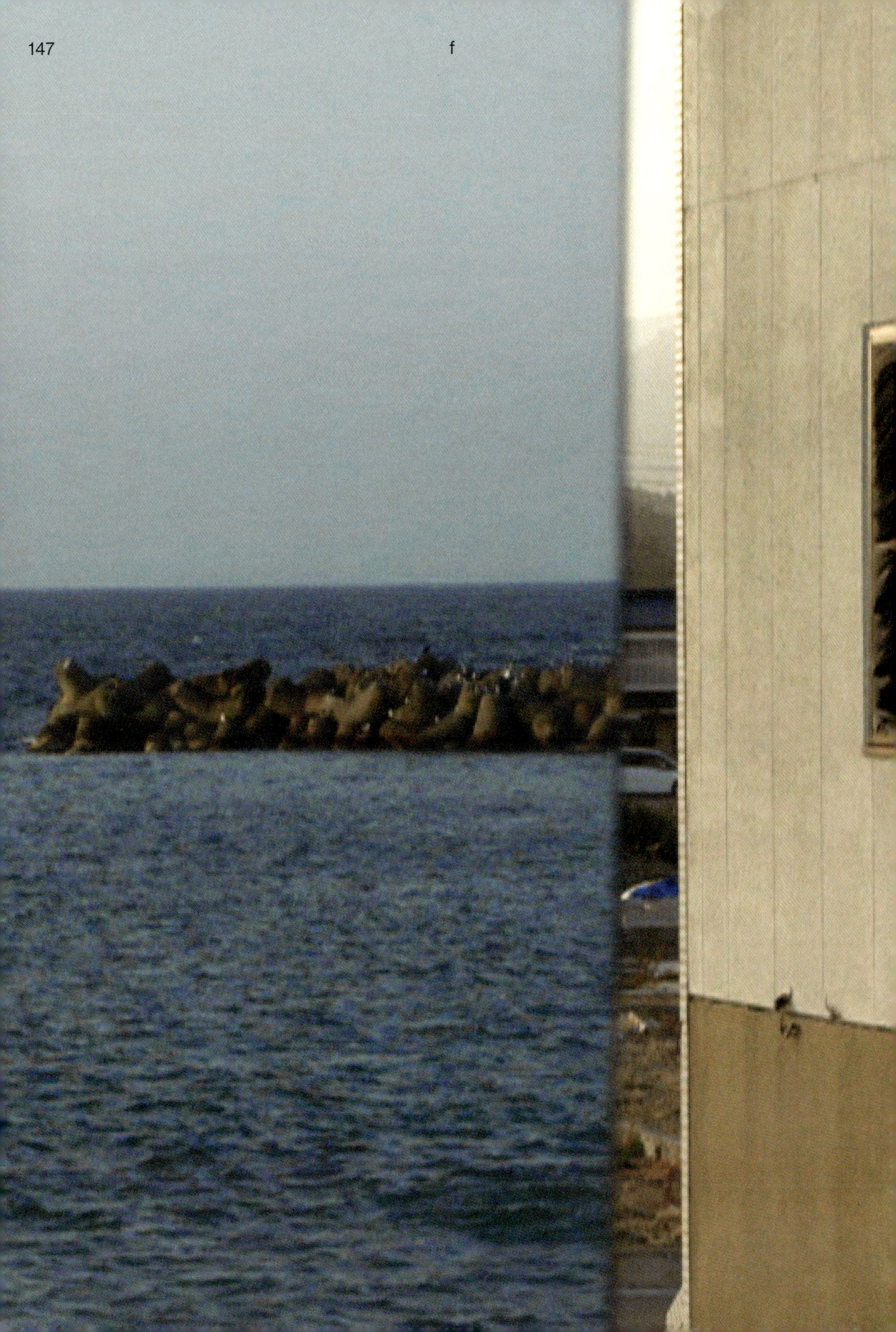

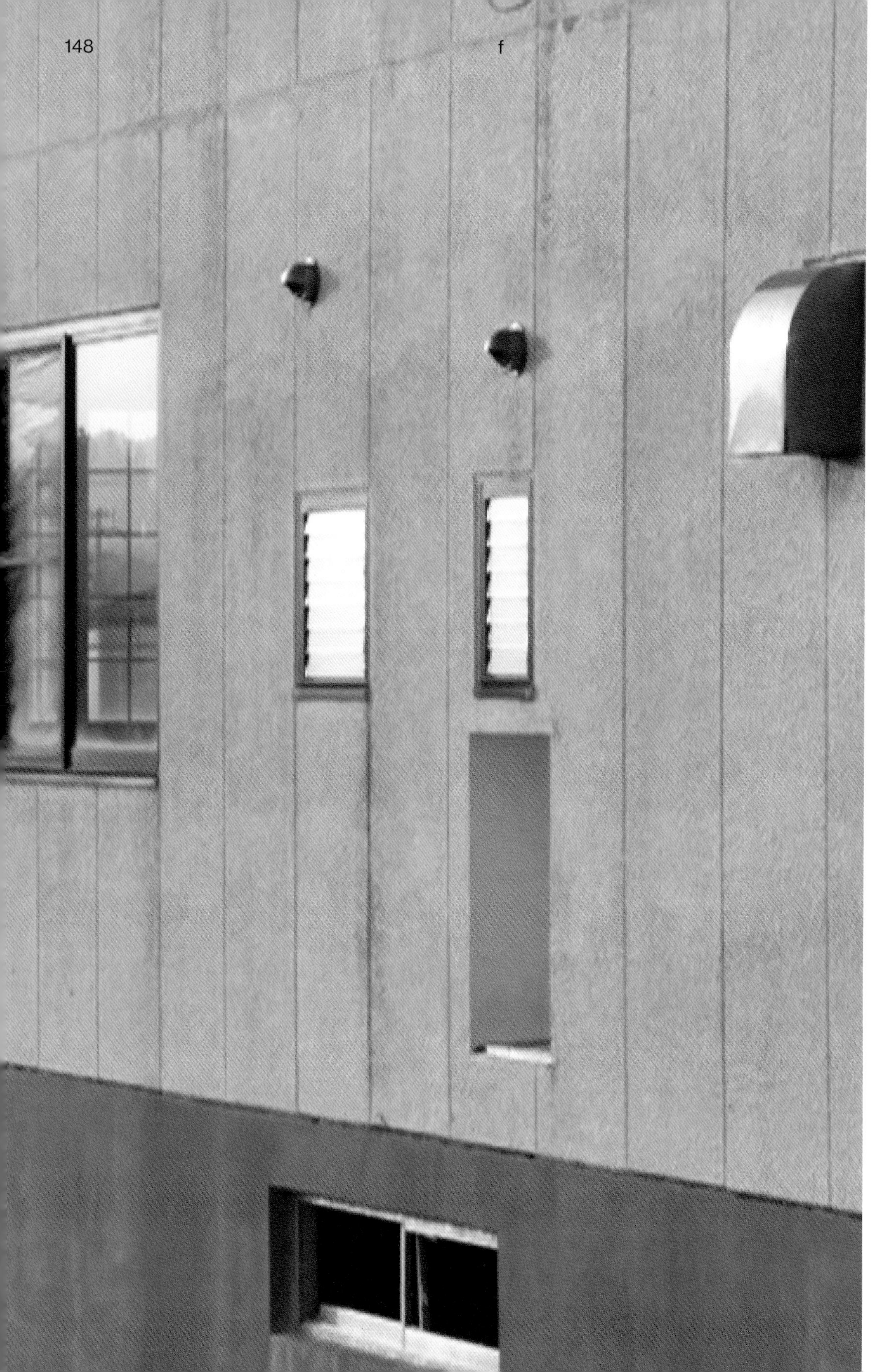
f

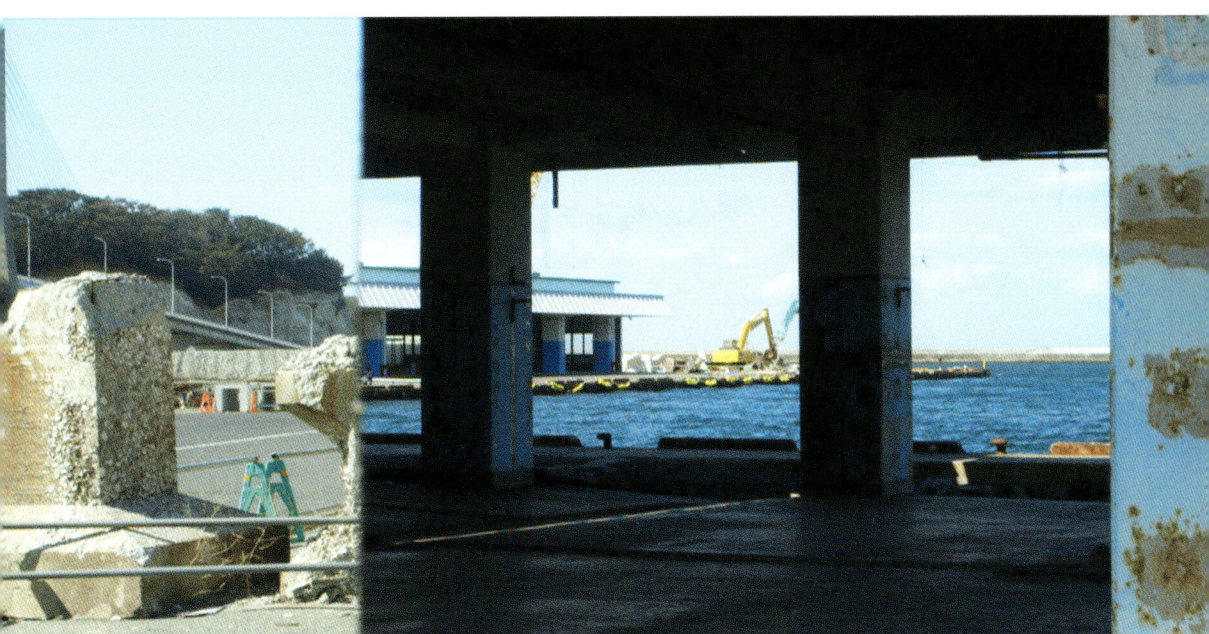

f

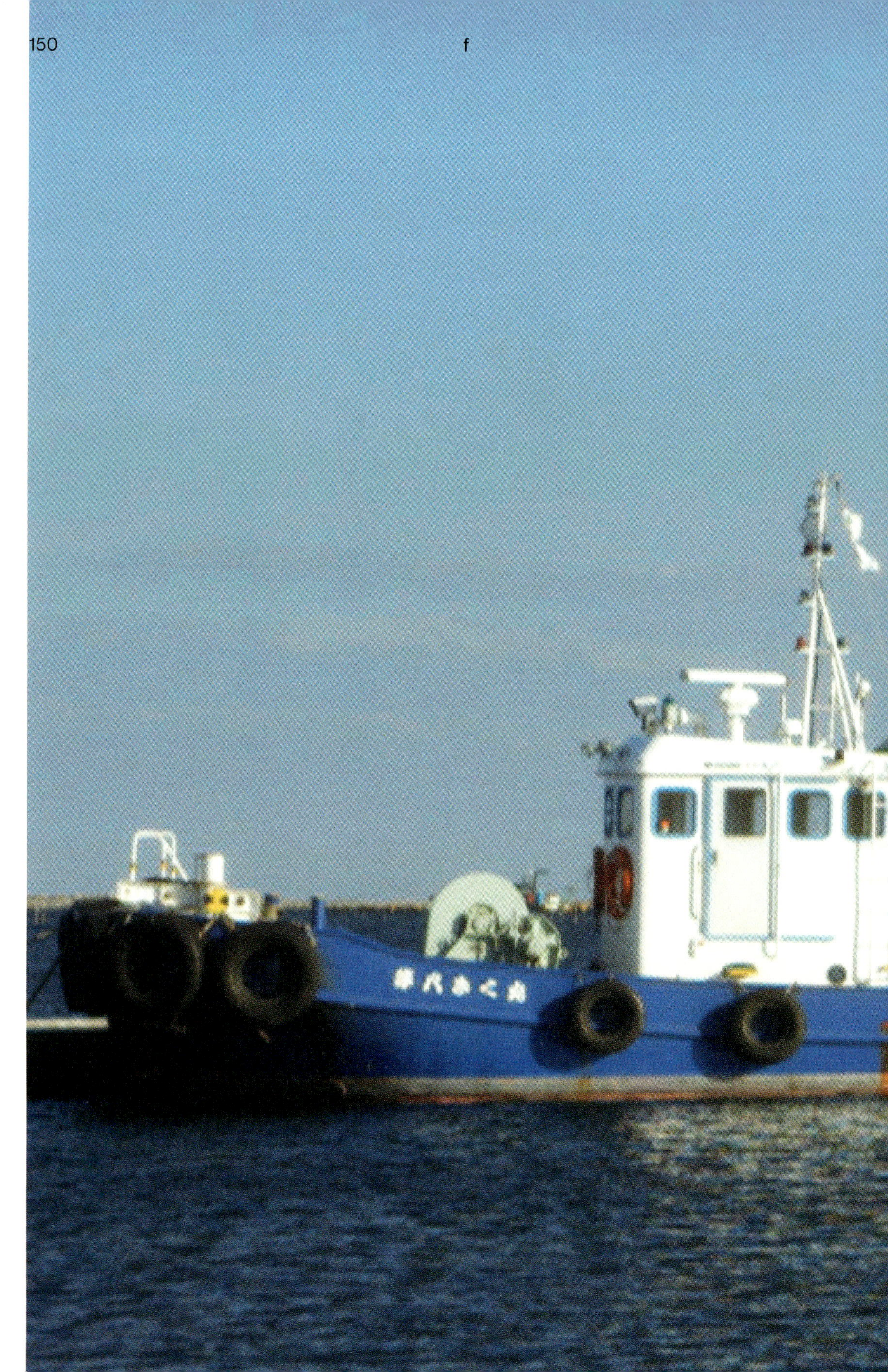

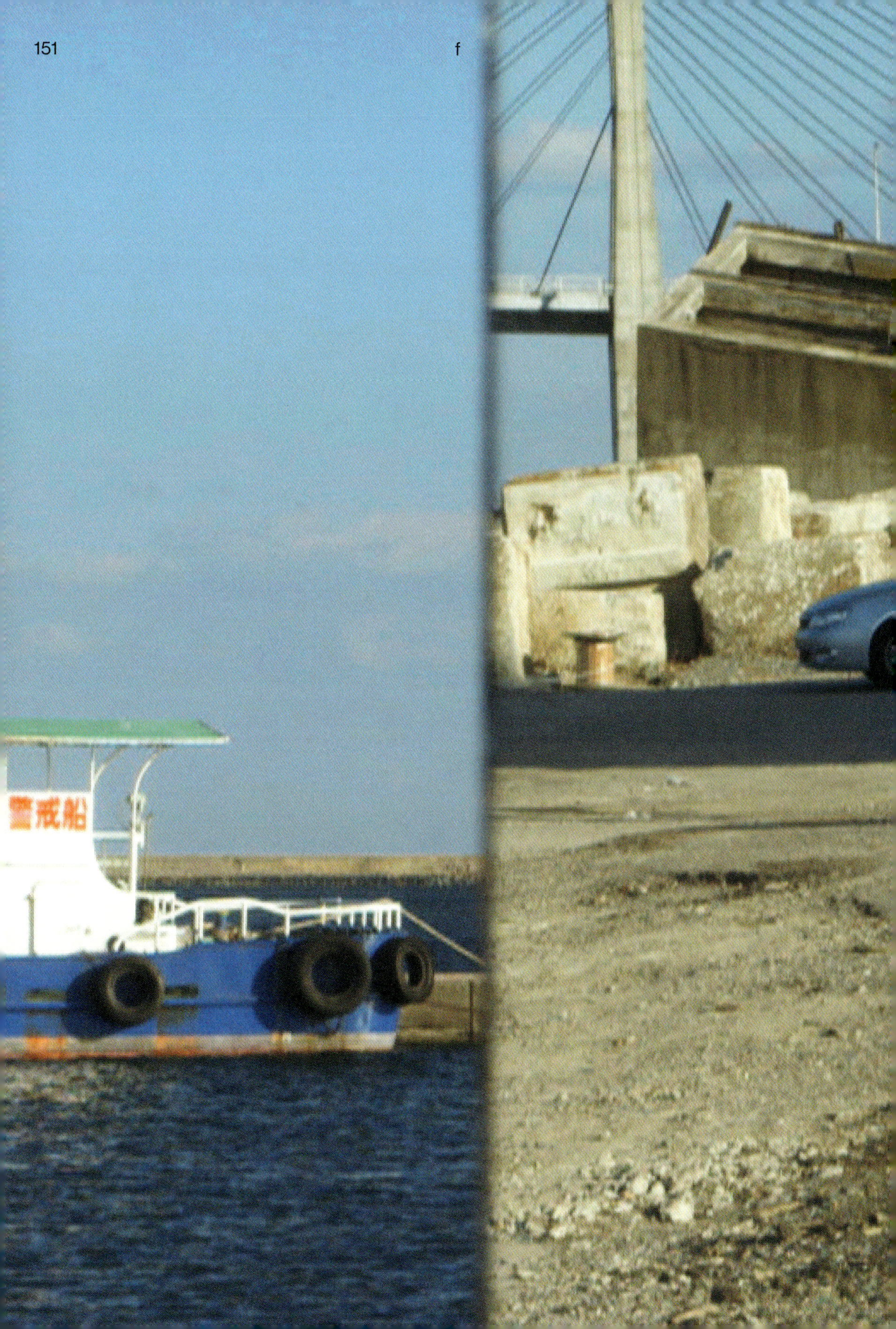

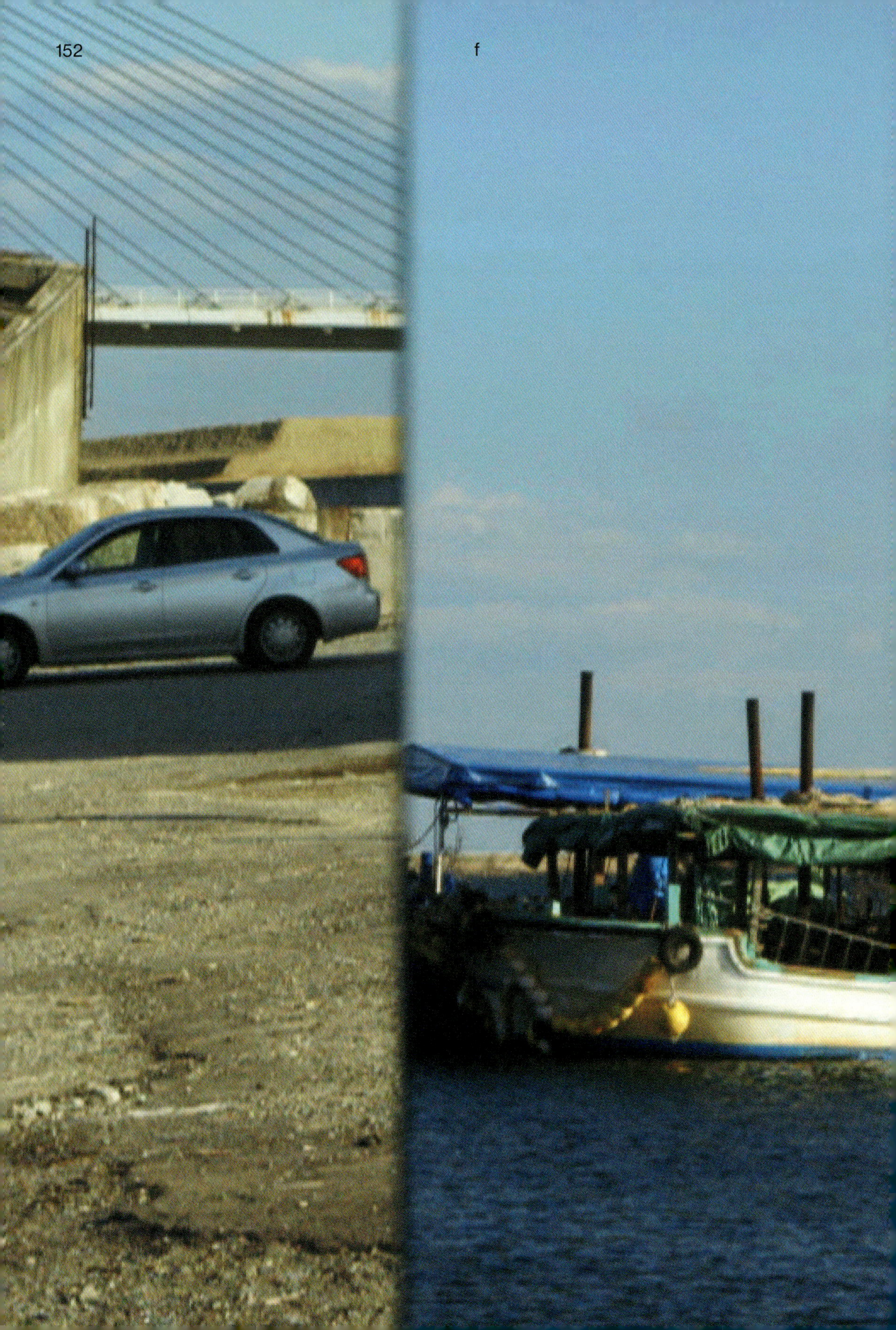

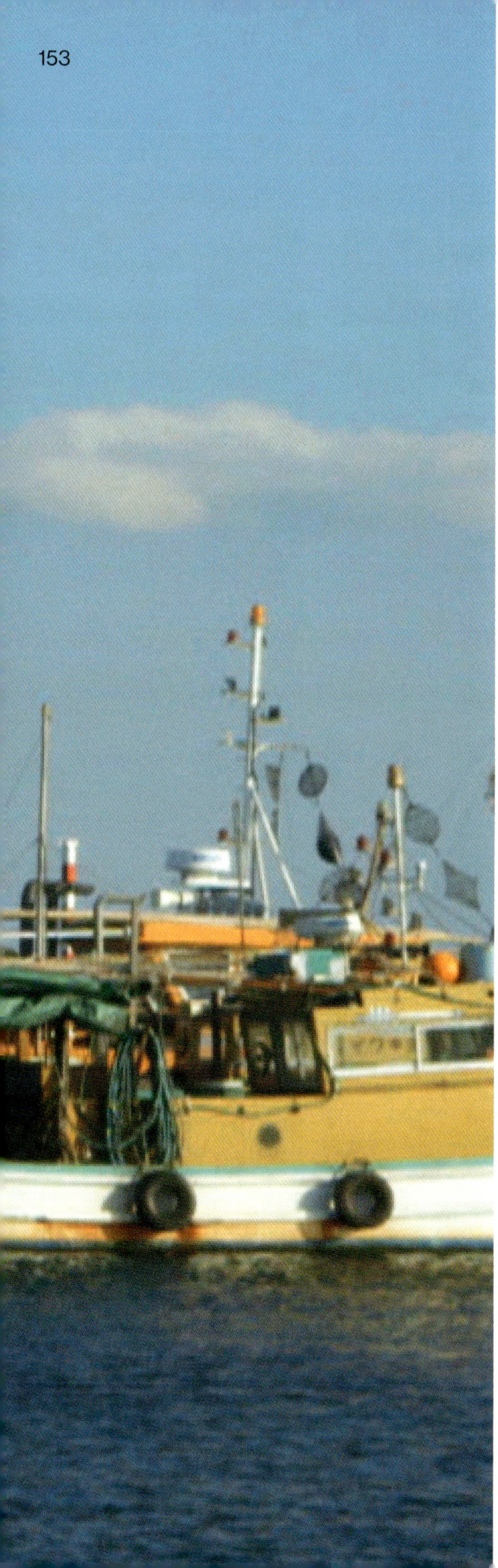

f

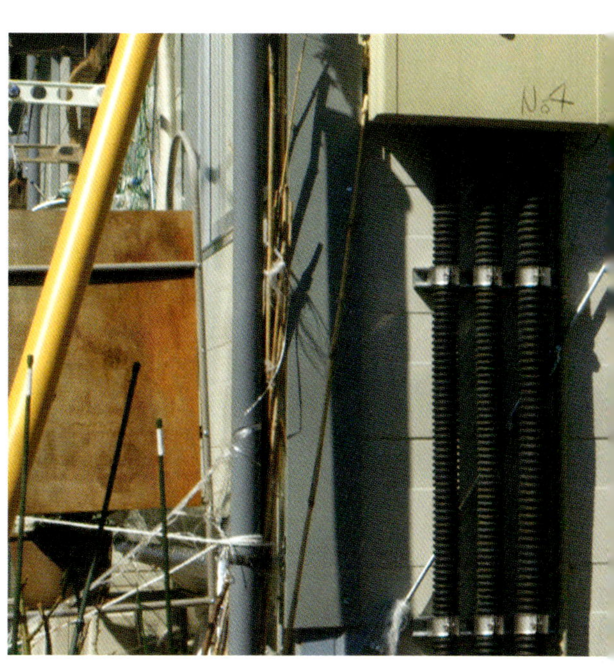

f

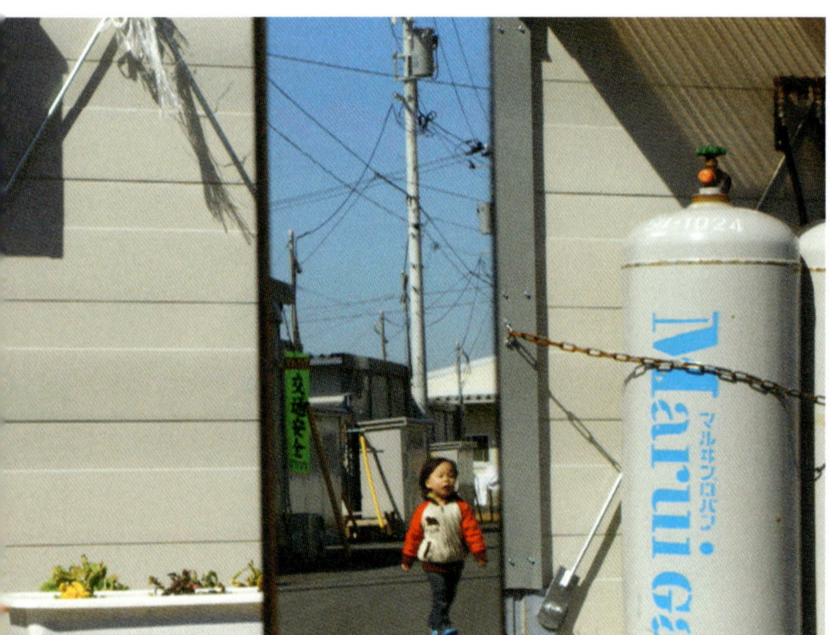

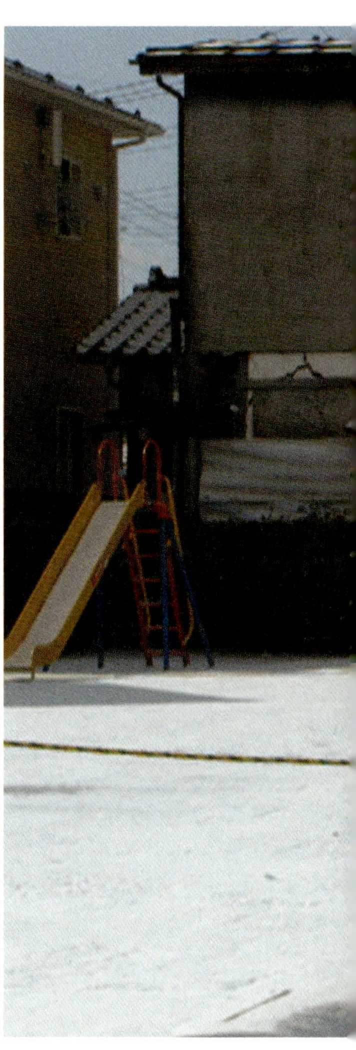

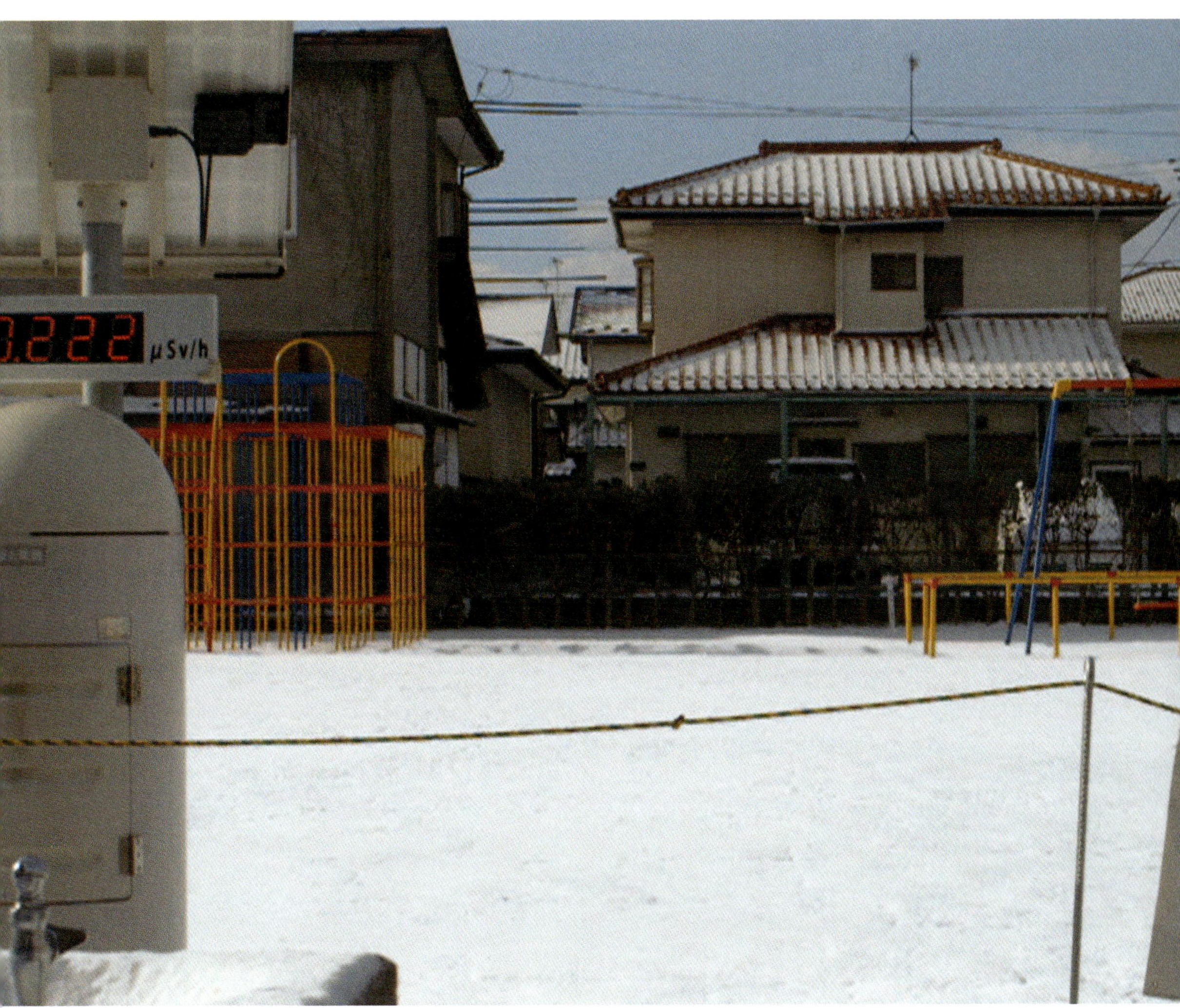
0.222 μSv/h

e

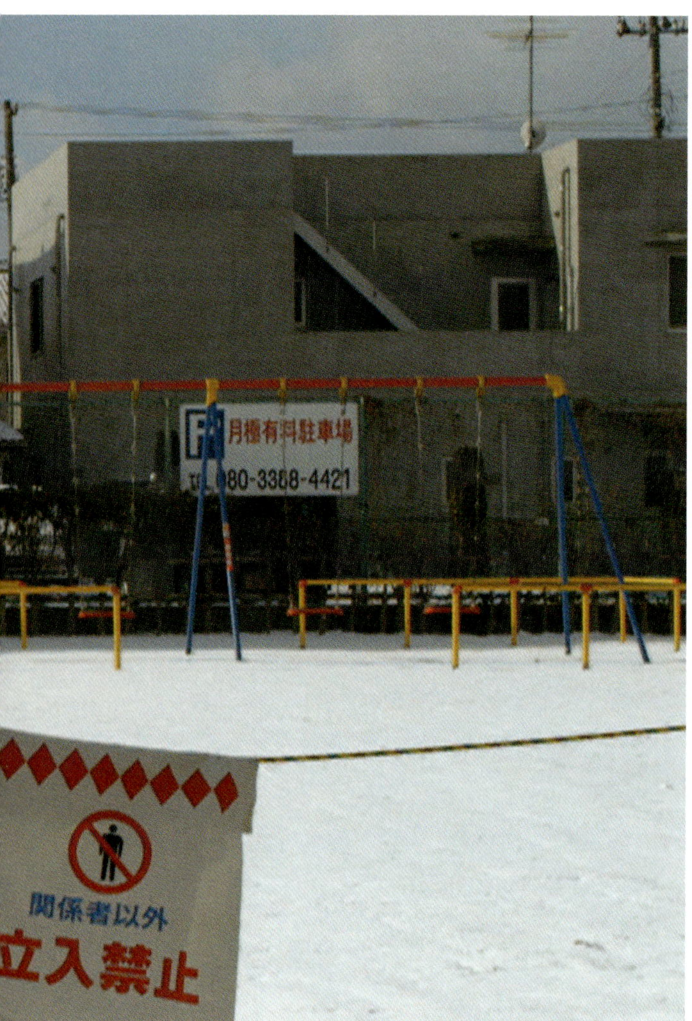

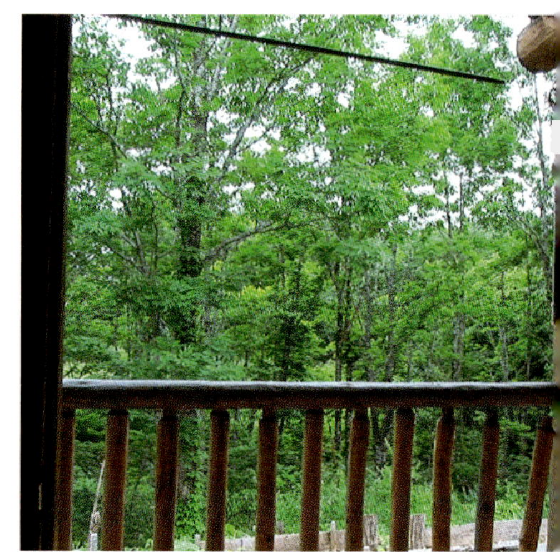

e

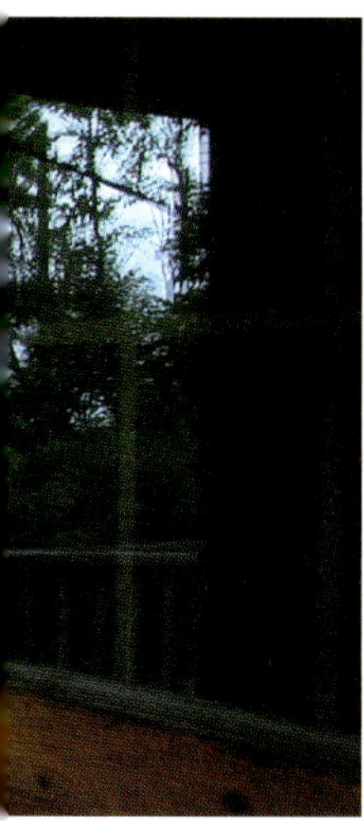
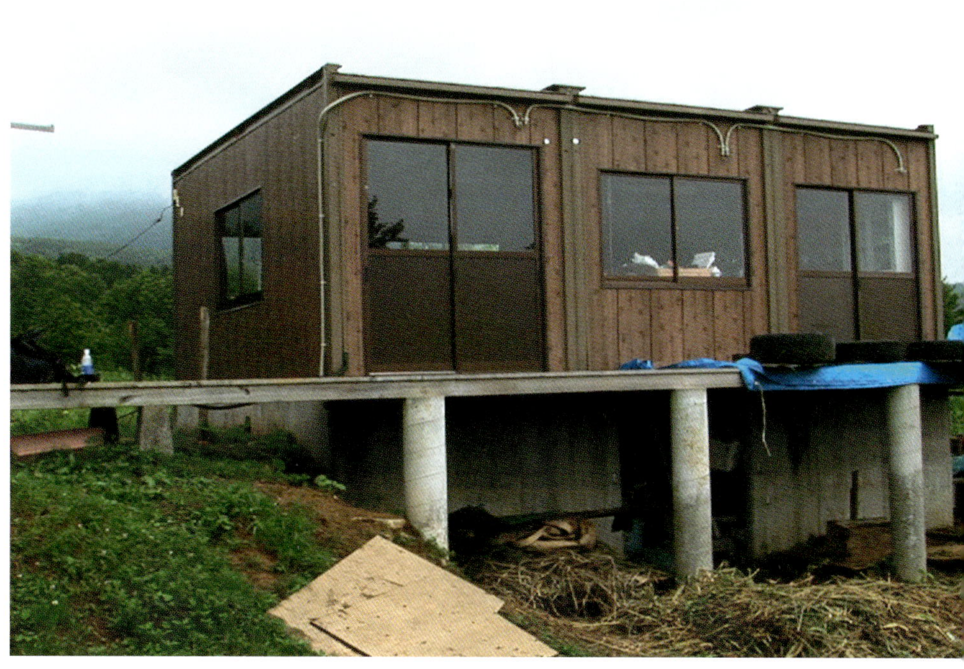
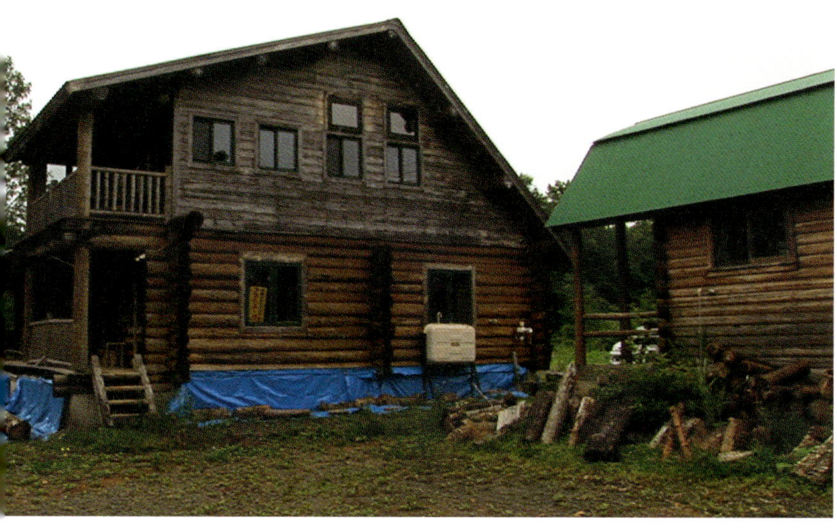

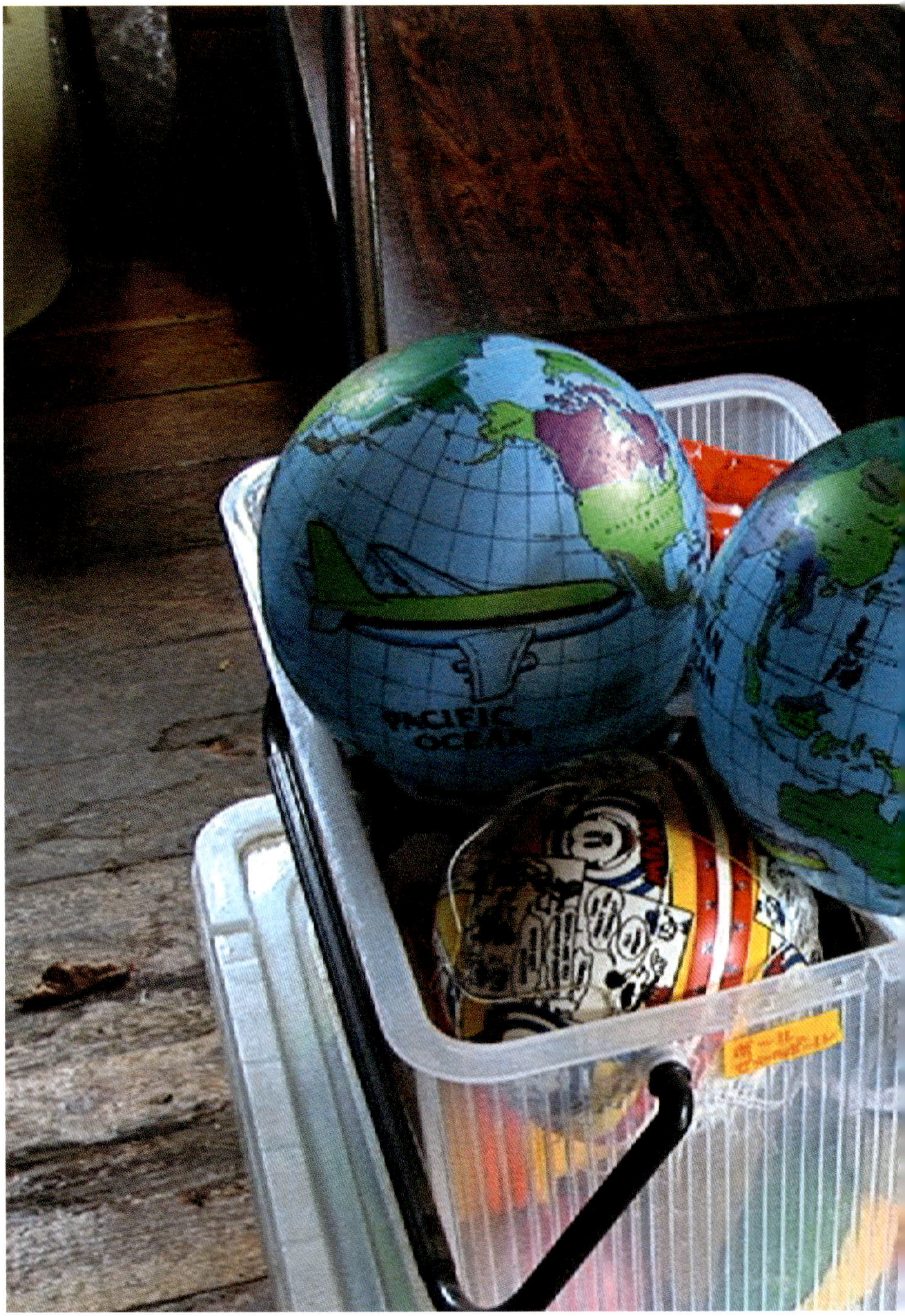

e

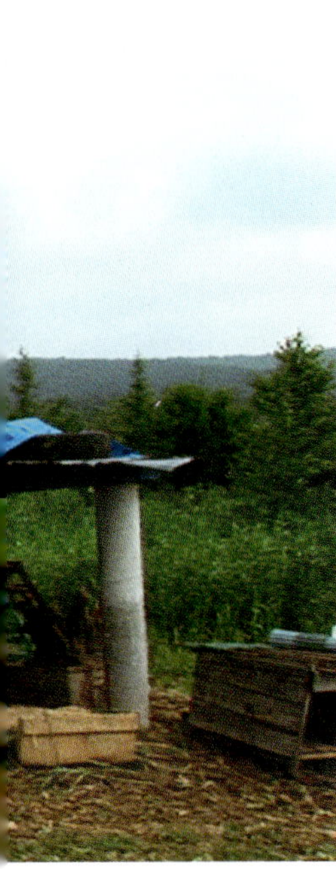

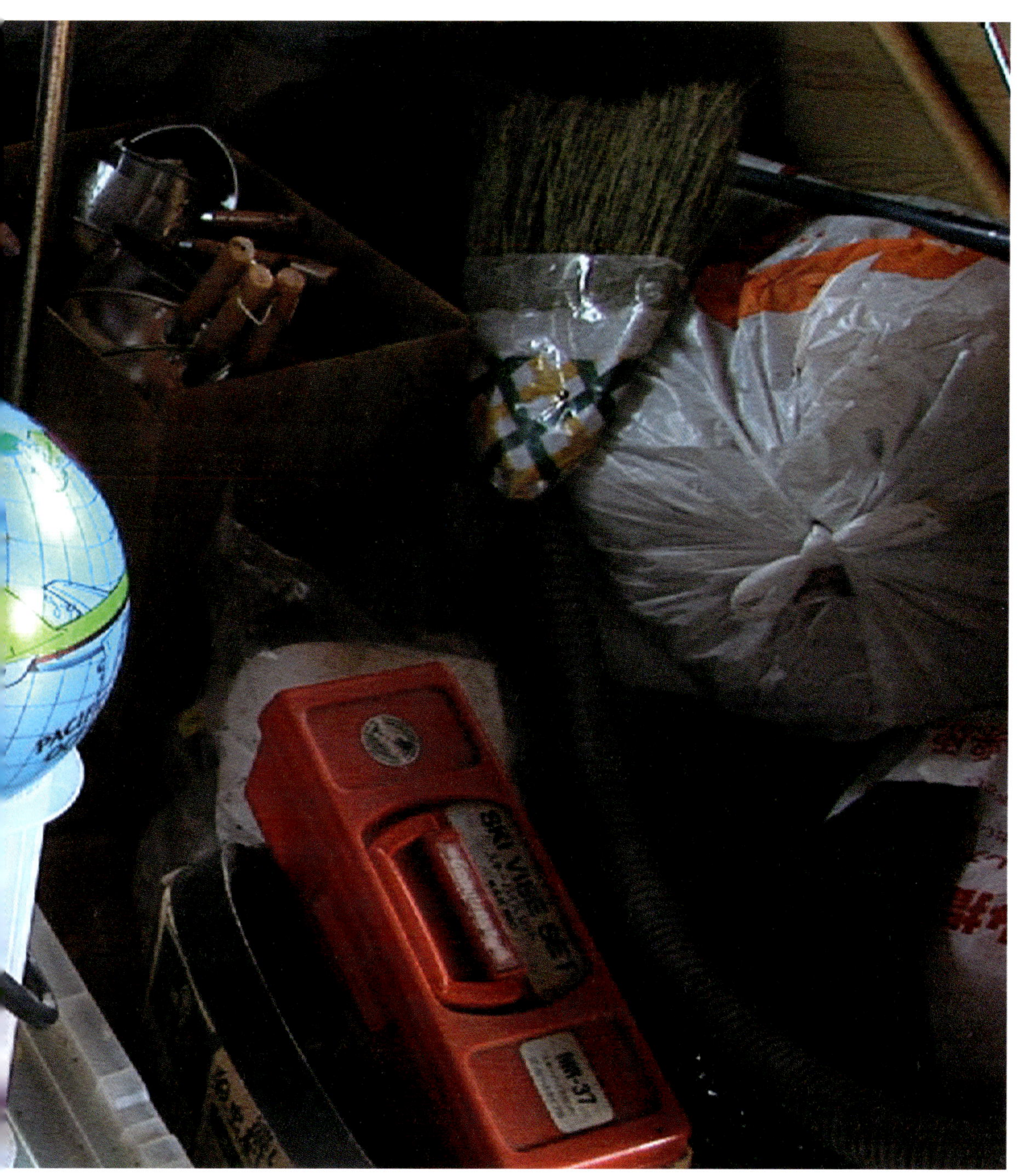

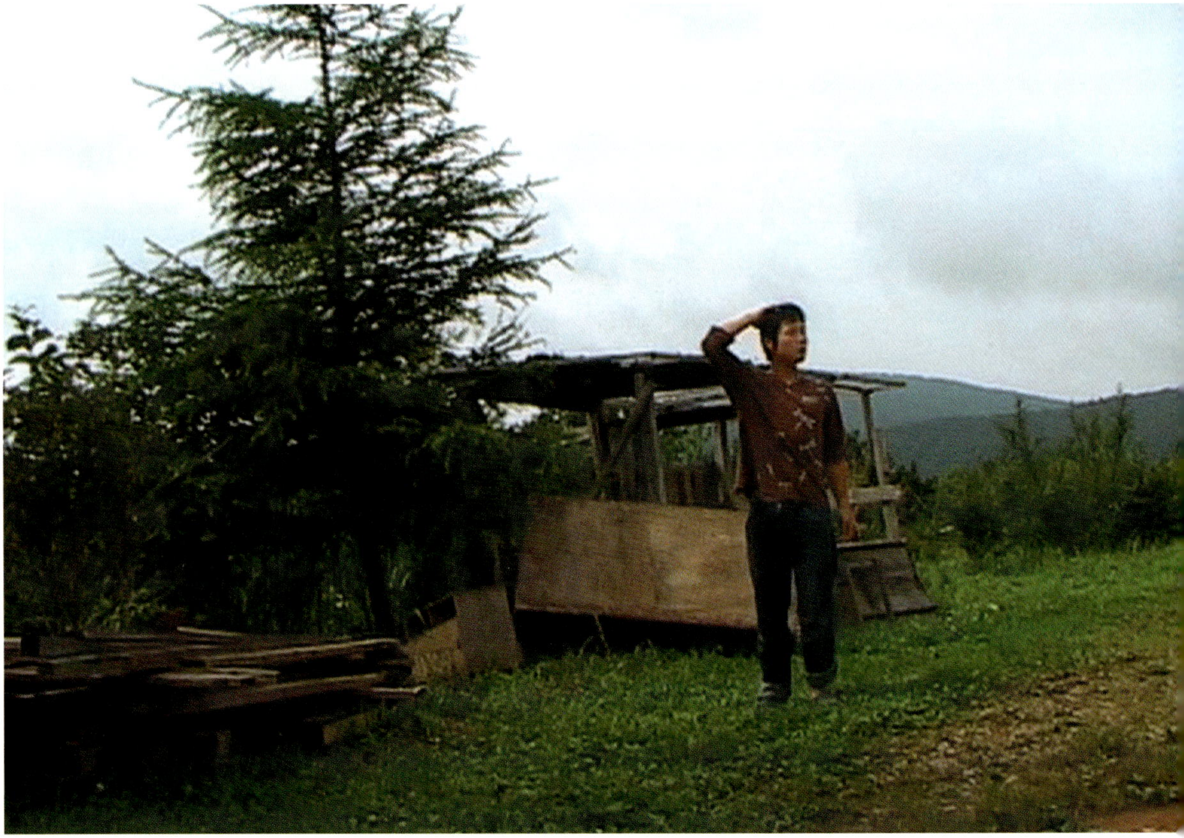

e

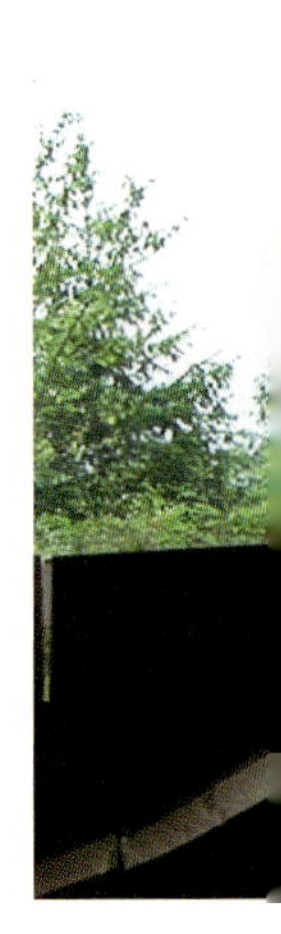

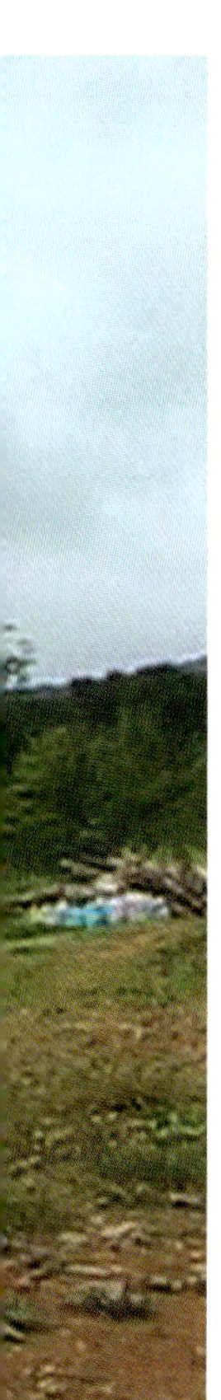

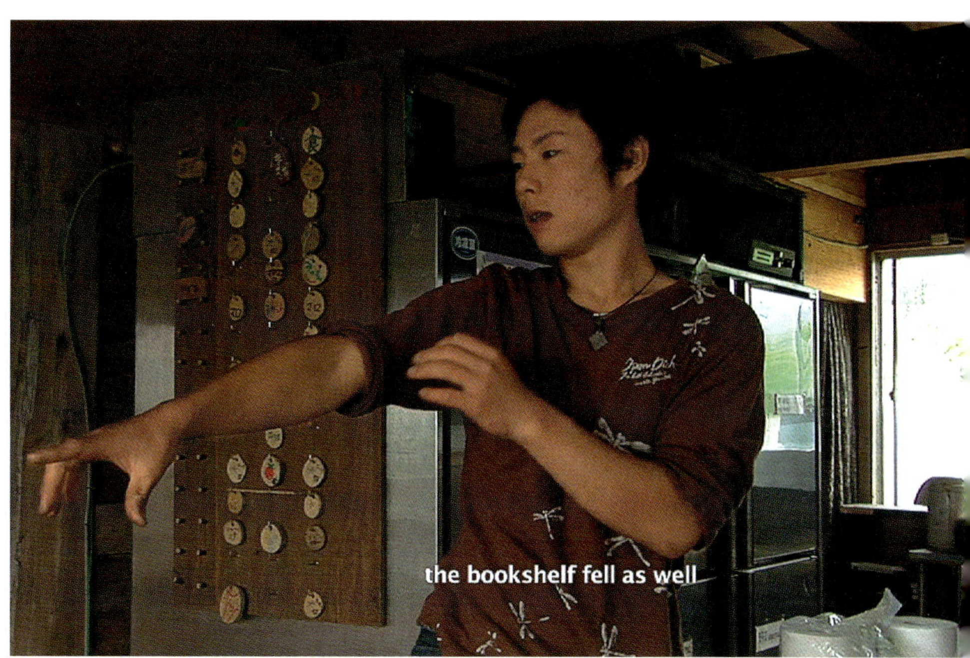
the bookshelf fell as well

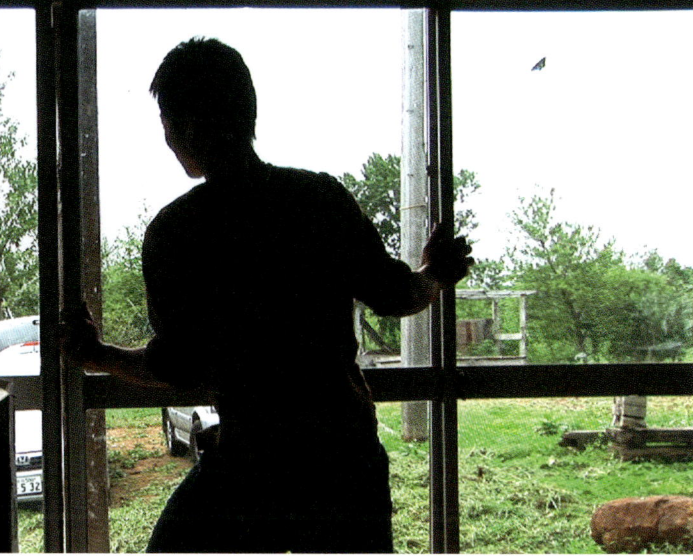

e

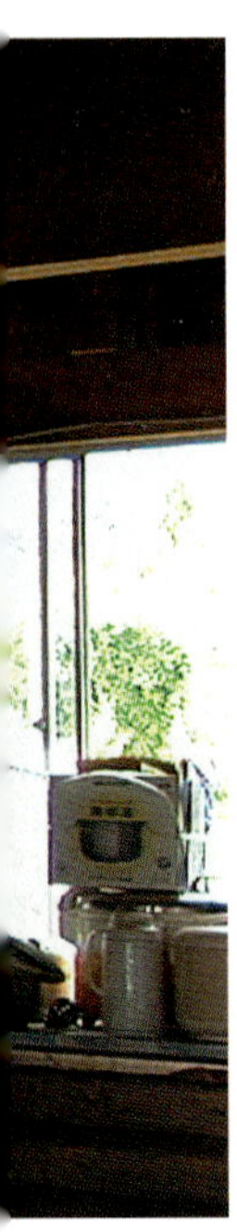

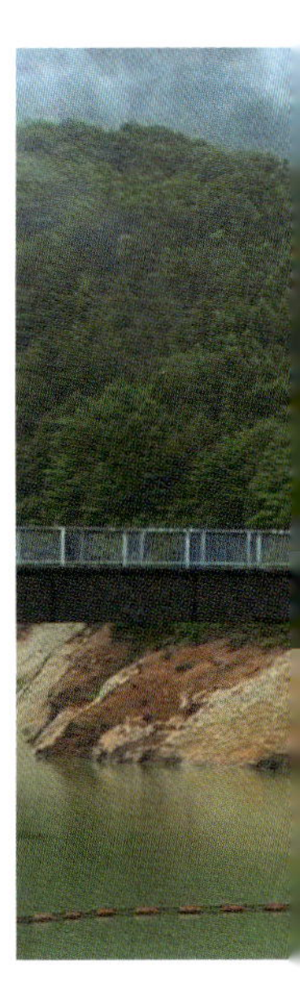

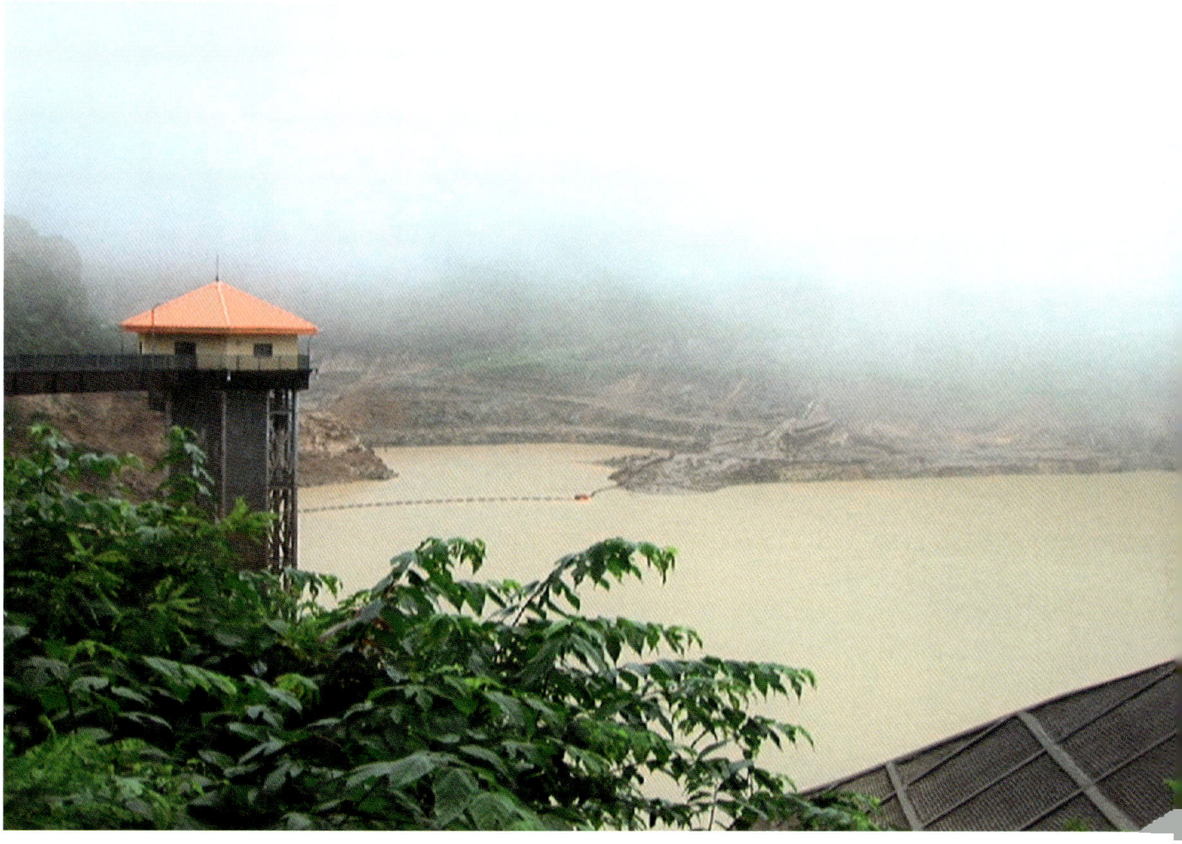

e

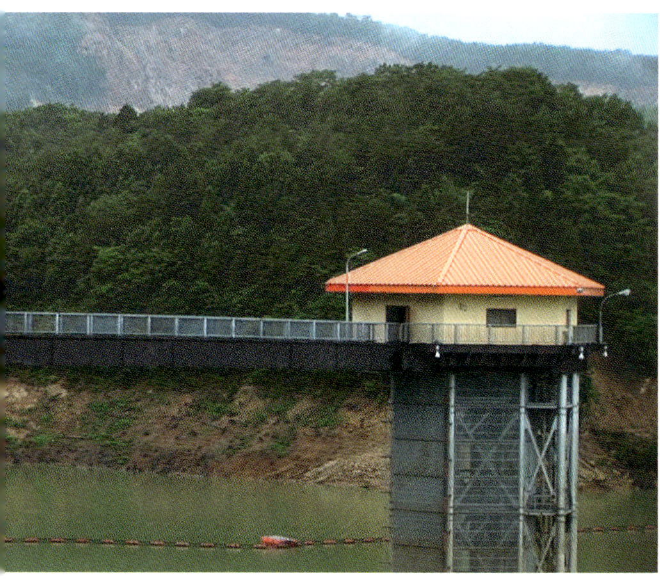

Director of the onsen

I don't know how long it lasted.
The landscape was difficult to describe.
I saw the dam falling and the ground, too.
It looked like a volcanic eruption.
Then a tsunami occurred.
I had never experienced such a strong earthquake.
It was really something!
The mountain, 100 tons of ground falling all
    of a sudden. "Boom"!
More than an earthquake,
it was like a bomb explosion.
 – Did it make a heavy sound?
Yes, it was really something.
The dam didn't break.
It is very strong,
I think it can't break.
Some water was turning like the Niagara Falls,
like this,
it was swirling.
If you go into the mountains, you'll see.
There are a lot of places like in these photos.
It was a huge earthquake.
I don't know how to describe the landscape.
I don't know how to put it.
When the ground fell,
at that moment,
some trees were swallowed while still standing.
A mountain as heavy as a hundred tons was falling!
You can't really tell from here, but you can see
    when you are there.
All kinds of specialists came,
even some from Kôchi.
They say that the shock is a gold mine in terms of data.
The specialists say that the landscape should
    be preserved so they can study it.
It really was a huge earthquake.

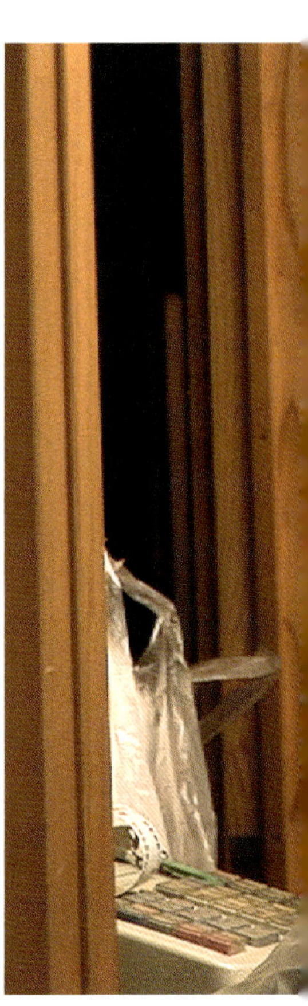

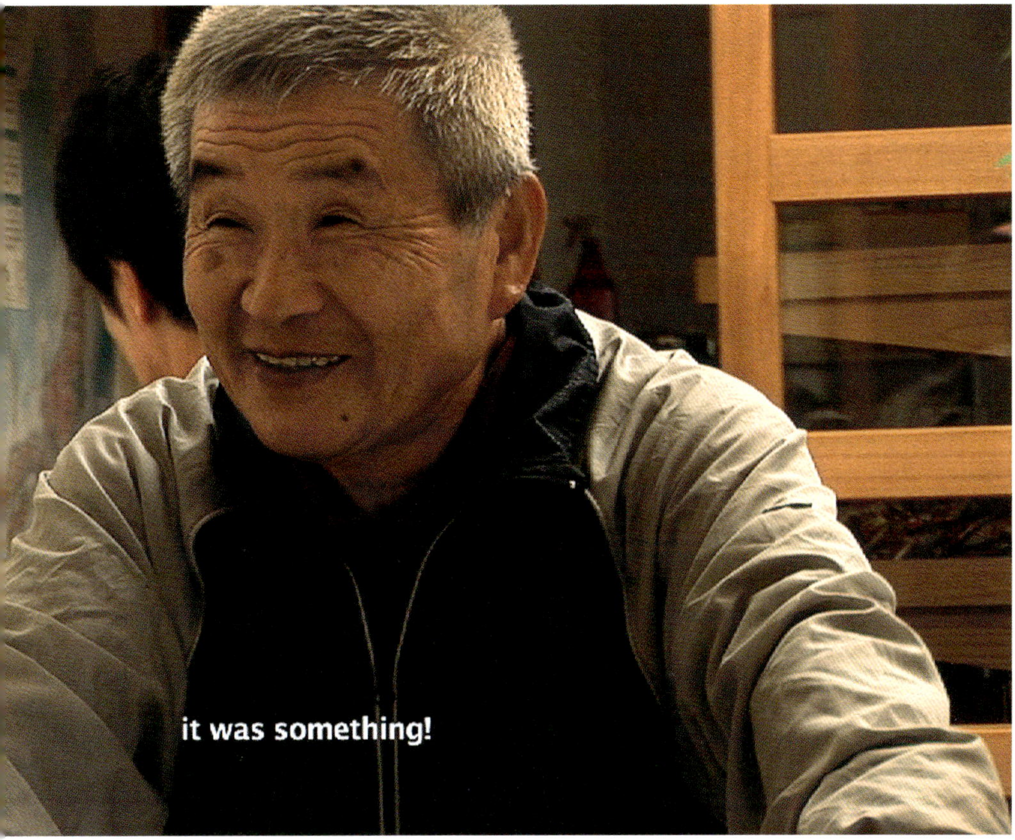

it was something!

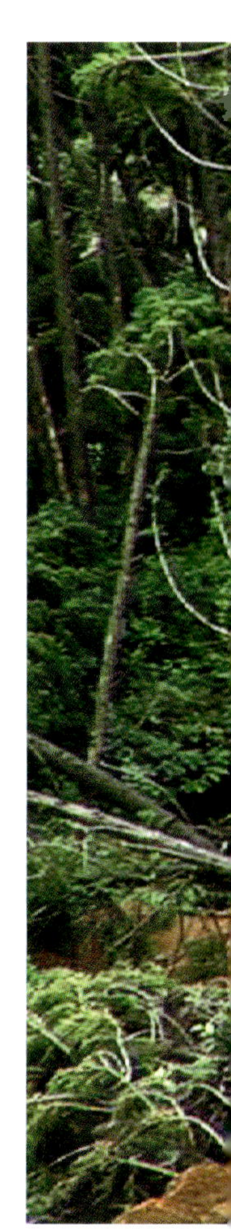

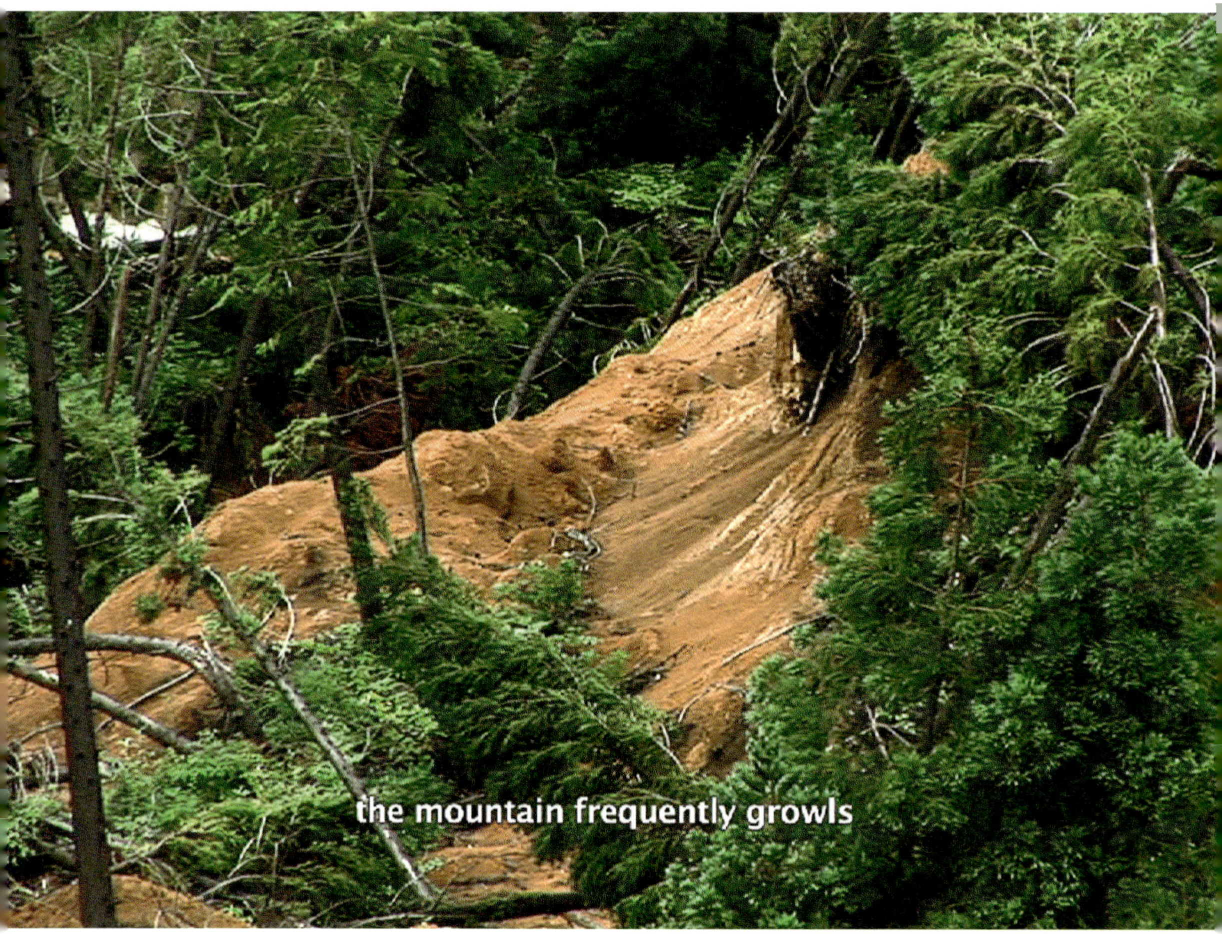

e

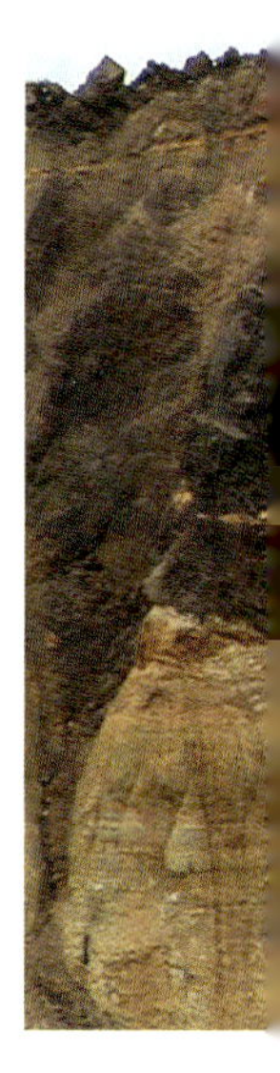

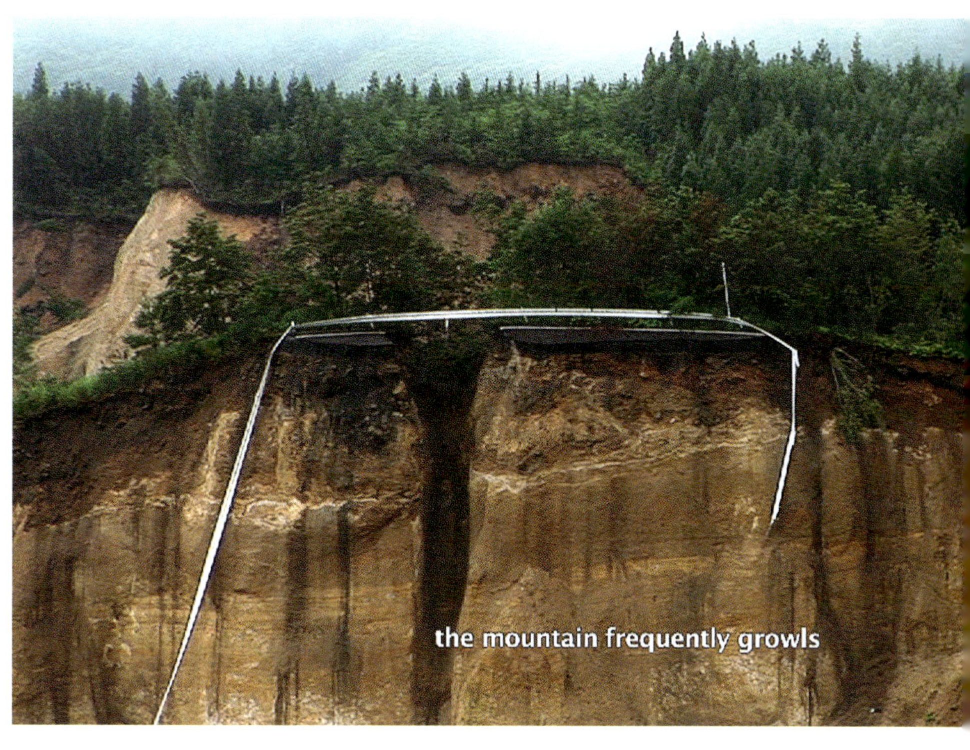

the mountain frequently growls

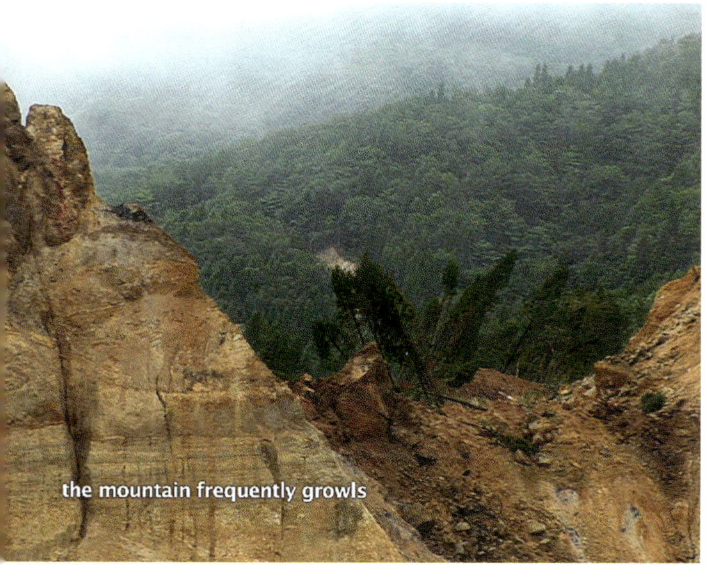

the mountain frequently growls

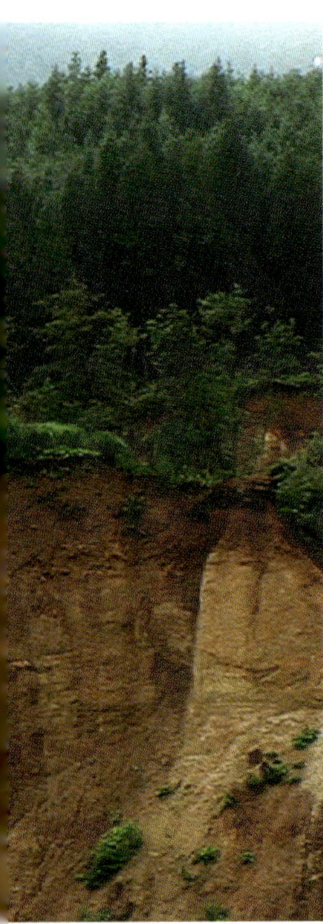

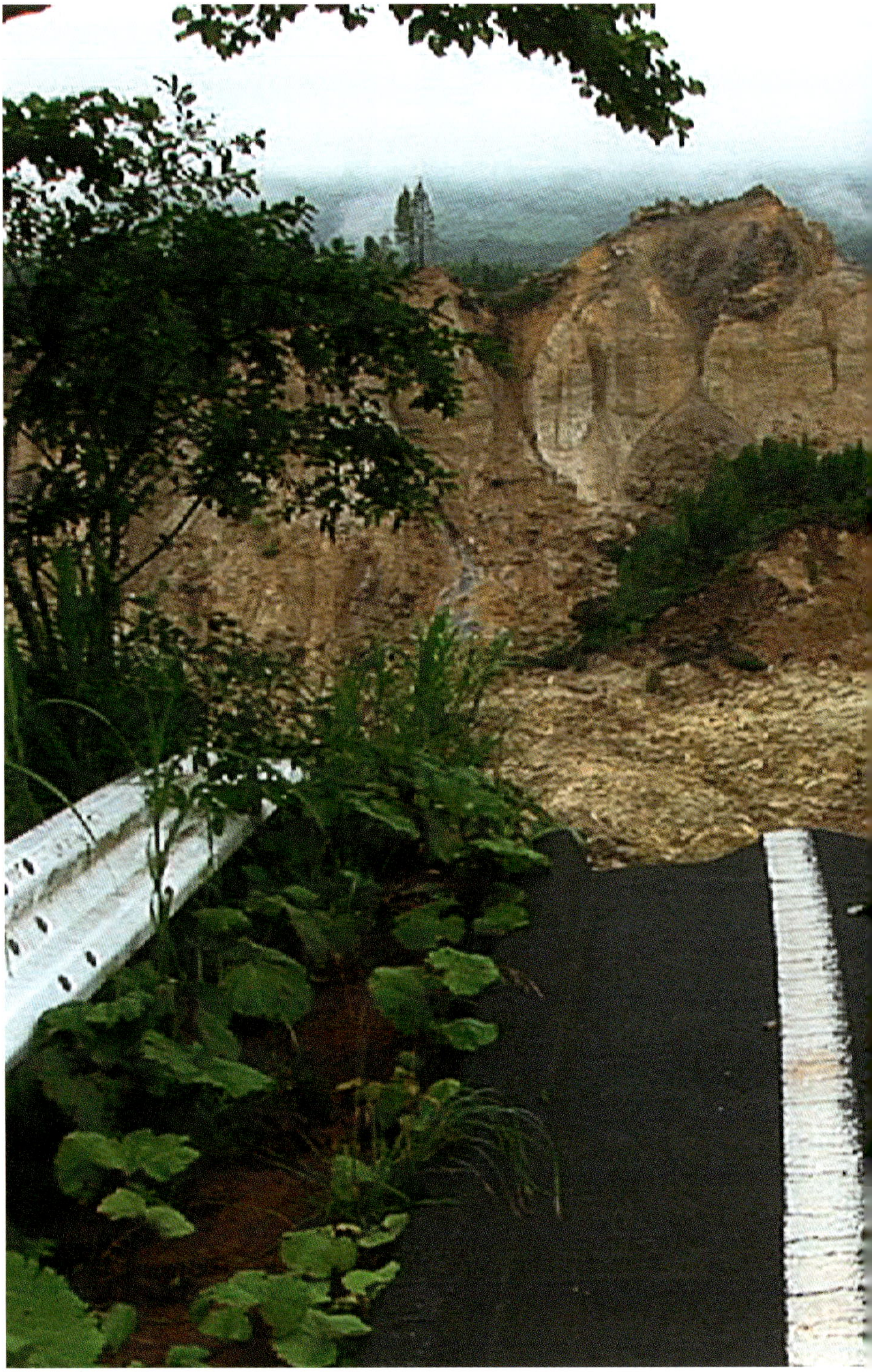

e

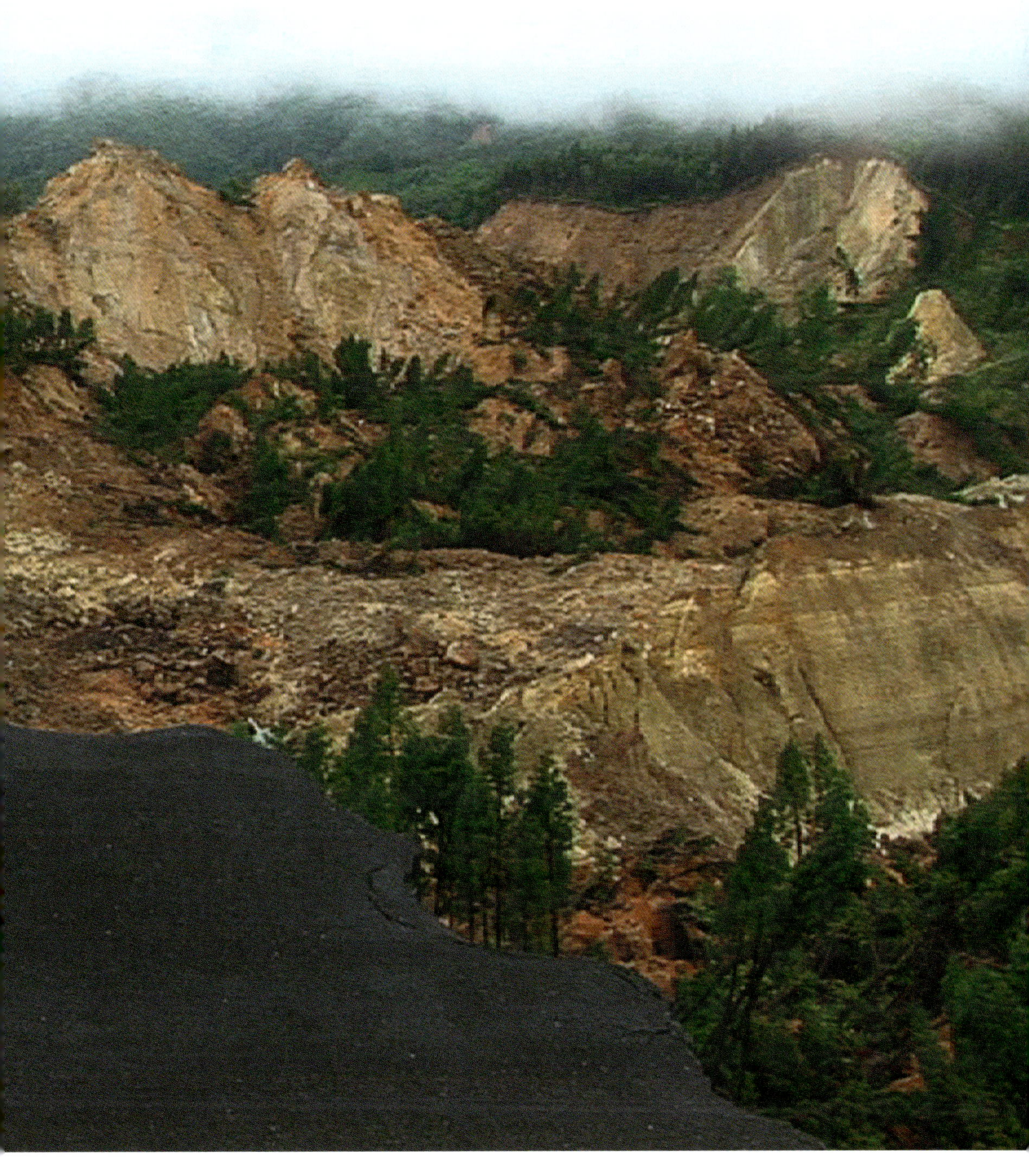

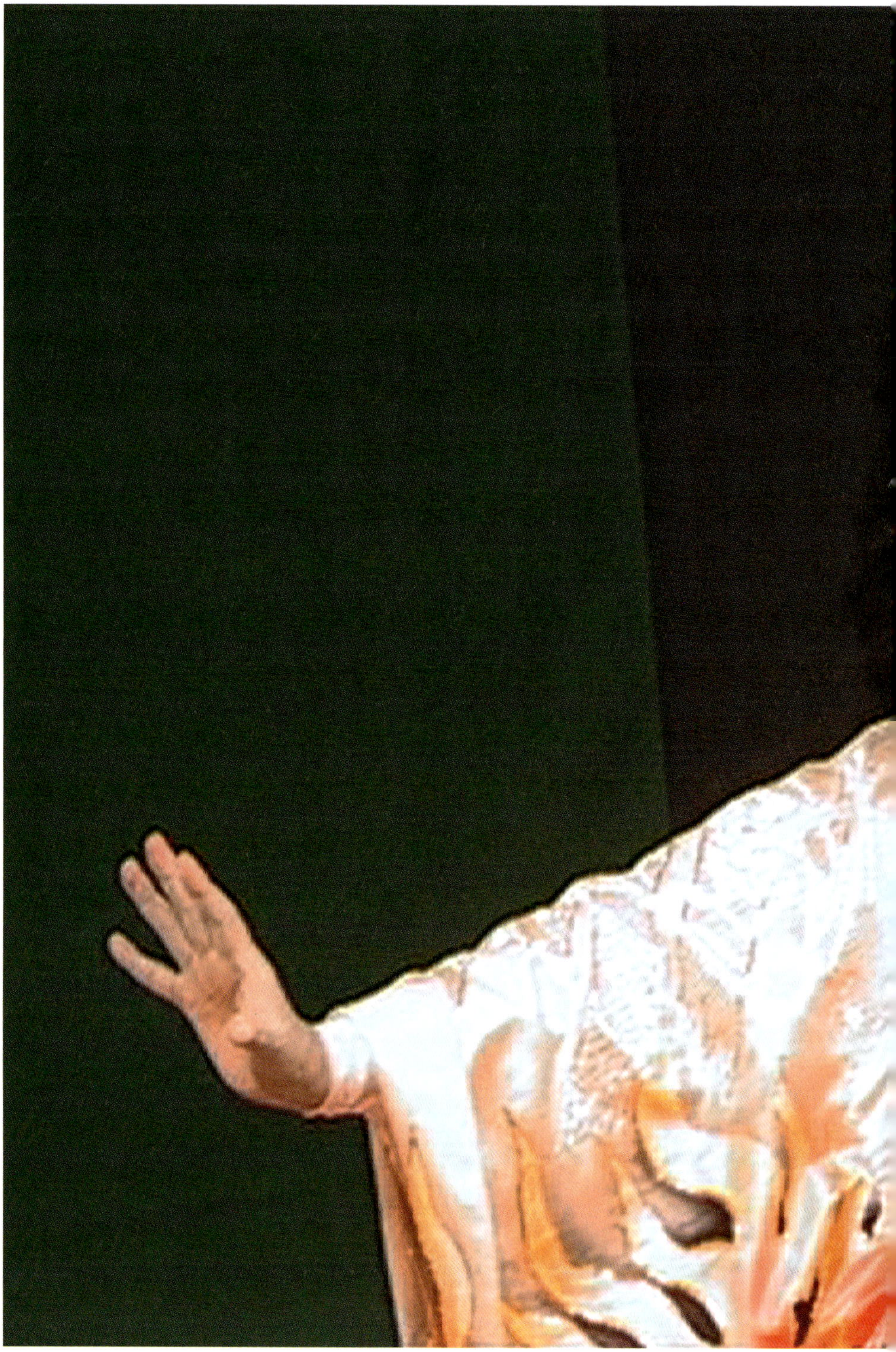

e

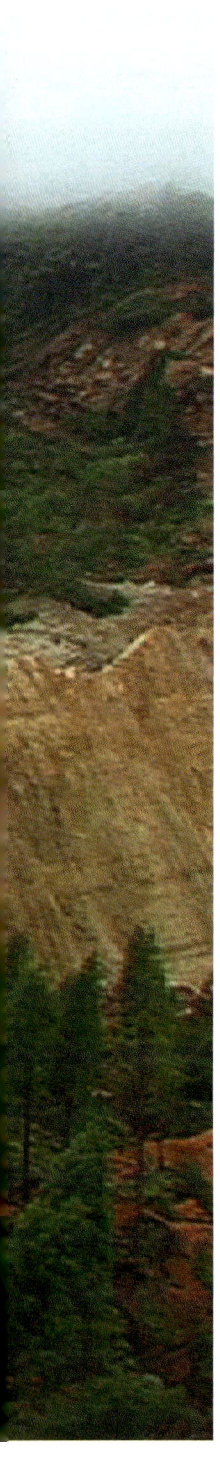

e

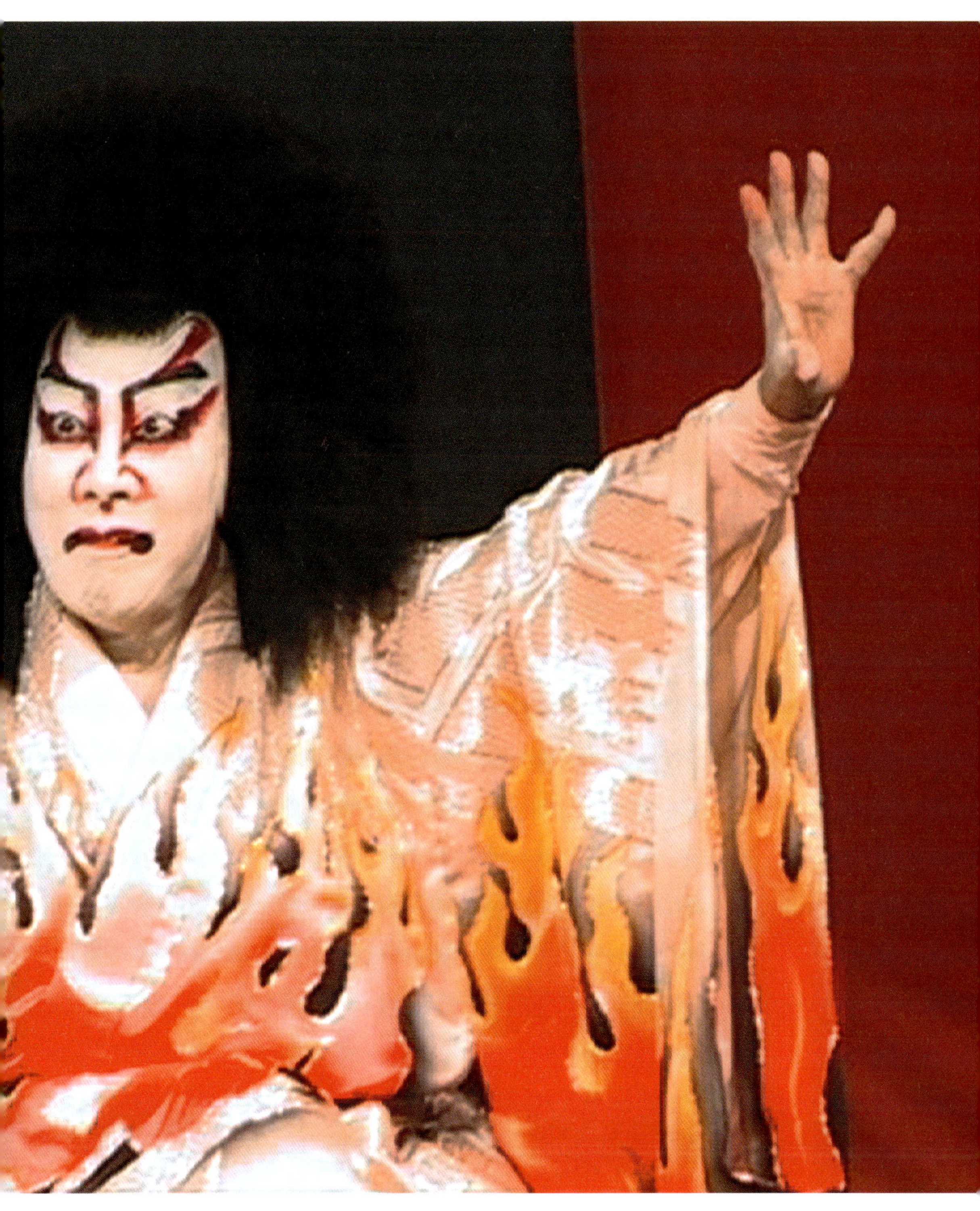

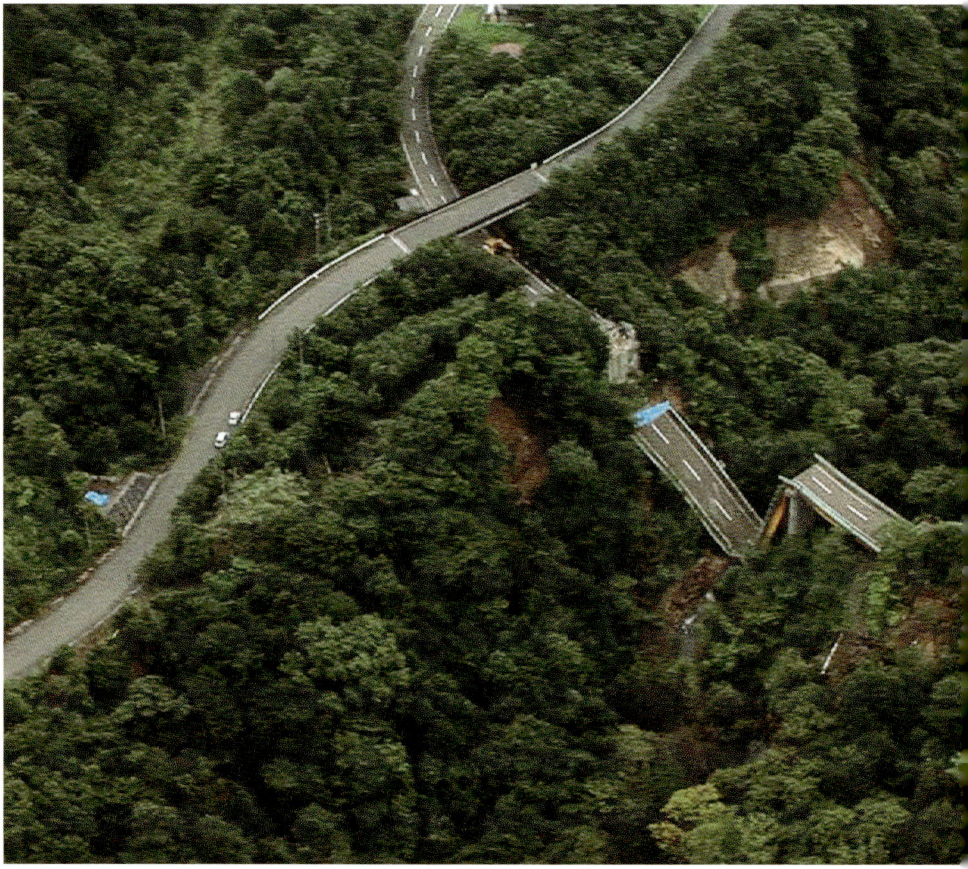

e

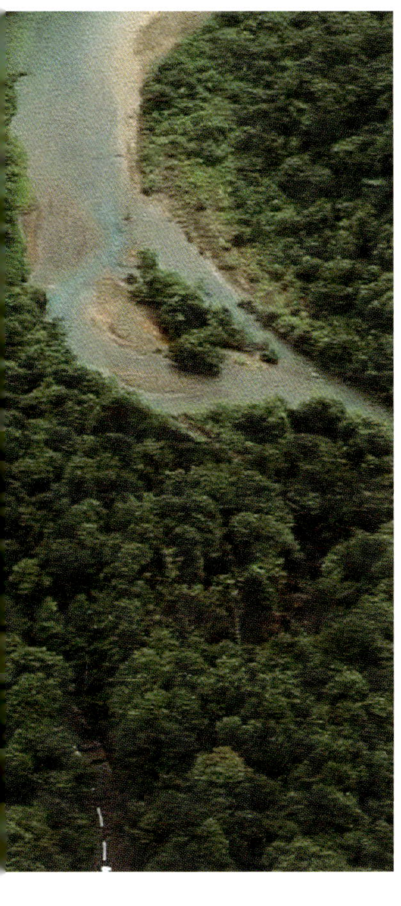

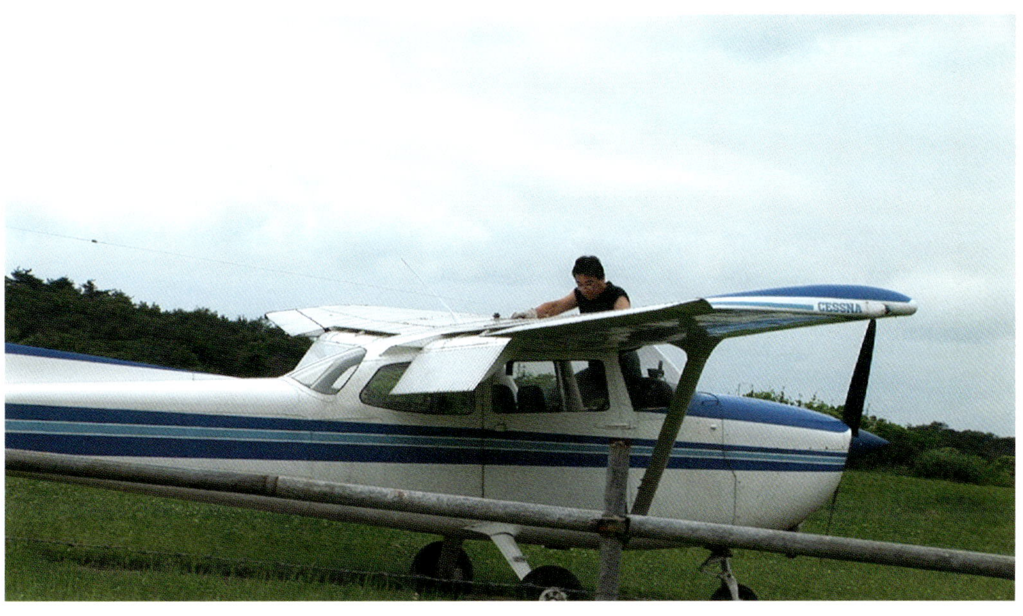

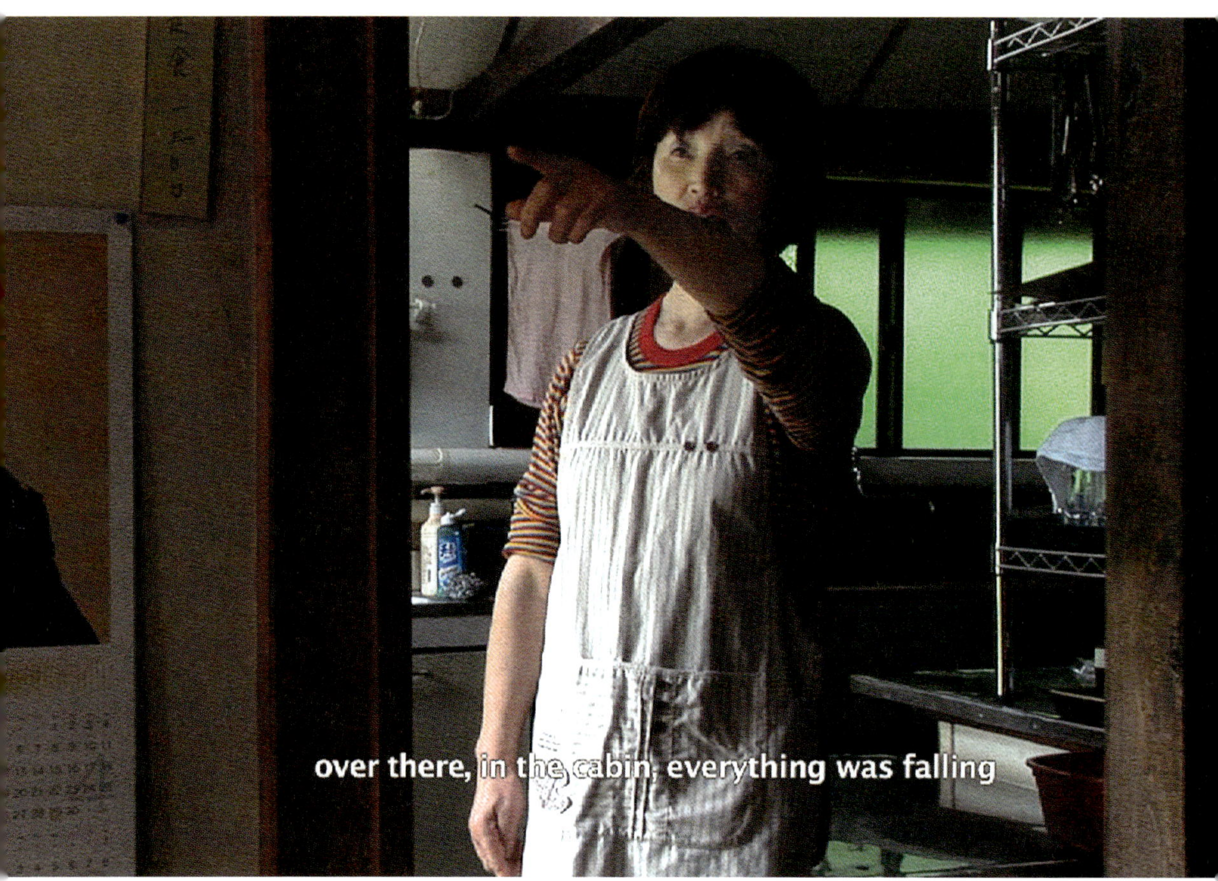
over there, in the cabin, everything was falling

Manager of the fishing company

The mountain frequently growls.
Generally it happens in winter,
but that winter, the growling was happening
   almost every day.
It's like the sound of the air force training.
The sound was coming from the depths
   of the ground, "Doo, doo, doo."
Saturday is the day when the trash is collected.
They collect it twice a week,
from where the snowplows are.
It was when I was taking the trash down.
Because it was Saturday,
I thought that maybe some clients would buy
   fish from me.
So I went to get them.
And the earthquake started when I got out
   of the car and put the fish crate down.
At the time, I didn't know what was going on.
Over there, in the cabin,
everything was falling.
The water in the fish tank splashed out
with a loud sound, "Daboom, daboom."
I understood how serious the situation was,
but I could not stand up,
and I instinctively crouched down.

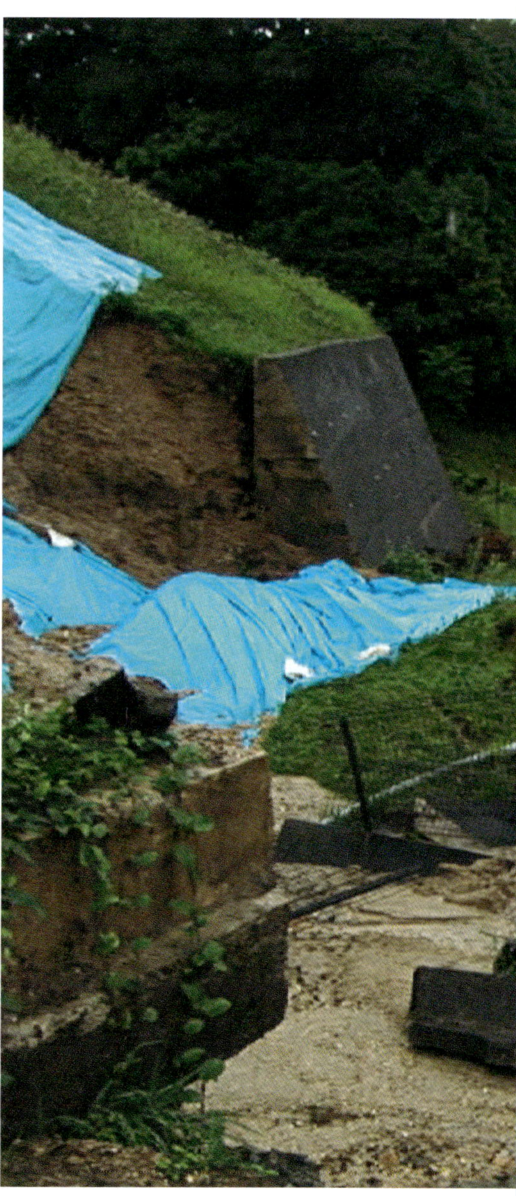

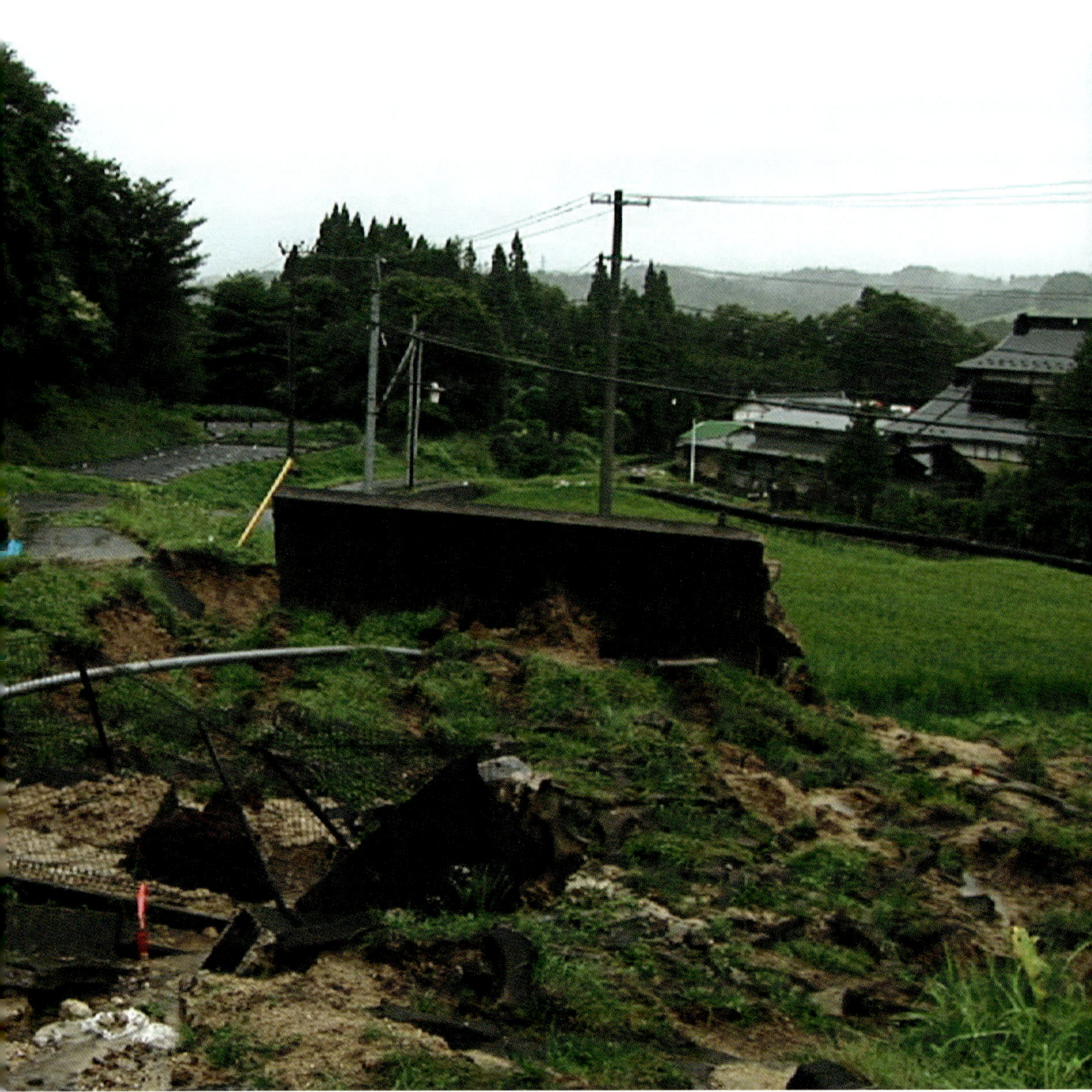

e

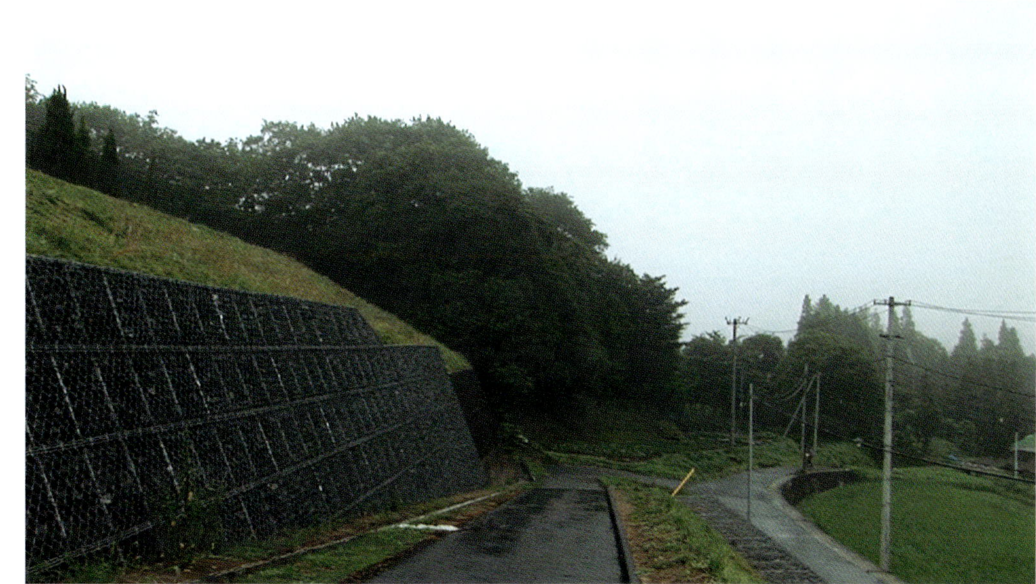

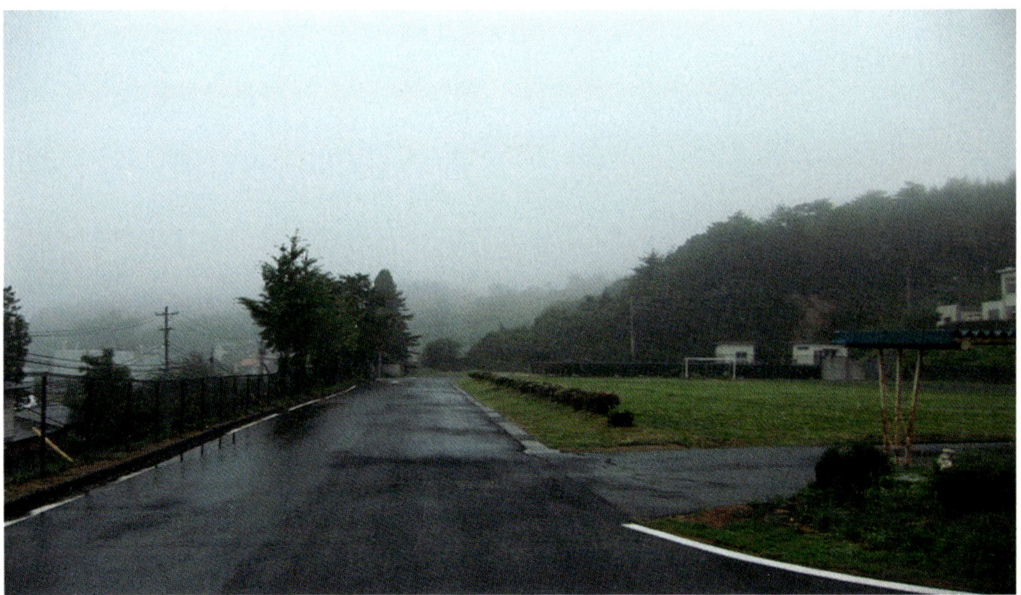

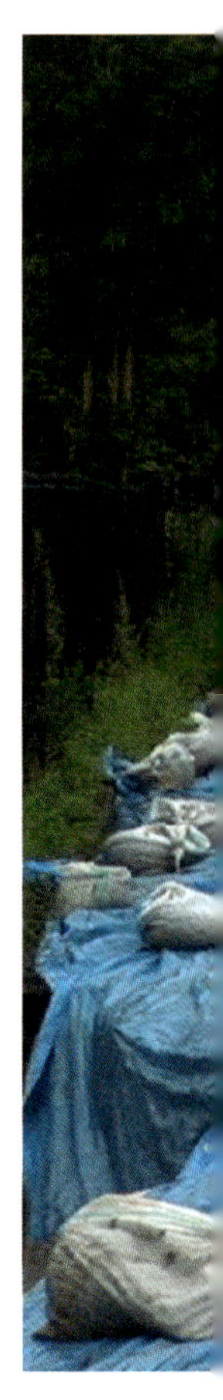

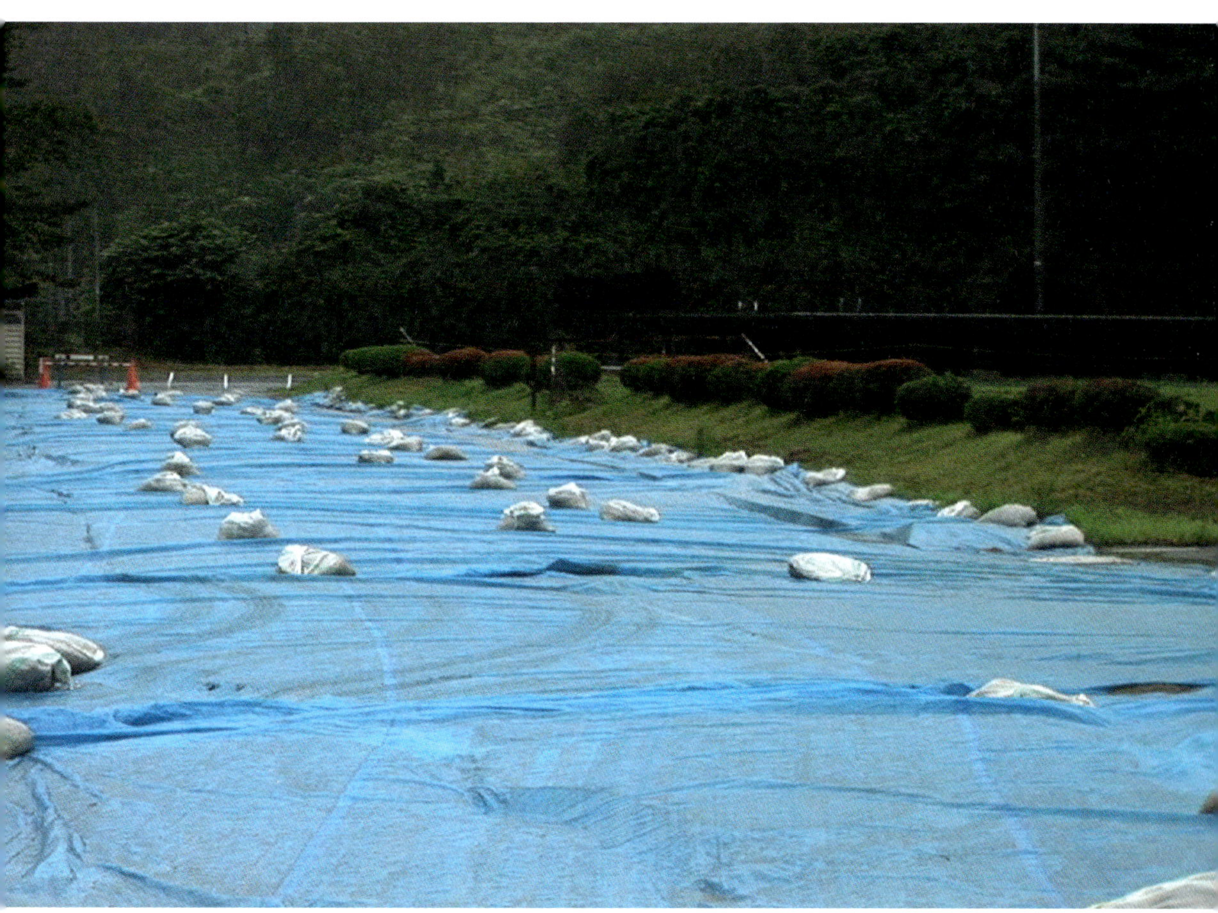

e

e

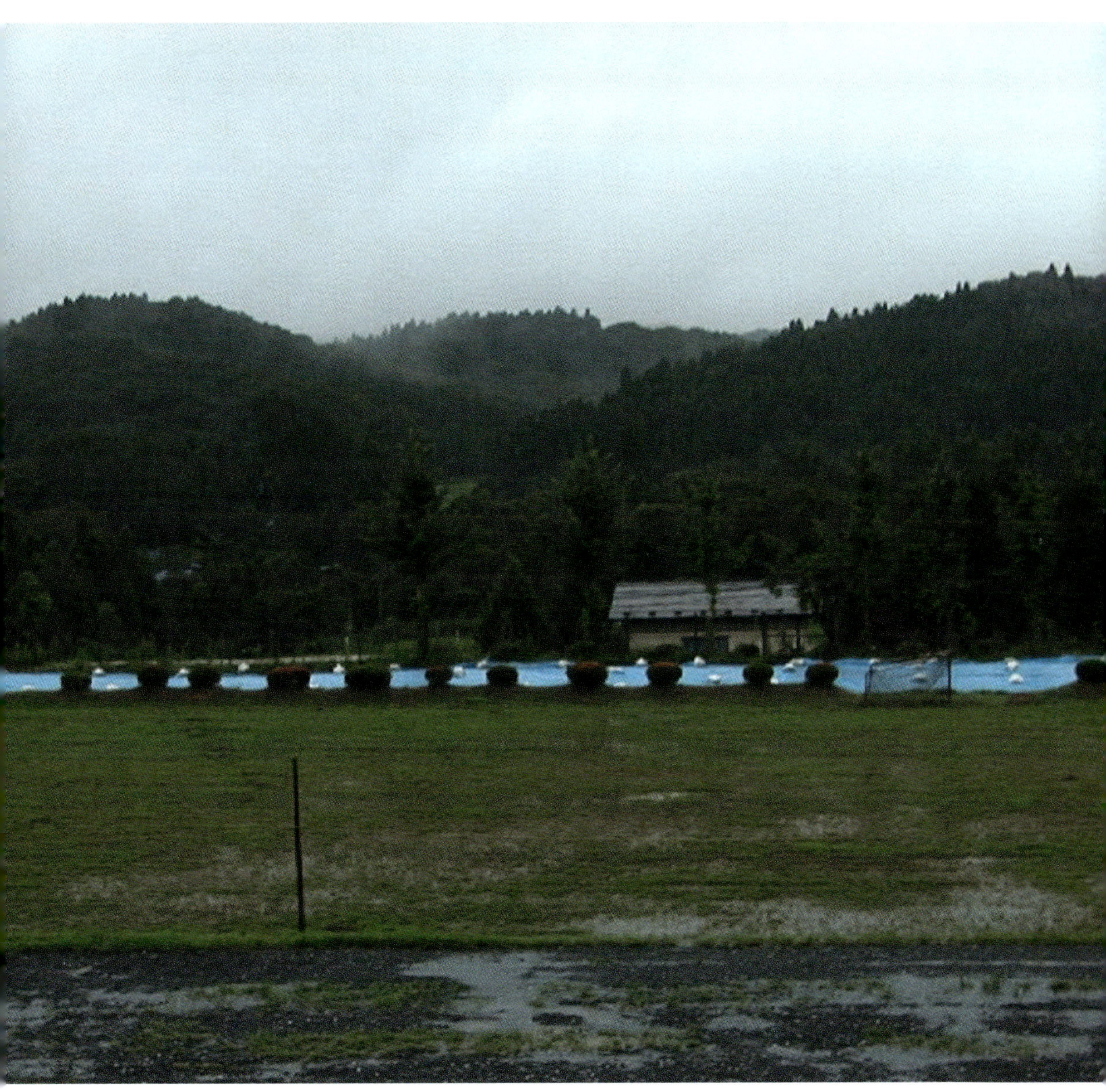

e

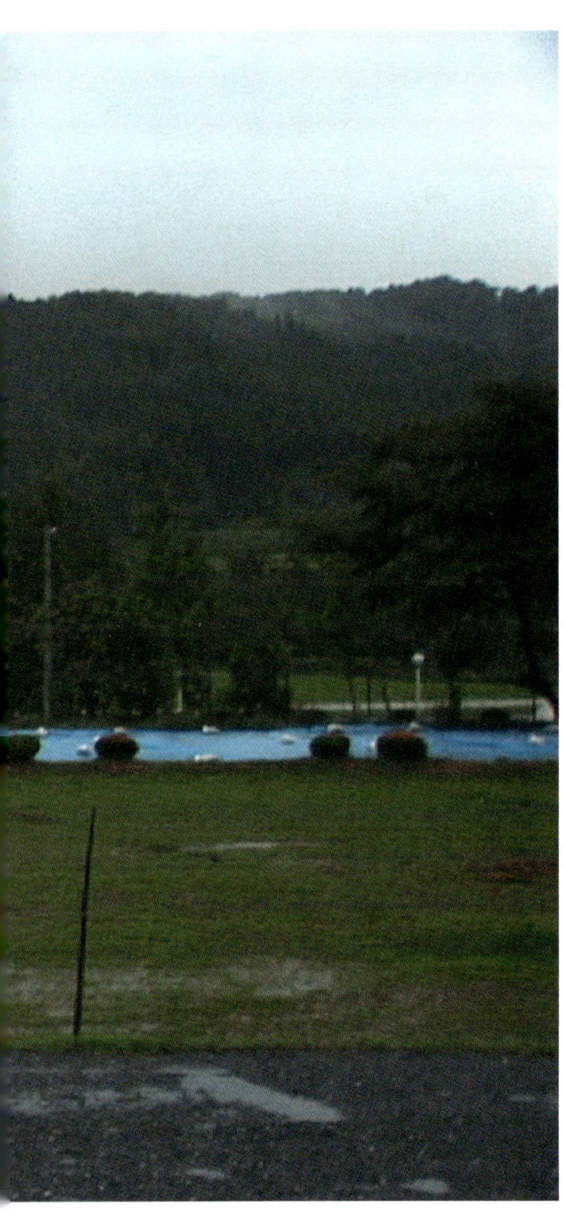

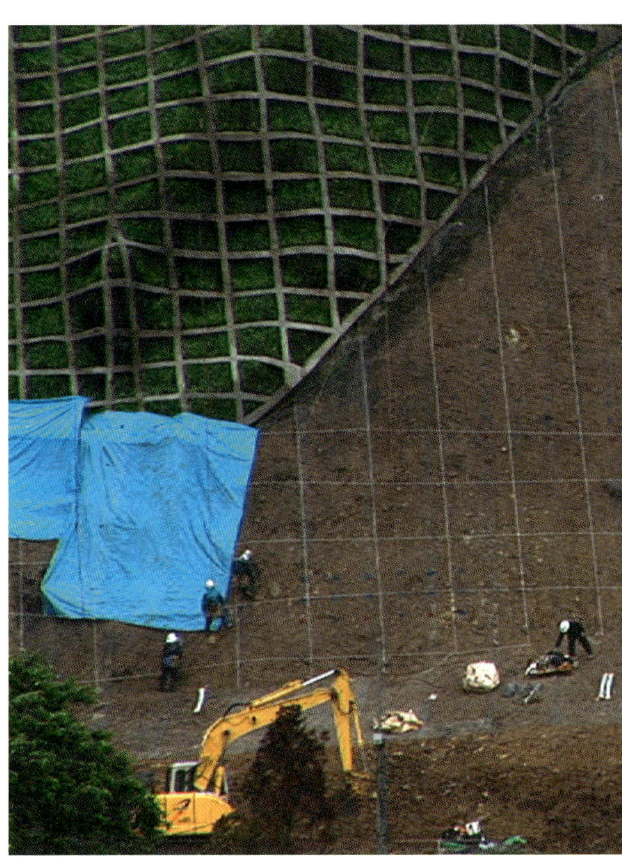

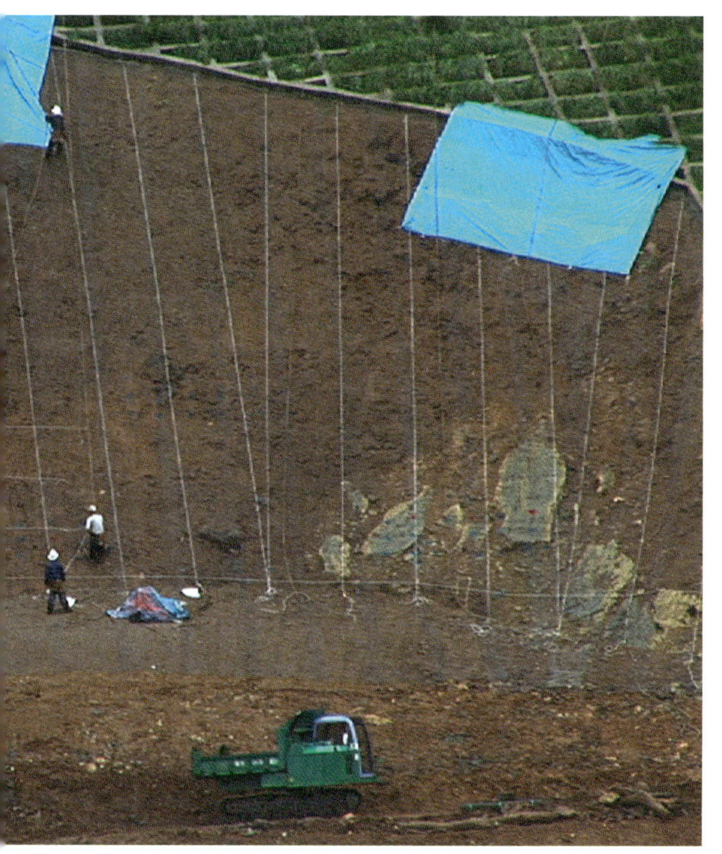

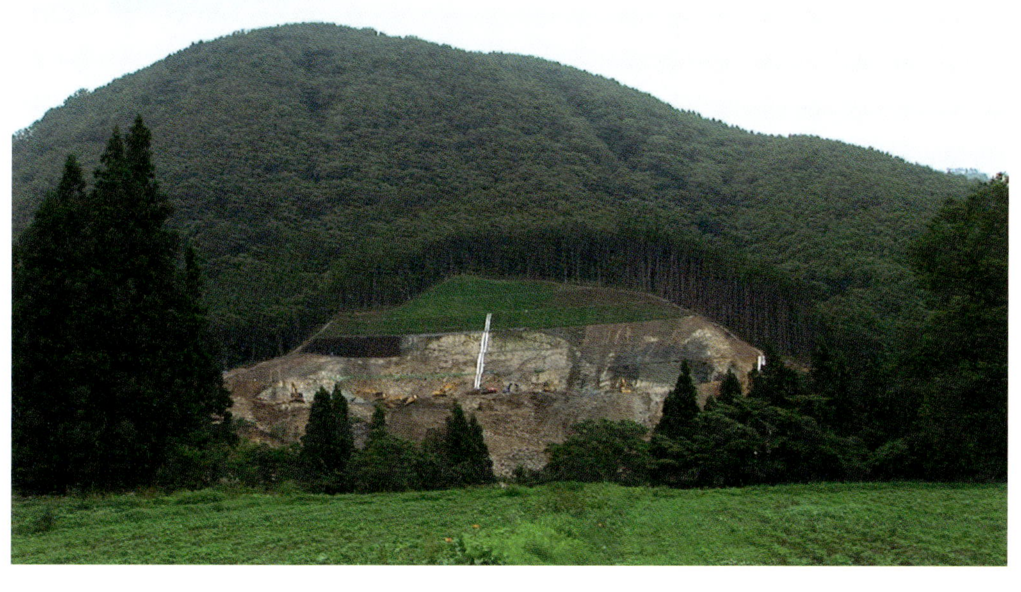

e

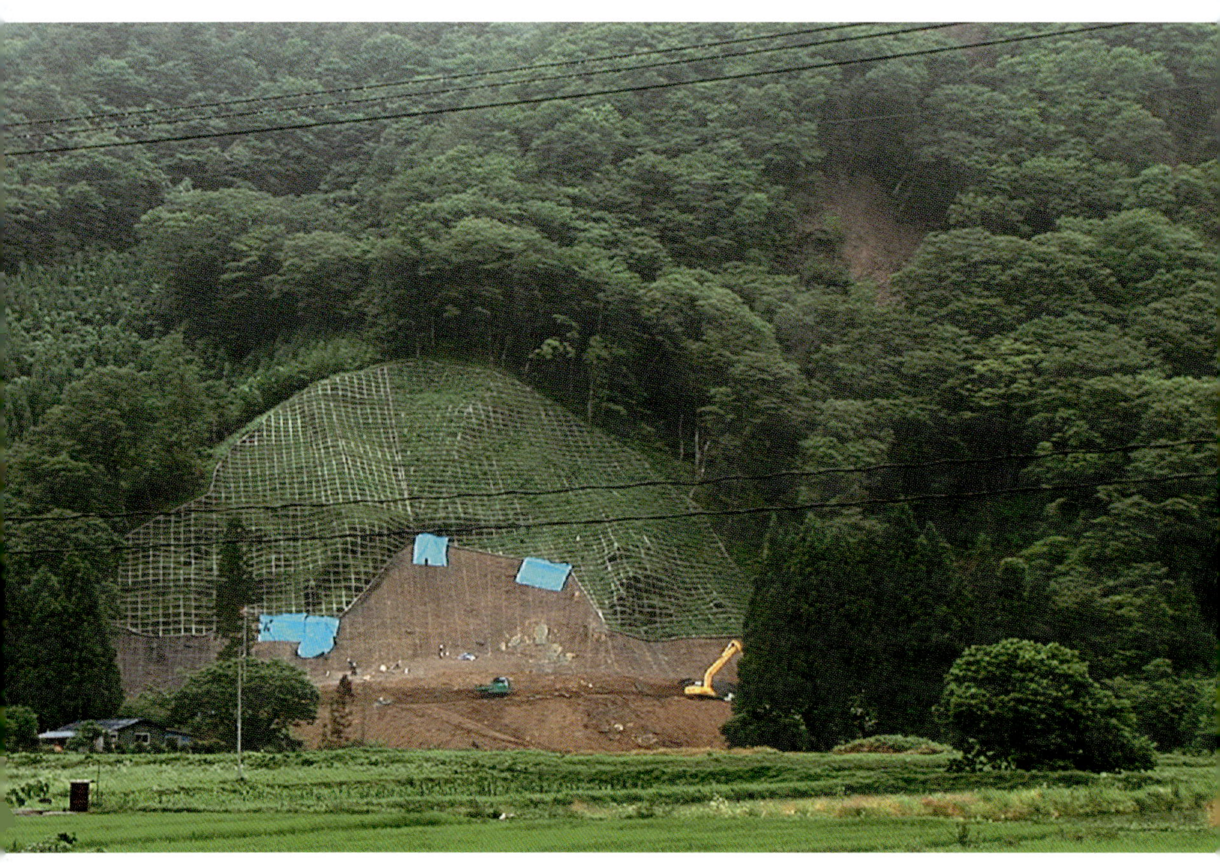

Marta Gili

*Interview
with Natacha
Nisic*

*Entretien
avec Natacha
Nisic*

Marta Gili: According to Heraclitus, the true nature of things is hidden, and yet we are constantly trying to understand and "decipher" what it is that separates the hidden from the visible. Science and religion also try to provide answers to some of these questions. For you, what is the role of artistic discourse here?

Natacha Nisic: As you say, we strive to understand the world. I really like that expression, because it contains its own negation. You can take it with humor, humility, or deep despair, but this lack is a given. Art is incomplete, it does not profess, does not demonstrate, does not inscribe thought or action in a globalizing movement. When I started the *Catalogue de gestes* in 1995 [p. 10 + 15-25], I was thinking of the visions tending toward exhaustiveness of nosographic registers or the photographs on those sheets by Eadweard Muybridge, but also Gerhard Richter's *Atlas*: a mixture of admiration and distance at the very idea of aiming at an exhaustiveness of forms, a completeness of knowledge. The *Catalogue de gestes* was thus supposed to contain a contradictory principle in its very conception: the promise of a kind of exhaustiveness, as in "cataloguing," "making an inventory," and its very impossibility, by deciding to make it an open, potentially incomplete work. The conceptual form of this work constitutes a kind of paradigm of my conception of artistic activity, a *double bind* between the will to fix, to mark in a precise time, and the very impossibility of doing so, because it is fleeting, ephemeral, simple and vain.

M.G.: In most of your works, the search for spirituality or occult forces is presented not as a form of detachment or a flight from reality, but as an immanence, an affirmation of the inseparability of the visible and the invisible. If that dimension is, it seems to me, present in *Catalogue de gestes*, it becomes more obvious in your latest works.

N.N.: In my more recent works, which bring into play the representation of religious worlds, my questions gain an added value. Giorgio Agamben notes that ritual is still the place where narrative is associated with gesture. Without that basic link, gesture loses all meaning or reason to exist. Now, whether in *Carmel* (2008), *Princess Snow-Flower* (2011) or, more recently, *Andrea* (2012), I filmed situations for which I had little or no access to the liturgical narrative, to the semantic body of ritual. For example, in South Korea, on an island

fifty kilometers from Seoul, I filmed a woman who people had told me was a shaman (*Princess Snow-Flower*) [p. 37 + 72–78]. She was very talkative but I didn't understand either her actions or her words: all I saw was her body subject to violent tension. I filmed without knowing, as if the actions were going to bring an answer to the unintelligibility of the situation, I filmed actions without stories, caught up as they were in the intensity of their movement. In fact, I experienced a very similar situation in a Carmelite convent in Lisieux. My lack of a Christian upbringing meant that for me the sisters' ritual acts became inscribed in a history that connects me to the history of painting and cinema. I'm thinking of Alain Cavalier or Robert Bresson. This baring of an "en-soi of the body," without narrative, silent, was a guiding line in the elaboration of the *Catalogue de gestes*, but also many pieces that followed immediately afterwards, such as *"Attitudes," la salle d'attente nº 1* (1997) [fig. 1] and *"Attitudes," la salle de projection* (1999) [fig. 2]. In these two pieces, the bodies of the people in a position of waiting or attentiveness in front of an invisible film are projected onto seats. The visitor can join this fictive community by sitting on the chair, but the point above all is to effect a montage of associations of actions without a story, reduced to their "pure" function, detached from any explicit context.

Thus, whether in my older or more recent pieces, two movements tend paradoxically toward the same concern with de-fragmenting the real. The first uses the forms of sacred language and ritual, from which a first layer of narrative has to be detached, and the second deals with the most banal everyday reality, decontextualizing the actions and attitudes that surround us to make them accessible to a new form of narrative. In this way they are sacralized, not in a frozen religious form, but in a new register of association, like an emergence, a fracturing of the unconscious.

M.G.: The narrative apparatus of your latest installations, in which narrative is presented in several time phases and moments, marks a clear break in your approach.

N.N.: What is affirmed in my latest works – especially since *e* [p. 138 + 156–184], made in 2009 – is the attraction to a form of narrative that would combine speech with characters and landscapes. In the case of *e*, three phases of this narrative are played out: before the catastrophe, which contains an element of insouciance, the suspended time where "it" happens, which is a paradoxical subjective time because the few seconds of the earthquake are experienced as an eternity by those who live through it, and afterwards, which is a time that bears the visible or invisible stigmata of the event and must be redefined, reinvented. The linearity of this story in three phases is only a surface effect, an abstract construction that can occur only with an external or remote distance, like that of the witness, the stranger, or with adequate temporal distance. It's an effect of perspective, that is to say, a construction of the narrative where the vanishing lines and axes can come together at one or several points, and something of the diffraction or break can then be reconstructed. The installation set-up with three simultaneous screens demands that the viewer grasp multiple meanings: they must choose and associate the elements of a subjective montage in a threshold situation. The inherent incompleteness of the set-up is associated with enveloping elements such as sound, mixing natural ambiences, with strident birds and insects, and deep, almost tellurian frequencies. The movement of withdrawal in relation to the incompleteness of meaning is offset by other elements of the language of forms and sounds.

M.G.: In "Notes on Gesture,"[1] Giorgio Agamben, who you quoted, describes the invention of cinema as an act of safeguarding and recording gestures that would otherwise be lost. Do you also see yourself as an archeologist of gesture?

N.N.: In 2007 I started making *Nord* [p. 10], a piece of work in northern France, in the Lille-Roubaix region, which bears the scars of a now-lost economic grandeur. I felt intuitively that the bodies resisted ruin. Gestures, by grafting themselves onto a ritual, onto a tradition, as in the case of cock fighting, or in a close relation to work, in particular textile manufacture, would thus establish a singular narrative that would put itself forward as resistance.

In the piece called *e*, I also filmed the suspended gesture of a very great kabuki master, Ichikawa Danjūrō XII [p. 170–171], in a suspended time of the action called *mie*. It seemed to me that this gesture signified the pitch of catastrophe, but also the memory of past and future gestures.

M.G.: What is the "suggestive memory" that you mentioned in your exhibition "Effroi" [p. 11 + 138] at the Musée Zadkine in 2005?

N.N.: The word *effroi* (dread) is what came to me when I blew up a photograph of a reservoir by the railway track of the camp at Birkenau and discovered the figure at the center. It is a figure without a face, a specter whose presence and form I couldn't explain, and which acts as a point of no return, rather like in the film *Blow-Up* by Michelangelo Antonioni, a dead point of vision, such that "behind each image a murder is hidden." At Auschwitz, in each bit of earth, in each drop of water, ashes are hidden. The image in this reservoir has no body or name, it is at the limit of perception, of thought.

M.G.: You belong to a generation of contemporary artists who question the problematics of representation through a wide variety of supports – fixed and moving images, language, narrative, etc. How do you situate your work in relation to other artists of this generation?

N.N.: I was born a year before 1968, and I think that my childhood years were bathed in a world of deep transitions: a conservative world crumbling, as for example were family models, moral, educational and cultural codes, and a utopian movement, or at the very least an aspiration to a form of freedom, in which my parents were personally very involved, as if carried by a wave, the zeitgeist that you cannot escape. Then, in the 1980s, my father was one of the pioneers of experiments with video in France, what we now call "video art." After that he made documentaries. What I remember from that time is a twofold movement: a liberating diffraction, carried by a strong utopian desire, and at the same time a fragmentation linked to separations and ruptures. I could see this twofold movement in historical events that were seminal for me: the fall of the Berlin Wall – I was there for my studies at the time – and then the war in Yugoslavia, which we felt acutely, despite the geographical distance. These were transitions, from the Cold War to a "globalized" world, from a world of information and the production of binary images to a plethora of modes and possibilities of representation and dissemination. To that were very naturally added theoretical questions about the notion of representation, given that there was no "an-ideology" of images. So I shared the works and concerns of directors and artists like Harun Farocki, Hartmut Bitomsky, Aurelia Mihai and Maja Bajevic, but also Gillian Wearing and Eija-Liisa Ahtila.

Then came Japan, a decisive experience. That was in 1999. Since that time I have constantly been weaving new connections, whether living

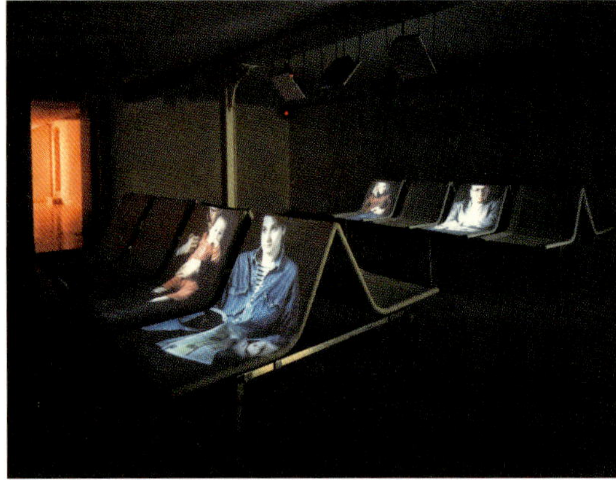

fig. 1

Natacha Nisic, *"Attitudes," la salle d'attente n°1*, 1997, 16 seats in canvas and aluminum, 5 video projections, color, each 10' View of the exhibition "Remise en forme," Galerie Xippas, Paris, 1997–1998

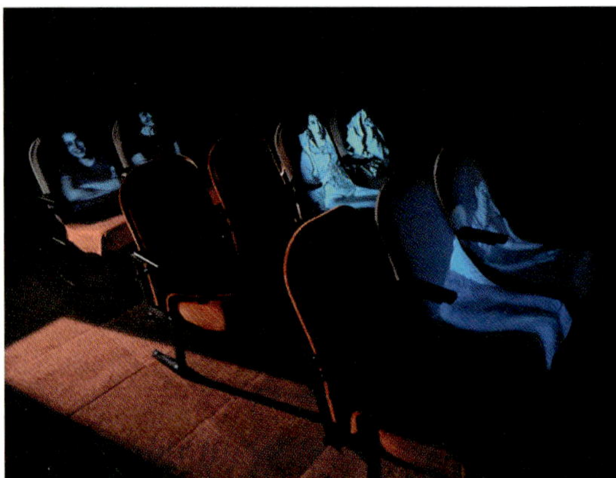

fig. 2

Natacha Nisic, *"Attitudes," la salle de projection*, 1999, 20 cinema seats, 3 video projections, color, each 42', monitor and surveillance cameras View of the exhibition "La salle de projection," L'atelier, Centre National de la Photographie, Paris, 1999

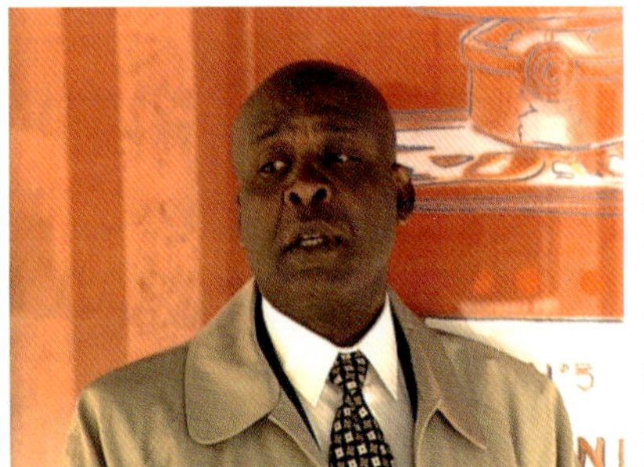

fig. 4

Eija-Liisa Ahtila, *Where is Where?*, 2008, 6 HD video projections, 16/9, color, DD 7.1 sound, 52'

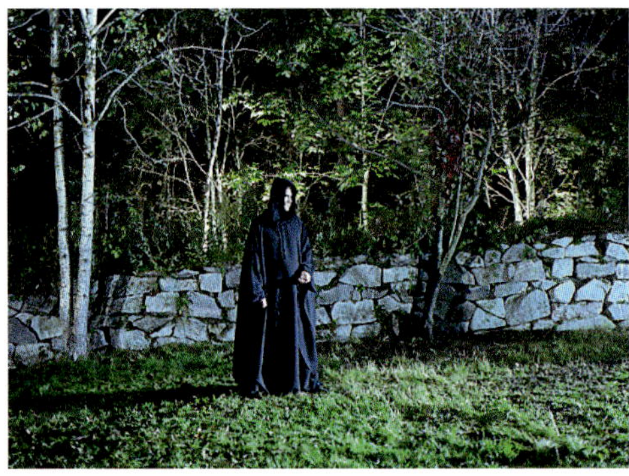

fig. 3

Gillian Wearing, *10–16*, 1997, video projection, color, sound, 15'

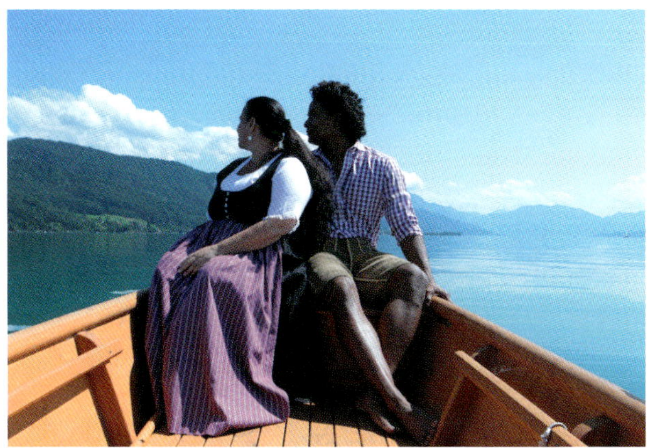

fig. 5

Natacha Nisic, *Le Ciel d'Andrea*, photograph of the shoot, July 2013

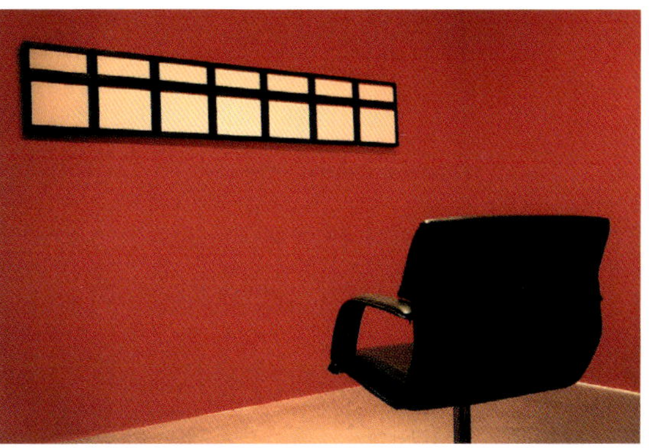

fig. 6

Natacha Nisic, *Indice Nikkei*, 2003, soundtrack, 5', 14 drawings in pencil on paper, seats.
View of the exhibition "Haus/raus-aus," Le Plateau – Frac Île-de-France, Paris, 2003

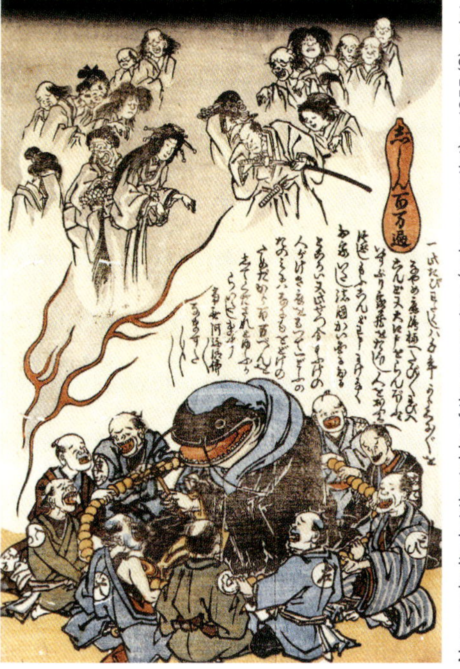

fig. 7

Namazu invited at the table of the carpenters (unknown artist), c. 1855 (?), print. Saitama Prefectural Museum of History and Folklore, Omiya

abroad or through artistic collaborations, as with the composer Jean-Luc Hervé or the choreographer Mié Coquempot. It was also in Japan that I met Park Chan-kyong. I shared his vision of historical and ideological power relations, of frontiers, war and religion, all important subjects that speak to me of a world that has not made the transition from the Cold War, where several historical temporalities still cohabit.

M.G.: At the Jeu de Paume and elsewhere, I have had the opportunity to exhibit several of those artists you say you feel close to – Maja Bajevic, Harun Farocki, Gillian Wearing, Eija-Liisa Ahtila. I can see issues that you share with the last two in particular, such as exchanges of identity (for example, in *10-16*, which Wearing made in 1997) or reparation rituals carried out through several time frames (I am thinking of Ahtila's 2008 piece *Where is Where?*).

N.N.: The set-up in *10-16* [fig.3] permutes genders and ages. Wearing invents rituals for the accession to speech and creates a difference that resembles the work of psychoanalysis: there is revelation, perturbation and, perhaps, reparation. What is hidden, unsayable, declares itself. I am thinking of the sisters in the Carmelite convent who, in contrast, have taken the vow of silence. That silence fills my gaze on the locations of *Princess Snow-Flower*. The heterogeneous objects, the landscapes where agricultural ruins sit alongside kitsch modern constructions are the only "vestiges" of a speech that cannot emerge, whether because of the "closure" of the monastery or that of language. In *Where is Where?* [fig.4], Eija-Liisa Ahtila stages elements of a historical culture that is repressed in France. She conveys an other's gaze on the other, and that distance here allows a critical distance that struggles to assert itself in France. That's a position I can identify with.

M.G.: Who is Andrea, this woman with multiple histories, woven between the West and the East, the visible and the invisible, the describable and the indescribable?

N.N.: Andrea is the spiritual daughter of Kim Keumhwa, a famous shaman but also a "living cultural treasure" in Korea. Andrea is German and lives in Bavaria. I met her after my travels in Korea, where Park Chan-kyong told me about her. After a first installation, *Andrea* [p.36–37], in 2013 I decided to complete and extend the story of her life and of

the strange powers surrounding it in the piece *Andrea en conversation* [p.41–72] and in a long documentary film, *Le Ciel d'Andrea* [fig.5]. These different works show the unusual circumstances that led Andrea to become a Korean shaman. This was a personal and cultural revolution, a matter of life and death.

Andrea is a central figure, between two contrasting worlds: western Europe, heir to the rationalist thought of the Enlightenment, which has constantly sought to consolidate the concept of civilization, the base of a society with frontiers that are more or less porous to what it has designated as barbarism since Ancient Greece; and the East, a remote figure masked by the temptations of Orientalism, a reading of the Other as inaccessible, sometimes frightening, but seductive in its exoticism. Andrea's path is unique, it brings together our classical pantheon, her own Catholic heritage, and a complex, rich cosmology from China and Korea.

In South Korea, shamanism is a pocket of resistance to the violence of history. Shamans are mainly women. To be a shaman is a form of ostracism, but it is also a position, a recognized social role, a power in the patrilineal world created by men.

Filming Andrea is a way of thinking about the position of the filmer / filmed couple, and thereby that of the viewer. Part of Andrea's life remains unexplained, mysterious, out of the common. This mysterious element must not be turned into spectacle. On the contrary, the camera sticks to the objectivist tradition, and could be seen as taking a position analogous to poetic writing. I am thinking of Charles Reznikoff and the American objectivists for whom the utterance, in its very structure, is already a displacement of language. Because there's nothing exotic about Andrea's practice in Bavaria, it is perfectly legible, integrated into the everyday landscape. For Andrea, wearing a Korean *hanbok* comes more naturally than a traditional Bavarian costume, but for an outside eye both outfits are at once attractive and strange.

Also, the extreme singularity of Andrea's narrative has to do with the fact that it seems haunted by as many *virtual* presences as *actual* persons. How does one represent these worlds of the absent and the living? How do you get the visible and the invisible to cohabit? Here I remember André Bazin, for whom the ontological question of the transition from photography to cinema is a matter of more than purely mechanical progress.[2] Illusion is not a grammar of cinema but its very function, its ontological nature, which engenders the spectator's scopic pleasures. To bring together Andrea's real and virtual worlds is, quite simply, to talk about cinema. To talk about perceptions, of the real or realities. It is not about constructing an illusionist or even naive vision. The choices of *mise-en-scène* are constructed in this interstice between presence, absence and memory.

M.G.: What *mise-en-scène* do you see for *Andrea en conversation*, a new nine-channel version of *Andrea* conceived specially for the exhibition at the Jeu de Paume?

N.N.: It will be a dialogue between two apparatuses of perception and narration: film and installation. The form of the installation stipulates ambulation, a space extended to the moving body. In this apparatus, the images, sounds and words concerning Andrea are included in an open physical and mental ensemble. As a spectator, the visitor to the exhibition is sometimes inattentive. They create a singular, internalized montage of the signs and images put before them. The exhibition space emphasizes the fragmentation of narrative, the loss of a single, linear meaning in favor of a non-authoritarian, fragmentary construction of the narrative. The installation offers an indiscipline of the gaze. As for the film, it maintains a heterogeneous structure and the linearity of the narrative is fragmented by the different image sources, visual and aural correspondences, complex time shifts.

M.G.: You also explore all these invisible forces or these elusive specters in situations whose reality is as overwhelming as it is incomprehensible, as in *Indice Nikkei* [fig. 6 + p. 193–196]. What is the story behind that piece?

N.N.: The first version of *Indice Nikkei* was made in 2003 for my solo show "Haus / raus-aus" at Le Plateau – FRAC Île-de-France. At the time it seemed to me that the stock exchange and the financial systems were at the heart of our fragility, a fragility in the sense of an opaque world that we as citizens could not grasp, understand or therefore influence, if only by the power of thought. Ten years later, this analysis has become a cliché and the "crisis" of 2008 marked a new stage in our perception of the idea of catastrophe. The piece's structure, built around echoes, and the walls painted red and the chalk on the walls – these are ways of staging the effects of saturation and

dizziness produced, among other things, by a deep feeling of impotence. The curves are astonishingly similar to the fractures in the rock in Kurihara Mountain after the earthquake of 2008. The forms of these curves were later "interpreted" as an act of resistance by the soprano Donatienne Michel-Dansac, whom I invited to take part in the project.

M.G.: This element of the unknown, whether the mystery that characterizes *Andrea* or the opacity of financial systems in *Indice Nikkei*, seems to take other forms in *e* and *f*.

N.N.: There are unpredictable "natural" forces like the ones that cause earthquakes. I thought up *e* after I heard about a famous Japanese legend, about Namazu, the catfish [fig. 7]. Japan, it says, sits on a giant catfish whose movements create earthquakes. The catfish is held by the god Kashima, but Kashima is an unreliable god and whenever he goes away the catfish stirs. What struck me were the many prints showing Namazu invited to dine at the table of the carpenters feasting in his honor. Thanks to him, work and wealth have returned, while the townspeople are weeping in the ruins. Namazu is not a tragic figure, because he also brings the promise of renewal.

These unforeseeable forces enable us to develop our adaptive relation to the world and place man within a whole, an ensemble where he is both passive and submissive, and the active force. However, when it is a matter of "forces" such as nuclear danger or the play of global finance, these forces originate in an idea of man's omnipotence. Whether harnessing energy or in the mindboggling calculations of machines and computers, "civilized" man is competing with unpredictable forces, dominating them, and thinks that he controls them. This excess engenders a vertigo, a fear that carries within it the negation of man. In the face of that, all I can offer are extremely simple acts: the vocal creation by Donatienne Michel-Dansac for *Indice Nikkei* or, for *f* [p. 143–156], the use of mirrors found on the site of the tsunami, which therefore witnessed the disaster of the tidal wave and survived it.

1. *Trafic*, no. 1, winter 1991, p. 33–34.
2. See André Bazin, *What Is Cinema?*, University of California Press, 1968.

—

Translated from French by Charles Penwarden

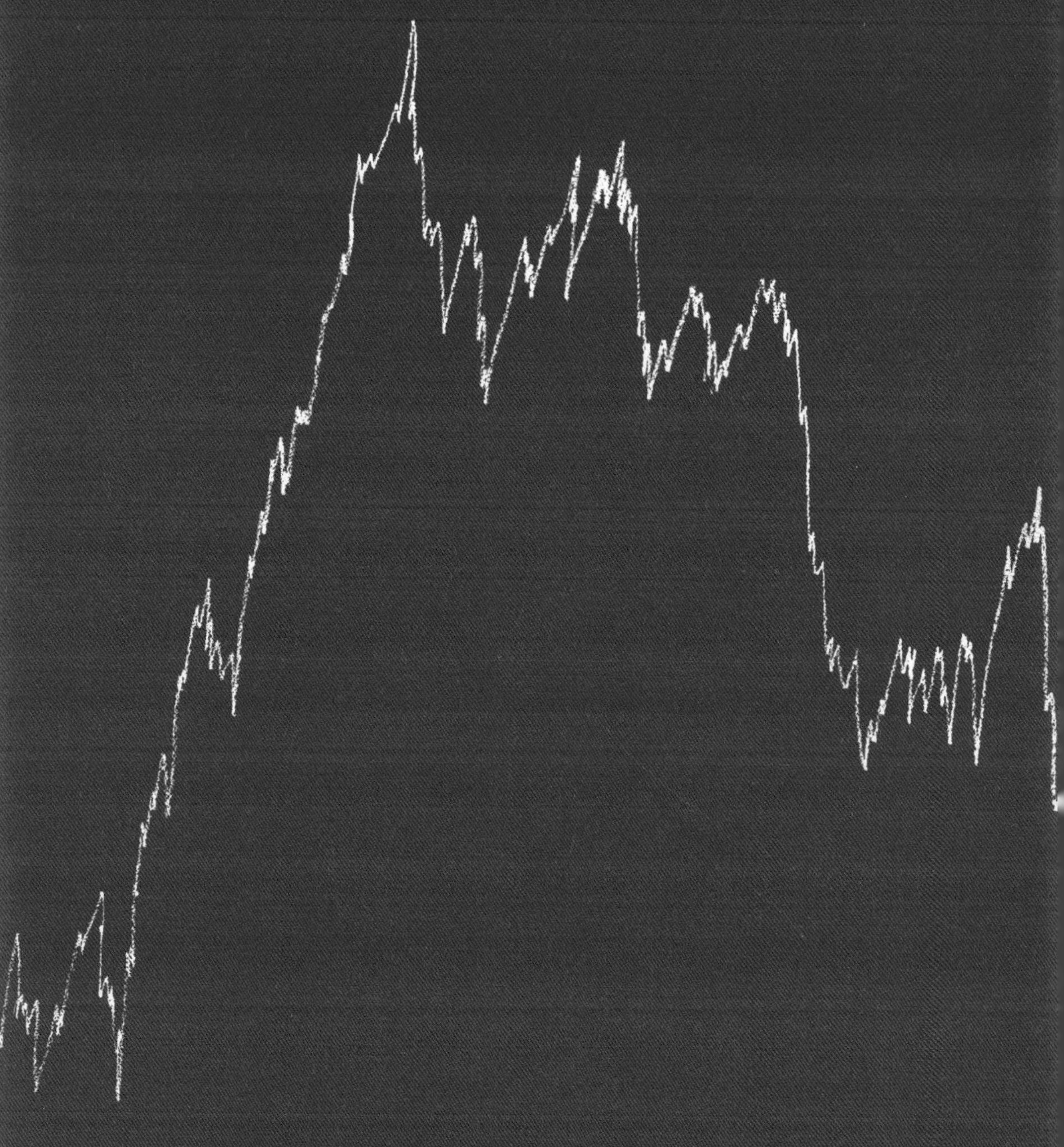

Indice Nikkei

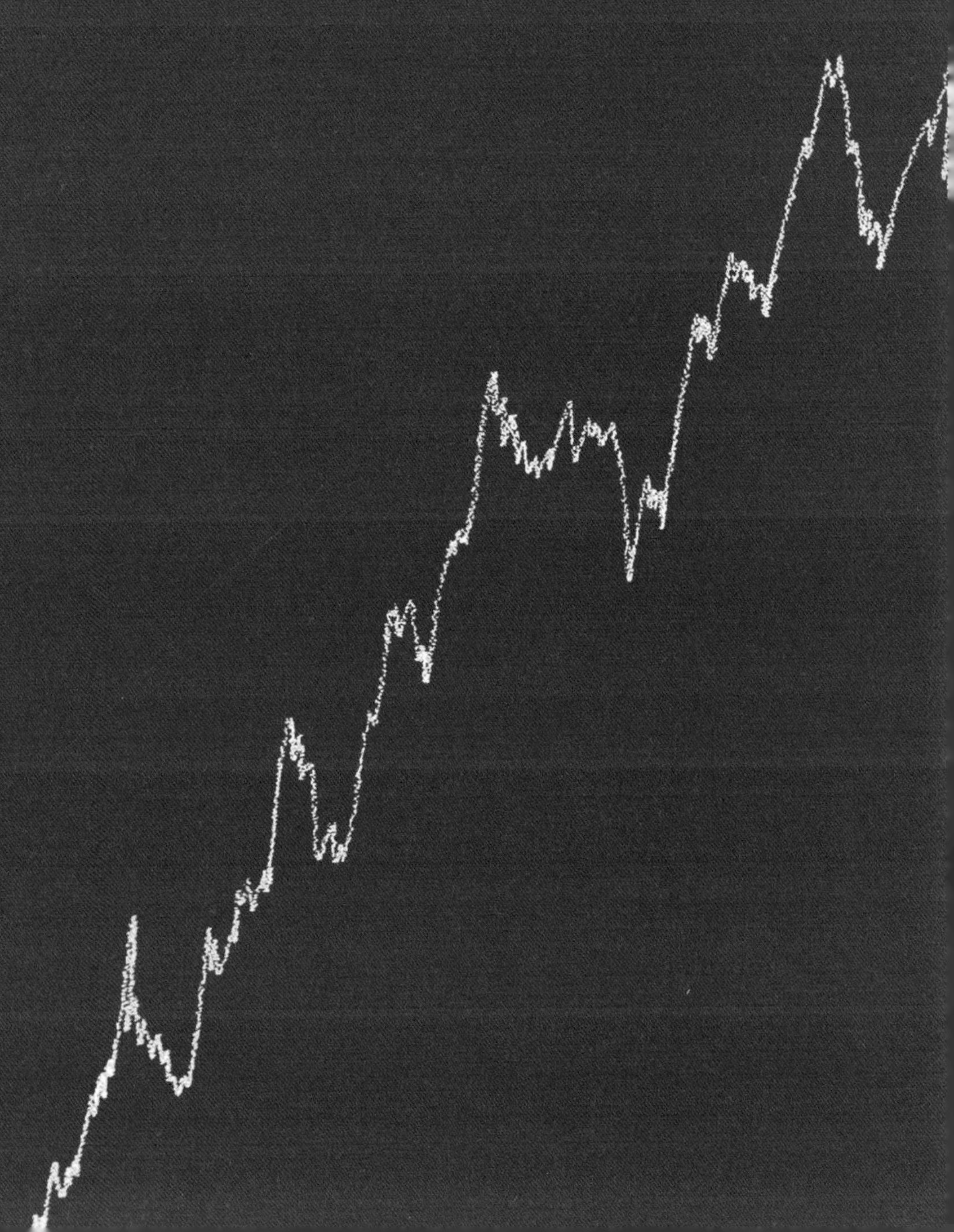

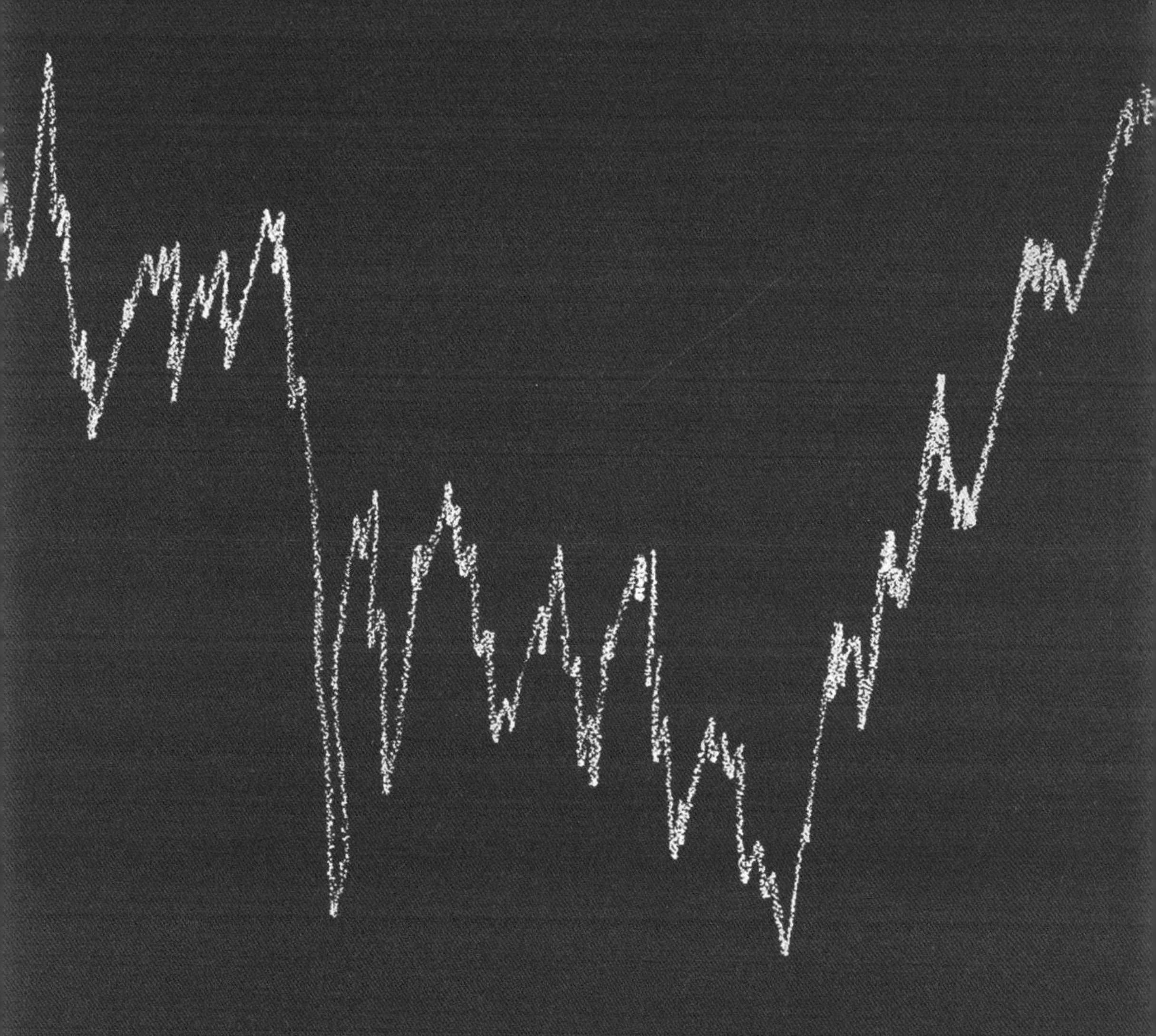

 Indice Nikkei

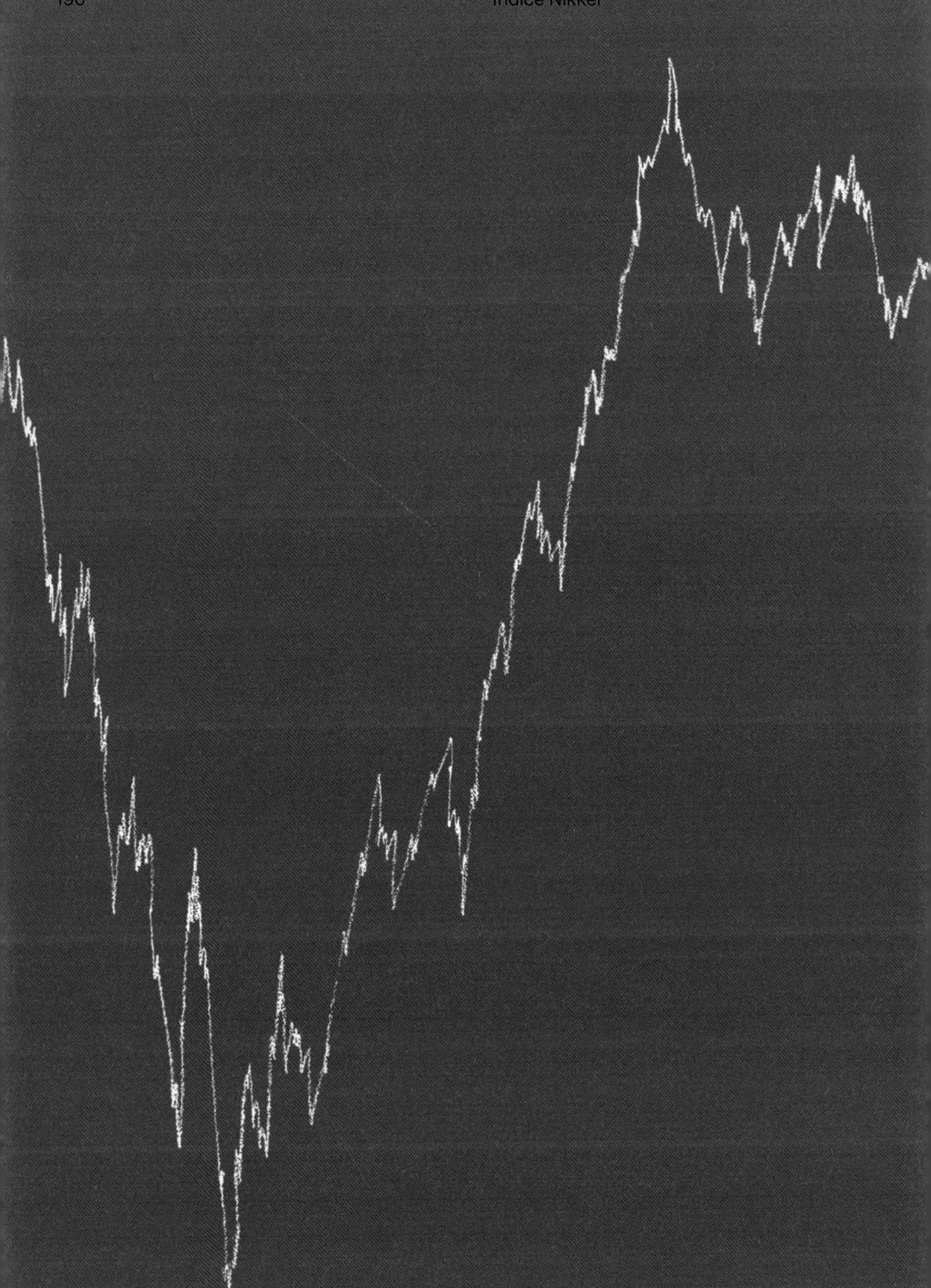

Born in La Tronche, France, in 1967. Lives and works in Malakoff, France

TRAINING

2004
— Screenwriting workshop, La Fémis, École Nationale Supérieure des Métiers de l'Image et du Son, Paris

1989
— Deutsche Film- und Fernsehakademie, Berlin

1986
— École Nationale Supérieure des Arts Décoratifs, Paris

GRANTS AND RESIDENCIES

2007
— Villa Medici, Rome

2006
— RIAA – Residencia Internacional de Artistas en Argentina

2002
— Cité Internationale des Arts, Paris

2001
— Villa Kujoyama, Kyoto

2000
— Senatsverwaltung für Bildung, Wissenschaft und Forschung, Berlin

1997
— FIACRE – Fonds d'Incitation à la Création, Ministère de la Culture et de la Communication, France

SOLO EXHIBITIONS

2013
— "Natacha Nisic. Écho," Jeu de Paume, Paris

2012
— "K. W. Complex. Natacha Nisic / Park Chan-kyong," Atelier Hermès, Seoul
— "Aurélie Sement / Natacha Nisic," Grandes Galeries de l'ESADHaR, Aître Saint-Maclou, Rouen

— "Chantal Akerman, Natacha Nisic, Marguerite Duras," Galerie Florent Tosin, Berlin

2011
— "My Corean Dream," Maison des Arts de Malakoff
— "Princess Snow-Flower," Galerie Florent Tosin, Berlin

2010
— "(s'entretenir) [2]," Atelier de Création Radiophonique, France Culture, Paris
— LOOP Barcelona, Barcelona, Galerie Dominique Fiat's stand

2009
— "e," Galerie Dominique Fiat, Paris

2007
— "Nord," Villa Medici, Rome
— "Forget me not," Domaine Départemental de Chamarande

2005
— "Effroi," Musée Zadkine, Paris

2004
— "Hand-Made," Galerie Xippas, Paris

2003
— "Haus / raus-aus," Le Plateau – Frac Île-de-France, Paris

2002
— "Fill-Ile," Iteza Gallery, Kyoto
— "La Méthode B," Tokyorama, Palais de Tokyo, Paris

2001
— "3 × 36 aide-mémoire," Sai Gallery, Osaka

2000
— "Natacha Nisic," Kunstbank, Berlin
— "Zu vermieten," Galerie Karlheinz Meyer, Karlsruhe

1999
— "La salle de projection," L'atelier, Centre National de la Photographie, Paris
— "Le S. C. sans peine," Galerie Anton Weller, Paris

1995
— "Pleine campagne," Galerie d'Art Contemporain, Auvers-sur-Oise
— "Natacha Nisic / Gilles Picouet," Galerie ART'O, Aubervilliers

SCREENINGS

2012
— *Le textile est mort mais les gens vivent encore*, "D comme documentaire," Gaîté Lyrique, Paris

2011
— "Kunstabend," K21 Kunstsammlung Nordrhein-Westfalen, Düsseldorf
— *e*, Festival video_dumbo, New York
— *e*, Rencontres Internationales Paris / Berlin / Madrid, Centre Pompidou, Paris, Museo Nacional Centro de Arte Reina Sofía, Madrid, Haus der Kulturen der Welt, Berlin
— *Catalogue de gestes*, "Un dimanche, une œuvre," Centre Pompidou, Paris

2009
— *En découverte*, Festival Remise, Bludenz

2008
— *Carmel*, "Hello Darkness," K21 Kunstsammlung Nordrhein-Westfalen, Düsseldorf
— *Nord* and *Carmel*, Centre Pompidou, Paris

2007
— *La Porte de Birkenau*, performance of the work *Different Trains* by Steve Reich, Parco della Musica, Rome
— "Le Regard ordinaire," retrospective of films by Natacha Nisic, Villa Medici, Rome
— *En découverte*, Villa Medici, Rome
— *Le textile est mort mais les gens vivent encore*, "Cinem'art," Auditorium dell'Arte, Rome
— *La Porte de Birkenau* and *Effroi*, "Trying to Land," MACRO – Museo d'Arte Contemporanea di Roma, Rome
— *Effroi*, Paris Tout Court, Festival International du Film Court de Paris

2006
— *Catalogue de gestes*, "S. 8", Centre Pompidou, Paris
— *Le Suicide des objets*, "Video club," MAC / VAL, Vitry-sur-Seine
— *En découverte*, Festival Manca, Nice
— *Hand-Made*, 5th EMAP – Ewha Media Art Presentation, Seoul

2005
— *En découverte*, "Objets parallèles," Festival Némo, Auditorium de la Videothèque de Paris
— "Rétrospective Natacha Nisic," Galerie Remparts, Toulon

GROUP EXHIBITIONS

2012
— "Le Plateau : 10 ans !," Le Plateau – Frac Île-de-France, Paris

2011
— "Big Picture (Orte / Projektionen)," K21 Kunstsammlung Nordrhein-Westfalen, Düsseldorf
— "Fragmentations: trajectoires contre nature," Domaine Départemental de la Garenne-Lemot, Gétigné-Clisson / Musée d'Art et d'Histoire, Saint-Brieuc
— "Bien à vous," Red Brick House, Yokohama

2010
— "The Yvonne Rainer Project," British Film Institute, London
— "Between me and you," Rencontres Internationales Paris / Berlin / Madrid, La Tabacalera, Madrid
— "Yebisu International Festival for Art & Alternative Visions," Metropolitan Museum of Photography, Tokyo

2009
— "elles@centrepompidou. Artistes femmes dans les collections du Musée national d'art moderne," Centre Pompidou, Musée National d'Art Moderne, Paris
— "Art et territoires," Hospice d'Havré, Le Fresnoy – Studio National des Arts Contemporains, Tourcoing

– "Là où je ne connais personne," Centre du Vieux-Colombier, Frac Bretagne, Rennes

2008
– "FEW," Wattwiller
– "Yokohama collection 08," Yokohama

2007
– "Spazi aperti," Accademia di Romania, Rome

2006
– "Paris-Belgrade," French Cultural Center, Belgrade

2005
– "À table(s)," Domaine Départemental de Chamarande

2004
– "Territoire et Déplacement," Centre Arc-en-Ciel, Liévin
– "Fenster zum Hof," NGBK, Berlin
– "Tempered Ground," Museum of Garden History, London

2003
– "Flambant vu. Corps, spectacles," Galerie Séquence, Chicoutimi
– "Une sélection 1998–2003," Frac Bretagne, Rennes
– "Histoire de gestes," Le Quai, Mulhouse
– "Para ver de otra manera," Festival International Huesca Imagen, Museo de Huesca

2001
– "Contemporary Utopia," Latvian Center for Contemporary Art, Riga
– "Plan B," with Herbert Schwarze, hARTwareprojekt, Dortmund

1999
– "Zauber*haft," Waldschlösschen, Dresden
– "Kyushu Contemporary Art Adventure," Inter Media Station, Fukuoka
– "Extra*et*Ordinaire," Le Printemps de Cahors

1998–1999
– "Aller-retour," Bonner Kunstverein, Bonn; Stadtgalerie Saarbrücken, Saarbrücken; Stadtgalerie im Kulturviertel, Kiel

1998
– "Élizabeth Creseveur, Rose Gibbs, Natacha Nisic, Mélik Ohanian, Jana Simpson," Galerie Jennifer Flay, Paris
– "Regard fatigué," with Christophe Marchand-Kiss, Akademie Schloss Solitude, Stuttgart

1997
– "Remise en forme," Galerie Xippas, Paris

1994
– "Chez l'un l'autre," Galerie Anton Weller, Paris

SELECT BIBLIOGRAPHY

INTERVIEWS

"Natacha Nisic / L'art au risque de la mémoire," interview with Catherine Francblin, with the participation of Philippe Forest, *Entretiens sur l'art*, Fondation d'Entreprise Ricard, September 20, 2005 (online report: http://fondation-entreprise-ricard.com/conferences/entretiens/art/natacha-nisic/).

Natacha Nisic, interview with Éric Corne and Maëlle Dault, account of the discussion of April 3, 2003 in connection with the exhibition "Haus / raus-aus," Paris, Le Plateau–Frac Île-de-France, 2004.

"Spectre. Natacha Nisic," in Réra, Nathan (ed.), *De Paris à Drancy ou les Possibilités de l'art après Auschwitz*, Pertuis: Rouge profond, 2009, p.57–71.

MONOGRAPHIC STUDIES AND SOLO EXHIBITION CATALOGUES

Galdo, Luisa, *Natacha Nisic, "Come l'invisibile diventa visibile." La Shoah – I Gesti*, contemporary art history thesis, supervisor Simonetta Lux, Sapienza–Università di Roma, Facoltà di Lettere e Filosofia, 2011.

Haus / raus-aus. Natacha Nisic, Brussels: La Lettre volée / Paris: Le Plateau–Frac Île-de-France, 2003; texts by Éric Corne and Christophe Marchand-Kiss.

K. W. Complex, Natacha Nisic / Park Chan-kyong, Paris: Fondation Hermès, 2013; texts by Natacha Nisic and Park Chan-kyong.

Natacha Nisic. Écho, Paris: Jeu de Paume / Arles: Actes Sud, 2013; texts by Beck Jee-sook, Philippe-Alain Michaud, and Florent Perrier, interview with the artist by Marta Gili.

Natacha Nisic. Effroi, Paris: Musée Zadkine / Paris-Musées, 2005; text by Annette Becker, foreword by Noëlle Chabert, artist's statement by Natacha Nisic.

Natacha Nisic. Pleine campagne, Auvers-sur-Oise: Office Municipal de la Culture, 1995; texts by Christophe Domino and Véronique Pittolo.

GROUP EXHIBITION CATALOGUES

À table(s), Chamarande: Domaine Départemental de Chamarande, 2005; text by Christophe Domino.

Aller et retour: 35 Jahre Deutsch-Französisches Jugendwerk, Bonn: Bonner Kunstverein / Sarrebruck: Stadtgalerie Saarbrücken / Kiel, Stadtgalerie im Kulturviertel: 1999; text by Annelie Pohlen.

Ateliers 1997–2002. Centre national de la photographie, Paris: Centre National de la Photographie, 2002; edited by Régis Durand and Claire Jacquet; text by Christophe Marchand-Kiss.

Big Picture. Orte / Projektionen: zwölf kinematographische Installationen, Berlin: Kerber, 2011; edited by Doris Krystof.

Contemporary Utopia – Mūsdienu Utopija, Riga: Laikmetīgās mākslas centrs (Latvian Center for Contemporary Art), 2001; edited by Frank Wagner.

Dynasty, Paris: ARC–Musée d'Art Moderne de la Ville de Paris / Paris-Musées, 2010; edited by Patrice Hergott and Christian Wahler; text by Doris Krystof.

Elles@centrepompidou: pionnières, feu à volonté, corps slogan, eccentric abstraction, une chambre à soi, le mot à l'œuvre, immatérielles, elles@design, architecture et féminisme? Artistes femmes dans la collection du Musée national d'art moderne-Centre de création industrielle, Paris: Centre Pompidou, 2009; texts by Quentin Bajac and Camille Morineau.

*Extra*et*Ordinaire. Le Printemps de Cahors. Photographies & arts visuels*, Arles: Actes Sud, 1999; texts by Christine Macel et al.

Flambant vu. Corps, spectacles, Chicoutimi: Galerie Séquence, 2002; text by Sylvain Campeau.

Huesca Imagen. Para ver de otra manera, Huesca: Diputación Provincial de Huesca, 2003; edited by Liliana Albertazzi.

Le Plateau, 10 ans, Frac Île-de-France, Paris: Le Plateau–Frac Île-de-France, 2012.

Ossip's studio: mémoires d'atelier, expérience de production, Paris: Musée Zadkine / Paris-Musées, 2008; texts by Noëlle Chabert, Hubert Lucot, Jérôme Mauche et al.

Plan B – Kunst Raum Stadt, Dortmund: Hartware MedienKunstVerein, 2001; texts by Hans D. Christ, Iris Dressler, Diana Ebster et al.

Remise en forme, Paris: galerie Xippas, 1997; text by Liliana Albertazzi.

Temper Ground, London: Museum of Garden History / Parabola, 2004; edited by Eliza Williams.

Yebisu International Festival for Art & Alternative Visions 2010: Searching Songs, Tokyo: Metropolitan Museum of Photography, 2010; edited by Keiko Okamura, Hiroko Tasaka, Masako Immaki, and Jiro Iio.

ESSAYS

Becker, Annette, and Debary, Octave (eds.), *Montrer les violences extrêmes*, Paris: Créaphis, 2012.

Brenez, Nicole, and Lebrat, Christian (eds.), *Une histoire du cinéma d'avant-garde et expérimental en France*, Paris: La Cinémathèque Française / Hazan, 2000.

Parfait, Françoise, *Vidéo, un art contemporain*, Paris: Éditions du Regard, 2002.

ARTICLES

Ackermann, Tim, "Bilder der gezähmten Welt," *TAZ Berlin*, July 31, 2004, p. 29.

Bach, Jana J., "C. Akerman, M. Duras, N. Nisic," *Zitty Berlin*, February 2013, p. 132.

Benhamou-Huet, Judith, "Trois galeries dans le vent. De jeunes artistes français et allemands à découvrir," *Les Échos week-end*, no. 19177, June 11–12, 2004, p. 6.

–, "Les tabous de Natacha," *Les Échos week-end*, no. 18903, May 9, 2003, p. 4.

Berelowitch, Irène, "Videolettres," *Télérama*, no. 2371, June 21, 1995, p. 72.

Blazevic, Dunja, "Destruction de l'image, image de la destruction," *Art press*, no. 192, June 1994, p. 46–50.

Brignone, Patricia, "L'image-geste," *Omnibus*, no. 30, October 1999, p. 12.

Campeau, Sylvain, "Opsis mobile," *Papel Alpha*, no. 6, 2002–2003, p. 51.

Champagne, Aurélie, "Vision de l'indicible, Natacha Nisic, 'Effroi,'" *Zurban Paris*, no. 260, August 17–23, 2005, p. 76.

Colard, Jean-Max, "Natacha Nisic," *Les Inrockuptibles*, special issue "Printemps de Cahors," supplement to no. 203, June 16, 1999, p. 9.

Corne, Éric, "Pariz / Beograd, srodnost po izboru," *Danas* (Belgrade), April 15–16, 2006, p. 3.

Cosar, Sascha, "Wenn das Schaf zum Telephon Hörer greift," *Bonner Kultur*, no. 304, December 31, 1998, p. 24.

Couturier, Élisabeth, "Les hommes au placard, les femmes au musée !," *Paris Match*, no. 3131, May 25–June 3, 2009, p. 30–31.

Delaporte, Ixchel, "Supermarché, objet d'art," *L'Humanité hebdo, la semaine télé*, December 11, 2004, p. 23.

Dhellemmes, Bertram, "'Effroi' de Natacha Nisic, musée Zadkine, Paris," *L'Architecture d'aujourd'hui*, no. 361, November–December 2005, p. 12–13.

Douaire, Pierre-Évariste, "Natacha Nisic," *Parisart*, June 2004 (online: http://www.paris-art.com/galerie-photo/Natacha %20Nisic/Natacha %20Nisic/4388.html).

Escalle, Clotilde, "Les traces de la mort," *Tageblatt* (Luxembourg), no. 142, June 21, 2005, p. 17.

Farine, Manou, "Femmes. 'Elles' envahissent Beaubourg," *L'Œil*, no. 614, June 2009, p. 36–43.

Fau, Alexandra, "Les artistes et l'Holocauste" (*Art absolument*), no. 16, spring 2006, p. 62–68.

Francblin, Catherine, "Natacha Nisic. Musée Zadkine," *Art press*, no. 316, October 2005, p. 88.

Gamba, Mario, "Come interpretare quest'altro Reich," *Il manifesto*, April 5, 2008.

Jarton, Cyril, "Natacha Nisic, pour la vie," *Beaux Arts magazine*, December 1996, no. 151, p. 37.

Ko, Miseok, "Religious Encounter of Tradition and Modernity, of Orient and Occident," *Dong-a Ilbo*, November 20, 2012, p. 22 (in Korean).

Kröner, Magdalena, "In der Wollfaden-Metropole," *Die Tageszeitung*, June 28, 2000, p. 15.

Krystof, Doris, "Catalogue de gestes," Centre Pompidou, Musée National d'Art Moderne, collection of films (commentary online: http://collection. centrepompidou.fr/ mediaNavigart/oeudoc/fra/ GE/NE/GENERATION-AUTO-1500000000-5910000309.htm), 2009.

Lamy, Frank, and Lavrador, Judicaël, "Le tour des galeries," *Beaux Arts magazine*, no. 241, June 2004, p. 42.

Lee, Doeun, "Chosun Seen by a German Monk, and + α," *JoongAng Sunday*, November 4, 2012, p. 25.

Lee, Mihye, "House of Healing," *Vogue Korea*, December 2012, p. 234 (in Korean).

Lee, Seulbi, "K. W. Complex," *Monthly Art*, December 2012, p. 140–145 (in Korean).

Lemaître, Isabelle, "Domaine départemental de Chamarande, ou un centre d'art contemporain arrivé à son rythme de croisière," *Flux News*, July 2005, p. 23.

Lequeux, Emmanuelle, "Le Centre Pompidou glorifie les femmes au risque de les placer dans un ghetto," *Le Monde*, May 29, 2009, p. 20.

–, "Natacha Nisic. Plongée dans les eaux troubles de la mémoire,"

Beaux Arts magazine, no. 255, September 2005, p. 124.

–, "Un instant de mémoire révélé," *En ville*, no. 7, June 2005, p. 49.

–, "Natacha Nisic. Aide-mémoire," *Beaux Arts magazine*, no. 228, May 2003, p. 35.

Lesauvage, Magali, "La loi du genre. elles@ centrepompidou," *Fluctuat*, June 8, 2009 (online: www.fluctuat.net/6853-elles-centrepompidou).

Marcelis, Bernard, "extra et ordinaire, le printemps de cahors," *Art press*, no. 249, September 1999, p. 90.

Marchand-Kiss, Christophe, "Et compagnie," *Action poétique*, no. 182, December 2005, p. 82.

Martínez, Beatriz, "La distorsión líquida," *Cahiers du cinéma España*, no. 45, May 2011, p. 10–12.

Mauche, Jérôme, "Hand-Made / Fait main: Natacha Nisic," *Synesthésie*, 2004 (online).

Moulène, Claire, "Natacha Nisic, *Haus / raus-aus*," *Les Inrockuptibles*, March 26, 2003, p. 70.

Müller, Michael-Georg, "Wiederaufstehen nach dem Beben," *NRZ*, March 19, 2011.

–, "Kunst: Japaner glauben an eine neue Ära," *WAZ-NRZ*, March 18, 2011.

Mura, Giannina, "Bambini tra le ceneri e il mare," *Il manifesto*, September 14, 2005, p. 15.

"'My Corean Dream.' Natacha Nisic," *Libération*, special pullout, September 19, 2011, n.p.

Naphegyi, Caroline, "Natacha Nisic," *Le Journal des expositions*, no. 40, November 1996, p. 6.

Nisic, Natacha, "Projet d'investissement de la salle de projection du CNP," *Journal du CNP*, no. 6, January 1999, p. 11.

Nowak, Ewa Isabella, "Haus / raus-aus," *Arteon*, no. 10, July 2003, p. 10–11.

Nuridsany, Michel, "Video, appartements et chambres d'hôtel. La jeune création passe à l'attaque," *Le Figaro*, September 3, 1996, p. 23.

Pittolo, Véronique, "Natacha Nisic: The Time of the Movement," *Katalog*, vol. 9, no. 4, autumn 1997, p. 58.

Ramade, Bénédicte, "Natacha Nisic, hors de la maison," *L'Œil*, no. 545, March 2003, p. 99.

Rebischung, Jean-François, "Souvenirs d'ouvriers entre mains d'artistes," *Nord Éclair*, June 12, 2009, p. 17.

Reneau, Olivier, "De la video chez les impressionnistes," *Technikart*, no. 3, December 1996, p. 94.

Sardá, Juan, "Cita con la vanguardia," *El Mundo*, May 20, 2011.

Schaeffer, Ute, "Experimente in Labor Europa," *General Auzenger*, December 16, 1998.

Sipp, Thomas, "Le mois du film documentaire," *Bref*, no. 75, November–December 2006, p. 2.

Soyer, Carine, "Aller-retour: les pérégrinations créatrices de quatre artistes," *Jalouse*, no. 61, June 2003, p. 84–87.

Thély, Nicolas, "Natacha Nisic, artiste en construction," *Aden*, March 12–20, 2003, p. 27.

Vanbremeersch, Sandra, "Natacha Nisic. Haus / raus-aus," *Parisart*, June 2003 (online: http://www.paris-art.com/ graff/haus--raus-aus/ nisic-natacha/4077.html).

Viau, René, "Natacha Nisic... vivre ?," *etc*, no. 63, September–October–November 2003, p. 69–71.

Villeneuve, Mathilde, "Natacha Nisic," *02*, no. 35, autumn 2005, p. 43.

Wanzelius, Rainer, "Schluchzende Töne aus alter und neuer Welt," *Westdeutsche allgemeine Zeitung*, May 25, 2000.

Yáñez, Jara, "'Extranjero' y 'valor trabajo.' A través de la frontera," *Cahiers du cinéma España*, no. 33, April 2010, p. 19.

RADIO

France Culture, *Direct*, March 23, 2009; "Journée Claude Lanzmann."

France Culture, *Ultra contemporain*, July 2, 2005; exhibition "Effroi," Musée Zadkine.

France Culture, *In situ*, April 17, 2002; on the subject of the artist's studio.

France Culture, *Trans / Formes*, October 20, 1999; exhibition "Extra*et*Ordinaire," Le Printemps de Cahors.

France Culture, *Peinture fraîche*, June 21, 1999; exhibition "Extra*et*Ordinaire," Le Printemps de Cahors.

Radio Aligre, January 1998; exhibition "Remise en forme," Galerie Xippas, Paris.

Radio FG, January 1996; exhibition "Natacha Nisic / Gilles Picouet," Galerie ART'O, Aubervilliers.

TELEVISION

Arte Video Night, October 2011; interview between Dominique Fiat and Natacha Nisic.

TV Belgrade, April 2006; exhibition "Paris-Belgrade," French Cultural Center, Belgrade.

Direct TV 8, July 21, 2005; exhibition "À table(s)," Domaine Départemental de Chamarande.

Arte, *Exhibition, la chute*, April 2004; interview with Natacha Nisic about her work *Le Suicide des objets*.

FILMOGRAPHY

Des témoins racontent, le Titanic, video, color, sound, 22', Paris: Arte France Développement / Cherbourg: Musée de la Mer, 2012.

Les Carriers, video, color, sound, 16', Tercé: La Carrière de Normandoux, 2008.

L'important est que cela soit mis en eaux, video, color, sound, 17', Domaine Départemental de Chamarande, 2007.

Une histoire de topinambours, video, color, sound, 16', Domaine Départemental de Chamarande, 2007.

Christoph Hein. À mi-mots, video, color, sound, 41', Paris: MK2 TV / Arte, 2006.

Maternelles. Dominique, video, color, sound, 13', Paris: La Cinquième / MK2 TV, 2003.

Histoires d'écrivains, Hélène Lenoir, Jacques Roubaud, video, color, sound, 2 × 13', Paris: La Cinquième / MK2 TV, 2002.

Kyoto, voyages, voyages, video, color, sound, 41', Paris: MK2 TV / Arte, 2002.

Le Dessous des cartes, video, color, sound, Paris: Arte, 1995–2013.

Au sujet d'un secret entre vous et moi, color, sound, 8', Paris: Télérencontres, 1992.

Durable, 16 mm, color, sound, 19', Berlin: DFFB / Paris: ENSAD / Ex Nihilo, 1991.

LIST OF WORKS

Works presented in the exhibition at the Jeu de Paume are marked with an asterisk.

[p. 10 + 15–25]
Catalogue de gestes (extracts)*
1995–...
Digitalized Super 8 films, color, each between 1' and 2' 30"
Centre Pompidou, Musée National d'Art Moderne / Centre de Création Industrielle, Paris (gift of the artist)

[p. 188]
"Attitudes," la salle d'attente no. 1
1997
Installation, 16 canvas and aluminum seats, 5 video projections, color, each 10'
Production: La Sept Video, Paris, Centre National des Arts Plastiques, Paris, Galerie Renos Xippas, Paris
Fonds National d'Art Contemporain

[p. 188]
"Attitudes," la salle de projection
1999
Installation, 20 cinema seats, 3 video projections, color, each 42', monitor and surveillance camera
Assistant director: Vincent Royer
Production: La Sept Video, Paris, Centre National de la Photographie, Paris
Collection of the artist

[p. 189]
Indice Nikkei
2003
Installation, soundtrack, 5', 14 pencil drawings on paper, seats
Production: Le Plateau – Frac Île-de-France
Collection of the artist

[p. 193–196]
*Indice Nikkei**
2003–2013
Installation, 2 soundtracks, each 10', chalk drawings on red paint, 2 seats
Sound design: Donatienne Michel-Dansac
Sound: Jean-Yves Pouyat, Éric Marciszewer
Collection of the artist

[p. 137]
La Porte de Birkenau
2005
HD video projection, color, 3'
Director of photography:
Muriel Coulin
Production: Mémorial
de la Shoah, Paris, MK2 TV,
Paris
Permanent installation
at the Mémorial de la Shoah,
Paris

[p. 137]
Mémorial des enfants
2005
Installation, 3,500 digital
prints on sheets of
Arche paper mounted
on backlit Macrolife panels
on a steel framework
120 m²
Production: Mémorial
de la Shoah, Paris,
Fin avril, Paris
Permanent installation
at the Mémorial de la Shoah,
Paris

[p. 11]
Effroi
2005
Video, color, 7' 30"
Camerawoman:
Natacha Nisic
Sound: Thomas Bauer
Production: Musée Zadkine,
Paris, Fin avril, Paris
Collection of the artist

[p. 138]
Effroi – La Vistule
2005
Color photography
110 × 80 cm
Production: Musée Zadkine,
Paris
Collection of the artist

[p. 11]
Effroi – Réservoir
2005
Color photography
200 × 135 cm
Production: Musée Zadkine,
Paris
Fonds National d'Art
Contemporain

[p. 10]
Nord
2007
Installation, 5 projections
of 16 mm films transferred
to video, color, stereo sound,
each 5' 50"
Director of photography:
Sébastien Buchmann
Assistant director of
photography: Lou Vernin
Video cameraman:

Olivier Menanteau
Editing: Natacha Nisic
Sound: Cyrille Lauwerier,
Nicolas Verhaeghe
Mixing: Hugues Petit
Assistant directors:
Émilie Dudognon,
Christine Crutel
Production: Centre National
de la Cinématographie, Paris,
Le Fresnoy – Studio National
des Arts Contemporains,
Direction Régionale des
Affaires Culturelles Nord-
Pas-de-Calais, Tourcoing,
Image / mouvement – Centre
National des Arts Plastiques,
Paris, La Mondiale, Paris,
Villa Medici, Roma
Collection of the artist

[p. 26–32 + 36]
Carmel
2008
4 rear projections, HD video,
colour, sound, each 25',
and 1 HD video projection,
color, 3'
Camerawoman:
Natacha Nisic
Director of photography:
Sébastien Buchmann
Assistant director of
photography: Lou Vernin
Key grip: Richard De Vadder
Grips: Valéry Lhomme,
Frédéric Oliver
Editing and sound:
Natacha Nisic
Post-production:
Bertrand Sart
Production:
Musée du Carmel, Lisieux
Permanent installation
at the Musée du Carmel,
Lisieux

[p. 138 + 156–184]
*e**
2009
Installation, 3 HD video
projections, color,
sound 5.1, each 19'
Video camera: Natacha Nisic,
Olivier Menanteau
Editing: Natacha Nisic
Post-production:
Bertrand Sart
Sound: Ikeno Tekeaki
Assistant: Jeffrey Lebeau
Mixing: Cyrille Lauwerier
Translation:
Sekiguchi Ryoko
Executive producer:
Akatsu Hiroko – Synapse Ent.,
Tokyo
Production:
Image / mouvement – Centre
National des Arts Plastiques,
Le Fresnoy – Studio National
des Arts Contemporains,

Tourcoing, Institut Français
du Japon, Paris, Galerie
Dominique Fiat, Paris, Arte
France Développement
Collection Fonds Régional
d'Art Contemporain Bretagne

[p. 37 + 72–78]
Princess Snow-Flower
2011
Installation, 3 HD video
projections, color, sound,
each 19'
Camerawork, editing
and sound: Natacha Nisic
Assistant: Vincent Royer
Production: GCC – Gyeonggi
Art Center, Korea, Galerie
Florent Tosin, Berlin
Collection of the artist

[p. 127–132, 137]
*Fukushima**
2011
Color pencil on Canson paper
75 × 315 cm
Collection of the artist

[p. 36–37]
Andrea
2012
Installation, 5 HD videos,
color, sound,
The Encounter: 13' 9",
The Souls: 8' 9",
Healing: 9' 27",
Archives: 10' 32",
The Voices: 8' 55"
Camerawork and editing:
Natacha Nisic
Sound: Jean-Yves Pouyat
Production: Fondation
Hermès, Paris,
Fondation Nationale
des Arts Graphiques
et Plastiques, Paris
Collection of the artist

[p. 41–72]
*Andrea en conversation**
2013
Installation, 9 HD videos,
color, sound, each approx.
10'
Camerawork:
Natacha Nisic
Director of photography:
Nathalie Durand
Sound: Jean-Yves Pouyat
Assistant director:
Charlotte Lessana
Editing: Natacha Nisic
Mixing: Jean-Yves Pouyat
Production: Jeu de Paume,
Paris, Seconde Vague
Productions, Paris
With the support of
the Fondation Nationale
des Arts Graphiques
et Plastiques, Paris
Collection of the artist

[p. 143–156]
*f**
2013
HD video projection,
color, sound, 20'
Camerawoman:
Nathalie Durand
Chief grip:
Kenichi Watanabe
Assistants:
Sugeeta Kajuto, Otake Nobu
Editing: Natacha Nisic
Sound: Natacha Nisic,
Philippe Langlois
Executive producer: Annick
Lemonnier – Epileptic Films,
Akatsu Hiroko – Synapse Ent.,
Tokyo
Production: Jeu de Paume,
Paris
Collection of the artist

[not reproduced]
*Fukushima**
2013
Color pencil on Canson paper
75 × 315 cm
Collection of the artist

[p. 189]
Le Ciel d'Andrea
2013
HD video, color, sound, 65'
Camerawork: Natacha Nisic,
Nathalie Durand
Editing: Natacha Nisic
Sound: Jean-Yves Pouyat
Assistant director:
Charlotte Lessana
Production: Seconde Vague
Productions, Paris, Centre
National du Cinéma et
de l'Image Animée, Paris,
Arte, Paris

JEU DE PAUME

This catalogue is
published on the occasion
of the exhibition
"Natacha Nisic. Écho,"
at the Jeu de Paume, Paris,
October 15, 2013
to January 26, 2014

Exhibition curators:
Natacha Nisic and Marta Gili

—

Director:
Marta Gili

General secretary:
Maryline Dunaud

Administration:
Claude Bocage

Communications
and sponsorship:
Anne Racine

Publications:
Muriel Rausch

Exhibitions:
Véronique Dabin

Bookshop:
Pascal Priest

Public programs:
Marta Ponsa

Educational projects:
Sabine Thiriot

Technical services:
Pierre-Yves Horel

—

Exhibition

Exhibition coordination:
Véronique Dabin

Registrar:
Maddy Cougouluègnes

Technical services:
Olivier Filippi

—

Catalogue

Editorial coordination:
Lætitia Moukouri

The Jeu de Paume
is subsidized by
the Ministry of Culture
and Communication.

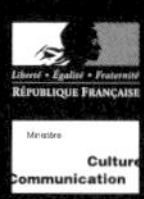

It is supported
by NEUFLIZE VIE,
principal partner.

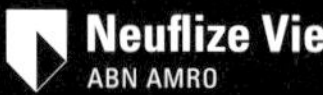

—

This book is published
with the support of
the Amis du Jeu de Paume.

—

Andrea (2012) and
Andrea en conversation
(2013) were selected
for support by the
sponsorship commission
of the Fondation Nationale
des Arts Graphiques
et Plastiques.

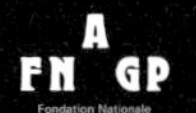

Acknowledgements

The Jeu de Paume wishes
to extend its warmest thanks
to Natacha Nisic for her
collaboration on the
exhibition and the book.

We would also like
to express our gratitude
to all the lenders who
agreed to contribute to
this exhibition:
— Centre Pompidou,
Musée National d'Art
Moderne / Centre
de Création Industrielle,
Paris
— Fonds Régional d'Art
Contemporain Bretagne
— Galerie Florent Tosin,
Berlin

The institution is also
deeply grateful to the
following for their invaluable
assistance in preparing
this project:
— Dominique Fiat,
Galerie Dominique Fiat,
Paris
— Philippe-Alain Michaud,
Centre Pompidou,
Musée National d'Art
Moderne, Paris
— Sandra Richard

and also to the following
people and institutions:
Eija-Liisa Ahtila,
Clotilde Escalle, Yumi Kang,
Doris Krystof, Anne-Marie
Miéville, Philippe Mothe,
Dominique Palmé, Ahran
Sohn, Ruth Waldburger,
Gillian Wearing, Le Fresnoy –
Studio National des Arts
Contemporains, Tourcoing,
Galerie Xippas, Paris,
Marian Goodman Gallery,
New York and Paris,
K21 Kunstsammlung
Nordrhein-Westfalen,
Düsseldorf, Maureen Paley,
London, Mémorial
de la Shoah, Paris,
Le Plateau – Frac Île-de-
France, Paris, Vega Film,
Zurich, and Video Data Bank,
Chicago

We would especially
like to thank the Galerie
Florent Tosin, Berlin,
in particular for its
generous support for
the catalogue.

Natacha Nisic wishes
to express her profound
gratitude to her producers
and partners for their
trust and commitment:
— Gérard Alaux, Fondation
Nationale des Arts
Graphiques et Plastiques,
Paris
— Régis Durand
— Dominique Fiat, Galerie
Dominique Fiat, Paris
— Akatsu Hiroko, Synapse
Ent., Tokyo
— Yvonnic Le Fustec, Arte
France Développement, Paris
— Annick Lemonnier,
Epileptic Films, Paris
— Caroline Naphegyi,
Tomorrow Land, Paris
— Luciano Rigolini,
La Lucarne, Paris
— Martine Saada, Arte
France, Paris
— Paul Saadoun, Seconde
Vague Productions, Paris
— Florent Tosin, Galerie
Florent Tosin, Berlin

The artist also extends
her warmest thanks
to all the people who
have supported and helped
her during the creation
of her works:
— Claire Aubret
— Benjamin Cordero
— Andrea Kalff-Cordero
— Hendrikje Lange
— Charlotte Lessana
— Julia Marchand-Nisic
— Park Chan-kyong
— Delphine Pellereau
— Sandra Richard
— Merryl Roche
— Vincent Royer
— Pascal Sottovia
— Han Sunhee
— Frank Tétart

and also:
— Master Kim Keum-hwa
— The community
of Benedictine monks
at Sankt Ottilien, Bavaria
— The community
of Benedictine monks
at Waegwan, South Korea
— The inhabitants and
mayor of the town of
Hisanohama, Fukushima
region
— Sugeeta Kajuto,
www.j-one21.jp

ACTES SUD

Editorial coordination:
Arnaud Bizalion

Head of partnerships:
Anne-Sylvie Bameule

Production:
Géraldine Lay

–

Editing:
Aïté Bresson
(French),
Bernard Wooding
(English)

Graphic design:
Maquette & Mise en page
– Hugo Anglade,
Thomas Petitjean,
Antoine Stevenot

Photoengraving:
Quat'coul

Photo credits

[p. 10] fig. 1: Courtesy
Centre Pompidou, Musée
National d'Art Moderne,
Paris; fig. 2: National Archives
at College Park (Maryland);
fig. 4: Courtesy Video
Data Bank – www.vdb.org
© Yvonne Rainer;
fig. 5: © Centre Pompidou,
MNAM-CCI, dist. RMN-
Grand Palais / image Centre
Pompidou, MNAM-CCI;
fig. 7: Ilmari Manninen
© National Museum of
Finland

[p. 36] fig. 1: Courtesy
Atelier Hermès, Seoul / Nam
Kiyong, 2012; fig. 2: Courtesy
K21 Kunstsammlung
Nordrhein-Westfalen,
Düsseldorf

[p. 37] fig. 3: Courtesy
Galerie Florent Tosin, Berlin

[p. 136] fig. 1: © Bibliothèque
Nationale de France;
fig. 2: © Tate, London 2013;
fig. 3: © RMN-Grand
Palais (musée d'Orsay) /
Hervé Lewandowski

[p. 137] fig. 6: © Mémorial
de la Shoah / Serge Klarsfeld
collection and private
collections

[p. 138] fig. 8: Courtesy
K21 Kunstsammlung
Nordrhein-Westfalen,
Düsseldorf; fig. 9: © Anne-
Marie Miéville and Jean-Luc
Godard / Ruth Waldburger –
Vega Film, Zurich

[p. 188] fig. 1: Courtesy
galerie Xippas, Paris /
photo: Frédéric Lanternier;
fig. 2: Photo: Michel N'Guyen;
fig. 3: Courtesy Maureen
Paley, London
© Gillian Wearing;
fig. 4: Courtesy
Marian Goodman Gallery,
New York and Paris /
photo: Marja-Leena
Hukkanen © Crystal
Eye – Kristallisilmä Oy,
Helsinki, 2013

[p. 189] fig. 6: Courtesy
Le Plateau – Frac Île-
de-France, Paris /
photo: Michel N'Guyen;
fig. 7: © Saitama
Prefectural Museum of
History and Folklore,
Omiya

© Natacha Nisic for
her works

© ADAGP, Paris, 2013 for
the works of Richard Serra
and Eija-Liisa Ahtila

© Actes Sud /
Jeu de Paume, 2013

Actes Sud
Le Méjan,
place Nina-Berberova
13200 Arles, France
www.actes-sud.fr

Jeu de Paume
1, place de la Concorde
75008 Paris, France
www.jeudepaume.org

–

Printed in August 2013
by Castelli Bodis, in Italy,
for Actes Sud

ISBN:
978-2-330-02379-9

Legal deposit 1st edition:
November 2013